WITHDRAWN

CURRENT ISSUES IN

NATURAL
RESOURCE POLICY

CURRENT ISSUES IN

NATURAL RESOURCE POLICY

edited by **Paul R. Portney**
with the assistance of **Ruth B. Haas**

contributors

Lee G. Anderson
Marion Clawson
Pierre R. Crosson
John W. Firor
Anthony C. Fisher
Kenneth D. Frederick
Winston Harrington
Hans H. Landsberg
Robert H. Nelson
John E. Tilton

Published by Resources for the Future, Inc., Washington, D.C.
Distributed by The Johns Hopkins University Press, Baltimore and London

Library of Congress Cataloging in Publication Data
Main entry under title:

Current issues in natural resource policy.

Includes index.
1. Natural resources—Government policy—United States—
Addresses, essays, lectures. I. Portney, Paul R. II. Haas, Ruth B.
III. Resources for the Future.
HC103.7.C87   1982   333.7'0973   82–47982
ISBN 0–8018–2916–X
ISBN 0–8018–2917–8 (pbk.)

Published by Resources for the Future, Inc., 1755 Massachusetts Avenue, N.W.,
Washington, D.C. 20036

Distributed by The Johns Hopkins University Press, Baltimore, Maryland, 21218
The Johns Hopkins Press, Ltd., London

RESOURCES FOR THE FUTURE, INC.
1755 Massachusetts Avenue, N.W., Washington, D.C. 20036

Resources for the Future is a nonprofit organization for research and education in the development, conservation, and use of natural resources, including the quality of the environment. It was established in 1952 with the cooperation of the Ford Foundation. Grants for research are accepted from government and private sources only on the condition that RFF shall be solely responsible for the conduct of the research and free to make its results available to the public. Most of the work of Resources for the Future is carried out by its resident staff; part is supported by grants to universities and other nonprofit organizations. Unless otherwise stated, interpretations and conclusions in RFF publications are those of the authors; the organization takes responsibility for the selection of significant subjects for study, the competence of the researchers, and their freedom of inquiry.

This book is a product of RFF's Quality of the Environment Division, Clifford S. Russell, director. It was edited by Ruth Haas and designed by Elsa Williams. The charts were drawn by Federal Graphics.

Contents

Foreword

All books and research papers published by Resources for the Future relate directly or indirectly to current policy problems. Even RFF reports on particular research investigations—publications that are designed for academics and other specialists—can and do affect the ways policymakers approach issues. RFF ideas sown in graduate schools around the nation bear fruit later in what might be called a "trickle-up" process—for instance, in congressional committee staffs.

The importance of such basic research should not be underestimated. Nevertheless, the nation is confronted with several pressing policy problems that require attention now; it cannot afford the luxury of years of lag time. Accordingly, at RFF we now are encouraging work that synthesizes and applies research results to a range of current problems. This volume presents such a synthesis for some important natural resource policy issues.

Two factors combined to create the need for such a book. First, all of the subjects discussed here are being debated in the public policy arena and legislation is probable for many of them. Everyone concerned—students of public affairs, public and private decision makers, citizens' groups, certainly members of Congress and their staffs—needs to be fully informed if rational debate and action are to be possible.

Second, many of the subjects addressed have been neglected by public policy analysts in recent years, mostly because energy and environmental policy have demanded so much attention that all other issues have been pushed aside. Both energy and the environment are addressed in this volume—they hardly could be omitted—but the reader will find the approach quite different than is typical.

It was not possible for RFF to allocate special funds for this project. As a result, the contributions by those on our staff were undertaken in addition to their regular responsibilities. Some of the authors from outside RFF donated their services, while modest honoraria were paid to others. Thus, the book has been created because a number of dedicated people believed in the importance of the problems and that a careful and thorough discussion based on years of research and acquired knowledge would be helpful. I am most grateful to all of them.

In particular, Paul R. Portney, senior fellow in our Quality of the Environment Division, deserves great credit for making this publication possible. He conceived the volume, identified the topics to be discussed, selected the prospective authors, and—with Ruth Haas's considerable assistance—saw it through to completion. More than is typical of an edited volume, this is his book.

Our experience at RFF has been that volumes such as this are among our more popular publications, despite the exceeding difficulty of obtaining funding for them. Portney's earlier volume, *Current Issues in U.S. Environmental Policy,* is a case in point. This book holds promise of being an even more popular sequel.

September 1982
Washington, D.C.

Emery N. Castle
President, Resources for the Future

Acknowledgments

As in any such undertaking, a number of individuals whose names do not appear on this volume contributed substantially to it. Emery Castle, Christopher Leman and Clifford Russell, all of RFF, read and commented extensively on first drafts of all the chapters, as did several anonymous outside reviewers. Individual chapters benefitted from careful reading by Raymond Arnaudo, James Crutchfield, Steven Freese, David Harrison, John Hoffman, Allen Kneese, Lester Lave, Thomas Lovejoy, Judy Lyman, James MacKenzie, Susan Peterson, Guilio Pontecorvo, Michael Sissenwine, Gary Toeniessen, and David Yardas. The chapters they read are better because of their constructive criticisms, although the authors bear full responsibility for the content of their chapters.

Finally, Susan Portney and Ramsay and Rebecca Midwood are due a vote of thanks. They put up with after dinner and weekend reading and writing that a better husband and father would have finished at the office. The editor appreciates their patience and dedicates this book to them.

September 1982   P.R.P.

CURRENT ISSUES IN
NATURAL
RESOURCE POLICY

1

Introduction

Paul R. Portney

Since the 1973 Arab oil embargo, concern about the adequacy of energy supplies in the United States has diverted attention from other natural resources. Recently, however, concerns about nonenergy resources have returned to the fore. This seems to be so for two reasons. First, for the time being at least, energy problems appear to be less pressing. By early 1982, for example, daily oil imports had fallen to 3.9 million barrels from their 1977 high of 6.6 million. More important, a new administration has come to Washington, one with some very different ideas from its predecessors about the proper stewardship of the country's natural resources. These differences appear to transcend questions of federal versus state or local management. Indeed, they seem to extend to the values attached to the development of natural resources as opposed to their preservation. This changing of the guard, then, has also refocused attention on the natural resource endowment of the United States and policies governing it.

Certain specific concerns are highlighting apparent shifts in natural resource policy. For instance, the nation is currently reexamining the principles behind the acquisition and management of its national parks, wilderness areas, wildlife refuges, and other publicly owned lands. Of particular concern is whether or not the protection of these areas from commercial development is rendering this country too dependent on potentially unreliable foreign sources of energy or so-called "strategic" minerals. Similarly, water shortages, particularly (albeit not exclusively) in the arid Southwest, have led policymakers to question whether there is enough surface and underground water to slake the nation's agricultural, industrial, and municipal thirst. Questions have also arisen both inside and outside government as to whether the country is running out of land that can be used to grow food for the United States and the rest of the world.

At the same time, housing price inflation has drawn attention to timber prices as one of many factors involved and in turn to the management of public and private forests and the rate at which trees are, or are not, harvested. The periodic collapse of certain of the world's ocean fisheries and the introduction of a new fisheries management policy in the United States has refocused attention on that important resource. Similarly, concern is mounting about the rate at which plant and animal species are being lost because of habitat modification and, in some cases, overharvesting. Finally, scientific evidence accumulated over the past decade has spawned a new concern. It is that both fossil fuel combustion and the manufacture and use of certain complex chemicals may be imperiling a less obvious but still quite important natural resource—the global climate. All of these specific issues, and others, have brought natural resources back into the spotlight.

It seems a propitious time to review the problems and policies related to the natural resource endowment of the United States. That is the purpose of this book. It deals in some detail with policies pertaining to public lands, nonfuel minerals, water availability, agricultural land, marine fisheries, endangered species, private forests, and climate.

As in any such review, however, certain topics must be omitted. Thus, energy resources and policy are not included, though these concerns do arise time and again in the discussions of public lands, water resources, agricultural potential, species endangerment, and climate problems. We have also drawn an admittedly arbitrary distinction in this book between natural resource policy and what might be called traditional environmental policy—that dealing with air and water quality, toxic substances, and hazardous waste disposal. Surely, clean air, fresh, pure water, and uncontaminated land could be treated as natural resources. They provide valuable amenity services, and their ability to assimilate a certain amount of pollution makes them doubly valuable. Nevertheless, Resources for the Future has recently reviewed this nation's policies to protect air and water quality and minimize exposures to toxic and hazardous substances.[1] Therefore, U.S. environmental policies are not discussed ex-

[1] Paul R. Portney, ed., *Current Issues in U.S. Environmental Policy* (Baltimore, Md., Johns Hopkins University Press for Resources for the Future, 1978).

cept where they influence other natural resource policies. To take but one example, water availability cannot be divorced from issues of water quality. Hence, the Clean Water Act comes up in the discussion of water availability.

THE ECONOMICS OF NATURAL RESOURCES

Several points may help the reader understand the analysis and recommendations of this book. The first is that since these chapters were written by economists, they reflect (in varying degrees) a particular point of view. To be sure, every effort has been made to ensure that the chapters are understandable to noneconomists. Indeed, policy- and lawmakers, business and environmental groups, and interested citizens form the largest part of the intended audience for this book. Nevertheless, the economist's concern with certain effects of natural resource or other policies is sure to show through.

Perhaps the most notable of these concerns has to do with whether or not a particular policy inhibits or facilitates economic *efficiency*. Economists seem always to be worried about efficiency, and this is offensive to many who may equate it with faster production lines, a disregard for human concerns, the downgrading of nature's bounty, and a more harried and less personalized style of life. Widespread as this impression may be, it is unfortunate because it is wrong. When economists extoll the virtues of an efficient natural resource (or other kind of) policy, it is because such a policy appears *in principle* capable of making some citizens better off while at the same time no one else is made worse off. In other words, efficient policies are those that do what appears to be the impossible. They produce "free lunches" by reallocating the natural, human, and capital resources at the disposal of the economy. If it is possible to add to the welfare of some without harming others, surely these are the kinds of policies the government should undertake.

In practice, of course, even efficient policies will work to the disadvantage of some, although by the very definition of economic efficiency, these policies must help the gainers more than they harm the losers—in other words, their benefits must outweigh their costs.[2] Since efficient policies will inevitably harm at least some citizens, they can be expected to encounter opposition. In fact, if those likely to be harmed by a policy are already poor, or belong to a future generation whose preferences cannot be represented in current decision-making, society may not wish to pursue even some efficient policies if there is no way to offset the

---

[2] For an excellent introduction to the subject, see Edward M. Gramlich, *Benefit-Cost Analysis of Government Programs* (Englewood Cliffs, N.J., Prentice Hall, 1981).

losses. When properly done, then, benefit-cost analysis not only totes up gains and losses, but, when possible, also shows how they are distributed across individuals, regions, and time. This information, too, is of great significance when natural resource or other policies are being considered.

The important point is that when economists talk about efficiency in natural resource policy, they try to take into account *all* the gains and losses that may result. These include the solitude or scenery a wilderness area offers, the camping and hiking that goes on in national parks, the protection of delicate or unique ecosystems, and all other nonmarket activities that may compete with more commercial and less aesthetic activities and that should be valued on an equal footing with them.[3]

This concern for efficiency is one reason for the esteem with which economists view an economic system organized around private transactions between informed and consenting parties, a system sometimes referred to as the "free market." Under certain, admittedly quite restrictive conditions, such private transactions will result in an efficient overall allocation of society's resources. In other words, it will not be possible to improve on this allocation and make some citizens better off without at the same time making someone else worse off. That is the allure of the market.

One of the reasons there are government policies to regulate or otherwise influence the use of natural resources is that these resources illustrate almost perfectly several of the ways in which markets can fail to exist or function properly. These forms of market failure thus stand in the way of economic efficiency and establish a presumptive case for intervention. Since these market failures appear time and time again in each of the chapters, a brief and general description of several kinds of failure is provided here.

One absolutely essential precondition to private exchange is a well-defined and enforceable set of property rights. Yet several of the natural resources discussed in this volume are owned by no one, and thus in a sense are owned by all. These are the so-called *common property* (or open access) *resources,* examples of which are ocean fisheries, certain underground aquifers, and the atmospheric mantle surrounding the earth. It is both interesting and ironic that these resources are often mismanaged because of a *lack* of clear ownership—many people believe that it is the *fact* of ownership, particularly private ownership, that leads to unwise resource use.

[3] For a discussion of the valuation of some nonmarketed outputs, see John V. Krutilla and Anthony C. Fisher, *The Economics of Natural Environments* (Baltimore, Md., Johns Hopkins University Press for Resources for the Future, 1975).

The problem with common property resources is fairly straightforward. While it may be in the best interests of all to limit the rate at which such resources are exploited,[4] especially in the case of renewable resources, there may be no means of enforcing such limits, given that access is open to many. Therefore, so as not to be cheated out of their share, users accelerate their exploitation and may exhaust the resource or vastly diminish its future productivity. Thus, fisheries are harvested to near extinction, aquifers are drained faster than they can be recharged and are ruined, or the atmosphere is used as a dumping ground for potentially harmful gases.

If, on the other hand, ownership rights to these resources were clear and enforceable, a different pattern of use would no doubt emerge, one geared to preserving their long-term productivity (and hence profitability). True, the degree of exploitation might exceed that desired by the most devoted preservationist, but there is little doubt that the rate of exploitation would be slow in comparison with the open-access or common property case. In cases of common property resources, then, intervention of some sort is necessary to establish property rights and/ or limit directly the use of such resources.

Another form of market failure appears to be as much the rule as the exception in the case of natural resources—the *externality*. An externality occurs whenever transactions between two parties confer a benefit or a cost on a third party which is not taken into account in the deliberations of the first two. A positive externality benefits the third party, a negative externality causes harm. In such (obviously common) cases, either too little or too much of the externality-creating activity is undertaken.

The chapters that follow contain many examples of such external effects. For instance, the open space provided by a farm in an otherwise densely crowded metropolitan area may confer a benefit on all who pass by it. Unfortunately for the farmer who owns it, however, there is no way to charge for this benefit. Thus, in any deliberation about continuing to farm as opposed to, say, selling the property to developers, the farmer will reckon only the private gains from growing and selling the output of the farm. If, over the long run, these gains are less than the sale value of the farm, it may be sold, even though it would not be if the farmer could somehow profit from the scenic service his farm provides.

On the other hand, suppose that eroding soil from this same farm clouds an adjacent stream or contributes to the cost of dredging a harbor. In this case, an external cost is created which the farmer does not have

---

[4] When used in the context of natural resources, "exploitation" is not used pejoratively but rather as a synonym for extraction or removal.

to bear and which, therefore, does not enter into his decision-making. This points in the direction of *too much* farming relative to the socially efficient level. As one can see, externalities can cut both ways and quickly complicate decision-making.

Other activities involving natural resources are externality-ridden. For instance, private forests may provide aesthetic or recreation benefits to many, benefits which matter little to forest owners because they cannot be captured and turned into profit. Similarly, mining in wilderness or other outdoor recreation areas may greatly diminish the enjoyment of persons in adjacent unmined areas or so alter the habitat of a species that it may become extinct. Yet these very real costs may not be a part of the financial calculation that takes place when decisions are made to open new mines. Also, as a later chapter points out, the decision to produce and sell certain complex chemicals reflects the costs of labor, capital, and raw materials. It does not, however, reflect any of the potentially significant costs that may arise if the use of these chemicals results in atmospheric damage and eventual harm to human, plant, and animal life. In these cases, too, then, externalities may cause the private market to allocate resources inefficiently.

Very closely related to the concept of externality is that of a *public good.* To understand its importance to natural resource policy, consider for a moment its converse—the private good. Goods such as food, clothing, and fuel oil share several important characteristics. One is that if I eat an apple, wear a shirt, or burn a gallon of oil, no one else can eat that apple, wear that shirt (at the same time), or burn that gallon of oil. Another characteristic is that my purchase of the apple, shirt, or oil excludes you from purchasing that same unit. Thus, if you want the enjoyment of those private goods, you must buy them—a condition which is conducive to their provision by profit-motivated private parties.

Now consider a very different kind of "good," the preservation of a rare animal species threatened with extinction. Note, first, that the benefit that I may derive from this action in no way detracts from others' ability to benefit as well. More important, if the species is protected, there is no way I can be prevented from benefitting, even if I were unwilling to contribute to the cost of the preservation effort. In other words, I could "ride free" on the actions of those who did contribute. If everyone reasoned this way, of course, many important public goods would not be provided, even though it would be in the best interests of all to provide them.

These characteristics—the possibility of joint or simultaneous use, and the inability to exclude noncontributors—help define public goods and, as the example above indicates, national parks, wilderness areas, and scenic rivers and trails are excellent examples of such public goods. So, too, are the preservation of species, the protection of global climate, and other important natural resources discussed in this book. The very fact that they are public goods is often sufficient to ensure that they will not be provided in sufficient amounts, if at all, by the private sector. This is another reason, then, for government intervention in the area of natural resources.

These frequently occurring features of natural resources—their "publicness," common property aspects, and/or the externalities that arise when they are used or extracted—are an important reason why unregulated private transactions between individuals may not provide the right mix of wilderness areas, farmland, private forests, mineral exploration, water use, ocean fishing, species preservation, and atmospheric protection. They go a long way in explaining why economists take a strong interest in the scope and form of natural resource policy. Readers would do well to take note of the many places where these market failures appear in the ensuing chapters.

At the same time, it is important to note that natural resource policy in the "real world" may have nothing to do with economic efficiency whatsoever. In fact, as an attribute of policy design, efficiency is often more noticeable in the breach than the observance. In other words, federal water policy, to take an example from chapter 7, originally was designed to help open up the West. Even though that goal has been accomplished, and even though the perpetuation of those policies often leads to blatant misallocations of water resources, they continue because those who benefit from them are politically effective in arguing their point. While they are always concerned with the efficiency implications of policy, each of the following chapters also has another important goal: to describe what is actually happening to a particular resource and why it is happening, even where (perhaps particularly where) economic considerations play a small role. Thus, the politics of redistribution is as important to some of these chapters as the economic point of view.

This leads to another interesting observation. Even when the government intervenes in the name of efficiency, those efforts may be as prone to failure as the system they seek to correct. It is unfair, in other words, to compare an obviously imperfect market system with an idealized regulatory system unblemished by human or institutional imperfection. Thus, readers should try to see how perverse bureaucratic incentives, "capture" of regulatory bodies by regulatees, difficulties with centralized information collection, scientific uncertainty, or other similar problems frustrate natural resource management where efficiency is a goal. Each chapter contains such examples.

OVERVIEW

The plan of the book is this. In chapter 2, Robert Nelson addresses perhaps the most controversial issue in natural resource policy today—the public lands. He points out that these vast areas (the federal government owns more than half of five states and more than a fourth of the total land area of the United States) are important for a number of reasons. For instance, federally owned land may contain as much as half of future U.S. oil and natural gas reserves, as much as two-thirds of future coal reserves, and about half of this country's current inventory of softwood sawtimber. Equally as important, the federally owned national parks and forests, wilderness areas, wildlife refuges, and other natural systems provide a major share of the recreation and wildlife preservation enjoyed in the United States today.

Nelson identifies three major issues revolving around the public lands today. The first is the conflicts that inevitably arise about the uses to which those lands will be put. For instance, should more commodity production take place on federal lands, or should those lands be preserved in perpetuity for recreation and other nonextractive uses? If the former, what areas should be developed and how can this be done in the least environmentally disruptive way? If the latter, which of the often conflicting recreational uses should be permitted, and under whose jurisdiction should the recreation take place?

Once this difficult allocation of public lands to competing uses has been made, Nelson argues, a second major problem must be faced. How much oil, gas and coal, timber, and other commodities should be produced on those lands which are devoted to commodity production? While private companies make decisions like this all the time, the calculus of the federal government is a more complex one, and is further complicated by the fact that the output of some of these lands is large enough to influence the market price of the commodities produced. This creates a centralized planning task of almost unmanageable proportions.

Finally, Nelson considers the past performance of public land management in the United States and asks whether it might be time to consider alternatives to current philosophies. Among the alternatives he identifies as worth considering are an overhaul of the existing system of federal ownership and management; a devolution of ownership to the states of at least some land now federally owned; and, finally, the sale to private parties—on terms attractive to the federal government—of some lands acknowledged to be best devoted to commodity production.

In chapter 3, Hans Landsberg and John Tilton examine the dependence of the United States on a number of nonfuel minerals, and discuss what should—or should not—be done about it. They begin by pointing out the relative size of mineral production in the U.S. economy, how much smaller nonfuel mineral imports are compared with fossil fuels, and how frequently concerns arise about "mineral shortages" (the current "crisis" about strategic mineral supplies, it seems, is not all that new). They also point out that it is not necessarily unwise to rely on foreign sources for mineral supplies—import dependence cannot be equated with vulnerability to supply disruption. In fact, they argue that it is infeasible to become completely self-sufficient with respect to certain important commodities.

Landsberg and Tilton identify producer cartels, competition for limited supplies, and supply disruptions as three threats to imported minerals. While each must be taken seriously, there are reasons to believe that none of these threats is critical. For instance, producer cartels may be effective in the short run (for several years, say), but can be thwarted by materials substitution as well as dissension between cartel members. Competition for foreign supplies can be partially alleviated by the new discoveries that may result when prices rise, as well as by dampening of demand. Politically motivated supply disruptions are a possibility, of course. Even here, however, there are forces that would tend to moderate the threats posed. For example, even nations unfriendly to the United States generally need the hard currency generated by minerals sales. This will make it difficult for them to harm the United States through supply cutoffs.

Finally, Landsberg and Tilton examine recent U.S. minerals policy and outline what they think is a sensible basis for future policies. The major components of the latter, they feel, ought to include above all else an up-to-date stockpile. Other components should be a plan to allocate supplies when and if shortages arise, an honest appraisal of the mineral-producing capability of the public lands and the environmental laws governing mineral discovery and production, and a policy of facilitating minerals substitution where possible.

In chapter 4, Winston Harrington and Anthony Fisher take up the issue of endangered species. They begin by pointing out how very important plant and animal diversity is to mankind. This importance extends beyond their use as food and fiber, building materials and the like. Plants and animals are also the source of beneficial drugs and medicines, provide invaluable information on the evolution of all species, as well as human biology, and cleanse and renew the support system upon which all life depends. In addition, as the authors point out, plants and animals make an aesthetic contribution to our lives that is virtually impossible to measure. Unfortunately, as Harrington and Fisher argue, species are disappearing at an increasing rate—extinctions are currently running at a rate of 1,000 per year worldwide and may reach 10,000 per annum by the end of this decade. Much of this loss is caused by the activities of mankind—perhaps surprisingly, more through economic activities that affect species' habitats than by direct harvesting, as in the case of whales.

Harrington and Fisher turn next to current policies to protect against species loss. While the Endangered Species Act of 1973, as amended, may have had some adverse effects on economic development, the authors conclude that this effect has been small enough that no major changes in the act seem required. They also point out, however, that most of the extinctions that scientists fear will take place over the coming years will occur, not in the United States, but elsewhere in the world—most notably in the tropical rain forests of South America, Africa, and other continents. Since these areas fall well beyond the reach of the Endangered Species Act, Harrington and Fisher discuss briefly a few international approaches to species preservation that may hold out some hope of success.

In chapter 5, Lee Anderson calls attention to U.S. policy governing marine fisheries. The focal point for his discussion is the Fisheries Conservation and Management Act (FCMA) of 1976. Anderson begins by placing the marine fishing industry in the context of both national and regional economies: while it is small in the former context, it is important in several regions. He then discusses the bioeconomics of unregulated fisheries to show why some form of regulation is essential, and points briefly to previous regulatory approaches.

Anderson then discusses in detail the 1976 law and the shape it has taken to date, including the fisheries management plans that are its primary products. Although there is room for efficiency-enhancing improvements through FCMA, so far it appears that efficiency has been a minor concern in plan formulation. Anderson explains why and suggests ways in which this state of affairs might be improved.

In chapter 6, John Firor and Paul Portney look at a most important natural resource, the global climate. They do so because climate can be and is being affected by mankind in ways which may eventually be quite harmful. Firor and Portney concentrate on two primary threats: that arising from the increasing concentrations of carbon dioxide and other gases in the atmosphere, which have the potential to warm the atmosphere to a troubling extent; and that arising from the manufacture and use of chlorofluorocarbons (or CFCs), chemicals which can work their way into the stratosphere and break down the ozone "shield" that protects all living things from the sun's harmful ultraviolet radiation.

After discussing these threats in some detail, Firor and Portney identify a set of characteristics common to these two climate problems which makes them difficult to deal with. These include an almost pervasive uncertainty about many aspects of the problems, the distant horizon over which the problems are expected to arise, the uneven distribution of the consequences of climate change, and the conflict between preventing these climate changes and other quite important national goals. The authors conclude with several recommendations for future "climate policy," including a call to devote far more attention to these potential problems than they are currently receiving.

Water and its availability (or lack thereof) is the subject of chapter 7. Kenneth Frederick begins by reviewing the sources and uses of fresh water and pointing to a number of special problems which make an overall assessment of water availability difficult. These include regional imbalances in water supply and demand, temporal variability in rainfall, and occasional impairment of water quality by pollution or saline deposits.

The major part of this chapter is devoted to the question of whether or not the United States has enough water to meet its many needs—agricultural, energy-related, recreational, municipal, and so on. The answer is affirmative, subject to at least two very important caveats. The first is that the institutions through which water currently is priced—or, discouragingly, more often given away—must be changed so that those who use such a valuable resource are made to pay its full cost. Only in this way will the proper incentives to conserve water rather than squander it be felt.

This change will have to take place at both the state and federal levels. At the former, it will require considerable modification of the rules governing the transfer of appropriative water rights and those governing irrigation and water conservation. At the federal level, it will require major changes in the amount and timing of the charges levied on those using federally provided irrigation water. Such changes would go a long way toward allocating water to its highest and best uses, and ensuring that opportunities to conserve it are seized upon.

The other caveat is the quality of available water, which is important to Frederick's optimistic assessment. Unless both surface and groundwaters are protected against increased salinity and conventional and toxic pollution, adequate water supplies could become a serious local, state, or even national problem. Ensuring protection would be facilitated, Frederick argues, by a more carefully targeted Clean Water Act as well as a more coordinated national approach to groundwater management.

The fate of U.S. agriculture is influenced by factors discussed in the chapters on endangered species, climate, and water availability. In chapter 8, Pierre Crosson discusses another problem for U.S. agriculture—the perception of inadequate agricultural land to meet increasing demands for food and fiber. He begins by pointing out that three factors—growth of export demand, a slowdown in the rate at which yields have grown, and conversions of agricultural land to other, nonagricultural uses—have combined to put new pressure on existing and potential croplands. But he argues that the last of these, land conversions, has been the least important of the three and is unlikely to be a serious problem in the future. Other more worrisome problems exist.

Crosson points out that increased crop production in future years will come at a cost—both in economic and environmental terms. With respect to the latter, for example, the primary problem is soil erosion. That is, as less desirable cropland is brought into production, erosion is likely to increase, causing problems for both farmers and for others adversely affected. In addition, recourse to less productive lands, and the additional fertilizer they require, implies that food prices will increase as well. Thus, although Crosson is confident that food demands can be met, it will be at a higher cost to society.

What response might this call forth? Rather than attempt to limit exports or artificially restrict the conversion of agricultural land, Crosson suggests that basic technological research should be the focus of ameliorative policies. Candidates for federally sponsored research are projects that would improve the photosynthetic capability of plants, enhance nitrogen fixation, improve soybean yields, and promote conservation tillage. Crosson concludes by analyzing the current direction of federal erosion control policies.

In the ninth and final chapter of this book, Marion Clawson directs our attention to an often overlooked natural resource, the privately owned forests in the United States. These forests, which provide a major share of total timber harvested in the United States each year, do face some problems. They include various forms of trespass, illegal harvesting for firewood and other uses, and an inability to capture some of the benefits that would result from better management (water quality enhancement, for example). On the whole, however, Clawson suggests that these problems are not of great importance, and indicates that the private forests are healthy, well run, and capable of generating on a sustained basis even larger amounts of timber than are currently being produced.

It is tempting to search for some common theme or solution that runs through all these chapters. This temptation should probably be resisted. The problems that arise in each chapter differ in seriousness, origin, likelihood, and amenability to correction. Some—such as water shortages or overfishing—are present-day problems for which solutions exist, even if they are not currently being employed. Others—such as the adequacy of agricultural land or dependence on imports for "strategic" minerals—may be much less serious than they at first seem. There may be steps that can be taken to lessen both the perception and the reality of the problems that do exist. Finally, still other problems may be more speculative and perhaps more distant. Climate change and, to a lesser extent, species endangerment come to mind here. Nevertheless, these problems could be the most serious of all and, furthermore, the most difficult to address if they do arise. Thus, the natural resource policy issues raised in this book span a number of dimensions.

As suggested above, however, a great many (though not all) of the problems to be discussed in the following chapters can be understood as failures of private markets to achieve efficiency. Solutions do exist for many of these failures and include such familiar remedies as public provision of services, corrective taxation to remedy negative externalities, direct regulation, or sponsorship of research. The real test comes in designing and packaging such remedies so that they are not only economically efficient, but also politically saleable. That is the true mark of good policy analysis.

2

The Public Lands

Robert H. Nelson

ORIGINS

At the end of the American Revolution, seven of the original thirteen states had claims to western territories. Between 1781 and 1802, however, these states ceded their western lands to the national government, about 237 million acres in all. Under the procedures for becoming a state established by the Northwest Ordinance of 1787, federal lands were not transferred to newly formed states. As a result, the federal government would continue to own large areas of public lands, even in states admitted to the Union.[1]

Various acquisitions and purchases in the nineteenth century greatly expanded the area of the United States from 538 million acres in 1802 to its present size of 2.3 billion acres. The greater part of the newly acquired acreage became part of the public lands, except in Texas and Hawaii, which did not have any original federal lands.

[1] Paul W. Gates, *History of Public Land Law Development* (Washington, D.C., Government Printing Office, 1968) pp. 72–74.

[2] For leading histories of public land disposal, see Gates, *History of Public Land Law Development*; Benjamin H. Hibbard, *A History of the Public Land Policies* (Madison, Wis., University of Wisconsin Press, 1965—original 1924); and Roy M. Robbins, *Our Landed Heritage: The Public Domain 1776–1970* (Lincoln, Neb., University of Nebraska Press, 1976—original 1942).

Throughout the nineteenth century, the basic policy of the federal government was to dispose of the public lands and the issues posed were as controversial then as they are now.[2] Early American legislative history was dominated by public land debates, Henry Clay once remarking that "no subject, which has presented itself to the present, or perhaps any preceding Congress, is of greater magnitude than that of the public lands."[3]

Much of the land went to new states in the form of education grants. At first these consisted of one section (equal to a square mile) per township (36 square miles), but this rose to two and then four sections after 1896. If the designated sections were not available, the state could make "in lieu" selections on other federal lands within its boundaries. Indeed, several of the western states, including Utah, Arizona, and Colorado, are only today completing their in lieu selections, partly because of litigation over the selection procedures. Alaska received by far the largest single land grant, 104 million acres, when it became a state in 1958, although the actual transfer is still only halfway completed. While most of these grants are past history, the recent "Sagebrush Rebellion" has again raised the issue of state land grants, in some cases proposing that most of the remaining public lands be transferred to the states.

The idea that some public land should be retained by the federal government developed slowly. Setting aside the Yellowstone area as a "public park" in 1872 was an early step toward retaining these lands.[4] The national forest system, another form of retention, was begun in 1891 and expanded most rapidly during the presidency of Theodore Roosevelt. The remaining public lands were available for homesteading until the Taylor Grazing Act of 1934 effectively ended this practice in most places.[5] The lands not previously disposed of or included in a particular public land system—often the poorest lands, which no one wanted—were eventually placed under the administration of the Bureau of Land Management (BLM).

Since 1934 there have been only minor changes in the extent of the public lands outside Alaska. Table 2–1 shows the current public land ownership by state; 52 percent of the total land in twelve western states

[3] Quoted in Frederick Jackson Turner, "The Significance of the Frontier in American History," in George R. Taylor, ed., *The Turner Thesis: Concerning the Role of the Frontier in American History* (Boston, D.C. Heath, 1956) p. 13.

[4] For the history of the national parks, see John Ise, *Our National Park Policy: A Critical History* (Baltimore, Md., Johns Hopkins University Press for Resources for the Future, 1961).

[5] For the history of the disposal of the public rangelands, see Louise E. Peffer, *The Closing of the Public Domain* (Stanford, Calif., Stanford University Press, 1951).

TABLE 2–1. Federal Land Acreage, by Agency, by State[a]
(thousands of acres)

State	BLM	Forest Service	National Park Service	Fish and Wildlife Service	Total federal	Federal percent of total state
Alabama	3.3	643.8	6.6	48.5	1,122.3	3.4
Alaska	73,600.0[b]	22,894.7[c]	51,015.2[c]	76,058.9[c]	226,200.0[b]	60.3[b]
Arizona	12,588.9	11,270.7	2,696.0	1,588.4	32,014.3	44.0
Arkansas	1.6	2,476.2	93.0	193.9	3,358.3	10.0
California	16,609.4	20,369.7	4,500.0	234.6	46,702.1	46.6
Colorado	7,993.9	14,414.2	600.0	56.9	23,607.9	35.5
Connecticut	—	—	1.1	0.2	9.3	0.3
Delaware	—	—	—	24.6	40.9	3.2
Dist. of Columbia	—	—	6.9	—	12.8	32.9
Florida	1.2	1,097.9	2,062.0	452.9	4,040.9	11.6
Georgia	—	862.9	36.7	469.3	2,277.4	6.1
Hawaii	—	—	245.0	255.8	660.6	16.1
Idaho	11,945.9	20,422.8	86.9	85.2	33,759.6	63.8
Illinois	—	260.7	—	117.0	606.6	1.7
Indiana	—	186.2	8.0	7.8	496.6	2.1
Iowa	—	—	1.7	73.6	227.4	0.6
Kansas	0.7	108.2	0.7	51.4	733.0	1.4
Kentucky	—	667.3	79.3	2.2	1,414.4	5.5
Louisiana	7.2	597.7	1.2	276.2	1,098.6	3.8
Maine	—	51.2	38.4	30.3	134.8	0.7
Maryland	—	—	37.7	26.1	203.0	3.2
Massachusetts	—	—	29.2	12.0	79.9	1.6
Michigan	0.9	2,728.3	618.4	107.1	3,467.4	9.5
Minnesota	43.6	2,796.1	134.4	442.8	3,423.0	6.7
Mississippi	0.6	1,140.6	106.7	107.3	1,730.6	5.7
Missouri	0.2	1,463.1	62.7	55.6	2,195.6	5.0
Montana	8,141.6	16,752.7	1,220.5	1,137.7	27,740.6	29.7
Nebraska	9.4	351.7	5.8	156.9	712.2	1.4
Nevada	48,844.8	5,146.0	697.6	2,362.7	60,506.1	86.1
New Hampshire	—	700.2	4.1	2.2	721.9	12.5
New Jersey	—	—	34.7	37.9	151.5	3.1
New Mexico	12,840.5	9,244.4	248.5	383.0	25,873.7	33.3

is owned by the federal government. More than half the land is federal in five states: Nevada (86 percent), Utah (64 percent), Idaho (64 percent), Alaska (60 percent), and Oregon (53 percent). Even in California, one of the most industrial and urban states in the nation, 47 percent of the land is federally owned.

Although public land policies occupied center stage in national debates until the early part of this century, after World War I they receded from national view and kept a much lower profile until the late 1960s. However, the public lands have played a critical role in the environmental and energy policy debates of recent years. Their sheer size and

TABLE 2–1. Federal Land Acreage, by Agency, by State[a] (*continued*)
(thousands of acres)

State	BLM	Forest Service	National Park Service	Fish and Wildlife Service	Total federal	Federal percent of total state
New York	—	13.2	33.7	23.5	245.9	0.8
North Carolina	—	1,162.7	374.2	136.1	2,050.9	6.5
North Dakota	68.1	1,105.5	71.3	1,272.6	2,386.4	5.4
Ohio	0.1	175.3	11.5	8.7	345.3	1.3
Oklahoma	7.0	293.2	9.2	141.0	1,590.0	3.6
Oregon	15,745.1	15,615.8	171.3	507.4	32,313.7	52.5
Pennsylvania	—	508.8	31.9	9.2	732.6	2.5
Rhode Island	—	—	—	1.0	8.0	1.2
South Carolina	—	609.4	20.9	189.5	1,176.4	6.1
South Dakota	276.4	1,995.3	183.3	458.4	3,492.3	7.1
Tennessee	—	622.0	263.2	82.4	1,853.9	6.9
Texas	—	782.6	1,087.4	255.5	3,408.7	2.0
Utah	22,052.6	8,045.9	2,009.2	101.7	33,530.0	63.6
Vermont	—	279.9	1.2	5.8	295.6	5.0
Virginia	—	1,617.4	299.3	103.7	2,409.7	9.4
Washington	311.2	9,052.6	1,909.9	181.1	12,472.7	29.2
West Virginia	—	967.1	2.4	0.3	1,097.1	7.1
Wisconsin	0.3	1,498.7	63.0	220.8	1,867.7	5.3
Wyoming	17,793.1	9,253.3	2,391.1	74.2	30,329.6	48.7
U.S. total	248,887.7	187,327.8	73,626.2	88,774.7	636,929.6	28.1

Sources: Bureau of Land Management, U.S. Department of the Interior, *Public Land Statistics*—1980; Forest Service, U.S. Department of Agriculture, *Report of the Forest Service: Fiscal Year 1980 Highlights* (July 1981); U.S. Department of the Interior, *Annual Report of Lands Under Control of the U.S. Fish and Wildlife Service as of September 30, 1980, and Addendum*—December 2, 1980; National Park Service calculations provided to author.

[a] Most recent acreages available—BLM and total federal for 1979; Forest Service, National Park Service and Fish and Wildlife Service for 1980. Includes federal acreage only, thus excluding private holdings within national park and forest boundaries.

[b] Lands expected to remain federal after State of Alaska and native selections are completed—BLM estimate as of March 1982.

[c] Lands after enactment of Alaska National Interest Lands Conservation Act of 1980—agency estimates as of March 1982.

the fact that they contain extremely valuable environmental assets and energy resources make it very likely that issues surrounding their use will continue in the national spotlight for some time to come.

This chapter briefly describes the outputs of the public lands and the history of the conflict over preservation versus use of the land. It then examines three major issues of public land management. One of the most important is the standards and procedures by which public lands are set aside—in effect, zoned—for particular uses, such as preservation of wildlife or production of timber. Once it is decided that certain public lands will be available for mineral, timber, or other commodity production, a further major issue is the appropriate level of such production. A third fundamental issue is whether continued federal ownership of the public lands is desirable, or whether some parts of these lands might be more efficiently owned and managed by states, local governments, and/or the private sector.

OUTPUTS OF THE PUBLIC LANDS

Energy and Other Minerals

The Submerged Lands Act of 1953 established federal ownership of the outer continental shelf (OCS) beyond 3 miles (9 miles from Texas shores). The OCS contains 1.1 billion acres of land, an area almost equal to 50 percent of the U.S. land area. Since 1953, federal oil and gas leases on the OCS have yielded more than 5 billion barrels of oil, a little more than the current U.S. production from all sources in one and a half years. Federal lands have also yielded more than 44 trillion cubic feet of natural gas, a little more than two years at current U.S. rates of gas production. OCS leasing has also returned more than $40 billion in revenues to the federal treasury, including $6.3 billion in 1980. As shown in table 2–2, the OCS in 1980 produced 9 percent of the nation's oil and 23 percent of its natural gas. The Geological Survey estimates that 32 percent of still-undiscovered domestic oil resources and 27 percent of undiscovered domestic gas resources are located on the OCS.[6]

Production of oil and gas on onshore public lands is also substantial, particularly in Wyoming and New Mexico. In 1980, 149.7 million barrels of oil and 1.03 trillion cubic feet of natural gas were produced on onshore lands; this is equal to 5 percent of both total U.S. oil and total U.S. gas production. For the whole United States, including both offshore and onshore resources, the public lands are believed to contain 56 percent of undiscovered U.S. oil resources and 47 percent of undiscovered U.S. gas resources.

Large-scale production of the huge oil shale resources of the United States has regularly been predicted but has never materialized. The amount of oil they contain—more than 1.8 trillion barrels—exceeds the reserves in the Middle East.[7] The prime U.S. oil shale resources are

[6] Geological Survey, U.S. Department of the Interior, *Estimates of Undiscovered Recoverable Conventional Resources of Oil and Gas in the United States*, GS Circular 860 (1981).

[7] While "resources" and "reserves" are often used interchangeably, they are not the same thing. Total resources include those minerals that have been identified as well as those whose existence is only suspected. Reserves are those deposits that can be profitably

TABLE 2–2. Federal Oil and Gas Production and Undiscovered Resources

Type and location	1980 Production (millions/bbl)	Percent of 1980 U.S. production	1980 Royalties (millions)	Federal undiscovered resources[a] (billions/bbl)	Percent of U.S. undiscovered resources
Offshore oil, lower 48	277.4	8.8%	$837.2	14.8	18%
Onshore oil, lower 48	145.8	4.6	408.7	15.5	19
Alaska oil, offshore and onshore	3.9[b]	0.1	4.7	15.7	19
Total federal oil	427.1[c]	13.5	1,250.6	46.0	56
	(trillion cubic feet)		(millions)	(trillion cubic feet)	
Offshore gas, lower 48	4.64	23.0%	$1,295.3	98.1	17%
Onshore gas, lower 48	0.95	4.7	209.1	95.3	16
Alaska gas, offshore and onshore	0.08[b]	0.3	6.2	83.4	14
Total federal gas	5.67[c]	28.0	1,510.6	276.8	47

Sources: Geological Survey, U.S. Department of the Interior, *Federal and Indian Lands: Oil and Gas Production, Royalty Income, and Related Statistics* (June 1981); and U.S. Geological Survey, *Estimates of Undiscovered Recoverable Conventional Resources of Oil and Gas in the United States* GS Circular 860 (1981).
Note: Total U.S. oil production in 1980 was 3.147 billion barrels.
[a]Geological Survey estimates of "undiscovered recoverable conventional resources" are based in part on subjective probability procedures. They are approximate estimates based on the best available geologic judgments at a given time. The figures shown in this table are mean estimates.
[b]Production during 1980 occurred onshore only.
[c]Does not include production from federal naval petroleum reserves. In 1980 such production was 52.6 million barrels of oil and 59.3 billion cubic feet of gas.

located in the Piceance Basin in northwest Colorado, where about 80 percent are federally owned, including the areas with the highest quality deposits.[8]

Recent growth in U.S. coal production has occurred largely in the West, which is rapidly being transformed from a minor coal-production area into a major source of national supply. Western coal is now being burned partly because of its low sulfur content but more importantly,

extracted under *specific economic and technological conditions*. Thus, the size of reserves is not a fixed figure. It is important to keep this in mind when discussing possible mineral activities on public lands.
[8] For an examination of oil shale issues and prospects, see Congress of the United States, Office of Technology Assessment, *An Assessment of Oil Shale Technologies* (June 1980).

TABLE 2–3. Federal Coal Production and Reserves

State	1981 Federal production[a] (millions of tons)	Total federal reserves (millions of tons)	Federal percent of total state reserves	Projected total state 1990 production[b] (millions of tons)	1990 Total state percent of U.S. production
Colorado	11.5	9,900	61%	35.1	2.2%
Montana	15.4	77,200	64	109.7	6.8
New Mexico	8.9	3,700	82	64.1	4.0
North Dakota	0.2	3,200	32	50.8	3.1
Utah	8.6	5,600	85	48.8	3.0
Wyoming	49.9	40,400	73	256.5	15.8
Major federal coal states	94.5	140,000	66	565.0	34.9
Total 50 states	94.6	144,700	33	1,620.0	100.0

Sources: Bureau of Land Management, U.S. Department of the Interior, *Final Environmental Statement: Federal Coal Management Program* (April 1979); Bureau of Land Management, *Federal Coal Management Report: Fiscal Year 1981;* and Leasing Policy Development Office, U.S. Department of Energy, *The 1980 Biennial Update of National and Regional Coal Production Goals for 1985, 1990 and 1995* (December 1980).
    [a] Fiscal year 1981 production.
    [b] Includes projected production of both federal and nonfederal coal in each state. The DOE projections are in the high range compared with other 1990 coal projections, particularly for the state of Wyoming. The state government of Wyoming itself forecasts that 1990 coal production will be 168 million tons.

because of drastic rises in the costs of the chief competing forms of power generation—oil, gas, and nuclear power. By some projections, western coal will supply 50 percent of U.S. coal production by 1990.[9] About 60 to 70 percent of western coal is federally owned. In addition, perhaps another 20 percent, although nonfederally owned itself, is so intermingled with federal coal that the federal and nonfederal coal should be developed jointly. (Such intermingling is found, for example, in checkerboard areas of alternating federal and nonfederal square miles left over from the old railroad land grants.) The most active area for western coal development is northeast Wyoming and southeast Montana in the Powder River region, sometimes called the "Saudi Arabia" of coal. Federal coal production in the Powder River region has risen from less than 3 million tons in 1968 to 55 million tons in 1981 and may exceed 200 million tons annually by 1990.

Table 2–3 shows the distribution of coal production and coal reserve ownership among the major federal coal states. Total federal coal pro-

[9] See Bureau of Land Management, U.S. Department of the Interior, *Final Environmental Statement: Federal Coal Management Program* (Washington, D.C., Government Printing Office, April 1979).

duction in 1981 was 94.6 million tons, more than 10 percent of U.S. production. The potential for further increases in federal coal production is indicated by the fact that federal reserves represent about 33 percent of total U S. coal reserves.

Actual production of "nonenergy" minerals typically does not occur on federal lands, because successful mineral discoveries are usually "patented" and the lands thus are converted into private ownership. However, as chapter 3 points out, the public lands are believed by some to contain a major share of the nonenergy mineral resources yet to be discovered in the United States. In 1977, fully 94 percent of U.S. copper production, 93 percent of silver production, 75 percent of asbestos production, and 52 percent of lead production occurred on lands that were former federal claims or existing federal leases. In total, 33 percent of the value of U.S. nonenergy mineral production came from such lands.[10]

Timber and Forage

The renewable resource found on the public lands that has the highest market value is timber. In 1976, the most recent year for which the Forest Service has provided figures on total U.S. public and private harvests, federal timber supplied about 21 percent of the U.S. timber harvest.[11] As shown in table 2–4, the total federal timber harvest in 1980 was 10.3 billion board feet. In that same year, the federal government received $842 million in timber revenues. Most of the federal timber is located in the national forests, but the BLM also manages 2.4 million acres of prime timberlands in western Oregon. As with several other resources already mentioned, inventories available for future production substantially exceed the current share of production. The national forests alone contain more than 50 percent of the national softwood sawtimber inventory. Softwoods supply around 85 percent of national lumber supplies and include fir, pine, spruce, and other desirable types of lumber. In 1977 California, Oregon, and Washington alone contained 54 percent of the total softwood inventory in the national forests; another 16 percent was in Alaska.

Rangeland forage has by far the lowest value of any of the important commodity outputs of the public lands; total federal grazing fees from 220 million acres of rangeland (plus additional forest land grazing) were

[10] U.S. Department of the Interior, *Background Papers: Draft for Public Review and Comment of the Report on Nonfuel Minerals Policy Review* (April 1979) p. III–5.

[11] Basic data on public land timber and range production and resources are contained in: Forest Service, U.S. Department of Agriculture, *An Assessment of the Forest and Rangeland Situation in the United States* (January 1980).

TABLE 2–4. Federal Timber Harvests and Inventory[a]

Location of timber	1980 Federal harvest volume[b] (million board ft)	1980 Federal harvest value[c] (millions $)	1980 Average sale value (per 1,000 board ft)	1977 Federal softwood sawtimber inventory (million board ft)	Percent of U.S. softwood sawtimber inventory
California	1,478.0	$123.8	$83.8	160,000	8.1%
Oregon					
Nat'l forests	2,511.4	348.1	138.6	252,800	12.7
BLM lands	1,139.9	348.3	305.6	50,000	2.5
Total Oregon	3,651.3	696.4	190.7	302,800	15.2
Washington	1,121.1	109.1	97.3	134,000	6.8
Total West Coast	6,250.4	929.3	148.7	596,800	30.1
Alaska	451.1	7.2	16.0	186,900	9.4
Idaho	657.3	25.7	39.1	99,700	5.0
Montana	434.3	16.2	37.3	64,100	3.2
Total Northern Rockies	1,091.6	41.9	38.3	163,800	8.2
Colorado	113.9	1.2	10.5	47,800	2.4
Utah	44.7	1.6	35.8	15,600	0.8
Wyoming	81.7	1.9	23.3	23,000	1.2
Total Central Rockies	240.3	4.7	19.5	86,400	4.4
Arizona	263.1	11.5	43.7	15,800	0.8
New Mexico	102.3	4.7	45.9	14,700	0.7
Total Southern Rockies	365.4	16.2	44.3	30,500	1.5
Total 50 states	10,344.7	1,083.4	104.7	1,058,400	53.4

Sources: U.S. Forest Service, Department of Agriculture, *Report of the Forest Service: Fiscal Year 1980 Highlights* (July 1981); Bureau of Land Management, U.S. Department of the Interior, *Public Land Statistics— 1980;* and Forest Service, U.S. Department of Agriculture, *Forest Statistics of the U.S., 1977—Review Draft* (Washington, D.C., Government Printing Office, 1978).

[a] Includes Forest Service and BLM timber harvests.

[b] Forest Service harvest volume based on actual harvest; BLM volume based on volume of timber sold in 1980.

[c] Forest Service value based on actual value of timber harvested; BLM value based on value of BLM timber sales in 1980.

only $40.5 million in 1980. About 2.1 million cattle and 2.3 million sheep consumed 10.3 million "animal unit months" (AUMs) of forage in 1980 on the public rangelands managed by BLM. An additional 8.7 million AUMs of forage were obtained from rangelands and forest lands managed by the Forest Service. It is estimated that the public rangelands provide about 30 percent of the total forage supplied from grazing in eleven western states, but less than 5 percent of the total national forage supply of all kinds.[12]

While public forage is of very minor importance to the national economy, it is highly significant to some individual ranchers. It is not uncommon for a rancher in the Southwest to obtain his entire forage supply from public lands—"yearlong" grazing. Further north, a more typical forage supply pattern would be private hay in the winter and early spring, BLM grazing during the late spring and early summer, Forest Service grazing through the rest of the summer, and grazing on private pastures and BLM land in the fall. Ranchers have permits to a certain amount of grazing in a particular area (an "allotment") on BLM and Forest Service rangelands. Such grazing permits effectively are assigned indefinitely to owners of particular ranch properties and are transferred virtually automatically to any new purchaser of the property—often thereby adding a large "permit value" to the sale price of the ranch. A fairly small number of ranchers benefit the most from access to these public lands; fully 64 percent of the AUMs of public land grazing are held by 12.3 percent of the rancher "permittees," involving fewer than 4,000 individual ranch operations in all.[13]

Recreation, Wilderness, and Wildlife

In addition to the commodities discussed above, the public lands provide a number of other very important "outputs" which are not usually exchanged in traditional private markets. These include camping, hiking, and other recreational activities, the preservation of wilderness areas and wildlife, as well as the protection of sites that are of historic or natural interest. Some of the "outputs" of the public lands—on-site recreation, for example—can be enjoyed only by participants. The preservation of wilderness areas or endangered wildlife, however, may provide satisfaction to many who might never visit particular sites. Fees are charged for some noncommodity uses, although these are generally well below typical charges for private recreation. In 1981, for instance, the

[12] A report from the secretary of the interior and the secretary of agriculture, *Study of Fees for Livestock Grazing on Federal Lands* (October 21, 1977) p. 3–4.
[13] Ibid., p. 4–40.

normal entry charge at national parks was $1–2 per car for visits in some cases lasting up to 15 days. If visits at all the units of the national park system are included (many of which have no fee), the average charge per visitor was only about 5 cents per day in 1981.

The national park system was established in 1916. By then, eleven national parks, including Yellowstone (1872), Yosemite (1890), Mt. Rainier (1899), and Glacier (1910), had already been created by individual acts of Congress. The national park system has grown rapidly in recent years, from 26 million acres in 1960, to 79 million acres in 1981. The Alaska National Interest Lands Conservation Act of 1980 alone added 44 million acres. Visits to full-fledged national parks rose from 27 million in 1960 to 47 million in 1980.

By 1981, the national park system contained not only 48 national parks, but also 78 national monuments, 64 national historic sites, 17 national recreational areas, 12 national preserves, 10 national seashores, 4 national lakeshores, 4 national parkways, and a number of other types of facilities, including the White House. The management philosophy of the national park system has been to preserve as far as possible plants, wildlife, landscape, and geology in their natural condition, but to make these assets highly accessible to the general population.

The first unit in the national wildlife refuge system was established by President Theodore Roosevelt in 1903 when he designated 3-acre Pelican Island off the Florida coast as a Federal Bird Preserve.[14] Like the national parks, the refuge system has grown very rapidly in recent years, reaching 88.7 million acres with the addition in 1980 of 54 million acres of new refuge lands in Alaska. The refuge system differs from the national park system in that there is considerable hunting and fishing, grazing, crop production, and even some timber harvesting and mineral leasing on these lands. The number of visits grew from 14 million in 1966 to 23 million in 1980, about half the number of visits to the national parks.

More Recent Recreation Systems

The national wilderness system was formally established by Congress under the Wilderness Act of 1964, which designated the first 9.3 million acres of the system and created procedures for review of additional lands. Prior to 1964, the Forest Service had already identified a number of wilderness areas administratively, but wilderness proponents preferred statutory assurances against later changes in use. Under pressure

[14] Fish and Wildlife Service, U.S. Department of the Interior, *Final Environmental Statement: Operation of the National Wildlife Refuge System* (November 1976) p. II–5.

from such groups, the Forest Service in 1972 began an intensive review of the national forests to identify further areas suitable for wilderness classification. Dubbed "Rare I" (for *R*oadless *A*rea *R*eview and *E*valuation), this review was finally abandoned inconclusively in 1974 after an adverse court decision and severe criticism from environmental groups. The Carter administration in 1977 began a second major wilderness review of 62 million acres of roadless lands ("Rare II"), which was completed in 1979. As a result, the Forest Service recommended 15 million acres to Congress for wilderness designation (6 million in Alaska), further study of 11 million acres, and against wilderness designation for 36 million acres, which would be allocated to "multiple use." The Bureau of Land Management is now examining 24 million acres of its land outside Alaska for possible wilderness designation.

By 1979 the size of the wilderness system had grown to 19 million acres, 80 percent of which was in national forests and by 1981, with the addition of more than 50 million acres of Alaska wilderness, the system reached 80 million acres. The largest part of wilderness acreage is now in the national park system (35 million acres); the national forest system contains 25 million acres; and the wildlife refuge system contains 19 million acres. Construction of roads, harvesting of timber, and recreational use of mechanized vehicles or equipment are prohibited in wilderness areas. Hunting and fishing are allowed and existing livestock grazing can continue, although new range improvements in many cases cannot be installed.

The national wild and scenic rivers system and the national trail system—both established by Congress in 1968—also serve as major sources of recreation. As of early 1982, 61 rivers running for 6,936 miles had been approved by Congress for the wild and scenic rivers system; an additional 88 rivers were designated for further study.[15] Congress has also designated 21,102 miles of national trails, including the Lewis & Clark, Appalachian, and Pacific Crest trails.

The National Forests and the BLM Rangelands

The national forest system is not usually considered one of the national recreation systems. However, 234 million recreational "visitor days" (defined to be 12 hours) were spent in the national forests in 1980. If

---

[15] Wild rivers are free of impoundments and have unpolluted water and shorelines that are basically primitive. They are generally inaccessible except by foot. Scenic rivers have no impoundments and shorelines or watersheds that are largely primitive. They may be reached by road or railroad. To qualify for inclusion in the system, a river or river segment must be free flowing, have high quality water, and possess one or more outstanding scenic, recreational, geologic, fish and wildlife, or historic or cultural values.

these were to be valued conservatively at $5 per day (a minimum price for a full day of just about any privately sold activity), the total value in 1980 of recreation visits to the national forests would have exceeded $1 billion, which is more than 50 percent higher than the receipts from timber sales. Moreover, 89 percent of timber-sale value in 1980 was generated by the 45 million acres of national forest lands in California, Oregon, and Washington—only 24 percent of the total system acreage. In short, with the possible exception of these West Coast forest lands, the national forest system should really be considered as one of the prime national recreation systems.

The number of recreation "visits" to the national forests climbed from 7 million in 1930 to 134 million in 1964. The states with the heaviest recreational use of the national forests are California (58 million visitor days in 1980), Colorado (22 million), Oregon (19 million), Arizona (18 million) and Utah (14 million). The most popular recreational activities include camping (57 million visitor days in 1980), fishing (17 million), hunting (16 million), and winter sports (14 million).

If there has been insufficient official recognition of recreation on the national forests, the gap between perception and reality is even greater for the public rangelands managed by the BLM. More than 65 million visitor days were spent on BLM rangelands in 1980; they would be worth more than $300 million if recreational visits were valued at $5 per day, compared with grazing revenues of $24.6 million. Future trends will almost certainly widen the dominance of recreational value over commodity values for much of the BLM rangelands. This has happened on private rangelands as well; on the Edwards Plateau in Texas, where there are no public lands, ranchers have commonly earned considerably more from hunting access fees—up to $50 per person per day—than from their livestock operations.[16]

Preservation Acts

The public lands also contain many important historical, geological, archeological, and paleontological assets; plant and animal systems; and other elements of the national heritage. Their preservation has become a high priority item and a major influence on public land management. As shown in table 2–5, the flow of legislation to preserve the national

[16] Charles W. Ramsey, "Potential Economic Returns from Deer as Compared with Livestock in the Edwards Plateau Region of Texas," *Journal of Range Management* vol. 18 (May 1965) pp. 247–250. See also C. Robert Taylor, Bruce R. Beattie, and Kerry R. Livergood, "Public vs. Private Systems for Big Game Hunting," paper prepared for a conference on "Property Rights and Natural Resources: A New Paradigm for the Environmental Movement," Montana State University, Bozeman, December 1980.

heritage greatly speeded up about twenty years ago, reflecting a growing sense that something important was being lost in the headlong national pursuit of "progress." Areas of historical as well as natural interest were included in the legislation. For example, the National Historic Preservation Act of 1966 created the Advisory Council on Historic Preser-

TABLE 2–5. Preservation Legislation Enacted by the U.S. Congress

Law	Year enacted	Main preservation provision(s)
Yellowstone Park Act	1872	Created first national park.
Antiquities Act	1906	Created system of national monuments.
National Parks Act	1916	Created National Park System.
Wilderness Act	1964	Created national wilderness system.
National Historic Preservation Act	1966, 1980 amend.	Expands scope of historic preservation, directs federal agencies to examine impacts on historic properties.
Wild and Scenic Rivers Act	1968	Created national wild and scenic rivers system.
National Trails System Act	1968	Created national trail system.
Bald Eagle Protection Act	1969, 1972 amend.	Forbids killing of bald and golden eagles and protects habitat.
National Environmental Policy Act	1969	Requires study of environmental impacts associated with major federal actions.
Wild and Free-Roaming Horse and Burro Act	1971	Provides for federal management and protection of wild horses and burros.
Endangered Species Act	1973	Bars federal actions that would jeopardize an endangered or threatened species.
Eastern Wilderness Act	1975	Extended wilderness system into East, creating first eastern wilderness areas.
Federal Land Policy and Management Act	1976	Requires wilderness review of BLM lands.
Surface Mining Control and Reclamation Act	1977	Requires restoration of mined land to original condition.
Endangered American Wilderness Act	1978	Added 1.3 million acres of new wilderness.
National Parks and Recreation Act	1978	Made important additions to the wild and scenic rivers system, national scenic trails system, and national wilderness system.
Public Rangelands Improvement Act	1978	Sets goal to restore rangelands to earlier productivity.
Archeological Resources Protection Act	1979	Requires permits for site excavations and artifact removal, provides other protections for archeological resources on federal lands.
Alaska National Interest Lands Conservation Act	1980	Establishes large new national parks, wildlife refuges, wilderness areas, and other "conservation system units" in Alaska.

vation, gave a new prominence to the National Register of Historic Places, and generally provided a much stronger mandate for historical and archeological preservation. In early 1982, the BLM employed a total of 142 professional archeologists, 10 historians, and 3 anthropologists to ensure that such considerations were included in land management decisions.

The legislation outlined here has formed a preservation system that can be seen as a unique American outdoor museum. Europe pioneered art and history museums; libraries; preservation of churches, castles, and palaces; and other such elements of its heritage. With its national parks, wilderness areas, wild and scenic rivers, and protection of endangered species, America has pioneered the preservation of the heritage of the natural world. That America should develop such a contribution to the museums of the world is due in large part to the central place of the land in American history and in the shaping of the American character. The public lands play a large role in government preservation efforts both because many of the most unique natural features are located on these lands, and because it is easier to provide special government protection on such lands.

AN OLD DEBATE: USE VERSUS PRESERVATION

The basic purposes and assumptions of public land management were formed around the turn of the century and have not changed very much since then. The intellectual inspiration was derived mainly from two movements with quite different objectives, conservationism and preservationism. The influence of these two movements and their past battles is still seen in many current policy issues concerning the public lands.

In the first 100 years of the nation, little attention was paid to preserving the heritage of nature. There were still vast areas of forbidding if potentially productive lands open to the west; the "wilderness," while offering freedom from the restraints of civilization, was also something to be conquered.[17] However, the radical and sometimes disquieting social transformations accompanying industrialization and urbanization after the Civil War also produced a strong counter urge to remember and preserve aspects of the past. Indeed, by the latter part of the nineteenth century, a full-fledged preservation movement had emerged in the United States.

[17] See Roderick Nash, *Wilderness and the American Mind* (New Haven, Conn., Yale University Press, 1967).

A key turning point was the year 1890, which historian Frederick Jackson Turner singled out as the critical dividing line in all of American history, marking the closing of the western frontier.[18] In that year Yosemite, Sequoia, and Kings Canyon national parks were created, in significant part as the result of efforts by the famous naturalist, John Muir, the founder of the Sierra Club in 1892. The General Revision Act of 1891 included provisions to establish a system of forest reserves; although a little unclear, it appears that the actual congressional intent was to preserve the forests much as national parks.[19] New York state in 1894 similarly set aside 3 million acres in Adirondack Park that have been preserved in an undeveloped state to this day.

As matters turned out, however, the General Revision Act became the founding legislation for the national forest system, not the national park system. The prospect of setting aside such large areas in forest reserves aroused strong opposition among westerners who, in a foreshadowing of later conflicts, wanted the lands kept available for commodity uses. Owing in part to the efforts of Gifford Pinchot, who would become the first chief of the Forest Service in 1905, a compromise was achieved whereby the forest reserves would be retained in federal ownership, but the management philosophy would emphasize multiple use over preservation. The triumph of this philosophy, which later became known as conservationism, was reflected in the enactment of the "Organic Act" of the Forest Service in 1897. The modern Forest Service and the BLM still embrace conservationism as the basic management philosophy of the public lands.[20]

The conservationist philosophy was not only a necessary political accommodation to demands for use of federally retained lands, but a powerful ideology in its own right. Conservationism, like preservationism, had roots in a sharp reaction to unsettling events of the late nineteenth century. The vast herds of buffalo had been extinguished in a few years; the seemingly inexhaustible pineries of the upper Midwest were largely cut in a few decades; overgrazing severely depleted the western ranges within a short time; millions of passenger pigeons were wiped out and other bird populations were severely depleted; gold and

[18] Turner, "The Significance of the Frontier in American History."

[19] Samuel T. Dana and Sally K. Fairfax, *Forest and Range Policy: Its Development in the United States* (New York, McGraw Hill, 1980) p. 56.

[20] For accounts of this history, see Gifford Pinchot, *Breaking New Ground* (New York, Harcourt, Brace, 1947); Henry Clepper, *Professional Forestry in the United States* (Baltimore, Md., Johns Hopkins University Press for Resources for the Future, 1971); Glen O. Robinson, *The Forest Service: A Study in Public Land Management* (Baltimore, Md., Johns Hopkins University Press for Resources for the Future, 1975); and Harold K. Steen, *The U.S. Forest Service: A History* (Seattle, University of Washington Press, 1976).

other mining towns rapidly boomed and then went bust; other events suggested a finiteness of resources that had not previously concerned most Americans.

A number of scholars have since pointed out that in many of these cases resources were exhausted rapidly because there were no private property rights on the public lands—the so-called "tragedy of the commons."[21] But most Americans of the time interpreted the overexploitation of natural resources as a result of the rapacious, undisciplined, and short-sighted behavior of private individuals and companies. They looked to government to ensure that natural resources would not be used up too rapidly, that they would be "conserved" for the future. This turn to government was not confined to natural resources; it was part of a broader progressive mode of thought which produced the Federal Reserve System, the Food and Drug Administration, the Federal Trade Commission, and other institutions still part of the government today.[22]

Widespread fraud and illegality attended the disposal of public lands to private parties in the latter part of the nineteenth century.[23] This led in turn to a wider suspicion and apprehension about private ownership of natural resources. It was only later that historians saw some major benefits in the unseemly establishment of private property rights, for it permitted escape from common-property resource problems and created incentives for the economic development that helped build the West. As later critics put it, congressional attempts to curb abuses never addressed the basic land law failings that caused these abuses in the first place; hence they "made it even more necessary for ranchers and others seeking to gain ownership . . . to resort to fraud in a more systematic way than they had before."[24]

The conservation movement was also very much a product of the scientific management movement of the time. In the business world, Frederick Taylor became a world hero—applauded even by Lenin—for demonstrating how scientific methods could greatly improve the efficiency of business production. Many Americans were convinced that virtually unlimited progress lay ahead, to be achieved on the foundations of scientific knowledge and method. In his leading study of the conser-

---

[21] Garrett Hardin, "The Tragedy of the Commons," *Science* vol. 162 (December 13, 1968) pp. 1243–1248; and Garrett Hardin and John Baden, eds., *Managing the Commons* (San Francisco, W. H. Freeman, 1977).

[22] For a classic study of progressive ideas, see Dwight Waldo, *The Administrative State: A Study of the Political Theory of American Public Administration* (New York, Ronald Press, 1948).

[23] See Hibbard, *A History of the Public Land Policies*, and Robbins, *Our Landed Heritage*.

[24] Gates, *History of Public Land Law Development*, p. 486.

vation movement, historian Samuel Hays emphasized its technocratic underpinnings:[25]

> The broader significance of the conservation movement stemmed from the role it played in the transformation of a decentralized, nontechnical, loosely organized society, where waste and inefficiency ran rampant, into a highly organized, technical, and centrally planned and directed social organization which could meet a complex world with efficiency and purpose. This spirit of efficiency appeared in many realms of American life, in the professional engineering societies, among forward-looking industrial management leaders, and in municipal government reform, as well as in the resource management concepts of Theodore Roosevelt. The possibilities of applying scientific and technical principles to resource development fired federal officials with enthusiasm for the future and imbued all in the conservation movement with a kindred spirit. These goals required public management, of the nation's streams because private enterprise could not afford to undertake it, of the Western lands to adjust one resource use to another. They also required new administrative methods, utilizing to the fullest extent the latest scientific knowledge and expert, disinterested personnel. This was the gospel of efficiency—efficiency which could be realized only through planning, foresight, and conscious purpose.

The scientific management espoused by conservationists for the public lands conflicted in many ways with the objectives of preservationists, who wanted the land left undisturbed, thereby precluding activities such as timber harvesting or mining. The split between conservationists and preservationists produced a complete break in relations between Pinchot and Muir during a famous controversy over a proposal to build a dam and reservoir in the then-beautiful Hetch-Hetchy Valley within Yosemite National Park. Pinchot strongly supported the project to supply water and power to San Francisco. Pinchot's position is described as reflecting the fact that he generally had "apparently no interest in the parks or in the preservation of great scenery."[26] Muir, by contrast, fiercely opposed the project, asserting that it defiled a national park of which "no holier temple has ever been consecrated by the heart of man."[27] The dam was eventually approved by Congress in 1913, reflecting the wider popular support at the time for the values of rational efficiency and scientific progress espoused by conservationism.

---

[25] Samuel P. Hays, *Conservation and The Gospel of Efficiency: The Progressive Conservation Movement, 1890–1920* (Cambridge, Mass., Harvard University Press, 1959) pp. 265–266. Reprinted by permission of Harvard University Press.

[26] Ise, *Our National Park Policy*, p. 87.

[27] Ibid., p. 88.

The enactment of the National Parks Act in 1916, the charter for the current national park system, established a land management system which, unlike the national forests, had preservation rather than multiple use as its basic objective. By then, preservationists had largely abandoned hope that the Forest Service would adequately defend their cause. The objectives of maximum use and preservation of nature apparently were too conflicting to reconcile in the same agency. The conviction that preservationist objectives are better served by formal segregation of lands from use-oriented systems has played a major role in public land management to the present day.

Neither the conservation nor preservation movements had much use for economic thinking, partly because the strong moral feelings and collective enthusiasms aroused by conservationism and preservationism were antithetical to the incentive of individual self-interest at the core of economic theories. Thus, although they were concerned with maximizing the use of public lands, conservationists seldom formulated this concept in economic terms. Expressing a common reaction, the Harvard economist Edward Mason once commented that conservationism "was a political movement. . . . Its economic analysis was practically non-existent, though it did emphasize the importance of sustained yield in renewable resources. The best it could do in defining the meaning of conservation was to say that it meant a 'wise use of resources.' "[28]

DECIDING THE USES OF THE PUBLIC LANDS

An Exercise in Zoning

Left to the private market, land use would be decided by the forces of competition—with the highest paying use prevailing. On private lands, governments have often chosen, however, to intervene extensively by means of zoning, subdivision controls, and other regulations. Indeed, zoning was explicitly intended by its architects to displace the market and provide instead for implementation of comprehensive public plans for land use. In practice, however, this objective has seldom been realized, partly because zoning restrictions on use of private property have created so much controversy.[29]

[28] Edward S. Mason, "Resources in the Past and for the Future," in Charles J. Hitch, ed., *Resources for an Uncertain Future* (Baltimore, Md., Johns Hopkins University Press for Resources for the Future, 1978) pp. 9–10. An exception to this criticism is the work of Siegfried von Ciriacy-Wantrup. See S. Ciriacy-Wantrup, *Resource Conservation: Economics and Policies* (Berkeley, University of California Press, 1952).

[29] See Robert H. Nelson, *Zoning and Property Rights: An Analysis of the American System of Land Use Regulation* (Cambridge, Mass., MIT Press, 1977).

While government intervention in the use of private property is not a problem on the public lands, controversies have arisen for other reasons. Fierce battles have broken out over zoning decisions to exclude extractive uses such as mining or timber harvesting from wilderness and other public land areas. These controversies are not unlike those attending many private zoning decisions. Public land zoning decisions often create major winners and losers; they play a large role in determining the levels of recreational, mineral, timber, and other outputs of the public lands—effectively rationing the services of the public lands among these outputs.

In theory, each parcel of public land should be put to the use with the highest social value. In practice, however, there are many obstacles to determining the social value of a specific parcel of land in a specific use. For recreation and other nonmarket uses, there is much uncertainty about the correct price at which to value these outputs. For instance, how much is it worth to preserve the breeding habitat for an endangered species? What value should be attached to a wilderness experience? For some marketable commodities the level of production on the public lands—itself influenced by public land zoning—is large enough to affect the market price of the commodity, again creating considerable uncertainty about the appropriate price.

There are equally formidable hurdles in determining the actual physical quantities of outputs gained or lost in public land zoning decisions. The potential for mineral production in an area often cannot be determined without a costly exploration effort (which may itself be environmentally disruptive); yet, such an effort frequently is uneconomic without prior guarantees that mineral production will later be permitted. The effects of habitat changes on wildlife populations and on related recreational activities are often poorly understood.

Much easier to understand, if not resolve, are the conflicts that arise between alternative uses of public lands. At least some mining will always be inconsistent with preservation of wildlife or wilderness. At least some timber harvesting will always be opposed by those who use public forests for recreation. At least some offshore oil and gas development will always be opposed by fishermen or others concerned about the possible aesthetic impairment of coastlines or a damaging oil spill.

Because it has been so difficult to establish "highest social value" in such cases, decisions about the uses of the public lands have been largely determined by political forces, much as in private land zoning. Indeed, in dealing with some zoning matters, such as the value of a wilderness area, or the importance of protecting habitat for endangered species, expert analysis is never likely to—nor perhaps should—displace political resolution. The decisions to use these lands for one purpose and not for another raise some of the most difficult and controversial issues of public land management.

Zoning Classifications

More than 100 years ago, the distinguished scientist, explorer, and first director of the U.S. Geological Survey, John Wesley Powell, argued that the arid lands in the West should be classified according to their best use and managed in a fashion most suitable to that use.[30] Powell had in mind separate use systems at a minimum for timberlands, irrigated farmlands, and grazing lands. Indeed, in a rough way the national forest system, Bureau of Reclamation project lands, and BLM rangelands correspond to the Powell typology.

Under early use categories such as a national forest, the act of classifying automatically transferred the land to a new agency. However, this has not been the case for the newer public land classifications such as wilderness areas. Each land agency thus has found itself directly allocating its own land among a number of competing uses.

Although the first U.S. zoning ordinance, in New York City in 1916, had only three broad use classifications—commercial, residential, and unrestricted—the urban trend has been toward much greater refinement.[31] Similarly, the public land agencies have introduced many new classifications. The BLM in recent years has been especially active in pioneering new use zones that include research natural areas, outstanding natural areas, cultural areas, primitive areas, areas of critical environmental concern, recreation lands, and wild horse ranges. In 1970 Congress created the King Range National Conservation Area on BLM lands along the California coast 200 miles north of San Francisco. Legislation has been introduced to create a Snake River Birds-of-Prey National Conservation Area to protect key raptor habitat on BLM lands in Idaho.

The California Desert Conservation Area contains 25 million acres—about a quarter of the total area of California—that are divided about equally between BLM and other landowners. One of the key features of the BLM plan for the area is a four-zone system, ranging from "controlled" zones with mainly wilderness uses allowed, to "intensive" zones.[32]

---

[30] John Wesley Powell, *Report on the Lands of the Arid Regions* (Washington, D.C., 1878). For an account of Powell's life and thinking, see Wallace Stegner, *Beyond the Hundredth Meridian: John Wesley Powell and the Second Opening of the West* (Boston, Houghton Mifflin, 1953).

[31] See Seymour Toll, *Zoned American* (New York, Grossman, 1969).

[32] Bureau of Land Management, U.S. Department of the Interior, *Final Environmental Impact Statement and Proposed Plan: The California Desert Conservation Area* (September 1980).

The BLM has established "unsuitability criteria" for livestock grazing, timber harvesting, and coal leasing; lands falling within the criteria are off-limits for these uses. Some of the criteria, such as excluding coal leasing from certain alluvial valleys, were in fact statutorily mandated.

The Forest Service has also employed zoning classifications widely. The Public Land Law Review Commission noted in 1970 that "within the total area of a national forest, there are established zones, each designated, in effect, for a dominant use to the total or partial exclusion of other uses."[33] A 1978 plan for an Oregon national forest allocated lands to nine use and management classifications, including those to "achieve high amounts of wood fiber and forage," "provide 'old growth' timber habitat," "maintain many primitive forest characteristics" and an "experimental forest and range" area.[34]

There are still large areas of public lands not zoned for any specific use. On those "multiple use" lands, agency managers have wide discretion to decide the best use. Although the principle of multiple use is sometimes said to provide an actual basis for making decisions, most students of public land management have concluded that it is in fact amorphous and offers little substantive guidance.[35] Multiple-use management is really management by agency administrative discretion in reponse to individual proposals. The lands managed under multiple use can be considered the public-land equivalent of the industrial or unrestricted zones commonly found in municipal zoning ordinances.

Congress has provided for the classification of the public lands in a number of ways: (1) by directly classifying certain public lands for a major use (e.g., a wildlife refuge) and then assigning management responsibility to an agency with a management philosophy suited to that use; (2) by creating a number of new zoning classifications (e.g., wilderness areas) and then retaining the right to approve agency proposals that certain lands be included within these classifications; (3) by formally creating other new zoning classifications and leaving it to the agencies to determine the lands falling within those classifications (e.g., alluvial valleys); and (4) by providing general authority for agencies to create their own zoning classifications and to designate lands falling within

[33] *One Third of the Nation's Land: A Report to the President and to the Congress by the Public Land Law Review Commission* (Washington, D.C., Government Printing Office, 1970) p. 51.

[34] Forest Service, U.S. Department of Agriculture, *Final Land Management Plan and Environmental Statement for Grande Ronde Planning Unit* (April 1978) pp. i, ii.

[35] John A. Zivnuska, "The Multiple Problems of Multiple Use," *Journal of Forestry* (August 1961); George Hall, "The Myth and Reality of Multiple Use," *Natural Resources Journal* vol. 3 (October 1963) pp. 276–290; R. W. Behan, "The Succotash Syndrome, or Multiple Use: A Heartfelt Approach to Forest Land Management," *Natural Resources Journal* vol. 7 (October 1967) pp. 473–484; and E. M. Sterling, "The Myth of Multiple Use," *American Forests* vol. 76 (June 1970) pp. 24–27.

these zones. This latter type of action is in fact a main function of land-use planning. If a plan genuinely resolves conflicts of uses in advance, it does so by matching up specific areas of land with specific uses, that is, it creates use zones. The National Forest Management Act of 1976 and the Federal Land Policy and Management Act of 1976 both require resolution of use conflicts on the public lands by means of formal land use plans.

Mining Withdrawals

Urban zoning becomes controversial when it is viewed as a means of excluding low- or even middle-income housing from a community. Zoning the public lands can be no less controversial. To be sure, the main use excluded on the public lands is not housing (although second homes are a potential use for many public lands), but rather, mining, timber harvesting, and other commodity production. Such users complain that they are unreasonably denied access to highly productive lands that would be most valuable in commodity production. In a fashion reminiscent of zoning debates in urban areas, public land zoning is also accused of benefiting an elite and well-off minority concerned with preserving its own recreation amenities while keeping out uses that would distribute economic benefits more broadly across the whole society.

One of the earliest forms of zoning on the public lands was to "withdraw" lands from a particular use. In 1906 Theodore Roosevelt withdrew 66 million acres of federal coal lands, preventing their sale to the private sector. Over the years, the public land agencies have withdrawn lands for many other purposes, such as national defense or for sites needed by the Bureau of Reclamation or other civilian agencies. The most controversial form of withdrawal has been to preclude lands from disposal under the Mining Law of 1872. This law provides that a prospector can stake a claim on public land and then, if he can show a valuable mineral discovery, obtain full private ownership (patent) to lands. Federal withdrawals of this sort have been made to protect particular areas from the destructive impacts which mining can have on sensitive environments.[36]

Large numbers of withdrawals were in fact made over time by the land management agencies, and in the 1970s the mining industry com-

---

[36] For a study of mining law on the public lands, see Robert W. Swenson, "Legal Aspects of Mineral Resources Exploitation," in Gates, *History of Public Land Law Development*. See also Congress of the United States, Office of Technology Assessment, *Management of Fuel and Nonfuel Minerals in Federal Land: Current Status and Issues* (Washington, D.C., 1979).

plained that it was finding itself shut out of an ever larger proportion of public lands. Not only had there been traditional withdrawals, but some of the new recreation systems also precluded mining. For example, although the Wilderness Act did allow mineral exploration to continue until 1984, the dampening effect of wilderness designation in most cases effectively precluded it.

A 1976 task force formed by the Interior Department sought to determine the cumulative impact of all kinds of withdrawals on the availability of public lands for mineral exploration. It found that, excluding the Alaska lands then in an uncertain status, 27 percent of federal land was completely closed to mineral exploration, 4 percent was highly restrictive, 18 percent moderately restrictive, and 52 percent had slight restrictions or none. The largest single category of closed lands was naval petroleum and oil shale reserves (24 million acres), followed by wildlife refuges (19 million acres), other military purposes (17 million acres), and national parks and monuments (15 million acres).[37] In order to determine whether further lands could he made available for mining, the Federal Land Policy and Management Act of 1976 directed that a full review of past withdrawals be completed within fifteen years and that withdrawals no longer necessary be revoked.

Total withdrawal is in fact a blunt instrument for achieving protection from the adverse environmental impacts of mining. However, under current law, public agencies find it necessary to exclude mining completely because they have no other mechanism to control mining impacts. A variety of proposals thus have been developed to replace the claim-patent system of the Mining Law with a discretionary leasing system similar to that for energy minerals. In their most naive versions these proposals simply suggest that the government lease copper, silver, and other "hardrock" minerals, just as it leases, say, coal. The problem is that no one knows where new hardrock deposits are located; the process of their discovery is typically arduous, time-consuming, expensive, and often environmentally disruptive. Any revision of the Mining Law must include an adequate incentive for industry to explore, which has traditionally been achieved by giving the explorer the rights to keep any valuable discoveries.

The Carter administration in 1977 proposed a new mining law under which industry would apply for a license to explore a given area and then receive an exclusive right to lease any minerals actually discovered. The government, however, would have the power to deny such a lease

[37] U.S. Department of the Interior, *Final Report of the Task Force on the Availability of Federally Owned Mineral Lands* (Washington, D.C., Government Printing Office, 1977) pp. 48–50.

if the projected impacts turned out to be environmentally or otherwise unacceptable. However, the mining industry successfully objected that the proposal went too far in protecting against adverse impacts and would kill off industry willingness to explore. The proposed change in the law made no headway.

A solution sometimes proposed would be for the government to deny permission for development following successful exploration only if mining companies were compensated for the costs of exploration. But this option raises formidable administrative problems in adequately measuring exploration costs and in avoiding incentives for companies to explore areas even when it is apparent that the government may well have to buy out the mining rights. The difficulty is compounded by the fact that only a small fraction of exploration efforts yield mineral deposits that are economic to mine (see chapter 3). If the government pays compensation for only the one successful mineral find, other failures would no longer be covered by the bonanza of this find. As a consequence, an acceptable compensation scheme would require that the government not only pay exploration costs for the one successful find, but also for all the other failures expected—an extremely complicated and expensive task.

Hence, even if it is not ideal, some form of withdrawal may have to be retained as a means of resolving conflicts between mining and other uses. Nevertheless, the current approach is a very primitive form of zoning, essentially allowing only two mining classifications, acceptable or unacceptable. It might well be desirable to create more zone classifications; mining might be allowed in some fragile areas, but under strict terms specified in advance by the zoning. Similarly, some kinds of mining might be allowed, and other types excluded by zoning. Underground mining, for example, might be acceptable in some places where surface mining is not, but of course the nature of the mineral deposit usually determines the mining technology. The fact that the mining law has survived for more than 100 years with little change is a strong indication that there are no easy solutions in this policy area.

Zoning to Exclude Timber Harvesting

Timber harvesting has traditionally been prohibited in national parks and, more recently, in some of the newer recreation systems, such as wilderness areas. Moreover, the Forest Service and BLM have been ruling out or tightly restricting timber harvesting in more and more areas to provide streamside buffer zones; to maintain scenic vistas along highways and rivers; on steep slopes where severe sedimentation or other environmental problems would arise; where forest regeneration would take too long (more than five years on BLM lands); in order to preserve forest old growth as wildlife habitat; and for other reasons.

Like the mining industry, the timber industry has complained that the cumulative effect of such zoning exclusions is to unreasonably restrict timber supplies. However, a number of economists contend that timber harvesting should actually be abandoned on still more lands because it simply is uneconomic. Most would agree, however, that the economic benefits of each zoning exclusion of timber harvesting should be examined closely to determine whether the benefits really exceed the costs. The American consumer has a significant stake in the national level of timber harvests; among other uses, lumber represents around 15 percent of the selling price of new homes.

A number of studies have in fact shown that the costs to the Forest Service of holding timber sales, including road costs, often exceed the revenues returned. One study examined 169,000 roadless acres in southwest Colorado which a Forest Service plan had proposed for timber harvesting. It was calculated conservatively that the timber would have to sell for at least $38.70 per thousand board feet to cover the costs of building logging roads and other Forest Service costs. Yet, the average successful sale price on similar timber was $2.65 per thousand board feet in the year the plan was issued.[38] In another case, the Natural Resources Defense Council found that, "although all but 45,000 of the 523,000 roadless areas in the Caribou National Forest in Idaho have been designated for 'multiple use' management, this forest has returned only 24 cents for every dollar spent on timber sales over the past five years."[39] Nationwide, an assistant secretary of the Department of Agriculture conceded that almost 22 percent of the Forest Service timber sale volume in 1978 did not cover sale costs.[40]

A more economically rational pattern of timber harvesting on the national forest system would produce some major regional shifts in harvest levels. The timber harvested in California, Oregon, and Wash-

[38] William F. Hyde, "Timber Economics in the Rockies: Efficiency and Management Options," *Land Economics* vol. 57 (November 1981) p. 632. See also William F. Hyde, "Compounding Clear-cuts: The Social Failures of Public Timber Management in the Rockies," in John Baden and Richard L. Stroup, eds., *Bureaucracy vs. Environment: The Environmental Costs of Bureaucratic Governance* (Ann Arbor, University of Michigan Press, 1981).

[39] Thomas J. Barlow, Gloria E. Helfand, Trent W. Orr, and Thomas B. Stoel, Jr., *"Giving Away the National Forests: An Analysis of U.S. Forest Service Timber Sales Below Costs,"* Natural Resources Defense Council (June 1980) p. 3 of background paper.

[40] Letter from M. Rupert Cutler, Assistant Secretary of the Department of Agriculture for Natural Resources and Environment, to James G. Dean (editor of *The Living Wilderness*), March 13, 1980.

ington in 1980 yielded revenues of $83, $139, and $93 per thousand board feet, respectively. By comparison, Arizona, Idaho, and Colorado timber yielded revenues of $44, $39, and $10, respectively. In the central Rockies, the Forest Service found that revenues from expanded harvests under consideration in 1978 on average would cover less than 50 percent of the costs incurred.[41] An economically sensible policy would eliminate public timber harvesting over wide areas of the Rockies, which happens also to be one of the prime scenic and recreational attractions of the nation.

Generally, the best timber is located conveniently in the lower elevations, while the best mountain scenery and other recreational attractions are at elevations too high for growing prime timber. Hence, even within California, Oregon, and Washington, it would be economically beneficial to exclude timber harvesting from many higher elevation sites and to zone them for recreational or other nontimber use. In short, both interregionally and more locally, the Forest Service could make economic and environmental gains by changing its timber harvesting patterns.

It is surprising that the Forest Service has not seized such an opportunity, which has hardly been a closely held secret. In 1976 Marion Clawson reported that "the geographic pattern of expenditure on national forests is economically unsound and wasteful," partly because "too much money is being spent on poor sites and not enough on good ones."[42] Such views were echoed in 1977, by Brock Evans, testifying as the director of the Washington office of the Sierra Club:[43]

> The basic timber management policy of the National Forest System today is one of "extensive management . . ." The alternative we are asking consideration of is one of "intensive management" which would consist of a higher level of commercial and precommercial thinning, planting and seeding, and pruning which would concentrate on those areas which have already been accessed by road systems and which in general contain the better quality timber growing areas. Our examinations of Forest Service data indicate that such an alternative is not only feasible and generally environmentally superior, but also economically more efficient.

[41] U.S. Forest Service, calculations made for the Carter administration "Timber Study on Alternatives for Increasing Supplies," memorandum of May 1978.

[42] Marion Clawson, *The Economics of National Forest Management* (Washington, D.C., Resources for the Future, 1976) pp. 75, 78.

[43] Statement of Brock Evans, Director, Washington office, Sierra Club, Before the Senate Subcommittee on Interior of the Appropriations Committee, Regarding the Forest Service Budget for Fiscal Year 1978 (April 19, 1977) pp. 1–2 of original submitted statement.

A change in management policy will not necessarily mean that conflicts between timber and recreational uses of the national forests will cease to exist. The nation will presumably want to preserve an ample acreage of old growth forests, some of which will turn out to have a very high economic value. Indeed, a substantial area of such forest land is now safely protected in Olympic National Park in Washington state, as well as in other portions of the national park and national wilderness systems. However, it may well be desirable to add to this land, either to increase the total preserved acreage, or perhaps for a better geographic distribution of old growth stands to provide public access.

The costs of preserving old growth can be quite high, however. Efforts to retain old growth to provide habitat for the northern spotted owl illustrate these potentially high costs. Although not federally listed, this owl is considered a threatened species by the state of Oregon. Its chief habitat is the old growth forests of the Pacific Northwest; protection of each pair of birds requires 300 acres of old growth timber, and some restrictions on harvests on 900 more acres. In its timber management plan for the South Coast-Curry forest area in southwest Oregon, the BLM in 1981 proposed to preserve old growth habitat for sixteen out of the twenty-five pairs of northern spotted owls identified in the planning area (another forty-four pairs were found on Forest Service lands in the area).[44] Such preservation involved reducing timber harvests by 21 million board feet per year, around $4 million per year in forgone timber sales, or $250,000 per year per pair of spotted owls.

Conflicts Among Recreational Uses

While conflicts between commodity and recreational uses of the public lands have received wide attention, those between different types of recreational use have been less noticed thus far, but are likely to become matters of increasing controversy. The famous Mineral King dispute, which concerned a proposed ski resort on a national forest site surrounded on three sides by Sequoia National Park, was an indication of this trend. The Sierra Club and other preservation organizations fought the project for many years, finally succeeding in 1978 when Congress placed the valley in Sequoia National Park, precluding its use as a resort. Other conflicts among recreational uses have concerned the use of motorcycles, snowmobiles, and other motorized vehicles, which are excluded from wilderness areas and some beaches. In 1972 the Nixon administration issued an executive order aiming to limit the areas of

[44] Bureau of Land Management, U.S. Department of the Interior, *Final Timber Management Environmental Impact Statement: South Coast-Curry* (1981) pp. 2-18, 3-36.

offroad vehicle use, which was then tightened by the Carter administration in 1977. Under the recently adopted plan for the California Desert Conservation Area, offroad vehicle use is excluded from "closed" zones (19 percent of the area); is allowed with restrictions in "limited" zones (77 percent); and is permitted without restriction in "open" zones (4 percent).[45]

The effect of wilderness zone designation is often to exclude competing nonwilderness recreation as well as commodity uses. The stringent controls on recreational use in wilderness areas have led some observers to propose the creation of new types of areas that still exclude commodity uses but allow more variety in recreation. Commenting on the Rare II process in his state, the governor of Montana, Thomas Judge, in 1978 recommended consideration of a "backcountry" zoning classification instead of wilderness for certain areas.[46] In 1979, Senator Mark Hatfield similarly suggested that some of the proposed wilderness area for Oregon be designated instead as an "Oregon Cascades National Conservation Area" with fewer restrictions on recreational use.

Even within existing wilderness areas, significant conflicts may arise in the future as it becomes necessary to protect such areas from the damaging impacts of large numbers of visitors. Alternative allocation schemes for permits would serve some populations better than others. A market pricing system would benefit the wealthy; a system of same-day permits would benefit those with time to spare in line; an early reservation system would benefit those who know the system and are both able and temperamentally inclined to plan well in advance. An extreme but not inconceivable option would be to exclude almost all entry into some wilderness areas—perhaps limit it to a few photographers and scientific researchers. This option would benefit most those strict preservationists whose enjoyment of wilderness comes simply from the pleasure in knowing of its existence.

Perhaps the greatest potential conflict among recreational uses, even though it has received little attention thus far, concerns second-home and resort development. The current policy to retain the public lands precludes sale of lots for second-home and resort development, even in the many areas where such sales might generate values of $5,000 or more per acre—far higher than any current use. Construction of private housing and other private facilities in forest areas might make possible much more intensive recreational use of the assets of these areas. Spec-

[45] *Final Environmental Impact Statement and Proposed Plan: The California Desert Conservation Area*, p. E–71.
[46] Comments reprinted in Forest Service, U.S. Department of Agriculture, *Final Environmental Statement: Roadless Area Review and Evaluation* (January 1979) p. V–22.

tacular mountain scenery and private development are not necessarily incompatible—as shown by the case of Switzerland.

DETERMINING COMMODITY PRODUCTION LEVELS

An Exercise in Central Planning

Once the public lands have been classified, and the basic land use allocations made, the level of production for each use in each area must still be determined. This section examines the determination of production levels on areas of the public lands where commodities such as minerals, timber, and forage will be primary outputs. Even in these areas, recreation often will be a significant activity, requiring considerable policy attention, and decisions about production levels will have to take into account existing environmental regulations. These recreational and environmental issues are important, but this section is concerned only with the level of production.[47]

The federal government has the option to sell or lease its natural resources and thereby to turn decisions concerning production levels over to the private sector. However, although the actual commodity production on public lands is almost always undertaken by lessees, the government usually imposes tight regulations concerning the time and rate of production, the level of resource recovery, the plan of operations, and other basic production decisions. The Mineral Leasing Act of 1920 even grants government agencies the authority to control the selling price of the lessees' mineral production, although this authority has not been exercised. Nevertheless, the government regularly faces the question of the price to be charged for the lease itself ("fair market value"). Such prices raise another set of important issues which are not discussed in this chapter.[48]

A particularly important government control over private commodity production on public lands is the "diligent development requirement," which specifies that production must begin within a certain time, typically soon after a lease to a public land resource is issued. Its purpose

[47] For discussion of such issues (if often ponderous), see the various programmatic and site-specific environmental impact statements by the BLM and the Forest Service for grazing, timber harvesting, coal mining, and other public land uses. The scholarly literature on these matters is surprisingly scarce.

[48] For discussion of such issues, see *Study of Fees for Livestock Grazing on Federal Lands* and U.S. Department of the Interior, *Final Report on Recommendations for the Secretary on Fair Market Value and Minimum Acceptable Bids for Federal Coal Leases* (December 1979).

is to prevent private speculators from holding public resources, a major public concern since the early conservation movement.

Diligence requirements have other less well understood and less desirable consequences. Speculation might also be labelled "private conservation," the withholding of a resource from the market because it will be more valuable in the future. The diligence requirement eliminates the possibility of private conservation, because the lessee would first lose his production rights. Public resources leased for private production must therefore be explored right away, whether or not such production properly allocates the resource use over time. As a result, the government must bear the full burden of assuring both sufficient development and adequate conservation. The diligence requirement was in fact a reflection of a general conservationist preference for public over private allocation of resources.

If production of natural resources held by the government does not affect output prices, the timing of production is a question of whether the value of the public resource is greater now or in the future—in the latter case discounted to calculate its "present value." However, government holdings of some natural resources—especially coal and timber—are so large that production can in fact significantly affect prices for these commodities. In this case, proper conservation of the resource becomes a complex matter. The government must prepare a full economic plan for present and future total production, both private and public. Since the government does not control private production, its objective typically becomes one of filling the gap between private production and the level of socially desirable total production.

It has not been widely recognized that commodity production decisions on the public lands are often exercises in central economic planning. The enactment of the Forest and Rangeland Renewable Resources Planning Act (RPA) in 1974, is, however, beginning to spur wider understanding that Congress really directed the Forest Service to undertake a large-scale central planning effort virtually unprecedented for the United States. A study of the 1980 RPA process made for the Society of American Foresters commented that "the RPA as amended requires a highly centralized and coordinated approach to planning." National quantitative goals and objectives for public land outputs must be assigned among regional plans and then further subdivided among forest planning areas. In this scheme, "the nationally defined goals and objectives become controlling."[49] During the 1970s, the Interior Department undertook some closely related central planning efforts for its coal program.[50]

[49] Society of American Foresters, *The RPA Process-1980: Report of the Task Force on RPA Implementation* (Washington, D.C., SAF, April 1981) pp. 9, 10.
[50] See *Final Environmental Statement: Federal Coal Management Program.*

OCS Oil and Gas Production

Federal oil and gas leases have traditionally required that active exploration leading to production occur within five years for offshore and ten
years for onshore leases. Although the offshore requirement is now
being changed to ten years in many cases, issuance of a lease will still
essentially commit OCS lessees to rapid exploration and then to production, assuming any oil and gas are actually found.

Rather than complicate matters, the government has effectively adopted
a simple rule to decide whether current OCS production is desirable. If
the oil and/or gas can be produced to yield higher revenues than the
cost of its production, the government has sought to have the resource
produced—assuming the environmental impacts are acceptable. In part,
such an approach reflects the power of compound interest; at a 10
percent interest rate the "present value" of a profit stream twenty years
in the future is less than 15 percent of the value of the same profit stream
today, hardly an encouragement to hold off production. Conversely,
the government would have to expect future oil profits twenty years in
the future to be almost seven times as great as they are today, in order
to justify holding oil in the ground on an economic basis.

However, we can now see—admittedly only with the benefit of hind-
sight—that it would actually have been economic in 1970 to hold some
part of U.S. oil in the ground until 1980, rather than produce it. World
oil prices rose by more than 1,000 percent over the past decade, while
the cumulative interest rates for the decade amounted to less than 300
percent. There may be future occasions when there will appear to be a
high likelihood of sharp price increases once again. Yet, ironically, the
mechanisms for conservation in such circumstances are weakest for the
publicly owned portion of U.S. oil resources. The scheduling of OCS
lease sales during the 1970s was actually driven by administrative considerations relating to the Interior Department's capacity to process sales
and industry's capacity to explore. In addition, the holding of OCS sales
in several cases was caught up in intense political maneuvering which
tended to restrain the rate of leasing and delay the opening of new
areas.[51]

The public and private incentives for production of OCS oil and gas
are also becoming more important as the Reagan administration seeks
to expand greatly the OCS acreage offered for lease. Prior to 1974, OCS
leasing was confined to the traditional areas of the Gulf of Mexico and
off southern California. However, OPEC price hikes generated new
interest in other areas that had not been so attractive to the oil industry

---

[51] For accounts of the political battles over OCS leasing, see the weekly issues of the
Coastal Zone Management Newsletter (Washington, D.C., Nautilus Press).

at lower world oil prices. After 1974, the government expanded the areas of OCS leasing to Alaska, the North and South Atlantic, and new areas off the West Coast. To date, the only commercially producible oil and gas discoveries resulting from the expanded leasing frontiers have been a few wells off California.

This discovery record has added weight to proposals to make much more OCS acreage available for exploration under a less confining system. Oil and gas exploration has always been a hit-and-miss proposition; many important finds have resulted from one person's "crazy idea." In Europe, the North Sea oil and gas fields were discovered only after several failures in the same areas in which oil and gas were later found by using newly formulated geologic concepts. The OCS leasing system in operation during the 1970s may have been too rigid to accommodate easily the chaotic, trial-and-error-filled learning process that has characterized past exploration.

An alternative approach would be to adopt a "preference right" leasing system for wide areas of the OCS. Under such a system, the government would continue to lease competitively the most promising oil and gas tracts. However, for the majority of tracts considered less promising, individual companies could apply at any time for a license to explore for some period, say five or ten years. If the environmental impacts were acceptable, the license would be issued. If the company then discovered oil and gas, it would automatically receive a long-term lease. The government would not receive any initial payment, but would share in the profits through production royalties, or more directly, adoption of a profit-sharing formula. For the reasons discussed above, any leases issued under a preference right system should allow longer development periods than current diligence requirements.

Coal Production

Unlike oil and gas, there is no single, given world price of coal to simplify coal calculations. Indeed, federal coal holdings and potential production are so large that federal actions can significantly influence the market price of coal. Moreover, as with oil and gas, a ten-year diligent development requirement eliminates an incentive a lessee might have to conserve the resource for later production.

Federal policy makers have considered asking Congress to abolish or significantly extend the period in which diligent development is required for coal leases. However, doubting the political acceptability of such a change, a compromise was instead proposed in the mid-1970s that involved both large-scale federal leasing and enforcement of diligent development requirements. The system effectively assumed that some number—possibly large—of federal leases would not be developed and would be returned to the government because they had not been diligently developed. This approach raised the prospect that coal development patterns would be distorted by production decisions made simply to avoid loss of a lease.[52]

Labelled the Energy Minerals Activity Recommendation System (EMARS), this proposed leasing system was publicly announced in 1976 but never got under way. It was rejected in 1977 both by the courts and the incoming Carter administration, which instead proposed a new coal leasing program with an explicit central planning framework.[53] The effort began with Department of Energy (DOE) "production goals" for the Powder River and other western coal regions, formulated initially for 1985 and 1990. The government would then calculate how much private sources and current federal leases would contribute to future coal production in the absence of any new federal coal leasing. Finally, the target for new federal leasing "needed" in a region would be set to fill any resulting future shortfalls below regional coal production goals.

Central planning for future western coal production, however, proved a trying task. A series of major shocks to government planners were delivered by 1979 OPEC price increases, the unexpectedly low growth of electric power use, rapidly shifting natural gas price and production forecasts, and other unpredicted events. Such factors caused changes in projections even at the national level; the instability of forecasts was further magnified when they had to be broken down into six western coal regions. In one admittedly extreme case, the 1990 DOE production goal for the San Juan River region in New Mexico was set at 58 million tons in 1978 calculations; dropped all the way to 17 million tons in 1979; and then rose back to 57 million tons in 1980. The key 1990 production goal for the Powder River region fell from 418 million tons as set in 1979 to 294 million tons as set in 1980, just one year later. On the demand side, DOE projections for use of coal synthetics in 1990 started off at 56 million tons in 1978; fell in a skeptical mood concerning synthetics to 28 million tons in 1979 goals; and then shot up to 198 million tons in 1980 in the aftermath of new OPEC price shocks.

It was equally difficult to estimate the amount of coal production likely to occur in the absence of any new federal coal leasing; depending

[52] For an account of federal policy debates in the 1970s concerning federal coal leasing, see Robert H. Nelson, *Federal Coal Policy* (Durham, N.C., Duke University Press, forthcoming 1983).

[53] This program is described in *Final Environmental Statement: Federal Coal Management Program.*

on how "serious" existing production plans of mining companies had to be, DOE surveys for the Fort Union coal region showed likely mining company production in 1985 of either 24 or 87 million tons. The coal leasing targets that emerged from such government calculations could have no greater reliability than the inputs. It is fair to say that central planning in this case turned out to be more like writing fiction than real planning.

By 1980, the Carter administration had various efforts under way to return to the earlier concept of leasing a large amount of federal coal and then letting market forces sort out how much would actually be produced. The Reagan administration has accelerated the move in this direction. While debate raged, the federal coal leasing program was suspended from 1971 to 1981, a decade in which a boom in western coal production got under way. This boom was possible only because, almost unnoticed at the time, large inventories of federal coal had already been leased in the 1960s; moreover, diligence requirements were simply not enforced for these leases.[54]

The federal coal leased in the 1960s created an inventory to sustain new production during the 1970s and 1980s in response to market demands. An inventory approach could be developed more formally into a new system of determining future federal coal leasing levels. Under such an approach, the government would lease sufficient coal to achieve some very ample inventory levels in a given region—say enough coal to accommodate projected growth in regional coal production for the next thirty years. As some of the federal coal moved from the inventory into an actual producing mine, new federal leasing would be undertaken to bring the inventory back up to the desired level. However, the ten-year diligence requirement still poses a major problem for this approach. The option to relax the requirement to a longer period such as twenty or thirty years—or perhaps even eliminate it—warrants consideration.

Timber Production

While the efforts to calculate regional coal production goals and to set federal coal leasing targets never got off the ground, a system to set harvest goals and sale targets for federal timber production has actually functioned for many years. As in the case of coal, federal timber inventories are so large that sales have the potential to substantially influence prices. Federal timber sales also carry requirements for diligent

---

[54] For a critical view of federal coal leasing in the 1960s, see Council on Economic Priorities, *Leased and Lost: A Study of Public and Indian Coal Leasing in the West* (New York, CEP, 1974).

harvesting of timber, within three years on BLM lands and varying up to a normal maximum of seven years on national forest lands.

The Forest Service method of planning timber harvests is based on biological and physical objectives. The fundamental objective is to maximize the physical volume of timber that can be produced in a continuous even flow over the long run—the Forest Service interpretation of "maximum long-run sustained yield." Employing data on existing timber inventories on the national forests, as well as growth projections for both this timber and the reforested lands, Forest Service computers calculate the maximum harvest level that can be sustained indefinitely without the harvest ever dropping off in the future. This maximum harvest becomes the "allowable cut" for a given timber area.[55]

The idea of maintaining a maximum flow of timber at an even long-run level has an obvious attraction. Such a policy would seem to be desirable, not only as a means of promoting the broader stability of timber markets, but also of local communities dependent on national forest timber. But, despite its apparent attractiveness, on closer examination the "even-flow" policy turns out to make little sense for the actual current circumstances of many national forests.

The national forest system still contains large areas of "old growth" timber that has never been cut. In such areas, the current inventory of timber is much larger than would ever exist in a long-run harvesting program where harvests have already occurred. A major issue in planning national forest harvests now and for a considerable time to come will be the proper rate at which to draw down the large one-time stocks of virgin timber. The even-flow policy, however, effectively ignores the existence of this one-time inventory; it simply sets the current harvest to equal the long-run equilibrium harvest after the inventory is gone.

With existing large inventories, as the Council on Wage and Price Stability put it in 1977, it is possible "to harvest additional volume for several decades without later ever falling below the harvest dictated by the long-run sustainable yield."[56] By precluding any current harvests above the long-run level, the Forest Service literally wastes the forgone timber harvesting opportunities in the short run. Study of harvest options on BLM lands in western Oregon showed that by departing from the even-flow policy, BLM could harvest 17 percent more timber for three decades without any loss in subsequent harvests. On one particular timbershed with an especially large old growth inventory, the even-flow

---

[55] Forest Service, U.S. Department of Agriculture, *Timber Harvest Scheduling Issues Study* (October 1976).

[56] U.S. Council on Wage and Price Stability, *Interim Report on Lumber Prices and the Lumber Products Industry* (October 1977) p. 24.

policy was preventing a 35 percent harvest increase for three decades that would involve no cost to harvest levels in later decades.[57]

The even-flow policy has other nonsensical if perhaps more subtle consequences.[58] It distorts public investment calculations by showing immediate large returns to timber investments that in fact will not show any real timber yields for up to 100 years (the "allowable cut effect"). This imaginary benefit shows up because, under an even-flow policy, any increase in long-run harvests allows greater immediate harvesting of existing old growth timber stands; this immediate increase is then counted as a real benefit attributable to the investment. Manipulations of forest area boundaries can increase or decrease allowable harvests, even though obviously no real change in the circumstances of timber supply has occurred. Finally, the even-flow calculations are based on federal timber alone; in cases where nonfederal timber is already being harvested at uneven rates, a federal policy to maintain an even flow will actually interfere with opportunities to stabilize the total flows of timber.

The Forest Service officially adopted the even-flow policy in 1973 and still adheres to it. In fact, the National Forest Management Act of 1976 formally mandates an even-flow policy, but then provides a loophole for departing from it for "multiple use" purposes. The Carter administration in 1979 directed that the Forest Service examine possibilities for such departures, an effort now being incorporated into the preparation of land use plans—few of which, however, have been completed. The Forest Service thus far has shown little enthusiasm for any changes in harvest policies.

One explanation for the stubborn adherence to the even-flow policy is its simplicity. The Forest Service has undoubtedly been concerned that abandoning this policy might lead the agency onto some unfamiliar ground. Forestry training has traditionally emphasized the calculation of the long-run equilibrium harvest (the "sustained yield"), a concept derived from European countries where the last excess timber inventories disappeared hundreds of years ago. There was no similar tradition of concepts and studies of how to draw down a one-time large stock of timber, the fortunate situation in which the United States to some degree still finds itself.[59]

[57] Robert H. Nelson and Lou Pugliaresi, "Timber Harvest Policy Issues on the O&C Lands," Office of Policy Analysis, U.S. Department of the Interior (March 1977) p. 31.

[58] See Thomas Lenard, "Wasting Our National Forests," *Regulation* (July/August 1981).

[59] For critical histories of Forest Service timber planning, see Ashley L. Schiff, *Fire and Water: Scientific Heresy in the Forest Service* (Cambridge, Mass., Harvard University Press, 1962); Sherry H. Olson, *The Depletion Myth: A History of Railroad Use of Timber* (Cambridge, Mass., Harvard University Press, 1971); R. W. Behan, "Forestry and the End of Innocence," *American Forests* vol. 81 (May 1975) pp. 16–19, 38–49; and R. W. Behan, "Political Popularity and Conceptual Nonsense: The Strange Case of Sustained Yield Forestry," *Environmental Law* vol. 8 (Winter 1978) pp. 309–342.

By adopting a simple biological standard to plan harvest levels, even if an economically irrational one, the Forest Service did at least avoid the central planning difficulties which afflicted the more economically based effort in federal coal planning in the Interior Department. An issue taken up in the next section is whether there are ways to escape a choice between these two problems.

Forage Production

As in its forests, the United States also inherited ungrazed rangelands that possessed a large one-time supply of forage. But unlike the forests, it took only a few decades of uncontrolled livestock grazing to exhaust this supply. Indeed, by the beginning of the twentieth century, much of the western rangelands were severely depleted by overgrazing. Today, it typically requires more than 10 acres of BLM lands to supply enough forage to meet the needs of a single cow for one month; a representative ranch of 200 cattle thus often requires 10,000 or more acres. Past overgrazing simply compounded the problems of arid lands that had very low productivity to begin with.

Although ranchers have traditionally exerted a dominant influence on rangeland management, the major event of the 1970s was a drive to extend Pinchot-style conservationism from the national forests to the public rangelands as well. The major forces behind this drive were conservationists and environmental groups, with the tacit encouragement of the BLM.

Following the same concepts that the Forest Service applied to timber harvesting, the BLM conceives its fundamental management objective to be to maximize the long-run sustained yield of forage that can be derived from the public rangelands, thereby "restoring" the rangelands to an earlier productive condition. Attempts in the 1970s by OMB and Interior Department economists to require economic viability of range improvement projects were perceived by many BLMers as one of the outside constraints that must be overcome.

Many ranchers also are not very concerned with economic benefits, judging by studies which consistently show negative or small returns to ranching.[60] Many in fact survive only by taking second jobs in the city, which enables them to remain a "rancher." The true motivation for many, if not most, full-time ranchers seems to be the way of life; the freedom of the wide-open spaces on the rangelands still exists, if not exactly in the Hollywood version. Such rancher motivations clashed in

[60] Arthur H. Smith and William E. Martin, "Socio-economic Behavior of Cattle Ranchers with Implications for Rural Community Development in the West," *American Journal of Agricultural Economics* vol. 54 (May 1972) pp. 217–225.

the 1970s with the effort to bring conservationism to the public range. Conservationism advocates scientific management, planning, and close government control over use of public resources, directly conflicting with precisely those values that appear to attract many people into ranching. In this case the conflict was further aggravated because conservationists sought major reductions in livestock grazing, both to reduce overgrazing pressure on the rangelands and to make more forage available for wildlife.

The resulting conflict in the 1970s between conservationists and ranchers turned the main efforts of these groups from range improvement to sparring with one another for future control over the rangelands. Under a court order resulting from a suit by the Natural Resources Defense Council, BLM was required in 1975 to prepare comprehensive plans for the future management of the public range. The court ordered preparation of 212 grazing environmental impact statements (later reduced to 144), the last of which would not be completed until 1988. The ultimate costs to the BLM will be perhaps $300 to $500 million, including inventories, land-use planning, and other EIS activities. The grazing EISs became the focus for BLM rangeland policy making in the 1970s.

The greatest economic irrationality on the rangelands does not involve the level of forage production itself, but the amounts of money spent on planning and deciding this production. One economic study found that "the entire EIS preparation and review process is appallingly tedious and costly. . . . The government is spending millions of dollars to prepare impact statements for projects with economic impacts which can hardly be measured."[61] The problem is suggested by the fact that the market value of permanent rights to one AUM of forage in most cases lies between $25 and $100. The basic decision confronting BLM is the extent of necessary reductions in livestock grazing; from a political standpoint, it is unlikely that livestock grazing could be reduced more than 25 percent on all BLM lands. This would amount to about 3 million AUMs, the value of which would range between $75 million and $300 million. In short, the direct economic value of the maximum feasible grazing reduction is less—possibly much less—than the planning costs being incurred to study just how large the grazing reductions should be.

The first grazing EIS—for an area around Challis, Idaho—provided an admittedly extreme example of uneconomic costs of decision making.[62] The direct costs of the EIS alone were $724,000, which even then

[61] T.A.P., Inc., *An Evaluation of the Economic Analysis Contained in Three BLM Grazing Environmental Statements* (April 1979) p. 18.

[62] Bureau of Land Management, U.S. Department of the Interior, *Final Environmental Statement: Proposed Domestic Livestock Grazing Program for the Challis Planning Unit* (January 1977).

did not include all the planning and other costs related to EIS preparation. The EIS analyzed total livestock grazing of about 20,000 AUMs, implying an EIS cost of $36 per AUM. Yet, permanent grazing rights in the area were selling for around $35 per AUM! In short, the BLM could have bought out most, if not all, of the grazing rights on its lands in the area for less than the direct cost of the EIS. In actual fact, the EIS was so severely criticized after its release that BLM was forced to disavow it, and then prepare a new one at further public expense.

As other investments, expenditures on decision making should not be extended beyond the point where the benefits (in the form of improved decision-making) exceed the costs. The ease with which the BLM exceeded this level is explained in part by the traditional conservationist antipathy to economic ways of thinking. It is also explained by the low value of the forage resource, which means that even major decisions about rangelands involve a small economic stake. Moreover, the intermingled private and public rangeland ownership patterns tend to require long and costly negotiations—with much controversy and confrontation between the BLM and ranchers—before any decisions can be reached. Recently, the BLM has been seeking to reduce planning and other decision-making costs, but this effort itself has provoked considerable controversy.

RETHINKING PUBLIC LAND MANAGEMENT

The Need for Change

Although Americans often think of themselves as nonideological, a bureaucracy must have some broad sense of purpose and direction—in a word, an ideology. As we have noted, the dominant ideology behind public land management has been conservationism.

The basic ideas of the conservation movement have not stood the test of time well. For instance, there is much less confidence today in the automatic character of human progress based on scientific advance. Experts are no longer trusted to the same degree; the idea that the political process should leave most administration as well as many key policy decisions to experts seems antiquated by now. Indeed, government decisions are seen as the inevitable result of compromise among highly politicized interest groups. The progressive faith in government planning and administration has given way to deep skepticism, leading spokesmen of diverse political views to agree that economic efficiency is usually better served by the market than by direct government control over production.[63]

Even in the private sector, large, highly centralized organizations are perceived as often rigid, unresponsive, and slow to adapt, in a word, "bureaucratic"—a malady only aggravated when the bureaucracy is in the public sector. The centralized institutions created to manage the public lands have changed little since their founding under conservationist principles. One of the major issues for the 1980s will be to assess whether, the original intellectual foundations having been greatly eroded, corresponding changes in the institutional products of conservationist thought are not also now needed.

The specific principles for public land management advocated by conservationism have not fared much better than the broader philosophy. The principle of multiple use was already challenged early in the twentieth century by such contrary steps as withdrawals (or prohibitions on certain uses), the Antiquities Act, and the creation of the National Park Service. Later actions—such as the creation of the National Wildlife Refuge System, the National Wilderness system, the National Wild and Scenic Rivers System, and other land classification efforts—have effectively created a zoning system for the public lands that conflicts with multiple use. The terminology of multiple use and the confusions it creates stand in the way of improving the public land zoning system— and in many cases even recognizing explicitly that such a system exists.

Another main tenet of conservationism, the principle of sustained yield, has been even less helpful in formulating forest and range policies. There is obviously no reason to object to the general proposition that yields from the public lands should be sustained—although a more traditionally American objective actually would be growing yields. Operationally, however, the public land agencies have interpreted the sustained yield principle in a specific way: the maintenance of a continuous even flow of output at the long-run biological potential of the lands. Such a concept takes little or no account of economic considerations. Remarkably, until the 1970s it was seldom even recognized explicitly that biological production must be a function of the level of economic investment—and that the latter requires some economic justification.

Attempts to introduce economic calculations into the determination of investment levels—mostly within the past decade—have thus far made little headway. For example, the insistence of the Forest Service on

---

[63] See Charles L. Schultze, *The Public Use of Private Interest* (Washington, D.C., Brookings Institution, 1977); Arthur M. Okun, *Equality and Efficiency: The Big Tradeoff* (Washington, D.C., Brookings Institution, 1975); and Milton Friedman, *Capitalism and Freedom* (Chicago, University of Chicago Press, 1962).

including the "allowable cut effect" as a timber investment benefit, despite its wide condemnation, shows the great difficulty of reconciling the conservationist and economic outlooks. The Forest Service adherence to the even-flow policy for timber harvesting in areas with large old growth inventories offers another example of the conservationist ideology triumphing over economic calculations—as well as ordinary common sense in this case. On examining the sustained yield principle, one expert was led to comment that "societies often find themselves in cul de sacs where progress is possible only if irrational beliefs are discarded. . . . Sustained yield forest management provides an excellent example of this situation."[64]

Another tenet of conservationism was its opposition to speculative holding of public resources, resulting in the imposition of strict diligent development requirements. Because "private conservation" was therefore precluded, the government has been required to decide the timing of production for nonrenewable public resources such as oil, natural gas, and coal. Yet, conservationism offered no economic framework for making such decisions; indeed, its precepts tended to inhibit the development of one. Recent attempts for the first time to follow through on the logic of central planning implicit in tight government control of resource development have been more show than substance.[65] The complexity of true central planning is only now dawning on the public land agencies. In the absence of satisfactory economic answers, the timing of energy production becomes mainly a political decision, where the normal span in elected office often favors current consumption over conservation for the future.

Conservationism also tended to ignore distributional questions, instead offering vague principles such as "the greatest good of the greatest number in the long run."[66] As a result, the political process also prevailed in the distribution of public land outputs. The results have been consistent with the widely observed tendency of political decision-making to favor concentrated and organized groups over diffused ones.[67]

[64] Anthony Downs, "Sustained Yield and American Social Goals," paper presented at a symposium on the economics of sustained-yield forestry, University of Washington (November 1974) p. 25.

[65] Christopher K. Leman, *Resource Assessment and Program Development: An Evaluation of Forest Service Experience Under the Resources Planning Act, with Lessons for other Natural Resource Agencies*, Office of Policy Analysis, U.S. Department of the Interior (August 1980).

[66] Pinchot, *Breaking New Ground*, p. 262.

[67] For the view that multiple interest pressures leave considerable agency leeway, see Paul J. Culhane, *Public Land Politics: Interest Group Influence on the Forest Service and the Bureau of Land Management* (Baltimore, Md., Johns Hopkins University Press for Resources for the Future, 1981).

The "ownership" of the public lands by all the taxpayers of the nation is by now more a consoling myth than a reality; in fact, various interest groups have steadily hardened their claims to continued receipt of specific benefits of the public lands. Ranchers hold permanent and even salable grazing permits to certain lands, and wilderness users have received a permanent commitment of large areas to wilderness recreation. Attempts to cut back on either rancher or wilderness entitlements encounter fierce and effective resistance. In this sense a considerable portion of the rights to use the public lands has already been transferred to private parties—de facto if not de jure. The congressional requirement in 1977 for private "surface owner consent" prior to the mining of underlying federal coal offers a recent instance where the practical effect was to establish new private rights in federal coal—reportedly now bringing rancher surface owners prices as high as $5,000 an acre and/or royalty interests as high as 3 percent.

The distribution of the financial returns from the public lands exhibits a similar pattern. Except for outer continental shelf leasing of oil and gas, the federal taxpayer derives little financial benefit from the public lands. By law, for example, the large revenues from oil and gas and other onshore energy mineral leasing are distributed 50 percent to the state in which the lease is located, 40 percent to the Reclamation Fund (used to pay for western water projects), and only 10 percent to the federal treasury. While the Reclamation Fund has been somewhat of an accounting fiction, the federal government also faces a sizeable loss in federal corporate income taxes because of the tax deductibility of mineral royalty payments. It is even possible in some cases that the imposition of a "federal" royalty will produce a negative net return to the federal government.

The much smaller revenues from the grazing fee are distributed 50 percent back to ranchers to fund range investments, 37.5 percent to the federal treasury, and 12.5 percent to the states. In 1978 the western states received $275 million as their share of the total revenues of the public land agencies within the Interior Department. This revenue was a net gain to the states, since no direct costs were imposed on them. The federal government, by contrast, received $363 million from its share of public land revenues, but also incurred $513 million in land management costs—a net loss of $149 million borne by the federal taxpayer.[68]

---

[68] Robert H. Nelson, *An Analysis of the Revenues and Costs of Public Land Management by the Interior Department in 13 Western States*, Office of Policy Analysis, U.S. Department of the Interior (December 1979).

The Forest Service in 1980 incurred costs of $2.1 billion while earning revenues of only $1.3 billion—resulting in a net "loss" of $800 million. Yet, it still paid 25 percent of its $625 million in total timber revenues to local counties. The wide failure to cover costs in public land management is especially notable in that such management in major part consists of the disposition of naturally created mineral, land, and other resources that entail no initial production costs. It would not seem unreasonable to expect that the costs of recreation and other nonmarket outputs of the public lands could be covered by positive net revenues in the sale of extremely valuable assets of oil and gas, timber, coal, and other resources of these lands.

Ideology and basic policy principles are not the only areas in which the public land agencies have been slow to respond to change. The original main outputs of the public lands, timber and forage production, now occupy disproportionate management time and attention. As a result, recreation and minerals production, more valuable current outputs, are neglected in comparison. Most of the top management officials of the Forest Service still come from a professional forestry background and those in the BLM from a range management background. The failure of present public land management extends, not only to commodity production, but also to recreation and wilderness protection in areas where that is more important than timber harvesting or grazing. The present system may be providing less commodity output *and* less environmental "output" than is possible.

All of these concerns might not be important if the public lands were somehow well managed despite outmoded ideology and other problems. But the preceding sections of this paper have shown that ideology can have very real consequences. The management of the public lands exhibits major economic inefficiencies in many areas. In some cases, such as the even-flow timber policy, these inefficiencies are direct outgrowths of economically irrational conservationist precepts.

The Interior Department was created to implement the greatest regional development policy in American history, the building of the West. As long as the federal government was installing infrastructure and making many of the other key decisions in western territories and later states, ownership of public lands by the federal government was a logical complement. But the western states have grown up; they are no longer the less developed part of the nation. Indeed, their energy wealth may be making them much better off than the rest of the nation. By 1985, Alaska is projected to receive more than $5 billion in oil and gas revenues. Wyoming and New Mexico are projected to receive more than

$1 billion in 1985 from oil, gas, coal, and other natural resource revenues.[69] The federal taxing of citizens in eastern and midwestern states to cover the costs of public land management may appear increasingly incongruous as these states suffer economic decline and the West booms.

The populations of western states are becoming more urban; new manufacturing industries are joining the traditional extractive industries. As the politics changes, western state governments are asserting greater control over their own state growth and development. With such trends, the federal ownership of large parts of western states loses much of its original justification. Many westerners, even those who recognize clearly that there may be financial losses involved, now prefer to control their own land use and other basic decisions. Commenting on the Sagebrush Rebellion, three westerners recently wrote that "historians and commentators on the western scene have often described the persistent colonial status of the West's most arid states. Lacking viable economies, these states have existed on federal subsidies for many years. Now, with prices for extractive resources (including the renewable ones) soaring, a natural response is to consider transfers of lands and rights." They concluded that "perhaps the rebellion marks a time for the intermountain West to stand on its own feet, cut the federal apron strings, and take the bad with the good."[70]

The record suggests it is time to examine alternatives to the current system of public land management. One response would be to seek revitalization at the federal level. At least in principle, such a proposal would be less politically controversial than other possible alternatives and might have greater prospects of wide public support. With a more incremental approach, there would be less opportunity for the law of unintended consequences to take hold. On the other hand, past revitalization efforts have tended to be swallowed up by the weight of traditional public land practice and bureaucratic inertia. The individual interest groups that benefit most from current land management policies may more effectively be mobilized to defeat piecemeal and gradualist reforms. The political prospects for real change thus might be greater by focusing a one-time national debate on more radical surgery. The diffuse taxpayers and other publics normally not heard could make their wishes felt.

The two leading proposals that have been made for more radical change in public land institutions are transfer of at least some of the

[69] Office of Policy Analysis, U.S. Department of the Interior, *Past and Projected State Revenues from Energy and other Natural Resources in 13 Western States: Background Report* (September 1981).

[70] Allen D. Lebaron, E. Bruce Godfrey, and Darwin B. Nielsen, "Sagebrush Rebellion: An Economic Analysis," *Utah Science* (Fall 1980) p. 90.

public lands to the states, or their divestiture to the private sector. Although both proposals are highly controversial, their advantages and disadvantages warrant examination. Probably neither alternative would ever actually be proposed for all public lands, but would be confined to certain lands with suitable characteristics.

Revitalization at the Federal Level

A revitalization of public land management under continued federal ownership would involve several elements. While it is easier said than done, the use classifications for the public lands should be updated to current circumstances and the public lands reclassified according to the best use of each area. The future direction of the national park system needs to be rethought, now that the prime natural assets of the nation have already been included within it. The national wildlife refuge system might evolve more toward the national park model, giving greater emphasis to preservation while also accommodating wider recreational use. The national wilderness system faces severe conflicts between the provision of recreation on the one hand and the preservation of areas in essentially natural states on the other. Recent proposals for "conservation areas" or "backcountry areas" are only two among many possible classifications of land for new recreational use systems.

A revitalization of public land management would entail much greater incorporation of economic calculations in the decision-making process.[71] Decisions to allocate land to one use should reflect at least an implicit calculation that this use has a higher value than others—including appropriate values for nonmarket outputs. Proposed investments should be evaluated to assess whether the returns received actually exceed the costs. Environmental and other regulations imposed on public land users should be similarly evaluated.

A revitalization at the federal level might well involve a reorganization of agency responsibilities. If major recreational use classifications are reformulated, existing recreational agencies may not match up with new recreational use systems. Wilderness areas might better be gathered within the National Park System; some of the newer urban, seashore, and other park system units might then be transferred to a separate federal agency for more intensive forms of recreation. Where commodities are being produced, new agencies might also be established. It might be well to create a new federal timber agency to manage all the prime timberlands now held by BLM and the Forest Service. A separate agency might be created to manage leasing of energy minerals.

[71] See John V. Krutilla and John A. Haigh, "An Integrated Approach to National Forest Management," *Environmental Law* vol. 8 (Winter 1978) pp. 373–415.

More sophisticated federal management could well result from a greater division of labor, matching specialized management skills to each major land use. A number of past studies—most recently in the Carter administration—have called for consolidation of federal land management under a single natural resources department; one of the major resulting gains would be the ability to reorganize the entire land management system. Creation of new federal agencies could make it easier to escape the tight hold of existing agency ideologies and traditions and to adopt innovative solutions.

It would seem obvious that once certain lands are designated for commodity production, production levels on the public lands should closely reflect economic factors. The difficulty of accomplishing this offers a major challenge for a revitalization of land management. Where the federal government is required to undertake central economic planning, it must develop extensive supply and demand projections, both for public and private producers, which are subdivided among the various public land regions and even subregions. It must then calculate socially preferable price and output levels for production from the public lands in all these areas. The task is formidable and the resources deployed thus far—intellectual as well as budgetary—have fallen well short of those necessary for success. Following the direction of the Resources Planning Act of 1974, the Forest Service has gone through two central planning exercises, to little satisfaction among those who have looked closely at the results.[72] Indeed, the suspicion grows that the task may be impossible as a practical matter, because of the huge data requirements, the complex interactions among producers and consumers, the possibility of many substitute forms of production, and numerous other complications.

An alternative economic solution would be to divide the public lands to be devoted to commodity production into much smaller units, each too small by itself to influence prices. Such units would then be instructed to maximize their own profits essentially as though they were private corporations. The issue raised here is in fact one long debated in the field of comparative economic systems—whether government production must be fully centralized, or can feasibly be decentralized under a system of "market socialism."[73] The Congress and the American public probably are only dimly, if at all, aware that existing statutory directions for the public lands seem essentially to require the adoption of a central economic planning system for production decisions.

[72] Society of American Foresters, *The RPA Process-1980*, and Leman, *Resource Assessment and Program Evaluation: An Evaluation*.

[73] See Wayne A. Leeman, ed., *Capitalism, Market Socialism, and Central Planning: Readings in Comparative Economic Systems* (Boston, Houghton Mifflin, 1963).

The best federal solution may in fact be to revoke at least some of the statutory requirements that compel central planning. One way would be to relax significantly or even eliminate the standard diligent development requirement. If this step were taken, the government could pursue various inventory strategies in leasing or sale of its resources; ample inventories of federal resources would be transferred to the private sector, free to be produced according to the signals of the market. Timber purchasers or coal lessees could wait twenty or thirty years to produce if they desired. As federal resources were actually committed to production, the inventory would be restocked again by new federal leasing or sales. To be sure, such an approach comes closer to an actual resource disposal program than would be consistent with traditional ideas of public land management.

A final key element of a revitalization strategy would concern equity matters. From the federal taxpayer's perspective, there is little to be said for a public land system that often serves as a conduit for subsidies to western individuals and governments. It would be more equitable to pass on a greater share of the costs of public land management to users who have no special claim to poverty. This could be accomplished by higher grazing, park, and other fees for direct users, and by greater cost-sharing in public land investments. The formulas for distribution of public land revenues should be revised to ensure that the federal taxpayer actually gains something financially from energy leasing and other valuable production from the public lands.

As a general proposition, the proposal to "revitalize" federal land management would command wide assent. However, examination of some of the particulars shows that they would be very controversial. Proposals for a formal zoning system and a reclassification of public land; a more businesslike ("economic") approach to production and other land decisions; creation of an effective central planning system (or alternatively, relaxation or even abandonment of diligent development requirements); and a new distribution of public land revenues would all generate strong opposition. The revitalization proposal initially appears less radical because it does not challenge the institutional forms and associated public land management ideology which date back to the early conservation movement. But actual practices have long since deviated from the original formal concept in many areas; revitalization would seriously threaten this development. Other alternatives for land management reorganization tend to have the opposite character; they would be fiercely resisted as a formal change in ideology, but in terms of actual practices they might well represent the more incremental step.

Decentralization to the State Level

Examination of the real workings of public land management shows that it is already very considerably decentralized to the state level—a consequence partly of the wide politicizing of land management decisions.[74] Not only do land agencies typically follow state and local wishes, but state and local governments derive the main financial benefits from the public lands. Indeed, the one substantive element that might be most radical about formal decentralization to the state level would be the transfer of current federal cost burdens to state and local governments.

Decentralization of land management to the state level would actually be consistent with broad currents in American thought. In 1977 the American Law Institute published a comprehensive model code for urban land zoning based on many years of study and debate among the nation's leading land use experts.[75] One of the basic principles of the model code was that land use control should remain at the local level, except for matters of clear state interest. The model code provided for state control only over major facilities and other "developments of regional impact" and over special "areas of critical state concern," an approach that has since been followed in a number of states. The model code's emphasis on decentralization in fact reflected a long-standing American view that government authority should be delegated to the lowest level feasible. The public lands are a major anomaly in this regard.

In fact, it is useful to think of the existing federal lands in this framework. The national parks can be regarded as early "critical areas" for the whole nation. The national wildlife refuges, wilderness areas, wild and scenic rivers, and other national recreation systems added further federal critical areas. An application of the model code principles to the public lands would then suggest that control over the remaining public land areas not deemed critical to the whole nation should be decentralized to the states. The states might themselves carry the logic a step further by designating their own critical areas on newly owned state land and then turning governing authority for the remaining lands over to appropriate local governments. Where protection of critical areas involves regulatory control over nearby private lands, state and local governments will have a major advantage over the federal government.

Such an approach offers the prospect of significant financial gains to the federal taxpayer. The financial benefits currently flowing from a few rich oil and gas and coal deposits could be protected either by retaining these limited resources in federal hands (perhaps as economically "crit-

---

[74] Culhane, *Public Land Politics.*

[75] American Law Institute, *A Model Land Development Code: Official Draft* (Philadelphia, ALI, 1977).

TABLE 2–6. Fiscal Impact of State Ownership of Public Domain
Lands Now Managed by the Interior Department (1978)

State	1978 Net state revenues, current federal ownership (000)	Net state revenues, transfer to state ownership (000)[a]	Net state gain or loss from transfer (000)
Alaska	$1,259.2	− $57,066.9	− $58,326.1
Arizona	954.4	− 8,966.2	− 9,920.6
California	10,628.9	739.9	− 9,889.0
Colorado	15,377.5	8,677.0	− 6,700.5
Idaho	2,341.3	− 10,668.3	− 13,009.6
Montana	7,959.2	947.6	− 7,011.6
Nevada	4,967.4	− 4,366.1	− 9,333.5
New Mexico	60,179.9	105,999.6	45,819.7
Oregon[b]	690.6	− 9,458.5	− 10,149.1
Utah	12,117.2	4,968.4	− 7,148.8
Washington	62.2	− 234.6	− 296.8
Wyoming	69,761.6	133,398.6	63,637.0
Total	186,299.4	163,970.5	− 22,328.9

Source: Robert H. Nelson, "An Analysis of Revenues and Costs of Public Land Management
by the Interior Department in 13 Western States," Office of Policy Analysis, U.S. Department
of the Interior (December 1979).

[a] Net state revenues are calculated based on the assumption that states would follow the
same pricing policies and incur the same management costs as the federal government now
does.

[b] The O&C timber lands are not part of the public domain lands.

ical areas") or by attaching an overriding royalty to any transfer of the
lands to the states. Even without such a step, the federal taxpayer would
have benefited financially in 1978 by transferring to twelve western states
all the surface and mineral rights in the public domain lands managed
by the Interior Department (excluding "O and C" timber lands in western Oregon, which are not part of the public domain lands).[76] As shown
in table 2–6, if the twelve states had owned the public domain lands in
1978, they would have incurred more in new management costs than
they would have gained in new revenues, producing a net fiscal loss to
those states of $22 million. If the transfer to the states had been limited
to the surface estate, the state losses would have been greater and,
conversely, the federal taxpayer would have experienced a net fiscal

[76] The O & C lands are railroad lands that have been repossessed by the federal
government. In 1866 the Oregon and California Railroad Co. received a grant to build a
line from Portland, Oregon south to California. Apparent violations of the contract terms
led to a long and complicated legal battle and in the end the government took back 2.5
million acres, commonly known as O & C lands. Today these lands have some of the
finest virgin Douglas fir forest to be found in the United States and are extremely valuable.
(Marion Clawson and Burnell Held, *The Federal Lands*, Baltimore, Md., Johns Hopkins
University Press for Resources for the Future, 1957.)

benefit of $133 million. Moreover, these calculations do not include $77 million in payments in lieu of taxes made by the federal government to western local governments in 1978.[77]

While federal taxpayers might benefit economically, the total environmental and recreation values involved are very likely much larger than the dollar sums just noted. Protection of recreational access for all Americans is another reason often given for retaining the public lands. However, most long-distance travel for recreation purposes is to national parks, wilderness areas, and other "critical areas" likely to remain under permanent federal control. In-state residents are the primary users of ordinary public lands. Moreover, state ownership of ordinary recreation lands would leave most, if not all, of them open for public recreation by all Americans. If considered necessary, the federal government could attach conditions to any transfer guaranteeing permanent public access to the lands—either through easements or other legal mechanisms.

The capacity and will of western states to protect recreational use of public lands is often questioned. Recreationists point to management of lands owned by the states themselves as a demonstration that state governments are predisposed to favor livestock, mining, and other commodity interests over recreation. This conclusion is suspect, however, for several reasons. First, and most important, existing state lands are typically in small isolated parcels, remnants of old education land grants, making it impossible to manage them effectively for recreation or any other purpose. Second, even if this problem did not exist, the past record would still not be a good indicator of likely future management. The western states are changing rapidly in their demographic and political makeup. California state government today is probably more oriented toward recreation needs of Californians than is the federal government. In any case, management of major new land areas would cause institutional change at the state level, greatly increasing the visibility of state land management, and thus very likely creating new constellations of political pressures favoring recreational use of state lands.

There is little doubt that most Americans favor a system of national parks and other national critical areas. Any transfer of other recreation lands to the states should probably begin with a comprehensive reexamination of existing federal lands to determine any further public lands that should be included in a national system. Even lands with potential for national significance might be held in federal hands. Indeed, the ongoing wilderness review of the national forests and BLM lands is accomplishing much of this task right now. The definition of "wilder-

---

[77] Nelson, *An Analysis of Revenues and Costs.*

ness" has become sufficiently vague and encompassing that in practice it comes close to "national critical area."

Divestiture to the Private Sector

Historically, divestiture of the public lands to private parties has frequently occurred in an incremental fashion and has almost always been accompanied by controversy. In the early nineteenth century, the government sought to sell public lands as a major public revenue source. This effort mostly failed when squatters simply entered the lands, could not be forced to leave, and were unable to pay much. The Homestead Act ultimately acknowledged the political and logistical inability of the government to oppose such pressures. Indeed, throughout the years prior to the Homestead Act, many easterners objected strongly to "giving away" their land to illegal squatters.

As noted earlier, the divestiture of federal rights has not stopped in the twentieth century; the "retention" of federal ownership of public lands has often been more in form than substance. As actually administered, the Taylor Grazing Act of 1934 might be characterized as a Homestead Act for rangeland grazing rights, giving these rights to ranchers whose level of grazing was established by historic use of public rangelands. Ranchers have in fact often derived significant benefits from maintaining the form of federal ownership along with the reality of many of the rights of ownership. For one thing, the federal grazing fee has often been less than the local property taxes many ranchers would have had to pay under their own ownership.

Divestiture of at least some public lands to private ownership would be consistent with the traditional American view to rely on the private sector for most functions. Even when the government does intervene in certain areas, the preferred approach is usually public regulation of private production, rather than direct public production. In this regard, as in others, the current extent of public land ownership is an anomaly in the American system.

There are, however, some sound justifications for public ownership of many recreational lands. As chapter 1 points out, the operation of private markets for recreation would be highly imperfect in many respects. A private owner of recreation lands would have to charge a fee to cover his costs and make a profit, even where there was no social cost to an additional recreationist. Because some recreationists would be kept away by a fee, the potential bid of a private recreational operator for lands would be less than the net social return to all recreational users in the absence of a fee (a case of the classic dilemma of the appropriate toll on an uncongested bridge).[78] Moreover, for dispersed types of recreation on public lands, such as ordinary sightseeing or hiking, the collection costs are likely to be a significant portion of—or even to exceed—the total potential fee collections, again causing private returns to fall well below the social return that could be achieved in the absence of a fee. If private land ownerships were not very large, recreationists could be confronted with the prospect of a new toll at every new property line. As size of private ownership becomes very large, it becomes very much like a private government. The assembly of units large enough for efficient recreation might itself require government condemnation powers.

Certain public land uses provide benefits to those who do not use the lands directly or immediately. For instance, some individuals benefit from the knowledge that recreation and wilderness areas exist, and future generations as well benefit from the protection such areas may provide for threatened plant and animal life. But no entrepreneur could readily convert benefits of this kind into profits.[79] Moreover, even where voluntary private donations would willingly be made for such purposes, the mail and other transactions costs of tapping large numbers of citizens are likely to be prohibitive. Even if I am willing to contribute 50 cents to preserve some proposed area (creating a large sum if many others join me), the costs of soliciting my contribution may well exceed 50 cents.

To be sure, even in the absence of such considerations, the tradition of free recreational use of the public lands might be inviolate. Open access to the public lands has become an element of national redistribution policy, making the lands equally available to rich and poor alike (assuming rich and poor can get to the lands equally). Adam Smith himself made an exception to his strong case for private land ownership in recommending that "lands for the purpose of pleasure and magnificence, parks, gardens, public walks, etc., possessions which are everywhere considered as causes of expense, not as sources of revenue, seem to be the only lands which in a great and civilized monarchy, ought to belong to the crown."[80]

On the other hand, some important forms of recreational use of land, such as second homes and resort development, would be greatly facil-

[78] For discussion of this dilemma, see Richard A. Musgrave, *The Theory of Public Finance* (New York, McGraw Hill, 1959).

[79] See Mancur Olson, *The Logic of Collective Action* (Cambridge, Mass., Harvard University Press, 1965).

[80] Adam Smith, *An Inquiry into the Nature and Causes of the Wealth of Nations* (Chicago, University of Chicago Press, 1976 edition) vol 2, p. 349.

itated by private ownership. Especially in the West, a new supply of land for such development would reduce its cost, putting private cabins and other facilities within the reach of a much larger part of the population. Once congestion begins to occur, as for much hunting, private ownership would allow direct pricing, which is frequently more efficient than other allocation methods, if not as acceptable on equity grounds.

It is interesting to note that private firms can provide even recreation deemed to be of critical national concern so long as points of entry are well defined. For example, Luray Caverns in Virginia differs little from Mammoth Cave National Park in Kentucky, although the former is privately operated.

While there are strong arguments for public ownership of at least some types of recreation lands, the case for public ownership of timber, livestock grazing, and other commodity lands seems much weaker. The introduction of economic efficiency into commodity production requires the rejection of habits of thought ingrained in the public land agencies over the past seventy-five years. The employees of public land agencies will not easily give up the biological approach to public land objectives. Biological concepts are not only practical tools in their mind, but in many cases are also moral imperatives. Many agency employees see the necessity of economic tradeoffs as an undesirable compromise of the agency's integrity. Public land agencies are strongly attached to concepts such as "multiple use," "sustained yield," and "even flow," even if they make little sense economically.

By contrast, the U.S. private sector has a different set of incentives which give a much greater weight to economic efficiency. Charles Schultze has urged greater reliance on private incentives for achieving many social objectives. One reason is that "under the social arrangements of the private market, those who may suffer losses are not usually able to stand in the way of change. As a consequence, efficiency-creating changes are not seriously impeded."[81] The tendency in recent years to try to supercede rather than guide the market

> has proven a costly bias. It has, with no offsetting gain, forfeited the strategic advantages of market-like arrangements. It has led to ineffective and inefficient solutions to important social problems. It has taxed, well beyond its limit, the ability of government to make complex output decisions. And it has stretched thin the delicate fabric of political consensus by unnecessarily widening the scope of activities it must cover.[82]

[81] Schultze, *The Public Use of Private Interest*, pp. 21–22.
[82] Ibid., p. 29.

The statutory basis for public land management currently is a confusing mixture of requirements to employ at the same time economic analysis and concepts that have little or no basis in economics. Although a case can be made that recent laws actually require an economic efficiency foundation for public land decisions, many contrary elements can also be identified.[83] The simplest way to ensure an economic approach might well be to turn production decisions over to private managers. As in most other sectors of the U.S. economy, government would then pursue nonmarket objectives by regulatory means and by financial incentives offered to the private sector.

The advantages of the private market as a planning and coordinating mechanism have been widely discussed, as have the major difficulties of central planning. Calculation of timber and mineral production goals and sale targets requires long-run predictive capabilities that have eluded government planners in many nations.[84] The demands for extensive central information require continuous assembly and updating of production plans throughout the private and public sectors.

A key advantage of the private sector is its greater innovative capacity and responsiveness to change. Even though private companies may also fall short in this regard (e.g., the auto industry), the penalties are usually greater than in the public sector, and the pressures to do better typically more urgent. The major innovations in timber management and production have in fact come from large timber companies rather than the Forest Service.[85] Indeed, a good case could be made that some of the current timber corporations more closely embody the actual Pinchot vision of scientific management of timber production than does the current Forest Service. More generally, the sophistication of American business planning as practiced by some of the most successful corporations sets an example which public sector planning rarely matches. In an irony of history, these private corporations have turned out in many ways to be the American embodiments of the progressive aspirations for the public sector.[86]

It is possible that private parties might also prove better than the government in managing wilderness areas, as well as areas where ordinary commodities are to be produced. If the ownership of existing wilderness areas were transferred to preservation organizations like the

[83] See Krutilla and Haigh, "An Integrated Approach to National Forest Management."

[84] See Michael Ellman, *Socialist Planning* (Cambridge, Cambridge University Press, 1979).

[85] For the history of industrial forestry, see Clepper, *Professional Forestry in the United States*.

[86] See Neil W. Chamberlain, *Private and Public Planning* (New York, McGraw Hill, 1965).

Sierra Club or the Wilderness Society, such groups might cover the costs of management in part by charging entry and other recreational fees. They might even be willing to tolerate some commodity production in some wilderness areas if that production was lucrative and did not impair the character of the area. For example, the Audubon Society has issued natural gas drilling leases in its Rainey Wildlife Sanctuary in Louisiana; the royalties, which come to almost $1 million annually, are used to further the Society's wildlife preservation activities elsewhere. In the view of the Audubon Society, the value of these additional activities outweighs any damage that might be caused by the carefully supervised drilling in the sanctuary. This suggests that even ardent preservationists are willing to accept some commingling of commodity and "natural" activities when the circumstances are right.

Yet, environmental groups often strenuously oppose any such commodity extraction in federal wilderness areas. This may stem from a belief that production will not be as carefully supervised in these areas as in the Audubon Society's preserve. But it is also attributable to the absence of a stake in the commodity production that might take place in some wilderness areas—in other words, the protestors lose nothing by opposing production. If they did, they would be forced, like the Audubon Society, to balance the competing benefits and costs of commodity production, a balancing that is conducive to good policy. This factor has led some observers to suggest that federal wilderness areas be divested to preservation groups.[87]

In recent years, dissolution of many of the governmental products of the progressive tradition has been high on the public agenda. The deregulation movement has sought to free the private sector from the tight reins of the Interstate Commerce Commission, Federal Power Commission, Civil Aeronautics Board, and other agency control. These agencies by and large did not achieve the disinterested expert decision making in the public interest that was originally sought. Instead, they tended to become captives of particular interests, often protecting these interests against forces of market competition.[88] The public lands represent a different type of progressive institution in that government is the direct resource owner and producer; nevertheless, many of the indictments of progressive regulatory institutions are similar to criticisms of public land

[87] John Baden and Richard Stroup, "Saving the Wilderness," *Reason* (July 1981) pp. 28–36.

[88] For a similar analysis of more recent regulation, see Bruce A. Ackerman and William T. Hassler, *Clean Coal/Dirty Air: Or How the Clean Air Act Became a Multibillion-Dollar Bailout for High Sulfur Coal Producers and What Should Be Done About It* (New Haven, Conn., Yale University Press, 1981). See also Institute for Contemporary Studies, *Regulating Business: The Search for an Optimum* (San Francisco, ICS, 1978).

management. "Deregulation" in the case of the public lands would consist, not in abolishing regulatory constraints, but in divestiture of at least some public lands to the private sector.

A Proposal for Public Land Reclassification

As the introductory chapter to this book points out, economists are often in search of efficiency—of ways to improve the lot of at least some individuals without diminishing that of others. A politician would understand this idea better as seeking to find compromises that make everyone happy. In actual fact, it seems possible that the existing system of public land management has such large ingrained economic inefficiencies and other irrationalities that basic institutional change could actually make all the current beneficiaries significantly better off.

Following a line of analysis dating back to J. W. Powell, the key to such general improvement would lie in an appropriate reclassification of the public lands.[89] The two broadest classes would be recreation lands and commodity production lands. By concentrating on what each type of land does best, the total output value of both recreation and commodity production could be increased. The private and public sectors should also do what each does best. The general record of the U.S. private sector in achieving efficiency in ordinary production compares very favorably with the U.S. public sector. On the other hand, the general record is better in the U.S. public sector in providing ordinary dispersed recreation such as hiking, fishing, hunting, and offroad vehicle use, as well as preserving wilderness areas and habitats for endangered species. The opportunities for such activities are more easily and widely available in the public land states of the West than they are in the East, where private ownership prevails.

The past twenty years have in fact been a fertile period for public land reclassification. The designation of wilderness areas and, more generally, the emergence of a de facto public land zoning system, have involved widespread land reclassifications, but they need to be carried further. For instance, one possible reclassification for the national forest system would be into timber production and recreation lands. It would probably make sense to divest to the private sector the 40 million or so acres—mostly in the Pacific Northwest—likely to be classified for timber production.[90] One way to accomplish such a divestiture would be to create new timber corporations and then gradually sell off the federal

---

[89] Powell, *Report on the Lands of the Arid Regions.*
[90] See Richard Stroup and John Baden, "Externality, Property Rights and the Management of Our National Forests," *Journal of Law and Economics* vol. 16 (October 1973) pp. 303–312.

shareholdings over some period, say fifteen years.[91] Divestiture terms could be set to ensure that public recreation continued on newly private timberlands as a secondary use; in many cases private timber companies now open their lands and even provide recreation facilities. Politically, it would be necessary to maintain at least part of existing revenue flows to local counties from timberlands—perhaps by making the counties shareholders in timber corporations newly formed from public lands.

On the other hand, the large majority of national forest lands could be classified into wilderness, backcountry, and other recreation systems. The federal government might continue to manage forest lands classified to be of critical national concern (such as wilderness); the states could then manage the remaining forest lands classified to be of more ordinary recreational interest. The release of even part of the federal funds now spent on uneconomic timber harvests would offer the chance for greater public spending on recreation.

The public rangelands might similarly be reclassified into two types: (1) livestock grazing lands and (2) recreation lands. The lands used mainly for livestock grazing could be placed under direct rancher management, perhaps under a 99-year or other long-term lease to the land itself (not to AUMs or other forage quantities). Terms would be set to ensure that state fish and game and federal wildlife agencies could make wildlife improvements on such grazing lands as desirable, much as they now do on private lands in eastern states. Rangelands classified for recreation could be managed by the federal government or by the states, depending on their value and national significance.

The potential for increasing both recreation and commodity outputs by reclassifying the public lands arises in several ways. First, greater production from commodity lands could be achieved by means of the more efficient production likely under direct private management. The greater benefit, however, would probably be expanded recreation on the public lands. Uneconomic commodity production would no longer conflict with recreation; instead, management attention would be focused on the needs of recreationists. Moreover, federal funds that are currently used inefficiently to support commodity production could be redirected in whole or in part to recreation. For example, as much as $50 million per year of federal funding that goes mainly for livestock grazing on BLM lands might be freed for rangeland recreation, an amount equal to five times the current direct level of BLM recreational funding. Even greater federal expenditures could be redirected to recreational

[91] See Robert H. Nelson, "Making Sense of the Sagebrush Rebellion: A Long Term Strategy for the Public Lands," paper presented at the Third Annual Conference of the Association for Public Policy Analysis and Management, Washington, D.C., October 23–25, 1981.

uses on the national forests. The real loser under the current organization of public lands is the national taxpayer, who might also benefit by return of some funds to the federal treasury.

Perhaps the greatest obstacle to public land reclassification is a wide fear that it would cause a loss of recreational access to the public lands.[92] However, even where lands were divested to the private sector, future public access could be maintained through access easements and other protective mechanisms. It might even be possible to increase public access by requiring ranchers and other owners of intermingled private lands to open their own lands as a condition for new long-term leasing of the adjacent public lands.

The most appropriate land use categories and the actual classification of existing public lands into these categories are potential matters for wide debate; there are valid pros and cons for all of the alternatives. The purpose of this chapter is to suggest the need for reclassification and to indicate some of the possibilities. A vehicle for addressing such issues might be a national commission for public land reclassification. The final resolution would be up to Congress.

CONCLUDING CAVEATS

Debates over public land policy are as old as the republic. They are inherently contentious because they very frequently involve control over property rights. Changes in public land policy usually benefit some parties while other groups see threats to the services they obtain from these lands. Zoning decisions to allocate public land among different uses are particularly important in determining gainers and losers and generate the same fierce conflicts seen in urban zoning.

These controversies do not stop once an area of public land is allocated to commodity production. Once this is decided, the level of production must be determined. Fair market value and other terms must be set. Regulations to protect the environment against adverse impacts of commodity production must be promulgated and enforced. Although recreation is perhaps not the primary use of the land, policies for recreation on lands open to commodity production must be formulated. All these decisions cause further significant conflicts.

The most contentious issue of all is the possibility of major changes in land tenure. Such changes would alter the distribution of public land

---

[92] Two examples of this concern are Ted Trueblood, "They're Fixing to Steal Your Land," *Field and Stream* vol. 84 (March 1980) pp. 40–41, 166–167; and Dan Abrams, "The Rebellion Is Getting Hot," *Jackson Hole News* (December 5, 1979).

benefits in a permanent way, whereas ordinary policy conflicts are more typically reversible in a new day. Moreover, changes in land tenure involve major symbolic considerations for many people. Indeed, it sometimes seems that the most important public land outputs are not a matter of actual uses of the lands but of the symbols they evoke. As a public rangelands committee assembled by the National Academy of Sciences recently noted:[93]

> Public rangeland supplies only a small amount of the national demand for meat, but an extremely large amount of the national demand for myths of free-ranging rugged individualists. . . . It is evident that public rangeland may be far better at producing the stuff of myth and national identity than economically prudent beef and mutton products. Yet, in the long run, the production and perpetuation of national myth may be one of the most valuable resources harvested from public rangeland.

For others, the public lands have served as a kind of battleground where symbols of good (the purity of nature) are saved from evil (modern industrial civilization). For still others, the very fact of public land management has had its own high "existence value" as a progressive symbol of public action to promote human progress. The public lands are seen as one of the main refuges from the corrupting taint of the private profit motive. If major change actually comes on the public lands, it may be mainly because new symbols of "federal colonialism" and "inept and oppressive bureaucracy" have replaced the earlier ones.

Study of the issues of the public lands thus may require an economics of myth and symbol as much as an economics of their direct use. Indeed, as a producer of myth the public lands are probably managed very efficiently; the rangeland program involves very minor sums compared with the billion-dollar agricultural subsidies to preserve the illusion of the yeoman farmer. The argument can be made that it would be better to leave well enough alone on the public lands.[94] Many economists may feel the urge to throw up their hands at such thoughts; yet, it is the romance of the public lands which gives them their compelling interest, and even leads many economists to study them. The fact that economic rationality is not necessarily the dominant influence does not in any case diminish the importance of its analysis.

[93] *Developing Strategies for Rangeland Management: A Report Prepared by the Committee on Developing Strategies for Rangeland Management* (Washington, D.C., 1981); The committee was assembled by the National Academy of Sciences, National Research Council, but disbanded before issuing a published official report (after running out of funds). The committee members then issued a summary report on their own.

[94] W. A. Kerr and A. Dooley, "Can Rangeland Projects Survive Cost-Benefit Analysis?" *Rangelands* (February 1982).

3

Nonfuel Minerals

*Hans H. Landsberg and John E. Tilton
with Ruth B. Haas*

The United States is one of the world's largest producers of minerals and at the same time it is one of the world's largest users of minerals and mineral products. For a variety of reasons, the country does not mine all the minerals it needs and thus relies on imports to supplement its supplies. The extent of this reliance is shown in figure 3–1. Almost all of the manganese, chromium, cobalt, bauxite, tantalum, and columbium consumed in the United States comes from abroad. Similarly, well over half of the country's supplies of tin, asbestos, nickel, cadmium, and zinc originate in foreign mines. Imports are significant even for copper, lead, and iron ore, which have long been considered major domestic mining industries. In short, figure 3–1 shows a country heavily dependent on outside sources for a number of important mineral commodities.

Minerals from abroad are vulnerable to a variety of interruptions. For example, sources can be overrun by insurgents, exports embargoed by hostile governments, or supplies sunk at sea. So it is perhaps not surprising that the concern over energy precipitated by the oil embargo and price hike of 1973–74 has in recent years been followed by an almost equally vociferous concern about nonfuel minerals, and strategic metals in particular. The call for energy independence that characterized the mid-1970s has now been succeeded by a call for mineral independence.

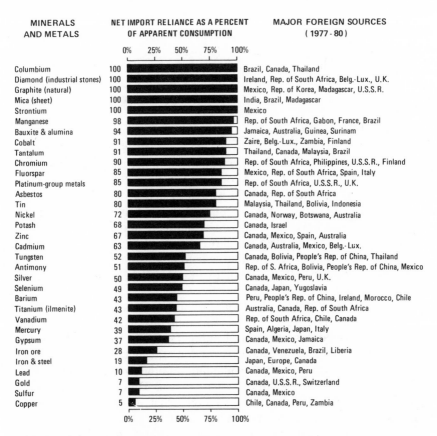

MINERALS AND METALS	NET IMPORT RELIANCE AS A PERCENT OF APPARENT CONSUMPTION	MAJOR FOREIGN SOURCES (1977-80)
Columbium	100	Brazil, Canada, Thailand
Diamond (industrial stones)	100	Ireland, Rep. of South Africa, Belg.-Lux., U.K.
Graphite (natural)	100	Mexico, Rep. of Korea, Madagascar, U.S.S.R.
Mica (sheet)	100	India, Brazil, Madagascar
Strontium	100	Mexico
Manganese	98	Rep. of South Africa, Gabon, France, Brazil
Bauxite & alumina	94	Jamaica, Australia, Guinea, Surinam
Cobalt	91	Zaire, Belg.-Lux., Zambia, Finland
Tantalum	91	Thailand, Canada, Malaysia, Brazil
Chromium	90	Rep. of South Africa, Philippines, U.S.S.R., Finland
Fluorspar	85	Mexico, Rep. of South Africa, Spain, Italy
Platinum-group metals	85	Rep. of South Africa, U.S.S.R., U.K.
Asbestos	80	Canada, Rep. of South Africa
Tin	80	Malaysia, Thailand, Bolivia, Indonesia
Nickel	72	Canada, Norway, Botswana, Australia
Potash	68	Canada, Israel
Zinc	67	Canada, Mexico, Spain, Australia
Cadmium	63	Canada, Australia, Mexico, Belg.-Lux.
Tungsten	52	Canada, Bolivia, People's Rep. of China, Thailand
Antimony	51	Rep. of S. Africa, Bolivia, People's Rep. of China, Mexico
Silver	50	Canada, Mexico, Peru, U.K.
Selenium	49	Canada, Japan, Yugoslavia
Barium	43	Peru, People's Rep. of China, Ireland, Morocco, Chile
Titanium (ilmenite)	43	Australia, Canada, Rep. of South Africa
Vanadium	42	Rep. of South Africa, Chile, Canada
Mercury	39	Spain, Algeria, Japan, Italy
Gypsum	37	Canada, Mexico, Jamaica
Iron ore	28	Canada, Venezuela, Brazil, Liberia
Iron & steel	19	Japan, Europe, Canada
Lead	10	Canada, Mexico, Peru
Gold	7	Canada, U.S.S.R., Switzerland
Sulfur	7	Canada, Mexico
Copper	5	Chile, Canada, Peru, Zambia

Figure 3–1. U.S. net import reliance of selected minerals and metals as a percent of consumption, January 1982 (estimates). Notes: Sources shown are points of shipment to the United States and are not necessarily the initial sources of the material. Net import reliance = imports − exports + adjustments for government and industry stock changes. Apparent consumption = U.S. primary + secondary production + net import reliance. Substantial quantities of rutile, rhenium, and zircon are imported but data are withheld to avoid disclosing proprietary information. (Figure courtesy of U.S. Bureau of Mines. Import-export data from the U.S. Bureau of the Census.)

In the minds of some, the Soviet Union is pursuing a "resource war" and has joined OPEC as a villain threatening the U.S. economy.

But is a resource war a real possibility or is it simply being used to justify a minerals policy that would open up more public lands to mining, a defense policy that would greatly strengthen the Navy and other military services, and a foreign policy that would treat South Africa and certain other mineral-exporting countries more favorably? Can the United States become self-sufficient in minerals production? More important, *should* it? This chapter examines the issues that arise out of these and other questions about mineral supplies—specifically, supplies of nonfuel minerals from abroad—and their implications for U.S. policy.

ROLE IN THE ECONOMY

Taken all together, nonfuel minerals play an important role in the U.S. economy. In their raw form, at or near the mine, the value of domestically produced minerals in 1979 was calculated at $24 billion, but the greater part of that sum was accounted for by cement, sand, gravel, stone, clay, and lime. Although these latter materials sell at per ton values as low as $2.50 (even metal ores, on the average, do not sell for much above $10 per ton), such large amounts are produced that in the aggregate they account for about two-thirds of the value of domestic mineral output.

Of this amount, only $8.5 billion, or about one third of the aggregate mineral value, is derived from metallic minerals and only iron ore and copper are valued at more than $1 billion per year. These two minerals make up 70 percent of the total value of domestic metallic mineral output and, with the exception of molybdenum, no other metal is produced at a value exceeding half a billion dollars a year. However, since the aggregate figure is often cited, many argue that it makes the minerals appear more valuable than they actually are.

The value of nonfuel minerals is also overshadowed by that of energy resources. In 1979, the value of domestically produced energy was in the neighborhood of $100 billion. Except for coal, each individual energy source—crude oil, natural gas, and hydro and nuclear energy jointly—was valued at more than all of the nonenergy minerals together. Comparisons for 1981 display an even greater difference. With oil prices decontrolled, crude petroleum in early 1981 was by itself pushing toward an annual value of $100 billion and natural gas will be next in rapid growth of value. One of the reasons for this disparity is the high per ton value of many of the energy reserves compared with minerals; crude oil, for example, sells at over $200 per ton.

When it comes to foreign trade, again the nonfuel minerals fade when compared with energy. In 1979, gross imports of nonfuel minerals totaled about $26 billion (of which 70 percent were metallic); net imports were about $8 billion. Moreover, of the $18 billion worth of metallic mineral imports, nearly 40 percent consisted not of ores but of processed, semi-fabricated iron and steel products. In the same year, gross U.S. energy imports totaled $60 billion, net energy imports $54 billion. In 1981, net energy imports had risen to $71 billion.

To help appreciate these differences, it is worthwhile noting that one day's petroleum imports equals in value that of two years of tungsten imports, six months of cobalt imports, or three months of platinum imports. In other words, trade in energy and nonfuel minerals is conducted on very different scales. This is true globally as well: of total world export trade, metallic mineral ores, concentrates, and scrap constituted only a little over 1 percent in 1978; fuels constituted 16 percent, and the gap widened appreciably in 1979 and 1980. When discussing issues involving nonfuel minerals, therefore, it is important to keep in mind these differences in scale and values. Judgments about energy supplies cannot be transferred wholesale to nonfuel minerals.

Another difference between energy and nonfuel minerals worth noting is that U.S. dependence on imports is not a recent development. This country acquired all or nearly all of its tin, nickel, chromium, and manganese from abroad even before World War I. It is true that import dependence appears on balance to be increasing. Over the past twenty years, for example, imports have captured a larger share of the domestic iron ore, bauxite, and zinc markets. In addition, more downstream processing is being done abroad. For example, foreign manganese and chromium ores, which used to be smelted in the United States, are now largely processed in South Africa and elsewhere. Similarly, much of the bauxite coming from Jamaica, Australia, and Surinam is refined into alumina before it is shipped.

A number of imported minerals have become more important because they are essential ingredients for many of the new specialty steel alloys and other materials developed in recent years. Since these materials possess special attributes, such as high strength-to-weight ratios or the ability to withstand corrosion at high temperatures and pressures, they are used extensively in the production of high technology and military equipment.

Despite this, as we shall see later, dependence on imports is not a bad situation in and by itself. A policy that emphasizes mineral self-sufficiency has costs of its own that must be taken into account when such policies are considered.

While foreign supplies may be interrupted, domestic mineral supplies are also exposed to risks. Labor disputes in the United States have periodically interrupted copper production, and inadequate precipitation has on occasions restricted generation of hydroelectric power in the Pacific Northwest, curtailing aluminum production. Furthermore, as we shall see in the following section, the extent of import dependence is just one of many conditions bearing upon mineral supplies.

MINERAL SUPPLIES

Four factors affect the availability of minerals to the United States and any one of them could conceivably cause disruptions or shortages. The first is the resource base. Clearly, mineral production requires a sufficient supply of ore deposits. How much do we have and how much will it cost to extract and process it? These are long-standing questions that must be viewed in a global context. They are also questions that have been taken up elsewhere and so will be discussed only briefly here.[1]

The second factor concerns the adequacy of investment in the mineral sector. Even with a rich endowment of mineral deposits, mines and processing facilities must be built to extract the ores and convert them into useful materials. The third factor concerns unanticipated surges in demand that occur from time to time, causing temporary shortages even when adequate capacity exists to service normal requirements. Such surges often occur during booms in the business cycle or during wartime.

Finally, mineral supplies may be affected by interruptions or constraints on production or trade. Shipments can be disrupted by cartels, war, civil disturbances, natural disasters, or deliberate embargoes by supplier countries. Since it is this form of short-term supply constraint, particularly with respect to imports, that is the focus of much current concern, it is discussed in some detail in the next section.

Factors Affecting Availability

The United States enjoys some preferential access to the minerals found and produced within its own borders. In an emergency, these minerals can be rationed by the government to those uses of highest national priority. In times of shortages, consumers can pressure the government to restrict mineral exports and thereby enhance domestic availability. Abroad, however, the United States must compete on an equal footing with other consuming nations for the available supplies. Indeed, U.S. consumers may find they are at a disadvantage as foreign consumers receive preferential treatment.

In the past, this has not been a significant problem. The number of major consuming countries has been limited, and the United States has been well served by a cadre of international mining companies, many headquartered in the United States. Through their worldwide exploration, development, and marketing activities, these companies have

[1]See, for example, the various sources cited in John E. Tilton, "The Continuing Debate Over the Exhaustion of Nonfuel Mineral Resources," *Natural Resources Forum* vol. 1 (1977) pp. 167–173.

ensured adequate mineral supplies for the United States and other consuming countries.

Many persons fear, however, that the future may be different. The growing economic nationalism found in developing and developed countries alike is hampering the operating ability of the multinational mining firms. At the same time, competition for mineral supplies is growing and is likely to become much more intense as Brazil, Mexico, Korea, and other developing countries become more industrialized and claim a larger share of the world's mineral output. Under such conditions, it is asked whether the United States can continue to count on minerals from abroad.

In examining this concern, we need to ask: Why not? Or more specifically: What would limit the flow of imports? The exhaustion of foreign mineral resources? Inadequate investment in the mines and facilities required to take minerals out of the ground and convert them into useful products? Discrimination against U.S. consumers, particularly during temporary shortages caused by unexpected surges in demand or by strikes and other interruptions in supply? Each of these possibilities is examined in turn.

RESOURCES AND RESERVES.   The popular perception of depletion is that the world is slowly, or not so slowly, using up its finite stocks of mineral resources. One day they will be gone, it is argued, and, like an automobile running out of gas, the industrialized world will grind to a halt. Modern civilization as we know it will cease to exist. Mankind, if it survives a turbulent transition period, will revert to a pastoral existence, requiring great changes in life-styles and much lower living standards.[2]

Those who subscribe to this view of depletion are fond of estimating life expectancies for various mineral commodities. The typical procedure is to take the reserves for a mineral commodity, or some multiple of reserves, and calculate how long they will last under various scenarios of future primary production. The results are generally alarming, indicating that within the next 100 years the world will run out of copper, lead, nickel, tin, zinc, and a host of other mineral commodities (see table 3–1).

Such results are also misleading. Reserves by definition include only those minerals contained in known deposits that are profitable to mine under existing legal, economic, and technological conditions, and so are

[2]The best-known version of this scenario appears in Dennis H. Meadows, Donnella L. Meadows, Jorgen Randers, and W.W. Behrens III, *The Limits to Growth* (New York, Universe Books, 1972).

TABLE 3–1. Life Expectancies of World Reserves, Selected Mineral Commodities

Mineral commodity[a]	1974 reserves[b]	1972-74 average annual production[b]	Life expectancy in years, at four growth rates[c]				Average annual production growth, 1947-74 (percent)
			0%	2%	5%	10%	
Antimony (Sb)	4.2×10^6	70.0×10^3	60	40	28	20	2.4
Arsenic (As$_2$O$_3$)	4.5×10^6	46.8×10^3	97	54	36	25	-0.6
Asbestos	87.0×10^6	4.0×10^6	22	18	15	12	6.5
Barite (BaSO$_4$)	181.4×10^6	4.3×10^6	42	31	23	17	4.1
Bauxite (ore)[d]	15.7×10^9	69.7×10^6	226	86	51	33	9.8
Bismuth (Bi)	113.4×10^3	4.2×10^3	27	22	18	14	4.4
Cadmium (Cd)	1.3×10^6	17.0×10^3	74	46	32	22	4.7
Chromium (ore)	1.7×10^9	6.5×10^6	263	93	54	35	5.3
Cobalt (Co)	2.4×10^6	25.3×10^3	97	54	36	25	5.8
Copper (Cu)	390.0×10^6	7.0×10^6	56	38	27	20	4.8
Diamond (industrial)	680.0×10^6	31.4×10^6	22	18	15	12	5.4
Fluorspar (90% CaF$_2$)	106.1×10^6	4.5×10^6	23	19	16	13	7.5
Gold (Au)	4.0×10^4	1.3×10^3	30	24	19	15	2.4
Ilmenite (conc.)[e]	516.9×10^6	3.4×10^6	150	70	44	29	9.5
Iron (Fe)	87.7×10^9	0.5×10^9	167	74	46	30	7.0
Lead (Pb)	145.1×10^6	3.5×10^6	42	31	23	17	3.8
Magnesium (Mg)[f]	...	5.1×10^6	...	...	...	...	7.7
Manganese (Mn)[g]	1.9×10^9	10.1×10^6	190	79	48	31	6.5
Mercury (Hg)	182.3×10^3	9.4×10^3	19	17	14	11	2.0
Molybdenum (Mo)	5.0×10^6	71.6×10^3	70	44	31	22	7.3
Nickel (Ni)	44.4×10^6	0.7×10^6	67	43	30	22	6.9

TABLE 3–1. Life Expectancies of World Reserves, Selected Mineral Commodities (*continued*)

Mineral commodity[a]	1974 reserves[b]	1972–74 average annual production[b]	Life expectancy in years, at four growth rates[c]				Average annual production growth, 1947–74 (percent)
			0%	2%	5%	10%	
Phosphate rock	13.0×10^9	99.4×10^6	128	64	41	28	7.3
Platinum group (metal)	1.9×10^4	0.2×10^3	117	61	39	27	9.7
Potash (K$_2$O)	80.7×10^9	22.2×10^6	3,638	217	107	62	9.0
Silver (Ag)	1.9×10^5	9.3×10^3	20	17	14	12	2.2
Sulfur (S)	2.0×10^9	46.8×10^6	44	32	24	18	6.7
Tin (Sn)	9.9×10^6	0.2×10^6	42	31	23	17	2.7
Tungsten (W)	1.6×10^6	39.0×10^3	42	31	23	17	3.8
Vanadium (V)[h]	9.7×10^6	15.7×10^3	462	131	71	43	11.1
Zinc (Zn)	118.8×10^6	5.6×10^6	21	18	15	12	4.7

Sources: U.S. Bureau of Mines, *Commodity Data Summaries 1972* (U.S. Bureau of Mines, 1972), and ibid. *1973, 1974, 1975, 1976;* Donald A. Brobst and Walden P. Pratt, eds., *United States Mineral Resources,* Geological Survey professional paper 820 (GPO, 1973); U.S. Bureau of Mines, *Minerals Yearbook 1948,* and ibid. *1974* (GPO, 1950 and 1976). Taken from John E. Tilton, *The Future of Nonfuel Minerals* (Washington, D.C., Brookings Institution, 1972).

a The notation in parentheses following the name of a mineral commodity indicates what the reserve and production figures actually measure. For example, for copper they measure contained metal (Cu), for ilmenite they measure concentrates (conc.), and for bauxite and chromium they measure ore (ore).

b Measured in metric tons except for diamonds, which are measured in carats.

c Life expectancy figures were calculated before reserve and average annual production data were rounded.

d Figures include only those ores that contain 52 percent or more aluminum.

e Figures are for noncommunist countries only.

f Production figure is based on 1973 and 1974 data. There are vast reserves of magnesium, and life expectancies would measure in centuries.

g Concentrate is assumed to contain 46 percent manganese for the production figure and 35 percent for the reserve figure.

h Production figure is based on 1972 and 1973 data and includes the output of only noncommunist countries.

not fixed stocks. Exploration and the discovery of new deposits are constantly adding to reserves. So too is the development of new technologies that permit the profitable exploitation of previously known but uneconomic deposits. Research on the extraction of iron from taconite, for example, has over the past several decades greatly enhanced world iron ore reserves. New techniques for mining and processing manganese nodules in the ocean may similarly enlarge manganese, copper, nickel, and cobalt reserves in the future.

So, just as gasoline can be added to the depleted tanks of automobiles, new deposits can be added to mineral reserves. Figure 3–2, for example, illustrates how cumulative world production would have reduced 1948 iron and copper reserves had there been no additions to these reserves since that time. The figure also shows that actual reserves grew, and grew substantially, despite the continual drain of primary production. Iron and copper are not unusual in this respect. World reserves for all major mineral commodities grew between 1950 and 1980.

Yet, clearly, just as there is an ultimate limit on the amount of petroleum available for refining into gasoline, only a finite amount of any mineral commodity can be extracted from the earth, if for no other reason than that the earth itself is finite. This might suggest that instead of relying on reserves to calculate mineral life expectancies, one should use the resource base. The latter is defined to include all of a mineral

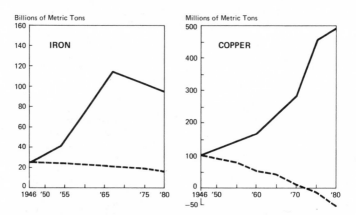

Figure 3–2. World reserves of contained iron and copper, 1946–80, and effect of cumulative production on 1946 reserves. (Redrawn from John E. Tilton, *The Future of Nonfuel Minerals,* Washington, D.C., Brookings Institution, 1977. Figures for 1975–80 are from U.S. Bureau of Mines, *Commodity Data Summaries*, 1980 and 1981, and United Nations, *Statistical Yearbook, 1978.*)

commodity found in the earth's crust, regardless of whether it is in a known deposit or profitable to recover. Thus, the resource base of any mineral commodity is indeed a fixed stock.

Mineral life expectancies based on the resource base tend to give more comforting results, but are no more appropriate than those derived from estimates of reserves.[3] Unlike gasoline, most mineral products can be recycled. Usage may dissipate the mineral or in other ways make recycling prohibitively expensive compared with primary production, but the world's stock of iron, lead, copper, and other mineral commodities is not diminished by use. Second, and more important, long before the entire earth's crust is chewed up for its content of a particular mineral commodity, the cost of producing that commodity would rise sharply and constrict demand.

For this reason, depletion should be properly viewed as a persistent rise in real mineral costs, rather than the actual running out of mineral stocks.[4] If production costs climb high enough, they can choke off mineral usage, and so may be just as disastrous as running out. However, looking at depletion this way, one can no longer conclude that it is inevitable, for while the exhaustion of high quality deposits tends over time to drive mineral costs up, new technology and other factors may offset this upward pressure on costs. Indeed, over the past century, the real costs of producing mineral commodities appear to have declined substantially.[5] This is due in large part to the application of new geophysical and geochemical techniques in exploration, the use of larger trucks and shovels in mining, better handling facilities and use of larger ships in the transportation of bulk commodities as well as advances in smelting and refining, and a multitude of other technological developments.

Whether new scientific and technological advances will continue to hold depletion at bay indefinitely is actively debated by scientists, economists, and others. Since the future course and consequences of new technology are intrinsically difficult to predict, this debate is not likely to be resolved in the near future.

---

[3]See John E. Tilton, *The Future of Nonfuel Minerals* (Washington, D.C., Brookings Institution, 1972) table 2–3.

[4]See, for instance, Anthony C. Fisher, *Resource and Environmental Economics* (Cambridge, England, Cambridge University Press, 1982).

[5]The classic study demonstrating this is Harold J. Barnett and Chandler Morse, *Scarcity and Growth: The Economics of Natural Resource Availability* (Baltimore, Md., Johns Hopkins University Press for Resources for the Future, 1965). An update of this view can be found in V. Kerry Smith, ed., *Scarcity and Growth Reconsidered* (Baltimore, Md., Johns Hopkins University for Resources for the Future, 1979).

What is clear, however, is that depletion will not occur quickly or abruptly. Even if technology should lose the upper hand, the rise in real mineral costs caused by the need to exploit ever poorer deposits will take place gradually over decades and perhaps even centuries. Thus, should depletion of foreign stocks threaten to raise the cost of mineral imports substantially, the United States would have ample time to develop domestic deposits and reduce its dependence on imports, assuming that lower cost domestic deposits were available. In fact, such a shift in the geographic location of mining would probably occur automatically in response to economic incentives. On the other hand, if lower cost deposits were not available in the United States, it would make no sense to exclude cheaper imports because depletion was forcing their price up. Such an action would simply accelerate and exacerbate the cost-increasing effects of depletion in the United States.

MINING INVESTMENT. Insufficient investment in new mines and processing facilities could also constrain foreign mineral supplies and keep them from increasing as fast as the anticipated growth in demand. Those who worry about this possibility point to the deteriorating investment climate found in many parts of the world. Rising economic nationalism, as noted earlier, has increased the political risks in a number of countries. In others, more restrictive policies governing the environment, worker health and safety, and public land use have inhibited new investment.

Again, however, this potential problem should automatically result in any desired reduction in imports since insufficient investment abroad will enhance the expected profitability of investment in the United States. Restrictions on imports to protect against interruptions would simply ensure that domestic consumers pay more for their mineral needs than their foreign competitors.

Of course, investment in the United States is not risk free. There is a great deal of uncertainty over possible changes in environmental regulations, federal land policy, worker health and safety standards, energy policy, and state severance taxes. Rising risks in the United States as well as abroad presumably increase the risk premium that investors demand. This, coupled with higher capital and energy costs in recent years, is likely to push mineral prices up, causing demand, and in turn investment, to grow more slowly than otherwise would be the case. In addition, investors as a group may underestimate the need for new capacity. While such developments may lead to perceived or actual shortages in the years ahead, restricting mineral imports would aggravate, not alleviate, such shortages.

THREATS TO IMPORTS

Three threats to imports are of particular concern—competition for limited foreign supplies, producer cartels, and supply interruptions caused by civil disturbances, war, and political embargoes.[6]

Competition for Foreign Supplies

Imports from abroad may at times be curtailed or cut off during periods of unexpected surges in demand or of interruptions in production. At such times, foreign producers may favor their own consumers. The issue here is not the cutoff of imports by war, embargoes, or other interruptions in production or trade but that U.S. consumers will find it difficult to compete for limited supplies during the times of shortages as a result of preferential treatment foreign producers may give their fellow countrymen.

While the possibility of such discrimination cannot be ruled out, U.S. customers presumably take it into account in making their decision to rely on imports. Restrictions on imports would simply limit their ability to make a rational tradeoff between the increased risk and lower mineral costs. Moreover, foreign producers are wary of openly discriminating against their foreign customers, for they are well aware that it encourages them to look elsewhere for supplies.

For this and other reasons, such discrimination is not widely practiced. Attempts to show that foreign producers of steel and copper reduce sales to the United States when mineral markets are strong and increase sales when they are weak have been unsuccessful.[7]

Overall, the argument that the United States should eschew mineral imports because it will face growing competition for them is not very convincing. Over the past thirty years, the United States has had to compete increasingly with other countries in international mineral markets. The mineral needs of Germany and Japan, in particular, have grown very rapidly. Yet the mineral resources and investment needed to accommodate their soaring needs, as well as the needs of others, were there in sufficient quantities.

---

[6]The material presented here is drawn from Tilton, *Future of Nonfuel Minerals*.

[7]See, for example, Richard M. Duke, Richard L. Johnson, Hans Mueller, P. David Qualls, Calvin T. Roush, Jr., and David G. Tarr, *The United States Steel Industry and Its International Rivals: Trends and Factors Determining International Competitiveness* (Staff Report of the Bureau of Economics to the Federal Trade Commission, U.S. Government Printing Office, November 1977), and Douglas B. Lauver, "Market Instability and U.S. Mineral Trade," *Materials and Society* vol. 5, no. 3 (1981) pp. 331–340.

Producer Cartels

In early 1974 the Organization of Petroleum Exporting Countries (OPEC) raised the price of oil by some 300 percent. This action shocked the industrialized countries and created widespread fear that similar efforts would soon follow with nonfuel minerals, particularly bauxite and copper, since the major exporters were predominantly developing countries and conditions appeared to favor the formation of cartels. One government official reflected the mood at the time when he wrote that the cartel formed by oil exporting nations is only the first in the new age of "commodity power."

Shortly thereafter, bauxite and copper producers did take some portentous steps. Jamaica increased bauxite taxes more than eightfold, in the process doubling the price of its bauxite exports. This unilateral action received considerable support from most other members of the International Bauxite Association, many of whom followed Jamaica's lead and raised their own bauxite taxes. In addition, members of the International Council of Copper Exporting Countries (CIPEC), responding to the sharp drop in prices during the latter half of 1974 and early 1975, announced an agreement to restrict their exports by 15 percent.

In retrospect, these actions appear far less threatening than they seemed at the time. The CIPEC effort was clearly a failure. Realizing their inability to control the volatile price of copper, the producing countries abandoned their efforts to stabilize and raise prices through a producers' cartel, and pushed instead for the formation of a copper commodity agreement under the auspices of the Integrated Program for Commodities of the United Nations Conference on Trade and Development (UNCTAD). A commodity agreement, unlike a cartel, involves the participation of consuming as well as producing states, and concentrates on stabilizing rather than raising prices.

In the wake of its sharply higher taxes, Jamaica experienced a dearth of new investment in bauxite mining. In fact, the country's output of bauxite plummeted by over 30 percent between 1974 and 1976. This was due in large part to a worldwide recession in the aluminum industry. Still, Australia, Guinea, and Brazil—countries that increased bauxite taxes modestly or not at all—continued to enjoy new investment and expanding production over this period. The message was not lost on Jamaica or the other Caribbean producers who closely imitated its tax initiative. In recent years, they have been more conciliatory toward the major aluminum firms and willing to grant some tax concessions.

These developments raise the question of why nonfuel mineral producers have not been able to imitate the OPEC cartel. Have they simply been stymied by the weak commodity markets that have generally prevailed since the middle of 1974? If so, will efforts to form cartels, so widely anticipated in the early and mid-1970s, recur and be more successful once the world economy improves? Or, are there more fundamental factors constraining the formation of mineral cartels?

To answer these questions, one must examine the conditions necessary for a successful cartel and assess the extent to which they pertain to the mineral industries. Although rather lengthy lists have been compiled, these conditions can be consolidated into the following:[8] (1) Production, exports, and reserves for the commodity must be concentrated in a small number of countries. Otherwise, the difficulty of negotiating an agreement acceptable to all parties becomes overwhelming. (2) Demand for the commodity must be relatively unresponsive to price or in economic terms, inelastic, so that an increase in price does not precipitate a sharp drop in sales. (3) The supply of the commodity from sources outside the control of the cartel also must be unresponsive to price or inelastic. Otherwise, efforts to raise price simply stimulate the flow of new supplies, which the cartel cannot control, onto the market. (4) The bonds among cartel members and their mutual interest in maintaining their association must be strong enough to withstand the temptation to cheat or to withdraw from the cartel.

The first of these conditions is satisfied for most mineral commodities. For example, ten countries account for over 75 percent of the production, exports, and reserves of bauxite and copper. The level of concentration is even higher for cobalt, chromium, manganese, platinum, vanadium, and many other mineral products.

The second condition holds for most mineral commodities in the short run, a period of up to three years, but not in the long run. Mineral demand is fairly insensitive to changes in price in the short run for two reasons. First, minerals are intermediate products used to make final goods, and not final goods themselves. In most instances, the price of a mineral commodity constitutes only a small portion of the total cost of the final good in which it is used. So an increase in its price is not likely to affect greatly the price, or the demand, for these final goods. Second, while a rise in a mineral's price will encourage the producers of final goods to consider the use of alternative materials, such substitutions rarely can be made quickly. Several years are often required to design a new production process, order new equipment, and retrain personnel. If new technology must be developed, the delay will be even longer. With ample time, such changes can be made, and it is for this

[8]Tilton, *Future of Nonfuel Minerals*.

reason that over the long run, the demand for most minerals *is* responsive to changes in price.

In appraising the third condition for a successful cartel, it is also necessary to differentiate between the short and long run. In the short run, an increase in price will stimulate a surge in supply from outside the cartel if considerable idle capacity exists in nonmember countries. It is primarily for this reason that cartels are difficult to maintain when the demand for minerals is depressed. Large public and private stockpiles may also increase the elasticity of supply from outside the cartel if they are released during periods of high prices. In the absence of such stocks, however, when the production of a mineral commodity approaches full capacity, the elasticity of supply in the short run becomes quite insensitive to price. No matter how high the price climbs, existing capacity inhibits any significant increase in output. Over the long run, of course, new capacity can be built outside the cartel. If the cartel controls all or nearly all of the world's reserves, this may require the development of marginal or submarginal deposits, and hence entail somewhat higher costs. Still, it can be done. Thus, the third condition may be satisfied in the short run, but not the long run.

As for the final condition, the internal cohesion of cartels seems to come unraveled with time. The study of past cartels reveals that after several years disputes tend to erupt among members over their relative market shares and other matters. This is not surprising, since it takes about that long for new sources of supply outside the cartel and the substitution of alternative materials to take their toll and force the cartel to contract its overall level of production. As a result, most cartels have lasted for only a few years and then collapsed. There are, of course, exceptions, such as the long-standing DeBeers diamond cartel. Also, despite some recent cracks in its structure, OPEC has managed to control the world price of oil for nearly a decade. These, however, are the exceptions.

In sum, the necessary conditions for a successful cartel may exist for a number of mineral commodities in the short but not the long run. This has led some to conclude that cartels pose little or no threat, for what rational producer would trade higher prices and profits for a few years for a long-term or even permanent loss of export markets? Others, however, are less sanguine, pointing out that public officials are often under great pressure to provide quick relief for existing problems, and so at times overlook or minimize the longer run consequences. Jamaica, after all, did sharply raise its bauxite taxes in 1974, despite the adverse consequences for future investment and output. It is difficult to determine whether this was done because the consequences were poorly perceived or because a rising imported oil bill and other internal ills required immediate attention. In any case, the possibility of future cartel efforts, though perhaps not great, should not be ruled out completely. If such attempts occur, they could have a significant impact on the prices of imported mineral commodities for a time, but they are likely to founder within a few years.

Civil Disturbances, War, and Embargoes

Twice during this century the United States has become embroiled in world wars, and both times strategic and critical minerals imported from the Far East, Africa, and elsewhere were restricted or cut off entirely. In some instances, the exporting countries were overrun by the enemy. In others, ocean supply lines were severed, or transport vessels were simply not available in adequate numbers.

The 1978 invasion of the Shaba Province in Zaire, and the resulting consequences for world supplies of cobalt, clearly illustrate the impact that such disturbances can have on mineral imports. The civil war in Angola during the 1970s, which interrupted copper shipments from Zambia and Zaire over the Benguela railroad to the west coast of Africa, provides another example.

Embargoes have been imposed from time to time by exporting states. They have also been imposed by importing countries. The United States, for example, has for many years prohibited nickel and other imports from Cuba, in an effort to persuade that country to modify its domestic and foreign policies. The United Nations embargoed chromium exports from Rhodesia (now Zimbabwe) to pressure the then rebellious British colony to accept greater black participation in its government.

These few illustrations indicate that in the past, mineral imports have at times been disrupted by war, civil disturbances, and embargoes. As for the future, there is unfortunately little to suggest that imports will be any more immune to such dangers.

In recent months, the suggestion of a "resource war" with the Soviet Union has attracted much attention. There has been some concern among certain groups that Soviet meddling in Africa, with the assistance of Cuban troops, is part of a long-term comprehensive plan to deny the West access to the mineral-rich resources of southern Africa. In the eyes of some, this strategy simply complements a Soviet thrust on Middle East oil, of which the invasion of Afghanistan was but an initial step.[9]

[9]The publications expounding this view are National Strategy Information Center, *The "Resource War" and the U.S. Business Community: The Case for a Council on Economics and National Security* (Washington, D.C., 1980) and World Affairs Council of Pittsburgh, *The Resource War in 3–D: Dependency, Diplomacy, Defense* (Pittsburgh, 1980).

Various motives for such a Soviet policy are offered. Some argue that the USSR is being forced by its own domestic resource needs to reach beyond its borders. Its past policy of self-sufficiency is collapsing, not so much because its internal resources are depleted, but more because it lacks the capability to develop them adequately.[10] Others maintain that the desire to deny vital minerals to the West is behind the Soviet drive, rather than internal needs which can still be satisfied from its own resources. Still others cite the lucrative opportunities for the Soviet Union and South Africa to create cartels in the manganese, platinum, chromium, and vanadium industries, should a new government more favorably disposed toward the Soviet Union come to power in Pretoria.

Opinions also vary over how the Soviet Union might pursue a resource war. Obviously, the country does not have the foreign exchange to outbid the West for available mineral supplies. Nor would such a policy make sense, unless the country actually needed these supplies for internal purposes. Even in this case, the result would simply be higher mineral prices, and—with time—an expansion of output in Africa and elsewhere. Moreover, mineral exports are hard-currency income for the USSR, whose manufactured goods do not enjoy a receptive world market.

The Soviet Union does have a large standing army, and has been building up its navy. This has led some to conclude it may plan sometime to move troops into the important mineral-producing countries.[11] So far, however, the Soviet Union has been very careful about committing its forces in large numbers overseas. Moreover, if a decision were made to directly challenge the West, an invasion of southern Africa would not appear to be a logical choice. The Near East is much closer and would involve far fewer logistical problems. In addition, the loss of oil from the Near East would more quickly and gravely threaten the economic and military strength of the West than the cutoff of minerals from southern Africa.

For these reasons, it seems more likely that the Soviet Union will continue striving to expand its power in Africa by exploiting tribal conflicts and by supporting indigenous opposition to white minority rule, particularly in South Africa and Namibia. Such a strategy entails much lower costs and risks. It also can exploit the antiimperialistic and anticolonial sentiments that are still strongly felt in many parts of southern Africa.[12]

[10]See the paper by Fine in *The Resource War in 3–D.*

[11]See *The "Resource War" and the U.S. Business Community.*

[12]For more on this possibility, see Steven J. Warnecke, "International Security Implications of Soviet Energy and Raw Materials Policies," *Probleme der Rohstoffsicherung* No. 92–93 (June 1981) pp. 127–148 (Bonn, Friedrich Ebert Stiftung).

It is difficult to predict just how successful the Soviet Union will be. When Marxist governments have come to power in the past, often with the help of the Soviet Union, as in Mozambique, Angola, Guinea, and Zimbabwe, they have not been willing to cut their economic ties with the West. To the contrary, they have generally tried to maintain and even increase their mineral exports, as a vital source of foreign exchange. Soviet pressure on these states to embargo trade with the West might well backfire, for they normally place their own national interests above those of the Soviet Union or world Communism.

Still, the vulnerability of mineral imports from southern Africa should not be underestimated. That area is passing through a turbulent and difficult transition period, as colonial status and white minority rule crumble in one state after another. The last significant holdout is South Africa, by far the greatest African supplier of mineral products to the West.

The front-line states of Mozambique, Angola, and Zimbabwe have all changed governments in recent years, and now are pushing for political change in South Africa. Namibia is likely to follow in the near future. It is uncertain how long the white-dominated government of South Africa can resist the pressure for change. Nor can it be known whether the shift toward greater black participation in government will occur peacefully or with considerable civil disruption.

What does seem certain, however, is that change will come. When it does, the possibility of an interruption in mineral production and exports cannot be ruled out. A period of instability could follow any shift toward greater black participation in politics, as a result of tribal conflicts and other rivalries. This has occurred, and continues to occur, in other African states.

Of the several threats to the mineral imports examined in this section, it is the threat posed by civil disruption, war, and political embargoes that in our judgment poses the greatest danger to the security of mineral imports, although we would not rule out the possibility of future attempts to form cartels, particularly at times of strong mineral demand. Moreover, of those commodities that the United States imports heavily, only a handful from southern Africa—chromium, manganese, cobalt, vanadium, and platinum—appear to be the most vulnerable.

IMPORT DEPENDENCE VERSUS VULNERABILITY

It is a common practice to equate import dependence with supply vulnerability: the greater the proportion of domestic consumption supplied by imports, the higher the risk of interruptions in these supplies and the more severe the resulting consequences. However, the level of import dependence is just one of a number of factors affecting the vulnerability of U.S. mineral supplies. Among the others are the following:[13]

1. The particular countries providing imports. Civil disruptions, political disturbances, and external invasions are much less likely to interrupt the flow of nickel from Canada than cobalt from Zaire. Canada, Australia, and European countries with close political and economic ties to the U.S. are not likely to engage in arbitrary actions to constrict supplies. On the other hand, the likelihood of a strike interrupting supplies is probably greater for nickel from Canada than for tin from Malaysia.

2. The diversity of foreign suppliers. The fewer the number of exporting countries and the more production is concentrated in one or a few regions, the greater the vulnerability of mineral imports. In recent years, for example, over half of the world's output of cobalt has come from Zaire, primarily the southern Shaba Province. As noted earlier, when rebels based in Angola invaded the Shaba Province in 1978, the impact on the world cobalt market was traumatic. The resulting shortages and sharply higher prices, however, have stimulated an increase in cobalt production elsewhere as well as cobalt substitution. This has increased the diversity of cobalt supplies, and thus has reduced the consequences of any future interruption in supplies from Zaire.

Alternative sources of supply, whether in the form of diverse suppliers or reserve capacity, can reduce vulnerability. For example, the iron and steel industries in the United States and Europe have for a number of years been operating below their potential. In an emergency, spare capacity could be activated to help make up for lost supplies.

Potential sources of supply are even more likely to exist. As pointed out earlier, although high quality deposits may be few in number and concentrated geographically, deposits that are economically marginal or submarginal are far more common and dispersed more widely. If supplies from the former are threatened, less attractive deposits can be developed. One of the more interesting illustrations of this possibility occurred in the late 1940s as the Cold War between the Soviet Union and the West heated up. In retaliation for U.S. restrictions on trade in high technology goods, the Soviet Union embargoed exports of its man-

---

[13]For a discussion of these factors and their effects on seven major metals—cobalt, chromium, manganese, aluminum, copper, lead, and zinc—see Leonard L. Fischman, project director, *World Mineral Trends and U.S. Supply Problems* (Washington, D.C., Resources for the Future, 1980). This study was part of a review of nonfuel minerals policy undertaken by the Carter administration.

ganese and chromium. The West at that time depended on these exports and dire repercussions were predicted. However, an expansion of manganese supplies from the Gold Coast (now Ghana), India, and South Africa and of chromium supplies from Turkey soon compensated for the lost Soviet supplies. The net result of the Soviet attempt to pressure the United States and its allies was simply the partial loss of two of its mineral export markets.

Nontraditional types of deposits may further expand the opportunities for developing alternative sources of supply. During World War II, for example, the United States, concerned about the vulnerability of its bauxite supplies from South America, developed new alumina refining techniques that could process the high silica bauxite found in Arkansas. This helped the country reduce its dependence on foreign bauxite from 54 to 20 percent of consumption between 1941 and 1943.

More recently, concern that the major bauxite-exporting countries might form a cartel has directed research efforts toward the production of alumina and aluminum from kaolin, anorthosite, and other non-bauxite ores that are found in large quantities in the United States. Manganese nodules are another new source of mineral supplies whose development would be accelerated if traditional imports were threatened. These potato-sized substances cover many parts of the ocean floor and contain large quantities of manganese, copper, nickel, and cobalt.

There is an important difference between actual and potential alternative sources of supply. Actual sources in the form of idle or under-utilized facilities are available immediately, or almost immediately, to fill the gap when imports are disrupted. This is not the case for potential sources. The expansion of existing facilities may require several years because new equipment must be ordered and installed. In addition, it may be necessary to hire and train new personnel. The development of entirely new facilities may require the construction of towns, ports, railroads, and other infrastructure, and take five years or longer to complete. The delay is likely to be even longer if nontraditional sources of supply, such as manganese nodules, are involved, for they require the development and testing of new mining and processing technologies as well as a favorable international framework. Thus, potential sources of supply can offer no immediate assistance in the event of an interruption in imports, unless the interruption is anticipated and the new sources of supply are developed prior to its occurrence.

3. Opportunities for material substitution. The demand for minerals is derived from the properties, such as strength, ductility, and corrosion resistance, that they impart to final products. Often different combinations of minerals can provide the same set of properties, or close

approximations. Thus, substitution can reduce the amount of a mineral used in a process or even eliminate it entirely. Silver, for example, is an excellent conductor of electricity, and can be used in place of copper wires. This is not normally done because copper is much cheaper. However, during World War II, government stocks of silver were used to help alleviate the copper shortage.

The opportunities for substitution are often not fully appreciated since substitution may occur at several stages of production. The use of tin in beverage cans, for instance, can be reduced by increasing the amount of enamel in the tinplate, by substituting aluminum sheet for tinplate, by replacing metal cans with glass or plastic bottles, and finally by switching to powdered milk, juices, and other beverages that are not usually sold in metal containers.

As will be seen in a later section, however, there are some limitations to substitution. In some end uses, the opportunities for substitution are minimal or nonexistent, at least with known technologies. Second, substitutes are of little value if they also are subject to supply interruptions when they are needed. To be useful, the supply of the substitute should be readily expandable. Third, it often takes time to substitute one material for another and existing facilities and technologies limit the possibilities for substitution in the short run.

4. The nature of material uses. The economic and strategic importance of goods that incorporate mineral products ranges from trivial to critical. In considering the consequences of a disruption in mineral imports, there is a natural penchant to focus on the most essential uses. During a crisis, however, presumably these would be the last sacrificed, either because producers could pay higher prices for whatever supplies were available or because the government would intervene, as is normal practice during wartime, to allocate supplies to the highest priorities. So the more a mineral product is used in less essential applications, the less serious the consequences of a supply interruption are likely to be.

5. Opportunities for recycling. Many mineral products are found in obsolete scrap (i.e., scrap from consumer and producer goods that have reached the end of their useful lives) and nonessential products that could be recycled should a cutoff in foreign supplies occur. Platinum, which the United States imports largely from South Africa, provides an interesting illustration. Since 1975, domestic motor vehicle manufacturers have been installing catalytic converters on automobiles to meet environmental regulations. Although the platinum contained in each converter is small—far less than a single troy ounce—altogether converters account for about a third of U.S. platinum consumption and constitute the country's largest single use of platinum. Since platinum

is not destroyed in this use, the domestic stock of this valuable metal traveling around in the nation's automobiles has grown rapidly since 1975. In an emergency, at a cost of somewhat greater air pollution, part or all of this traveling stock could be cannibalized and recycled for more critical uses.

The protection afforded by recycling may be limited by two time constraints. On the one hand, it may not be immediately available, if new recycling facilities must be built or present facilities expanded to handle the increased load. On the other hand, the stock of a mineral product contained in scrap and still in useful, though nonessential, products is finite and cannot replace imports indefinitely.

6. Level of private and public stocks. The U.S. government holds substantial quantities of chromium, manganese, cobalt, and other mineral commodities in its strategic stockpile. (This is discussed further in the section on policy options.) Domestic fabricators also maintain private stocks. In the event of an unexpected cutoff of imports, these stocks are immediately available to the country and so can prevent the disruption that otherwise would occur in the short run. Moreover, the existence of large stocks may reduce the likelihood of a supply interruption in the first place. An embargo imposed for political reasons, such as that discussed earlier for manganese and chromium, is not likely to put much immediate pressure on an importing country with ample stocks. Similarly, stockpiles may discourage producer cartels if producing countries fear these stocks would be released if output was artificially restricted in order to raise prices.

Because so many factors affect it, vulnerability of mineral supplies is not highly correlated in some simple fashion with the level of imports, but must be assessed on a case-by-case basis. Import dependence may be high and vulnerability low if alternative sources of supply are available, opportunities for material substitution exist, supplying countries are diversified and stable, consumption is largely concentrated on nonessential uses, and large public and private stocks exist. Conversely, vulnerability may be high even if imports supply little or none of the domestic market. For example, the United States, along with the rest of the world, experienced shortages of molybdenum from 1974 through 1979, even though the United States is the world's largest producer and exporter of this strategic mineral. This situation arose because a major addition to primary capacity, the Henderson Mine in Colorado, came onstream late from the point of view of the growth in demand and because a recession in the world copper industry reduced by-product molybdenum production. Thus, mineral self-sufficiency does not provide immunity against supply disruptions.

MINERAL POLICY

Concern over mineral resources has fluctuated for more than thirty years and most often this concern has been triggered by events that have had little or nothing to do with the security of supply. When industrial consumers find it difficult to meet their needs at prices they consider reasonable, they raise the cry of "shortage." The "shortage" disappears when prices go down.

Unusually heavy short-term demands, such as those of World War II, can lead to concern about dwindling supplies. The Paley Commission was formed in 1952 in response to just such a concern. As mentioned earlier, simultaneous economic booms can also increase the demand for nonfuel minerals. This sort of boom in the early 1970s led to another commission to study mineral supplies and government policy.

In all, three such commissions were appointed between 1951 and 1974 and in each case by the time their report was released the market had settled down and the commission had difficulty finding a receptive audience. It is not surprising then, that there appears to be no formal government policy, beyond broad generalities, that addresses nonfuel minerals.

Nevertheless, in recent years concern has focused on import dependence, and mineral legislation has been heavily preoccupied with encouraging a viable and strong domestic mining and mineral processing industry. In the Mining and Minerals Policy Act of 1970, Congress declares that, "It is the continuing policy of the federal government in the national interest to foster and encourage private enterprise in (1) the development of economically sound and stable domestic mining, minerals, metals and minerals reclamation industries, (2) the orderly and economic development of domestic mineral resources, reserves and reclamation of metals and minerals to help assure satisfaction of industrial, security and environmental needs, (3) mining, mineral and metallurgical research . . . and (4) the study and development of methods for disposal, control and reclamation of mineral waste products . . ."

The act does not specify the meaning of "economically sound and stable," or of "orderly and economic development," nor does it as much as hint at the terms on which the Congress would like to see the reconciliation of "industrial, security, and environmental needs" occur. Giving the secretary of the interior the authority to "implement" the act thus gave him more a motto to hang over his desk than a roadmap. It is not surprising, though perhaps unfair, that with the revival of concern over the U.S. minerals position, the Department of Interior has come in for a major share of the blame for what is seen by some as a lack of progress.

In frustration over the Interior Department's alleged neglect of the mining industry, and an interdepartmental mineral policy task force review established under the Carter administration in late 1977 that fizzled out, the mining interests in Congress introduced a new act and had the satisfaction of seeing it passed. The Minerals Policy, Research and Development Act of 1980 went considerably beyond its 1970 predecessor. Apart from the conventional recital of the fundamental importance of minerals to economic well-being and national security, the links to environment and energy, the interdependence of nations, and the importance of R&D, the act deplores the absence of a national materials and minerals policy and proceeds to lay down a large number of activities to be set up and "coordinated" by the Executive Office of the President.

Many specific tasks are spelled out: identifying materials needs; establishing a long-range assessment capability for materials demands, supplies, and needs; promoting an R&D program, both at home and in cooperation with other countries. Directions are given on implementing the stated policy. These include support for research to advance the science and technology of exploration, discovery, and recovery of nonfuel minerals; enhanced methods or processes for more efficient production and use of resources; improved and more conserving use of materials and better understanding of engineering designs; dissemination of information; establishment of an "early warning system" for supply problems; and assessment of any federal policies that affect the materials cycle. Finally, the act requires a sizable number of both one-time and periodic reports, including an assessment of materials needs for the next five years which would be revised annually, an assessment of critical material needs and steps necessary to meet them, and so forth.

It is obvious that the 1980 act goes far beyond that of 1970 in stating what kind of information is needed to evolve a minerals policy and where the responsibility might be placed for establishing the data-gathering and analytical capacity. On the other hand, the 1980 act does not advance beyond its predecessor in specifying the content of policy. It does not, for example, state the terms on which exploration and mining may occur on federal lands. It is silent on the extent to which national security considerations may justify exploration subsidies. It fails to recommend policies to foster investment in either domestic or foreign mining ventures. In short, it reasserts the importance of a "stable and sound" mining sector in the U.S. economy; requires that attention be paid to

long-term compatibility with environmental considerations, social issues, resource conservation, national security, and so on; assigns various
tasks to agencies and specifies a variety of reports to be made to the
Congress within one to five years. Even though it says all this in more
detail than the 1970 act, one finishes reading no less hungry than when
one began.

In late April 1981, Representative James Santini, the Nevada con-
gressman who has for some years been leading the fight for a more
explicit and aggressive U.S. minerals policy, introduced his "National
Mineral Security Act of 1981." It differs from the legislative undertak-
ings mentioned above in that it makes a number of specific recommendations, both of substance and procedure.

Among its substantive recommendations, the bill calls for a review
of all federal land not now open to entry for mineral exploration and
asks the secretary of the interior, upon industry request, to identify
tracts suitable for mining access after a specified review procedure.
Second, it recommends a number of fiscal measures to assist the mining
industry, including rapid depreciation and tax-free antipollution expenditures.

It would set up a three-man council of "wise men" in the Executive
Office of the President to oversee and coordinate mineral activities in
the federal government, especially with regard to carrying out the activities specified in the 1980 act and in the legislation proposed by Representative Santini. The bill, if passed, would be the closest the Congress
has come as yet in setting policy, as contrasted with making general
pronouncements. It marks a substantial advance, whether or not one
agrees with specifics.

Relevant Concerns

It should be clear that the overarching question for mineral policy is:
How much and what kind of insurance should be bought to protect the
U.S. economy against the possibility of supply interruptions or steep
price increases for one or more minerals? Ideally, the answer would lie
in an estimate of the expected damage from an interruption. This, in
turn, depends on the odds on the event occurring and its consequences.
While such estimates have been attempted, they are highly uncertain;
they also are often exaggerated. For example, the indisputable fact that
most contemporary products incorporate minerals is used to support the
assertion that supply deficiencies would bring the U.S. economy to its
knees. This leads ultimately to such meaningless exercises as saying that
6 million mineral workers (which includes workers in the metals and

chemicals industry) and 6 million agricultural workers create jobs for everybody else in the U.S. economy.[14]

Such misguided but not infrequently voiced notions suffer above all from failure to think of changes "at the margin" (i.e., suppose the U.S. iron ore or copper supply were reduced by 10 percent for a year or 50 percent for a month) rather than in aggregate terms (i.e., suppose the country were suddenly without iron or copper). But even at a more sophisticated level, attempts to calculate the economic impact of specific supply problems are seldom reliable or meaningful. A major reason is that any impact is largely dependent upon magnitude and duration of the triggering event, the mineral involved, and the state of the economy at the time. The evasive and remedial actions taken will also vary from mineral to mineral. Moreover, some of the consequences, while real and adverse (e.g., poorer quality goods and/or performance), are hard to translate into monetary losses.

It is obvious, nonetheless, that certain factors must enter into any attempt to assess impact: (1) What will be the size of inventories, including national stockpiles, at the time of disruption, and what will be the terms of access to these stocks? (2) How much idle capacity will be available for use? (3) How will the distribution of the remaining supplies be modified from the normal pattern? Will there be allocation priorities or pricing schemes that will contain the damage?

Unfortunately, the way in which a supply contingency will be played out in the market cannot be closely predicted. Pieces of the puzzle can be found, but it is unlikely that enough of them will be at hand to solve it. Moreover, the pieces will need to be fashioned from intimate, updated knowledge of each of the materials involved, its uses, and its customers.

Any assertion that a specified shortfall or price boost of a given material will reduce the GNP or employment by a stated percentage should be received with profound skepticism. What does seem clear is that high import reliance—or dependence as it has now come to be called—is a compelling reason for careful, continuously updated analyses of likely user and producer reactions to various contingencies under specified economic circumstances, limited to one material or family of related materials at a time. Such analyses are likely to yield a sense of relative significance and urgency of action, rather than specific damage estimates possessing a substantial degree of confidence. But even this is preferable to the broad generalizations—usually at both ends of the spectrum—to which policymakers no less than the public are typically treated.

[14]*U.S. Minerals Vulnerability: Natural Policy Implications,* Subcommittee on Mines and Mining, Committee on Interior and Insular Affairs, U.S. House of Representatives, 96th Cong. 2nd sess. November 1980, Washington, D.C.

The U.S. situation, for instance, is sometimes compared unfavorably with that of the Soviet Union. Fearful that foreign supplies might be cut off during a political or military confrontation with the West, the Soviet Union has strenuously followed a policy of resource autarchy. When forced to rely on foreign sources, it has turned primarily to its close neighbors and allies. As a result, of those minerals shown in figure 3–1, the USSR imports only mica, bauxite and alumina, fluorine, tin, tungsten, antimony, and barium, and in no case do imports constitute more than roughly half of the country's consumption. Moreover, it is a major exporter of many mineral commodities, including manganese, chromium, platinum, asbestos, iron ore, vanadium, and gold.

The United States, like the Soviet Union, could pursue a policy of resource self-sufficiency and greatly reduce its dependence on imports. The old adage, "minerals are where you find them," is obviously true, but misleading. It suggests that mineral deposits are limited to a few geographic regions and countries. While this may be true for the high quality deposits that can be mined profitably, as we have seen, mineral concentrations run the gamut from very high to very low quality and the lower quality deposits are dispersed more broadly. The United States is sufficiently endowed with subeconomic deposits to greatly reduce and, in many cases, completely eliminate its need for imports.

A policy of self-sufficiency would, however, have high economic and political costs. The use of poor domestic deposits obviously requires public subsidies or higher domestic mineral prices. While the costs might be modest in a few cases, they would be substantial in many others, such as manganese and chromium. Higher raw material prices would raise the costs of final goods, and make it more difficult for the automobile and other domestic industries that consume minerals in large quantities to compete with foreign producers. Politically, such a policy is inconsistent with the country's efforts to reduce inflation and foster freer trade and greater economic integration within the Western world. Cutbacks in mineral imports from developing countries might force these countries to seek more direct assistance from world lending organizations or to curtail their development programs. In short, a policy of self-sufficiency would undermine the role of the United States as the leader of the Western world.

Any mineral policy that is established for the United States must take an international view. The European Community and Japan are even more dependent than the United States on mineral imports (see figure 3–3). Efforts to become self-sufficient would be much more expensive and much less likely to succeed in Europe and Japan. Yet, self-suffi-

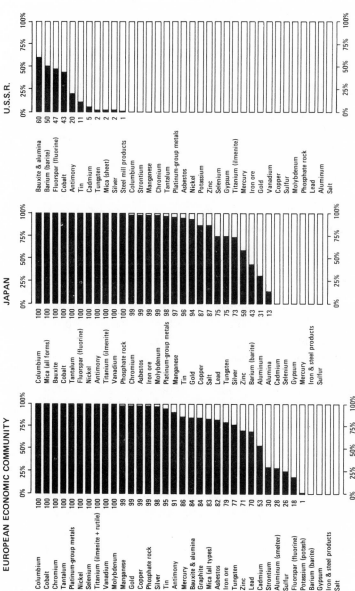

Figure 3-3. Net import reliance of selected minerals and metals as a percent of consumption, 1980. Notes: European Economic Community in 1980 included Belgium, Denmark, France, Federal Republic of Germany, Ireland, Italy, Luxembourg, the Netherlands, and the United Kingdom. The trade in columbium, tantalum, and vanadium is reported together for the EEC. Data for potassium, strontium, and graphite not available for Japan. (Courtesy of U.S. Bureau of Mines.)

ciency is of limited value to the United States if its allies remain highly dependent on imports.

It became painfully clear in the years after 1973 that even if this country could "solve" its energy problem, it would be of little avail if most friendly nations were unable to do so. No matter how well we managed our own affairs we would not remain unaffected. So it is with minerals. Markets are international, and supply and demand pulls and pushes are exerted from all directions. Even if this were not the case, for political reasons the United States would have to be concerned about serious economic problems induced by mineral shortages in Western Europe and Japan.

Moreover, confrontation between the "haves" and "have-nots," which is a significant aspect of the minerals issue, always lurks in the background; once it becomes an active factor, lack of a jointly agreed-upon approach can be very harmful. The same is true in relation to Soviet policy, if and when this would become an important element in U.S. mineral supply and demand, as some—we think mistakenly—believe it already is.

It is also important to devise mineral policies that impose a minimum of constraints upon the foreign and defense policies of the United States and its allies. The tie-in between oil imports and foreign policy, for example, circumscribes both energy and foreign policy. A parallel case in the materials field is that of southern Africa.

Because the Republic of South Africa and some of its northern neighbors are major exporters of a few important materials (manganese, chromium, cobalt, and the platinum group), U.S. policy toward these countries is heavily encumbered with mineral supply considerations. If the United States is "nice" to South Africa, it is bound to offend the black-ruled states to the north, endangering cobalt and chromium supplies, and if the United States offends South Africa, it may jeopardize manganese and platinum imports. At least so the conventional theory goes. There is, though, an opposing view; namely, that whichever way the political tide runs, materials exports will continue to flow, given the need of these countries to earn the funds to pay for both imports and their domestic expenditures. Neither side in this argument would question the desirability of divorcing, as far as is possible, materials issues and policies from foreign policy and defense considerations.

Policy Options

No single remedy will forestall or "cure" all material supply problems. The best insurance is a mix of policies that provides the most effective protection at the lowest cost. In evaluating alternative policies, it is important to distinguish between those that are designed to reduce the vulnerability associated with import dependence and those designed to reduce import dependence itself. The former tend to fall into the category of quick responses to unanticipated and general short-term problems caused by civil disturbances, embargoes, and other events; they include stockpiling and government intervention in the market.

Reducing our dependence on imports, on the other hand, requires long-term planning and decisions that often are based as much on political considerations as on economic ones. These include the mining of lands now protected by law, changes in environmental regulations, increased funding for research on materials substitution, and a protectionist trade and tax policy. With the exception of materials research, these are issues that affect a broad public and arouse strong emotions. They also have costs attached to them that in some cases are high. It is not surprising, therefore, that they are the most difficult decisions to make and the ones most likely to involve value judgments.

REDUCING VULNERABILITY TO SUPPLY INTERRUPTIONS. Among the measures in this category, a well-designed, up-to-date stockpile is likely to deserve particular consideration. Its major advantages are:

- The principal cost is the interest or the opportunity cost of the capital required to purchase the necessary stocks, as the cost of the material itself should be recoverable upon release. Indeed, since releases will be made only in extremely tight market conditions, the selling price is likely to be substantially above the acquisition price, helping to defray the interest and storage costs associated with stockpiling.
- Release of stockpiled materials can quickly make up for a reduction in imports and provide the breathing space needed to monitor and evaluate the situation before more extensive and usually much more costly long-term measures are adopted. Panic-triggered runs on available supplies, accompanied by steep price increases, are disruptive events that usually take time to bring under control. Well-timed stockpile releases may suppress them at the start.

The most potent arguments against stockpiles are:

- Unless continuously reviewed and changed in composition, they age quickly, so that when needed they fail to fit altered demand conditions.
- Releases made to adjust the composition of the stockpile to changing needs incidentally affect market prices and may depress do-

mestic production. The recent decision of the Reagan administration to reduce the silver stockpile in order to raise cash for acquisition of such materials as cobalt is a case in point. It aroused bitter opposition from circles interested in a lively silver market and was temporarily brought to a halt.

- Government may make acquisitions and releases for reasons other than emergencies. For example, as part of its battle against inflation, the Johnson administration released or threatened to release stockpiled materials to discourage domestic producers from raising their prices. The government has also on occasions sold from the stockpile in part to help balance the budget. Industrial producers can be expected to oppose such operations as undesirable government interference.

Weighing both the advantages and disadvantages of stockpiling, it is difficult to escape the conclusion that it is a relatively inexpensive, expeditious way of reducing the vulnerability associated with import dependence. Moreover, some of the cited drawbacks are partly amenable to correction. For example, under proposed legislation, revenues from stockpile sales would be available, without new appropriations, for other stockpile purchases.[15] In effect, the stockpile manager would be insulated to a greater degree from political pressures, or from industrial pressures filtering through the political process. Similarly, continuous review and adjustment to changing needs and technologies should not be outside the country's administrative inventiveness and capacity. On the other hand, the effects of nonemergency releases and acquisitions on markets are an unavoidable by-product of the scheme; they can be minimized by carefully timed and phased operation but not eliminated. In this connection, updating would have to include not only quantities but also quality and form. For instance, stockpiling chromium makes little sense if the capacity for processing chromium into ferrochromium is deficient.

Early in its existence the Reagan administration took action that suggests a revived interest in the stockpile. It ordered the disposal over the next three years of large amounts of silver (worth nearly $1 billion), diamonds, mercury, antimony, mica, and iodine, among others. Authority already exists for disposal of tin. Exact disposal schedules and amounts are laid down in the Omnibus Budget Reconciliation Act of 1981 (PL 97–35, August 1981). This act also authorizes $535 million for the purchase of materials and calls for annual and five-year materials

---

[15]The proposed National Materials Security Act of 1981.

TABLE 3–2. Purchase Priorities for
the U.S. Stockpile

Agricultural-based chemical intermediaries
Aluminum oxide
Bauxite, refractory grade
Cobalt
Columbium
Fluorspar
Medicinals (including opium salts)
Nickel
Platinum group metals
Rubber (including guayule)
Tantalum
Titanium (including rutile)
Vanadium

Source: Stockpile Report to the Congress October 1980–March 1981, Federal Emergency Management Agency, Washington, D.C.

plans to be transmitted to the Congress, as part of the annual budget preparation.

By late 1981, 5.2 million pounds of cobalt, worth $78 million, had been contracted for, and the administration has announced the intention to buy 1.6 million tons of Jamaican-type bauxite (of which 0.4 million tons are to be obtained through barter against U.S. farm products). These acquisitions would raise the cobalt holdings to 54 percent of the stockpile goal and bauxite to 50 percent. No other plans had been announced as of the end of 1981, but a priority list for future acquisitions has been released (table 3–2).

In this context, what is the current status of the stockpile and how does it operate? Its authority rests on the Strategic and Critical Materials Stock Piling Act of 1979. This act, among other changes in the legislation, which goes all the way back to 1939, established a three-year conventional war as the basis for setting stockpile goals. As noted earlier, it also set up a National Defense Stockpile Transaction Fund to receive proceeds from sales, which are then available for purchases, subject to congressional appropriation procedures. Management is in the hands of two agencies: the Federal Emergency Management Agency, which is in charge of policy and planning, and the General Services Administration, which does the buying, selling, and maintenance of the stockpile commodities.

The stockpile goals were most recently revised in May 1980. The actual holdings differ from goals in both directions: many items (to be precise, 37 groups and materials) are short of the goals, others meet goals or

TABLE 3–3. Major Stockpile Commodities or Groups in Stockpile[a]
(in order of value as of March 31, 1981)

Minerals	Value (million dollars)	Percent of goal
Tin	2,901	476
Silver	1,848	[b]
Chromium, chemical & metallurgical group	1,048	87
Tungsten group	862	59
Cobalt	816	48
Aluminum metal group	551	52
Manganese, chemical & metallurgical group	531	106
Industrial diamond group	479	143
Titanium sponge	440	17
Lead	433	55
Tantalum group	344	33
Zinc	321	26
Platinum	215	35
Beryllium metal group	177	87
Palladium	176	42
Rubber	172	14
Antimony	163	113
Fluorspar, acid grade	125	64
Aluminum oxide group	124	59

Source: Stockpile Report to the Congress October 1980–March 1981, Federal Emergency Management Agency, Washington, D.C.

[a] With a value of $100 million or more. Together these commodities account for 87 percent of the total stockpile value.

[b] The 1980 goal is zero.

are held in excess. In summary, the value of 61 family groups and individual materials in the stockpile, at March 1981 prices, was $12.6 billion. Of this amount, $5 billion represented excess over goals (mostly silver, tin, tungsten, and diamonds). Acquisitions to meet the 1980 goals would require some $12.5 billion, or, offset by disposals, $7.5 billion net. Table 3–3 shows the major items now held in the stockpile.

One final comment. As it stands, the national stockpile is designed exclusively to meet national emergencies and its content is geared to a three-year war. The new realities of vulnerability of supplies from sources other than war call for a fresh approach that would consider stockpiling to meet these types of contingencies. In this context, one would also want to give close consideration to the pros and cons of stockpiling by business rather than government—an option that might be useful even for the traditional stockpile, at least as a supplementary measure.

A second measure for reducing the vulnerability associated with import dependence entails government planning for market intervention in the event of an interruption of supplies. One of the fallacies in popular

presentations of such eventualities is the generally implicit assumption
that all customers will lose access to all supplies. This is not, of course,
the case. Existing supply lines will take time to be emptied, as will
inventories. Some limited, but quick, substitutions will be possible and
for that and other reasons the intensity of demand will vary among
users. Rising prices will move supplies to those users that can best afford
them at the higher cost. Government's admittedly difficult role will be
to safeguard the interests of those users who are priced out of the market
but whose function is considered to be in the national interest.

Government policies can also reduce vulnerability by encouraging
imports from relatively secure sources, secure because they are nearby,
located in politically stable areas, or for other reasons. The government
can similarly foster greater diversity in the origin of imports and thereby
limit the adverse effects of an interruption of supplies from any particular
source. Such policies take some time to implement and are likely to
involve some costs, for they force domestic consumers to use higher cost
imports. Such measures, however, can be kept in reserve and pursued
only when the need for them clearly arises. Stocks and government
intervention can provide immediate relief while new sources of supply
in more secure and reliable areas are developed. The latter can then
fulfill domestic needs after the available stocks are exhausted.

Reducing Import Dependence

The vulnerability associated with mineral imports can also be reduced
by increasing supplies from domestic sources and reducing dependence
on imports. A number of measures proposed in recent years to promote
greater self-sufficiency involve the use of public lands for mining, the
substitution of domestic mineral products for imports, protectionism,
and preferential tax treatment.

MINING AND PUBLIC LANDS.   Currently the most controversial policy
issue is whether the United States should expand its domestic mineral
supply by allowing exploration and mining on lands that have been set
aside for recreation or to preserve unique ecological areas. This question
is discussed in some detail in chapter 2 and is only briefly treated here.

Basically, the issue is one of development versus preservation. Domestic mining interests, and some politicians, claim that the land withdrawn under the provisions of the Wilderness Act of 1964 is too extensive
and contains mineral-rich areas that could reduce our dependence on
imports now. Their opponents point out that the public lands constitute
only a small percentage of the land available for exploration and de-

velopment, that the bulk of these lands have amenity values that exceed any benefits to be derived from the minerals they contain, and that those few areas that are mineral-rich should be held for the use of future generations, when they may be needed.

A dispassionate summary of the situation was attempted by the Office of Technology Assessment in 1979.[16] Briefly, OTA points out that it is no longer valid to assume that mineral activity is always the most valuable use of a tract of land; that the lower grade deposits being discovered are located at greater depths and are more expensive to find and mine; that the land base for renewable resource stocks has decreased as a result of population and economic growth; that there is increased appreciation of a host of nonconsumable resource uses; and that natural ecosystems provide valuable gene pools and materials for scientific study. Finally, ecosystems can be enjoyed without being damaged and their benefits can thus remain for future generations. Taken all together, the report concludes, these factors may well outweigh the value of mineral resources in a tract, "even when the social value of a secure domestic mineral supply is added to the private value of the deposit to a mineral producer." However, the changing values that have resulted in this weighting, OTA points out, may have serious adverse consequences on the domestic mineral industry ten to twenty years hence in an increasingly tight international minerals environment.

Given this, and the strong opinions voiced by both sides, it seems unlikely that decisions in this area will benefit much from objective calculations of relative merits and demerits. They are more likely to remain political decisions, whether by Congress, an executive department, or some other agency.

While there are vast tracts of land that could be mined before it becomes necessary to turn to areas protected for ecological or recreational reasons, mining interests argue that their operations would occupy only small amounts of land compared with the millions now restricted or closed to mining. However, even a small mining operation with its ancillary transport, housing, and other facilities could strike at the core reason for barring entry, namely preservation of the natural state of a specific area. Thus, it is not a statistical matter of a few hundred acres here and there, measured against millions left untouched, but of the compatibility of the two uses of the land *in a given location and context*. In other words, what matters is not so much whether it is right or wrong that entry is restricted on 30, 50, or 60 percent of federal lands—which typically represents the focus of the argument—but whether there is

---

[16]Office of Technology Assessment, *Management of Fuel and Nonfuel Minerals on Federal Land: Current Status and Issues* (OTA, Washington, D.C., 1979).

good reason to believe that a commercially viable mining operation could be established in a selected location and whether, weighed against the value of other services derived from that location, it is in the national interest to permit exploration and subsequent extraction.

Factors to be considered in a decision to permit mining would be the existence of alternative sources of supply; the estimated size of the deposit and its relation to total demand; the nature of the mineral use; the degree to which the site is disturbed; the cost of reducing such disturbances during or after mining; the attainment of supply stability by other means. In short, a site-by-site evaluation should be made.

Allied with the question of land withdrawals is that of the environmental effects of a mining operation—whether it affects an adjacent wilderness area or the surrounding vicinity. Sometimes, but not always, the problem can be "solved" by drawing boundaries to suit the occasion.

The Blackbird cobalt mine in Idaho is a good example. It is an old mine, last operated in 1959, and has produced 7,000 tons over a decade or so for the strategic stockpile. A National Materials Advisory Board report recently estimated that the mine might be able to produce 7 million pounds per year for thirteen years, which would amount to one-third or so of recent U.S. annual cobalt consumption. The mine, however, was located in a wilderness area. The Central Idaho Wilderness Act of 1980 drew the boundaries of the River of No Return wilderness so as to exclude the mine. Moreover, it provided that if cobalt was located within the adjoining wilderness area, recovery by open-pit mining would be permitted. However, by now the price of cobalt has dropped below the level at which production would be profitable, and no decision has been reached by the company involved, Noranda of Canada, to go into production. Only a strong federal effort would move things along.

For 1982, matters are frozen. The secretary of the interior will issue no leases in wilderness areas until after December 31, 1983, and in the meantime Congress is exploring what actions, if any, it should take on mining in wilderness areas.

In a sense, the mineral industry's complaints about the burden imposed by environmental regulations resolve into the same set of issues that affect federal land use, that is, the valuation and conciliation of differing objectives. Unfortunately, it is true that extractive industries tend to be highly visible polluters both because their processes literally stir up a great deal of dust and leave much residual waste behind, and because they frequently operate in terrains that make them conspicuous. The minerals industry is highly sensitive to the pollution control costs it has been facing and the House of Representatives' Subcommittee on Mines and Mining has the support of most members of this industry when it says that the "trend toward environment enhancement at any cost, regardless of economic impact, has led to excessive and unreasonable regulations which today threaten to stifle private enterprise and to cripple the basic industries of America, particularly the mining and minerals industry. Balance has been lost."[17]

Interestingly, the importance of nonmineral values is not called into question. "The Federal Government," the subcommittee's statement continued, "as a fundamental aspect of national mineral policy, must seek balance between the environmental, health and safety statutes and regulations on the one hand, and the need to ensure the reliable availability of strategic and critical minerals on the other."

This turns one again to the quest for other means of assuring reasonable stability of supply and price that might involve a smaller cost in both dollars and political friction. But decisions must eventually be made, and one side or the other will feel aggrieved. Again, therefore, the more closely decisions are keyed to a specific opportunity and site, the easier it will be to evaluate whether it makes good economic sense to make exceptions to general regulatory schemes. Evaluating the merits of specific actions is a different problem from that of managing vast federal lands on which minerals are only one of a large number of other national concerns. What is needed is a set of criteria and geological evidence that support opening up a specific site. In those terms, a "national policy" becomes a desirable goal.

What might such a policy look like? The above-mentioned Santini bill provides for nominations of tracts by industry and a subsequent decision by government, presumably based upon a set of criteria such as those suggested above. There are problems with this pragmatic, ad hoc approach. To be sure, it has the great merit of lifting decisions out of the ideological confrontation that pits "open up the land" versus "stop access to the land." However, mining firms would still demand some general criteria before spending funds on exploration. They would want to know, at least, whether successful exploration would automatically ensure the right to mine; whether proprietary data submitted for review would be protected and whether, if the application is turned down, they would at least retain a right of first refusal if the matter were ever reopened. In other words, it is difficult to see how the establishment of some general ground rules, whether or not they are called "national policy" could be avoided before industry would cooperate.

Similarly, environmentalists would want to know what criteria would go into decisions and what relative weight would be given to them in the contemplated wide-ranging cost-benefit reviews and decisions; whether

[17]*U.S. Minerals Vulnerability*, p. 2.

the approach would apply to *all* federal lands; and whether some way could not be found to divorce exploration, or at least those activities that are least disturbing, from decisions about the exploitation phase. Finally, many environmentalists would contend that any kind of exploration is environmentally adverse, and propose that some federal land be closed to exploration, even though this would preclude any assessment of its mineral wealth. A policy of basing decisions on specifics has much to recommend it, but there are general positions and arguments that should be considered and it is necessary to explore ways to meet valid concerns.

MATERIALS SUBSTITUTION. Substituting one material for another is done routinely by industries to increase productivity, lower materials or handling costs, or conform to government regulations. For instance, nickel and molybdenum are added to stainless and alloy steels to increase strength and corrosion resistance over a wide range of temperatures. Since molybdenum is more expensive, producers tend to minimize its use in favor of nickel. In times of short nickel supplies, however, producers have been known to stretch their limited nickel stocks by increasing the amount of molybdenum. Similarly, aluminum, plastic, or other materials can substitute for stainless steel in certain end uses.

Such substitution involves planning and, in some cases, retooling, and is not undertaken quickly or easily. It requires capital and time as well as information on the physical and chemical properties of the metals involved. For example, chrome bumpers and trim on automobiles can be replaced by rubber, plastic, and other materials, but this requires some redesign and modification of the production process, which may take several years to complete. If substitution requires the development of new product or process technologies, the implementation period will be even longer.

Consequently, although substitution can be used to reduce dependence on imported minerals, it typically requires a lengthy planning horizon. Despite its preoccupation with the welfare of the domestic minerals industry, the 1980 Minerals and Materials Act gives little attention to the possibilities of substitution or the need for research in this area.

Industries will carry on such research for their own products, but there is no incentive, or economic justification, for them to take account of the benefits their competitors and the country as a whole might receive in determining how much to spend on such efforts. As a result, without some government support, the level of research devoted to encouraging the substitution of domestically available minerals for imports is likely to be less than optimal.

Thought should be given to a stockpile, not only of materials, but of materials technology, with an emphasis on substitution possibilities for those metals obtained from insecure sources. Such government-sponsored research would not need to interfere with private efforts since these are geared to specific products and processes.

In setting up such a research program, three important questions need to be considered: (1) What is the time frame for substitution? (2) How can substitution possibilities be explored systematically, with government initiative and possibly funding? (3) How can the research results be transferred to the production line? Answering any one of these requires close cooperation between industry and government and judgments that may have to be based on less than ideal information.

For example, it is obvious that time frames for substitution will differ greatly. A recent study on chromium estimated that 30 percent of current U.S. chromium demand was instantly substitutable and another 30 percent could be substituted in one to five years.[18] Both technological considerations and quick response to price increases will determine which 30 percent of demand drops first. It is not clear what mechanism operates to remove the second 30 percent. Is it research by the individual user? Governmentally sponsored R&D? There are many generalities and few specifics in this area, especially institutional ones.

It is not sufficient to stop once substitute materials or processes have been developed. It is also necessary to be aware of the effect of substitution on the new mineral. For instance, if the supply of nickel were interrupted and users turned to molybdenum, which is a feasible substitute in some applications, how much substitution could molybdenum stocks and capacity support?

What is needed is a systematic and specific treatment of substitution which would point toward useful research—namely, exploring new and as yet unknown substitution possibilities. Both industry and government have a role to play in this undertaking.

PROTECTIONISM.   A protectionist trade policy, on the surface, appears to be a useful tool for encouraging the growth of domestic industries and promoting security of supply. However, it may have high costs.

A number of arguments have been made for trade controls—such as protection of domestic jobs or reducing the incentives for dumping. Here we concentrate on those arguments based on security of mineral supplies and reducing dependence on foreign imports, particularly imports from politically unstable countries.

[18]National Materials Advisory Board, *Contingency Plans for Chromium Utilization* (Washington, D.C., National Academy of Sciences, National Research Council, 1978).

Mineral consumers in this country generally do not choose to buy from insecure suppliers when they can obtain minerals at the same cost from more stable sources. Companies act to minimize disruptions and economic loss and will, as good business practice, discriminate in favor of more secure domestic supplies of minerals, as long as the cost of these supplies does not exceed the value of the security that is purchased.

However, there are times when it may be more economic to buy from insecure suppliers and, in acting in their own best interests, companies may not be acting in the interests of the country as a whole. While mineral consumers may adequately assess the risk of supply interruptions and lost sales for their own firms, they do not ordinarily consider the implications such interruptions may have for national security and foreign policy. As a result, they may import more than is desirable from the point of view of the country as a whole. Supporting this possibility is the belief that, if there is a serious military emergency, the government will allocate available mineral commodities. This means that those firms that have acted in the national interest (whether or not it was intentional) by investing in domestic supply sources will realize little or no benefit from their desirable behavior.

There is some truth in this view. Balanced against it, however, is the unlikelihood of any major world war lasting for more than six months or a year (if that long). Access to raw materials will be less important than supplies of existing military equipment. And a geographically limited war poses a relatively small threat to mineral supplies. Other supply interruptions, as an earlier section shows, will vary in cause, length, and severity, and can be dealt with on an individual basis.

There are two other concerns that appear to have some bearing on the issue of import dependence—control of prices through monopoly power and attempts to influence U.S. foreign policy. In the first case, if foreign producers' prices exceed those of domestic suppliers, imports will be displaced by domestic minerals. If foreign prices are lower than domestic ones, an effective protection policy will only ensure that U.S. producers' costs will be higher than the world monopoly price. Efforts to affect U.S. foreign policy are not likely to be successful either. As pointed out earlier, the USSR cut back manganese exports in 1948 in such an effort, but the principal effect was to encourage the United States to develop new sources of supply.

Thus, not only are the national security arguments for a protectionist policy not very strong, such a policy carries costs in the form of alienated trade partners, higher materials prices, and reduced supply options.

For reasons described already, the United States cannot afford a minerals policy that does not take into account the needs of its allies and neighbors. As a leader of the Western world, it has pursued political and economic policies to promote greater interdependence among countries. If the country now severely restricted imports of mineral commodities, it would undermine earlier policies and possibly threaten its position.

Decisions to restrict trade should not be made lightly. Since the costs, risks, and benefits of trade may vary greatly, depending on the mineral commodity as well as the timing and nature of the protection, restrictions must be evaluated on a case-by-case basis. Even where the advantages of restrictions appear to outweigh the disadvantages, lower cost alternatives should be examined and considered. Unfortunately, the information necessary for this sort of evaluation often is not available.

TAXES. Minerals enjoy percentage depletion allowances ranging between 5 and 22 percent, with most of the metals (except gold, silver, copper, and iron ore) at the high range. Companies are also entitled to expensing the costs of exploring and developing mineral properties (i.e., treating them as expenses deductible as costs in the income tax return of the year in which they are incurred rather than capitalizing them and charging them off just as other conventional capital items). While the oil and gas depletion allowance was highly controversial until it was finally abolished for all producers except independents in 1969, it has not been an issue for the nonfuel minerals. There is widespread agreement that these two tax regulations, originally enacted merely to simplify a difficult tax problem, have become incentives to mining and that a reduction or abolition would now be interpreted as a disincentive. There are few persons, if any, who are inclined to appear as advocates of such disincentives.

It is legitimate, however, to ask whether the depletion allowance is a particularly efficient incentive. The Treasury Department has raised substantial doubt as to both the general justification of special treatment and the specific way in which the subsidy is provided.[19] (The subsidy nature of the allowance lies in the fact, of course, that in time the producer recovers more than his full investment cost and that it accrues more quickly than would occur under normal capital cost recovery.) Assuming that the subsidy exists to increase output, one must ask why this would be desirable for many, if not most of the minerals involved, or, put differently, what social good (other than reducing reliance on imports) is served by raising output above what it would be in the unsubsidized case. Without answering this kind of question, it is not possible to evaluate the efficiency of the mechanism, that is, the rela-

---

[19]In General Accounting Office, "Assessing the Impact of Federal and State Taxes on the Domestic Minerals Industry" (EMD–81–13, June 8, 1981, Washington, D.C.).

tionship between the budgetary cost and the benefit in terms of mineral output.

Even accepting the usefulness of the allowance as an incentive, it can be faulted because it is levied on the gross income of the company but restricted to a maximum of 50 percent of net income and, therefore, helps those who are well off without the allowance and does little for the marginal producers—those with low net income who are precisely the ones that ought to be encouraged to produce. All in all, a careful comparison of the benefits of the depletion allowance is long overdue, but this is not one of the burning issues of mineral policy.

State-imposed taxes are a different matter. With the coming in fashion of high severance taxes for fuel minerals (on the grounds that the resulting revenues are required to pay for local environmental degradation and the depletion of the fixed asset) and the recent Supreme Court decision that upheld the Montana coal severance tax,[20] this is a matter of some concern. Where the taxes are levied on a per-ton basis and thus fail to relate to income or profits, they again act as disincentives for the exploitation of low-grade material, since the tax will represent a larger share of the revenue from low-grade than from high-grade material.

It is interesting that while severance taxes have received much attention, largely because some states have set them at high levels and have been accused by out-of-state customers as emulating OPEC in their exploitation of a seller's market, a GAO study has found that property taxes and occasionally state income taxes have a greater effect on the performance of mining firms than does the severance tax.[21] What all state taxes have in common is that they are typically not levied with an eye to their impact on mineral investment and production. Indeed, it is quite possible that a state's tax regime, as it affects mining operations, can work at odds with the federal fiscal regime. While tax policy does not presently rank high among mineral policy issues, neither should it be entirely pushed aside. It deserves greater attention as one of the ways in which the industry should or should not be assisted; though in such a judgment it is important to weigh whether the mining industry suffers discrimination compared with other industries and whether there are good reasons for giving it preferred treatment.

CONCLUSIONS

Ever since the Paley Commission released its report in 1952, resource analysts have pleaded for centralization of decision-making in mineral

[20]*Commonwealth Edison Co.* vs. *Montana.*

[21]In General Accounting Office, "Assessing the Impact of Federal and State Taxes on the Domestic Minerals Industry."

policy. Some would be content with a measure of coordination among various branches of the executive branch that deal with materials. Others would like to see new organizational structures set up, ranging from a small unit in the Executive Office of the President, to a new department. However, still others have cautioned against going very far in that direction and even see a danger in a move which would solidify the minerals establishment only to have it clash with those interests with which it interacts. Materials, they say, are just too varied and too ubiquitous to fit into a governmental unit.

What, then, can be said about U.S. mineral supplies and policy issues? First, supply concerns are not new, nor do they arise from any one source. Second, import dependence does not imply helplessness, and a policy of self-sufficiency has costs that are high economically and politically. Third, while the United States is vulnerable to supply interruptions, the cause and severity of the interruptions will vary, as will their economic impacts. Thus, each interruption must be judged separately. Fourth, while it is unlikely that the risks of interruptions can be completely eliminated, they can be reduced and the consequences mitigated in a number of ways—for instance, through stockpiling, substitution, recycling, and diversification of sources.

In deciding which of these measures are to be used, it is important to consider their effects, not only on the United States, but also on our neighbors and allies. Mineral markets are international and mineral policy must take this into account if it is to be effective.

Finally, while there is pressure from some sectors to ensure security of supply by opening up protected public lands to exploration and mining in the hope of finding new deposits of domestically scarce ores, such a policy can no more be based on a generalized case than can judgments about supply vulnerability. Wholesale judgments only lead to unproductive confrontation and ideological warfare. Instead, decisions should be based on general criteria but made on a site-by-site basis and should take into account the quality of the deposit, the nature and magnitude of the anticipated disruption, the economic benefits to be gained from extraction, alternative sources of supply, and the social value of leaving the site undisturbed.

The time was when mineral extraction was automatically considered the most valuable use of public land. Now, other national interests are involved and these must be given proper weight in decisions affecting the use of this land. These decisions will not be easy and, by the very nature of the issues involved, cannot be totally objective. But if a minerals policy is to be truly in the national interest, social, ecological, and environmental considerations must be put on the scale along with those of the minerals industries and the well-being of the economy.

4

Endangered Species

Winston Harrington and Anthony C. Fisher

As other chapters in this book point out, there are difficult problems associated with almost all valuable natural resources. At least some experts believe that the extinction of a great many plant and animal species is not only the most serious of these natural resource problems, but perhaps may be the most serious problem of any sort faced by mankind today.[1] While others would no doubt disagree with this assessment, there is widespread consensus that living resources are vital to mankind. This is so, not only because they directly provide food, clothing, building materials, and the like, but also for several other less obvious reasons. Thus, threats to their existence merit close attention.

The following section briefly discusses the contribution of plant and animal species to human well-being. Next, threats to the diversity of species are identified. These include not only direct harvesting (which threatens whales and certain other species), but also—and more important—ordinary economic activity that sometimes disrupts fragile habitats. The chapter then turns to those laws and policies of the United States that are designed to protect endangered and threatened species and identifies some of the controversies arising from the Endangered

The discussion of section 7 and the U.S. Endangered Species Act appeared in *Natural Resources Journal* vol. 21 (January, 1981) pp. 71–92.

[1] Edward O. Wilson, "Resolutions for the '80s," *Harvard Magazine* (January/February) 1980, p. 21.

Species Act of 1973, as amended in 1978. The chapter concludes with a discussion of the future direction of endangered species policy both in the United States and worldwide.

LIVING THINGS AS NATURAL RESOURCES

The well-known uses of living resources require little elaboration. This chapter concentrates instead on several less widely appreciated and quite diverse contributions of the plant and animal kingdoms, for example, medicines. While many medicines are comprised wholly of synthetic compounds, about half of all drugs prescribed in the United States contain some substance that originates in living resources.[2] Moreover, plants and animals can contribute significantly to medical research. For instance, the armadillo is the only other known animal species, apart from *Homo sapiens,* that is susceptible to leprosy. It thus figures prominently in efforts to eradicate a disease that strikes over 34,000 people worldwide each year.[3] The tropics are an especially important source of plants with potential for medicinal applications. Seventy percent of the 3,000 species known to have anticancer properties are found only in tropical moist forests.[4]

The fossil fuel resources upon which the world depends for much of its energy were, millions of years ago, living plants and animals. Plants which are now alive may play an important role in easing the world's energy problems in a much shorter period of time. One such possibility is the *Leucaena,* an exceptionally dense and fast-growing tropical tree that increases the nitrogen content of the soil in which it grows.[5] It appears to be an excellent candidate for biomass energy plantations, though it remains largely unstudied. Still more intriguing is the possibility of harvesting liquid hydrocarbons directly from plants. Some tropical species of the spurge family offer the promise, with some genetic improvement, of providing a renewable source of low-sulfur petroleum,[6] and the jojoba—a wild and rapidly growing plant found in Mexico—is coming into cultivation there and elsewhere, not only for the lubricating oil found in its seeds, but also for its ability to arrest the encroachment

[2] Norman Farnsworth and Ralph W. Morris, "Higher Plants—The Sleeping Giant of Drug Development," *American Journal of Pharmacy* vol. 148, no. 2 (1976) pp. 46–52.

[3] This example also points out that there are species that we may wish to become extinct—such as the organism that causes leprosy.

[4] National Academy of Sciences, *Ecological Aspects of Development in the Humid Tropics* (Washington, D.C., National Academy Press, 1982).

[5] National Academy of Sciences, *Leucaena: Promising Forage and Tree Crop for the Tropics* (Washington, D.C., National Academy Press, 1979).

[6] Paul R. Ehrlich and Anne H. Ehrlich, *Extinction: The Causes and Consequences of the Disappearance of Species* (New York, Random House, 1981) p. 74.

of desert areas. Interestingly, the jojoba's oil appears to be a good substitute for oil heretofore derived from the sperm whale, thus raising the possibility that the commercial development of one species may enhance another's chances for survival.[7]

In addition, the preservation of greater diversity today ensures that future options remain open. For example, the African oil palm was economically insignificant no more than twenty years ago. Today this plant is the world's second most important source of vegetable oil. Comparable prospective examples abound. For instance, a wild grass related to corn has been found in a remote, mountainous region of Mexico. Its key characteristic is that it is a perennial, whereas the domesticated (U.S.) corn crop must be planted annually.[8] If the wild strain could be successfully hybridized, considerable savings could result from eliminating the need to prepare and reseed corn cropland each year. Since annual seed and preparation costs for corn run about $60 per acre in the United States,[9] and since approximately 70 million acres are planted to corn each year, the annual savings from the introduction of a perennial could be on the order of $4 billion.

However, it should be pointed out that certain factors might tend to militate against such large gains.[10] For instance, yields of perennials might not reach those of the leading hybrid strains, and perennials might also require increased use of chemical herbicides and pesticides. In addition, the development costs of perennials could be great. On the other hand, if successful, perennials might produce other, less tangible benefits. For example, alleviation of the need to plow land annually could reduce the soil erosion thought by many to be a threat to U.S. agriculture (see chapter 8).

Other examples of the importance of species diversity are not difficult to find. Modern high-yield agriculture in the United States and elsewhere is heavily dependent on a continuing infusion of genetically diverse wild strains. For instance, wheat varieties in the Northwest lose their resistance to rusts (fungi) within about five years. To maintain current yields, new varieties must be introduced by combining genetic types that show promise of resistance.[11] Germplasm from wild varieties of peanuts found

[7] National Academy of Sciences, *Products from Jojoba: A Promising New Crop for Arid Lands* (Washington, D.C., National Academy Press, 1975).

[8] Noel D. Vietmeyer, "A Wild Relative May Give Corn Perennial Genes," *Smithsonian* vol. 10, no. 9 (1979) pp. 68–76.

[9] Personal communication with Professor Andrew Schmitz, Department of Agricultural and Resource Economics, University of California at Berkeley.

[10] We are grateful to Judy Lyman for pointing this out to us.

[11] Paul R. Ehrlich, Anne H. Ehrlich, and John P. Holdren, *Ecoscience: Population, Resources, Environment* (San Francisco, W.H. Freeman, 1977) p. 345.

in the Amazon region has greatly improved the resistance of domestic crops to certain diseases, at an estimated savings of $500 million per year.[12] To be sure, many plant breeders believe fears of the genetic vulnerability of U.S. agriculture are greatly exaggerated. One survey of corn breeders found that 83 percent were able to find most of the needed pest resistance in adapted domestic inbred lines. Nonetheless, germ-plasm collections are sometimes the only source of resistance to a particular disease or insect, and 87 percent of the respondents reported at least occasional use of such collections.[13]

The genetic information embodied in existing species can serve other purposes as well, and at least some of these are of considerable academic as well as popular interest. Moreover, the potential value of a species does not depend on how "advanced" it is; the greatest potential for pure science is sometimes found in those lowly, primitive species whose very names invite ridicule. A notable example is the Devil's Hole pup-fish. This fish, found only in a small rock basin in the Nevada desert, may help settle a debate in evolutionary theory between orthodox Darwinians and advocates of the "punctuated equilibrium" model proposed by Harvard paleontologist Stephen Jay Gould.[14] It should be noted that this species of pupfish is listed by the Fish and Wildlife Service as endangered, and thus is protected by the Endangered Species Act. Without such protection, the species might well have been extirpated several years ago by groundwater pumping in the vicinity of Devil's Hole.[15]

It is appropriate at this point to make an important observation: While many plants or animals have in the past or may in the future make

[12] National Academy of Sciences, *Ecological Aspects of Development in the Humid Tropics.*

[13] Donald N. Duvick, "Genetic Diversity in Corn Improvement," *Proceedings of the 36th Annual Corn and Sorghum Industry Research Conference* (1981), Chicago, Illinois, December 9–11, 1981.

[14] This disagreement is not over the existence of evolution, but over its timing. According to the orthodox Darwinians, the pace of evolution is steady but slow, with new species evolving only over millions of years. In contrast, the punctuated equilibrium model proposes that life forms exist for long periods with little change, and then speciate rapidly in response to altered environmental conditions. The importance of the pupfish to this debate is that it has apparently evolved as a separate species—perhaps even a separate genus—within the last 50,000 years. For a nontechnical account, see "Tiny Fish Looms Large in Evolution Debate," *New York Times*, April 20, 1982, p. C1.

[15] In U.S. v. Cappaert, 426 U.S. 128 (1976), the U.S. Supreme Court upheld a permanent injunction preventing groundwater pumping that would lower the water level in Devil's Hole. Although the Endangered Species Act was involved in this case because of the threat to the pupfish, the principal legal issue concerned the extension of the doctrine of federal reserved water rights to groundwater and also to *in situ* use of water. (Constance Boris and John Krutilla, *Water Rights and Energy Development in the Yellowstone River Basin* (Baltimore, Md., Johns Hopkins University Press for Resources for the Future, 1980) p. 34.

valuable contributions to science or agriculture, or other areas, it is surely not the case that *every* plant species will do so. Many, indeed most, species probably have no such utilitarian value. This does not always simplify the decisions that must be made when human activities threaten the existence of a species. There may be compelling philosophical or biological reasons to avoid endangerment or extinction. But it would be misleading to suggest that a miracle drug, a new cash crop, an answer to the energy problem, or the fate of the world's entire ecosystem lies behind each species.

One of the things that makes it difficult to formulate a policy for endangered species is the inability to determine on a species-by-species basis what mankind gives up if a species is forever lost. At the same time, we do know that the larger the numbers of species that are lost in a particular area as a result of natural forces or human intervention, the more likely it is that something of potential value will be lost. This is relevant since certain human activities, particularly tropical deforestation, can imperil large numbers of species at one time.

Before moving on to the scope and nature of the threat to natural populations, a general point should be made about biological diversity, a point that is relevant both to the values discussed in this section and the threats discussed in the next. Biological diversity refers to variation in the genetic characteristics of organisms and can exist on several levels: among different species that are members of a community of organisms, or an ecosystem; within a species, among different populations; and within individual plant or animal populations.[16] All three kinds of variation are crucial to the ability of a species to survive, to continue to evolve successfully in response to changes in its environment. This is because within a given population only certain individuals will be able to successfully adapt to a change, such as a new disease, a new predator, a reduction in food supply, or a variation in temperature. The smaller the population, the less the variability, and the greater the chance of extinction. And since variability is greater among different populations, and especially among different species, the argument for preservation is correspondingly stronger. Each species in a community responds to its environment in a unique way and the measure of its success is survival. This does not imply that the less abundant species are less important. In some instances a rare species may be a "keystone" that controls an important part of the structure and functioning of an ecosystem, or be of great importance if conditions change.

[16] Council on Environmental Quality, *Environmental Quality: 1980*, 11th Annual Report of CEQ (Washington, D.C., Government Printing Office, 1981) p. 38.

Biological diversity at all three levels is important for another reason. It is essential to the development of new products or medicines and agricultural advances. The basic idea in crop breeding, for example, is to introduce a new strain that has a characteristic that will enable it to ward off disease, say, or to grow more rapidly. Clearly, the less natural variation that exists, the less the chance of finding and introducing the desired characteristic.

There is one final point that might be made. In addition to the various material benefits of preserving diversity within and among species, there are less tangible but perhaps no less important aesthetic benefits. Rising attendance at national parks, increasing contributions to organizations such as the Nature Conservancy and the World Wildlife Fund, and population shifts to rural areas give some indication of the pleasure people derive from natural environments. Economists have tried to estimate the value of such pleasures, but it is difficult to be precise about experiences that are subjective. Still, the evidence that does exist suggests that these values may be substantial. In one study of the economics of dam construction in the Pacific Northwest, for example, it was found that the on-site recreational activities that would be lost if the dam(s) were constructed outweighed by themselves all the benefits of the project.[17]

THE THREAT TO GENETIC DIVERSITY

We have seen how natural populations and species, even those not currently being harvested, constitute a valuable resource. Yet this resource appears to be under unprecedented stress. The peculiar aspect of this problem is that it is the activities of "economic man"—both direct harvesting as well as direct and indirect habitat modification—that are largely responsible for the accelerating losses of species. This section sheds some light on this apparent inconsistency, and spells out in more detail the nature of the threat to species diversity. In other words, it tries to answer the questions: How are species being lost, and why?

The Extent of the Problem

Of all the threats to biological resources, habitat modification in its various forms is by far the most serious, according to all students of the problem. What form do these changes take and why are they made?

---

[17] John V. Krutilla and Anthony C. Fisher, *The Economics of Natural Environments: Studies in the Valuation of Commodity and Amenity Resources* (Baltimore, Md., Johns Hopkins University Press for Resources for the Future, 1975) chapters 5 and 6. This is a case study of the Hell's Canyon dam project.

Drainage of wetlands for coastal development is one of the most serious and far-reaching forms of modification, but conversion of land for houses, farms, and roads also destroys habitats. It is fairly clear that conversion of the very large tracts required for human settlement or crop production will destroy or drive off the wildlife once found there.

Agriculture presents an ironic case. It significantly depends on and benefits from population and species diversity, yet is one of the major threats to diversity. Modern agriculture seeks to increase productivity of the few edible plant species, which it does in part by breeding desirable features in harvested species, including high yields and uniformity. Both characteristics tend to reduce the number of varieties used at any one time. The gains of using such hybrids include yields several times higher than more primitive varieties, but there are also costs. For instance, in 1953 and 1954 wheat stem rust wiped out nearly three-quarters of the grain being grown for pasta (durum wheat) in the United States; in 1970 southern corn blight cost the United States a fifth of its corn crop.[18]

A second kind of habitat modification, less direct and perhaps for that reason less obvious than outright conversion, is chemical pollution. Scientific and popular concern with this problem can be dated to 1962 and Rachel Carson's *Silent Spring*. While her concern was chemical pollution caused primarily by pesticides (particularly DDT), there are other sources of chemical pollution. A recent focus of attention is acid rain. Oxides of sulfur and nitrogen are released when fossil fuels are burned in industrial or utility boilers, and automobile engines. Although there is considerable disagreement over the particulars, these oxides are dispersed into the air, sometimes over great distances, by tall stacks. While in the atmosphere, they convert to sulfates and nitrates, and join with water vapor to form dilute sulfuric and nitric acid. It has been shown that rain over large parts of the eastern United States and Canada, and over parts of Europe and Scandinavia, has increased in acidity and is more acid than rain falling in other areas, perhaps as a result of sulfur and nitrogen oxide emissions.[19] A species of Canadian trout appears already to be extinct, arguably as a consequence of increased acidity,[20] and the increasing sterility of lakes above 2,000 feet in the Adirondack mountains of New York state is by now well known.[21]

[18] U.S. General Accounting Office, *Better Collection and Maintenance Procedures Needed to Help Protect Agriculture's Germplasm Resources* (Washington, D.C., CED-82-7, December 4, 1981) p. 1.

[19] Gene Likens, Richard Wright, James Galloway, and Thomas Butler, "Acid Rain," *Scientific American* vol. 241 (October 1979) pp. 43–51.

[20] W. Keller, *Limnological Observations on the Aurora Trout Lakes* (Toronto, Ontario Ministry of the Environment, 1978) p. 2.

[21] For a good, general discussion of the problem, see Gene E. Likens et al., "Acid Rain."

Still another kind of habitat modification that appears to be having a serious impact on native populations and ecosystems is the introduction of exotic species—"biological pollution." New species have been introduced deliberately into areas where they do not normally occur, for reasons ranging from food production to aesthetics. A variety of sparrow introduced to the Americas by European immigrants displaced bluebirds, wrens, swallows, and other native birds by outcompeting them for food sources and nesting holes.[22] In other cases, exotic species have been introduced inadvertently. Old World rats that escaped from sailing ships have become major pests. Introduced species of fish have devastated native fish. This latter is a particularly serious concern in view of proposals for a new sea-level Panama Canal. Ecologists and biogeographers who have studied this project agree that perhaps thousands of extinctions could result from the inadvertent two-way exchange of marine species, with substantial changes in the ecological dynamics of both the Atlantic and Pacific oceans and their fisheries.[23] In summary, habitat modification in the forms of direct conversion of land, chemical pollution, and the introduction of exotic species has been and continues to be the major threat to the population and species diversity that is valuable to human beings.

In the United States, over 500 species are known to have become extinct since the year 1600, an average of one to two per year. By way of contrast, over a 3,000-year span during the Pleistocene period (a time of glaciation when many organisms died), fewer than 100 species were known to be lost in North America.[24] Moreover, the populations and geographic range of many species have declined markedly. Because the genetic compositions of different populations of a species are often different—the better to cope with local conditions—restriction of the range of a species may destroy genetic information even when it does not result in extinction.

Almost all the extinctions that have occurred in the United States have come about through destruction or limitation of natural habitat. Some habitats, moreover, have been much more heavily damaged than others. Two-thirds of the extinctions that have been verified in the United States have taken place in Hawaii, and the arid Southwest has accounted for another 17 percent. Not surprisingly, these extinctions are attributable far more to agricultural than industrial development.

[22] Clive Roots, *Animal Invaders* (New York, Universe Books, 1976) p. 127.

[23] J.C. Briggs, "The Sea-Level Panama Canal: Potential Biological Catastrophe," *Bioscience* vol. 19 (1969) pp. 44–47. Also, E. O. Wilson, "The Conservation of Life," *Harvard Magazine* vol. 76 (January 1974) pp. 28–31, 35–37.

[24] Paul A. Opler, "The Parade of Passing Species: A Survey of Extinction in the U.S.," *The Science Teacher* vol. 44 (January 1971).

In Hawaii, for example, most of the extinctions have been caused by the clearing of native forests for cropland and the introduction of exotic species, including domestic animals.[25] Nonetheless, habitat losses in the United States have not been—and are not anticipated to be—severe enough to cause wholesale loss of species. Concern about extinction still focuses on particular species, and policy in the United States has been formulated with this in mind.[26]

Elsewhere in the world, the problem of wholesale extinction appears much more serious. Entire plant and animal communities, not just individual species, are in jeopardy. Some scientists believe that 1,000 species are disappearing worldwide each year, and that this rate may reach 10,000 annually (or one per hour) by the end of the decade.[27] Indeed, by the year 2000 it is estimated that as many as two million of the perhaps three to ten million existing species could be gone, and more than half of all existing species could cease to exist by the end of the next century.[28] Extinction on this scale would clearly be a catastrophe.

Without minimizing the seriousness of this problem, it is worth noting the immense uncertainty surrounding such estimates. Virtually all the species whose extinction is feared are located in the world's tropical moist forests (TMF), an area about which very little is known even today. Extinction rates in the TMF zone are arrived at by first estimating the rate at which the primary forest itself is disappearing, and then estimating the effect of this disappearance (and habitat destruction) on the number of species. It would be well to examine these calculations in some detail.

Worldwide, the total area of the TMF zone is estimated to be 9 to 10 million square kilometers.[29] This primary forest is being converted to other uses at a rate in excess of 200,000 square kilometers per year, according to many experts, but this estimate has been arrived at by the most rudimentary calculations. For example, in a recent report of the

[25] Ibid.
[26] This is not to say that habitat destruction is no longer of any concern in the U.S. In particular, wetlands continue to disappear at the rate of 300,000 to 600,000 acres per year, and total wetlands acreage has declined from 125 to 75 million acres since 1850. National Academy of Sciences, *Impacts of Emerging Agricultural Trends on Fish and Wildlife Habitat* (Washington, D.C., National Academy Press, 1982).
[27] Norman Myers, "The Exhausted Earth," *Foreign Policy* no. 42 (Spring, 1981) pp. 141–155.
[28] Thomas E. Lovejoy, "A Projection of Species Extinctions," in G. Barney, *The Global 2000 Report to the President,* vol. 2 (Washington, D.C., Council on Environmental Quality, 1980) p. 328.
[29] A. Sommer, "Attempt at an Assessment of the World's Tropical Forests," *Unasylva* vol. 28 (1976) pp. 5–27.

National Academy of Sciences,[30] Myers asserted that the principal cause of forest conversion worldwide is shifting cultivation by "forest farmers," who clear small plots of land and cultivate them for a few years until the soil is exhausted or weeds take over, whereupon the farmers move on to other forested areas. This pattern is often called "slash-and-burn" agriculture. When the population of forest farmers is small enough so that the period between successive clearings of each area of the forest is twenty years or more, the disturbance is not permanent. In some parts of the world, in fact, slash-and-burn agriculture has been practiced for millenia.

However, population pressure has shortened the rotation period to the point where the forest is being permanently altered. Myers calculates the rate of forest conversion by forest farmers in the following way: First, it is estimated that there are about 20 million forest farming families worldwide. If each family clears one hectare per year—minimal practice according to Myers—the total conversion is 200,000 square kilometers per year. Myers admits that some of the land being cleared is secondary forest, and also that in some areas where primary forest is being cleared, population densities are low enough to allow sustainable use. Nonetheless, he believes at least half the total to be permanent destruction of primary forest. Myers continues, "When considered in conjunction with other factors—timber harvesting, planned agriculture, cattle raising, etc.—it becomes possible to credit that something approaching 200,000 square kilometers of TMF, and possibly even more, are being converted each year."[31]

It is easy to see that this calculation could be sharpened in several places by appropriate empirical studies. In fact, Lugo and Brown argue that the estimate appears to be undermined by the regional reports given in the same volume.[32] For eighteen of the countries discussed, Myers was able to provide individual rates of conversion. The primary forest areas of these eighteen countries comprise about 58 percent of the world's total TMF zone, and the sum of their depletion rates is 53,000 square kilometers per year. Extrapolating from these estimates gives a destruction rate for TMF of less than 100,000 square kilometers per year, less than half the rate given by Myers and others. Of course, this lower rate is still about 1 percent of the total TMF zone per year, which is a serious

[30] Norman Myers, *Conversion of Tropical Moist Forests* (Washington, D.C., National Academy Press, 1980).
[31] Ibid.
[32] A. Lugo and S. Brown, "Conversion of Tropical Moist Forests: A Critique," *Interciencia* vol. 7, no. 2 (1982) pp. 89–93.

matter if the consequences of deforestation are as severe as some scientists claim.

In fact, very little is known about the connection between the disappearance of the tropical moist forest and the extinction of species. At present, biologists have identified about 1,500,000 species of plants and animals. While everyone agrees that the known species represent but a small fraction of the total, no one has a very clear idea of the total number of species. Of the known species, about a million are found outside the tropics and only half a million within. Among animal and plant groups that are well known, however, the tropical representatives outnumber the nontropical ones by two to one. Scientists believe that another 500,000 nontropical species remain to be discovered, and extrapolating using the two-to-one rule therefore gives a worldwide total of about five million species.[33]

In any event, the effects of tropical forest conversion on the survivability of species are extremely difficult to predict. In part, this difficulty arises from the fact that "conversion" can range from land clearing to selective timber extraction, which "need not necessarily cause a qualitative change in the species complement."[34] Even when an area of forest is destroyed, moreover, effects on extinctions are uncertain. On the one hand, habitat alteration could have ramifications extending far beyond the region disturbed. The fish of the nutrient-poor waters of the Amazon and its tributaries, for example, depend on seeds from forest trees for a major part of their diet.[35] Destruction of the forest might therefore have unanticipated but dire effects on the number and variety of fish in the waters of the region, to say nothing of the effect on the species of the forest itself. On the other hand, in some cases habitat can be altered substantially without causing wholesale extinctions. Puerto Rico was 90 percent deforested and then allowed to recover without any significant loss of species, as far as is known.[36] Likewise, the virgin forest that once covered the eastern half of the United States has largely disappeared, but only a small fraction of species is known to have become extinct.

The purpose of this short critique of the estimates of extinction rates is not to discredit the studies producing such estimates, but to emphasize the immense uncertainty surrounding them. Most studies, in fact, are

[33] National Academy of Sciences, "Research Priorities in Tropical Biology" (Washington, D.C., National Academy Press, 1980) p. 35.

[34] Myers, *Conversion of Tropical Moist Forests,* p. 8.

[35] Michael Golding, *The Fishes and the Forest* (Berkeley, Calif., University of California Press, 1980).

[36] Lugo and Brown, "Conversion of Tropical Moist Forests: A Critique."

rather careful to qualify the numbers they produce. However, when the dramatic estimates often produced by these studies are picked up and repeated in the popular press, the qualifying context is left behind. In this way numbers often acquire a precision and authority far beyond the original intent.

The Economics of Extinction

The discussion of extinction rates in the preceding section should not be allowed to obscure the fact that extinction of species, especially in the tropics, may be an extremely serious problem. Thus there remains an apparent paradox to be explained: Considering the importance of species diversity, why are species being taken and habitats destroyed with so little thought for the consequences? Much of the explanation can be found in two concepts that appear repeatedly in this volume: externalities and common property resources.

Both problems are exemplified by whaling. Very simply, so many individuals of certain whale populations have been taken during this century that those populations as well as entire species have been unable to maintain themselves. Between 1933 and 1967, the number of whales taken on a global scale doubled, but the whale oil yield actually fell to little more than half the earlier number of barrels. The larger species, the blues and the fins, have been hunted to the brink of extinction, and by 1967 the industry was processing smaller species—seis and sperms and even minke whales (maximum length 30 feet).[37]

Why did this happen? Surely one reason is neglect of such nonextractive values as importance in ecosystem balance and possible future use of these species for other purposes. Unfortunately these values do not accrue to the whaling industry alone, but rather to all society. Thus, the industry does not take these values into account while harvesting and the resulting stock size is smaller than optimal for maintenance of the species.[38]

Something else is at work too: overexploitation of the whales as a common property resource. As explained in chapter 1, a common property resource is owned in a sense by no one, in a sense by everyone. Each individual whaler has an incentive to take more than he would if the whales he leaves were not subject to capture by his competitors.

[37] Ehrlich and Ehrlich, *Extinction*, p. 105.
[38] For a proof in the context of a formal bioeconomic model, see Anthony C. Fisher, "Economic Analysis and the Extinction of Species," University of California at Berkeley, Energy and Resources Group Working Paper ERG-WP-81-4 (November 1981) p. 8.

With all whalers, indeed all whaling nations, behaving in this fashion, the larger whales (at least) are threatened with extinction. Notice that the common property problem is distinct from the externality problem. That is, even were there no nonextractive external benefits associated with whales, too many would be taken in a common property regime. (See chapter 5 for a more detailed discussion of this problem in marine fisheries.)

The phenomena of common property resources and externalities also come into play in habitat modification. Forest farmers practicing shifting cultivation are exploiting a common property resource. Without ownership of the land, a farmer has little incentive to maintain its long-term productivity. Moreover, in virtually all of the cases described in the preceding section, the human agent captures most or all of the benefit when a habitat is modified, but bears little or none of the cost. A tropical rain forest cleared and planted to crops or denuded for fuelwood eventually might have yielded a valuable drug, or a renewable source of energy. These prospects, however, are not only highly uncertain and in the distant future, but also cannot be fully enjoyed by the individual who refrains from clearing and planting today. On the other hand, he can reasonably expect to reap all of the revenue from the crop grown on the land. The deck is stacked against preservation, and the results are not surprising. This is especially true when forests are cleared for fuelwood or crops by villagers. In these cases, fuel and food are a matter of life and death.

Another, more subtle effect can also bias decisions in favor of development in such a situation, even when conventional externalities are taken into account. We just noted that the discovery of an important drug or a renewable substitute for petroleum is a highly uncertain future event. If a forest were to be developed today, and some indigenous species lost, the possibility of making such discoveries in the future would be considerably reduced. However, the opposite is not the case—preservation for now does not preclude later development. It is the irreversibility of species loss that makes it such a serious problem. This same argument applies to preservation of diverse plants and animals for the aesthetic enrichment of future generations. Those generations could always choose to ignore diversity in favor of material enrichment if they so desire; but neither we nor they can enjoy the passenger pigeon or other now-extinct species no matter how badly that may be desired. That option was foreclosed for all and for all time a number of years ago.

LAW AND POLICY

Since 1900, the federal government has passed numerous statutes concerned with the protection of wildlife.[39] While many of them were motivated at least in part by a concern for particular species, the general problem of extinction of wildlife was not addressed until 1966, with the enactment of the Endangered Species Preservation Act, which directed the secretary of the interior, in consultation with wildlife experts, to publish a list of species threatened with extinction.[40] It also appropriated funds for acquiring lands on which listed species would be protected. The Endangered Species Conservation Act of 1969 extended protection to foreign species by authorizing their listing and limiting their importation into the United States.[41] In addition, the secretaries of State and Interior were directed to seek an international meeting to establish a treaty on the conservation of endangered species. This led, in 1975, to the Convention on International Trade in Endangered Species (CITES), which prohibited trade in specimens of endangered species among member nations except as specified in the convention.[42] By 1980, 58 nations had become signatories to the convention.

With the 1966 and 1969 acts, the first steps toward a national policy for protecting endangered species had been made. However, these acts were quite limited in substance. Neither contained any provision for actually protecting endangered species from harm except on the lands acquired pursuant to the 1966 act.

The first federal statute that prohibited individuals from directly harming an endangered species was the Marine Mammals Protection Act of 1972 which imposed a partial moratorium on the intentional or unintentional killing of marine mammals and the importation of products made from these animals.[43] Although the act provided significant protection for marine mammals, other endangered species were left unprotected.

Finally, in 1973, Congress adopted the nation's first comprehensive measure to protect endangered species, the Endangered Species Act, which modified previous legislation in several significant ways.[44] First,

[39] The first was the Lacey Act of 1900 [31 Stat. 188, current version at 18 U.S.C. §. 43 (1970)], which prohibited the interstate transport of wild animals killed in violation of state law. See Michael Bean, *The Evolution of National Wildlife Law* (Washington, D.C., Government Printing Office, 1977) for a history of federal wildlife legislation in the United States.

[40] 80 Stat. 926.

[41] 83 Stat. 275 (repealed 1973).

[42] 12 Int'l. Leg. Mats 1085 (1973).

[43] 16 U.S.C. §. 1361–2, as amended by the Fishery Conservation and Management Act of 1976, 90 Stat. 331.

[44] 16 U.S.C. 1531–43 (1976).

the secretary of interior was given authority to preserve endangered species within the United States. In language borrowed from the Marine Mammals Protection Act, it became unlawful to "take" (kill, capture, or hurt) an individual member of an endangered species. Thus, direct actions against endangered species were prohibited. It also made it unlawful to engage in foreign or domestic trade in endangered species, or to possess any species taken in violation of the act. In this way the act removed much of the financial incentive to harvest endangered species in the first place.

Second, it established a formal list of endangered and threatened species, together with criteria for inclusion on the list. The definition of species, furthermore, was broadened to include subspecies and distinct populations of listed species. This protected the small population of bald eagles and grizzly bears in the continental United States, for example, even though these animals remain relatively plentiful in Alaska.[45] Although species considered threatened under the 1966 and 1969 acts were automatically included in this list, additions could only be made through informal rulemaking procedures. It therefore became more difficult to add to the list than under the earlier acts.[46]

A third innovation in the 1973 act was a provision enabling any person to file a civil suit against the United States and any of its agencies to enjoin them from violating the act. The Endangered Species Act was thus of a piece with other contemporary environmental legislation that broadened access to the federal courts.

Finally, and perhaps most important, authority was provided to regulate the indirect effects of economic activity on endangered species. Specifically, section 7 of the act authorized the secretary of interior to designate, as appropriate, areas of "critical habitat" for particular species. In addition, all federal departments were required to ensure that actions authorized, funded, or carried out by them did not jeopardize the continued existence of endangered species or modify their critical habitat. These departments of government were to consult with the Fish and Wildlife Service (FWS) whenever there was a possibility that an endangered species would be affected by their actions.

This last requirement appeared to provide a way to stop a great many construction or other development projects which threatened endangered species, regardless of their social or economic benefits. While

---

[45] Some groups in industry now want to remove the protection of such animals in the lower 48 states. "It's Open Season on the Endangered Species Act," *Washington Post,* March 8, 1982, p. A11.

[46] In informal rulemaking, an agency first must publish a proposed rule in the *Federal Register,* giving interested parties an opportunity to comment on the proposed rule before issuing a final rule.

environmentalists hailed the measure, others were alarmed. Their fears were well expressed by Senator Jake Garn of Utah: "(T)here are enough obscure species of plants and animals to guarantee that nothing at all will happen in this country if no endangered species is ever to be disturbed in its corner of the environment."[47]

The Importance of Section 7: Its Effect on Economic Development

Section 7 soon emerged as the most effective and controversial provision of the 1973 act because it permitted the regulation of virtually all activities having possible impacts on endangered species.[48] Although only federal action was regulated, this limitation was not as restrictive as one might think. Most economic development having even modest environmental impact already required a number of federal permits. Federal agencies granting those permits were subject to the Endangered Species Act.

Also, although section 7 did not contemplate direct intervention by the Fish and Wildlife Service, the procedure that emerged provided FWS extensive opportunities for regulating projects through the biological opinion issued concerning the threatening effects of agency activities. If the FWS found an action would jeopardize the survival of a particular plant or animal, the action would have to be cancelled or appropriately modified.[49] The potential effects of section 7 on development were especially important in areas that had been designated as critical habitat for particular species.

It is useful to compare section 7 with section 102 of the National Environmental Policy Act, with which it has certain procedural resemblances. NEPA makes environmental quality an objective of national policy.[50] In particular, section 102 directs that federal programs give environmental objectives "appropriate consideration in decisionmaking along with economic and technical considerations." To that end, section 102(c) requires the preparation of an environmental impact statement

[47] Amending the Endangered Species Act of 1973: Hearings on S. 2899 Before the Subcomm. on Resource Protection of the Senate Comm. on Environment and Pub. Works, 95 Cong. 2 Sess. (1978) p. 45.

[48] Section 7 may have been the most important source of dissatisfaction with the 1973 Act, but it was not the only one. See R. Lachenmeier, "The Endangered Species Act of 1973: Preservation of Pandemonium?" *Environmental Law* vol. 5 (1974) p. 29.

[49] Although the possibility of balancing endangered species protection with other objectives had been allowed by the eighth circuit court in Sierra Club v. Froehlke, 534 F.2d 1289 (1976), this position was later rejected by the Supreme Court in TVA v. Hill, 437 U.S. 153 (1978). See Stromberg, "The Endangered Species Act of 1973: Is the Statute Itself Endangered?" *Environmental Affairs* vol. 6 (1978) p. 511.

[50] 83 Stat. 852 [codified at 42 U.S.C. §. 4332 (1976)].

(EIS) for most federal actions that may affect environmental quality. Similarly, the Endangered Species Act requires that federal agencies report the effects of their actions on endangered species (in fact, this determination is usually made as part of an EIS) and if necessary, that they consult FWS.

However, section 7 goes far beyond a requirement that agencies give appropriate consideration to effects of their actions on endangered species (presumably required by NEPA anyway). If the consultation determines that a proposed agency action poses a threat to the survival of an endangered species or its critical habitat, then the project *must* be altered or cancelled in order to remove that threat. In other words, rather than balance endangered species with other considerations, the act requires that adverse impacts on endangered species be avoided regardless of other objectives.

The consultation process thus raises the possibility of costly alterations or substantial delays for development projects. Regulations promulgated by the Fish and Wildlife Service and the National Marine Fisheries Service require that "(u)ntil consultation has been completed and a biological opinion has been issued, good faith consultation shall preclude a Federal agency from making an irreversible or irretrievable commitment of resources which would foreclose the consideration of modifications or alternatives to the identified activity or program."[51]

This regulation could stop work on a project by imposing lengthy delays while biological studies to determine negative impact on endangered species or critical habitat are completed. In one case, for example, FWS at first estimated that three years would be required to conduct the studies necessary to render a biological opinion.[52] Although these regulations apply only to listed species, some persons fear that the Endangered Species Act provides a "hunting license" for environmental groups who could stop any project by discovering some obscure species or subspecies in the affected area. Environmental groups could intervene both through the citizen suit provision and through FWS regulations that allow any person to petition for the review of the status of any species.[53] If, as a result of this petition, the species is listed, the project becomes subject to the act, and a consultation process must be initiated. The possibility of intervention thus creates considerable uncertainty for proposed construction projects.

[51] 50 C.F.R. §. 402.04 (1979).

[52] This estimate was made by the Denver regional office of the Fish and Wildlife Service in the biological opinion submitted to the Omaha District of the Corps of Engineers, December 15, 1977. It projected the effects of Grayrocks dam and reservoir on the survival of the whooping crane.

[53] 50 C.F.R. §. 17.13 (1969).

As a result, section 7 creates the potential to affect economic development severely. Has this potential been realized? What in fact have been the impacts of the act on economic development? A thorough answer to this question is beyond the scope of this chapter, inasmuch as the Fish and Wildlife Service has been involved in about 20,000 consultations with other federal agencies. *However, a preliminary examination suggests that in only a handful of cases has the act led to irresolvable conflicts between economic development and protection of endangered species.* We turn now to a brief overview of several cases to see how such conflicts have been resolved.

Litigation to Protect Endangered Species

1. *Mississippi sandhill crane.* In National Wildlife Federation v. Coleman, NWF brought an action to halt construction of a 6-mile segment of Interstate Highway 10 (I-10), which would have disrupted the habitat of the Mississippi sandhill crane, a subspecies consisting of only forty individuals.[54] The court of appeals found that the defendants had failed to ensure that their actions would not adversely affect the crane's habitat. An injunction preventing further construction was granted by the court. The highway was completed after the defendants made changes suggested by the Fish and Wildlife Service.

2. *Snail darter.* The plaintiffs sought an injunction against completion of the Tennessee Valley Authority's Tellico Dam in Tennessee on the grounds that it would cause extinction of the snail darter by flooding its habitat in the Little Tennessee River, the only place where these fish were known to exist. The U.S. Supreme Court ruled in TVA v. Hill that protection afforded endangered species by section 7 was absolute (TVA had argued that congressional appropriation of funds for the completion of the project after the listing of the snail darter was evidence of congressional intent).[55]

3. *Furbish lousewort.* This variety of snapdragon, long thought to be extinct, was rediscovered by the U.S. Corps of Engineers during preparation of the draft EIS on the Dickey–Lincoln project, a hydroelectric facility planned for the St. John River in northern Maine.[56] A compromise was worked out in which only some of the affected area would be flooded, but subsequent budget problems have made it unlikely that the project will be completed.[57]

---

[54] 529 F.2d 359 (5th Cir. 1976).

[55] 437 U.S. 153 (1978).

[56] "Furbish Lousewort Among 13 Plant Taxa Newly Listed by Service for Protection," *Endangered Species Technical Bulletin* vol. 3, no. 5 (1978)

[57] *Congressional Quarterly Almanac* vol. 35 (1979) p. 687.

4. *Whooping crane.* In Nebraska v. Ray, an injunction was granted to prevent completion of Grayrocks Dam in eastern Wyoming, partly because the resulting increased water consumption by a power plant would affect the whooping crane habitat in the Platte River channel 300 miles downstream.[58] A compromise was reached in which the power companies created a trust fund for purchasing downstream water rights to replace water used by the plant.

Between 1973 and 1978, the Endangered Species Act appears to have affected only a small number of projects, and only in a minority of those did a conflict arise that could not be resolved, suggesting that implementation of the act has not imposed major barriers to economic development. However, projects that were impinged upon were affected substantially, even if a compromise was reached. For example, the main feature of the agreement in the Grayrocks case was a substantial payment ($7.5 million) by the power plant consortium to purchase the downstream water rights. In addition, the Fish and Wildlife Service will presumably regard future depletions on the upper Platte as modifications of critical habitat and attempt to stop them. If FWS is successful, section 7 will effectively prevent further depletions from the upper Platte.

Thus, the total costs imposed so far by implementation of section 7 appear to be not very high, but they are distributed unevenly. For most people, the economic impact of section 7 has been negligible. The costs have been borne almost exclusively by those who might have benefited from canceled, altered, or delayed projects. This distribution of costs rather than the total itself may have influenced the movement to amend the act.

The 1978 Amendments

Largely in response to the Tellico Dam controversy, the Endangered Species Act was amended in 1978 to provide some balance between the need to protect endangered species and the need for economic growth and development.[59] The amendments instituted a procedure whereby these nonenvironmental objectives could be weighed against the goal of protecting endangered species.

In part, the 1978 amendments give formal congressional approval to regulations and practices previously established by the Fish and Wildlife Service. The act requires the preparation and implementation of recovery plans for conserving listed species. In fact, the Fish and Wildlife

[58] Nebraska v. Rural Electrification Administration, Nos. 76–1–242, CV–78–L–90 (D. Neb. Oct. 2, 1978).
[59] The Endangered Species Act Amendments of 1978, 92 Stat. 3751.

Service had already been preparing such plans for a number of years, and at the time of enactment, 18 plans had been completed and 64 recovery teams were preparing others. Similarly, the process outlined in section 7(a-d) of the act for interagency consultation is essentially the same as FWS regulations promulgated on January 4, 1978.[60]

Before beginning a development project or granting a permit to a private developer, each federal agency is required to request from the secretary of interior information on whether endangered species may be present in the region to be affected by the project. If the secretary advises that such a possibility exists, the agency must complete within 180 days a biological assessment to identify the endangered species. If a project could affect an endangered species, the secretary must submit within 90 days a biological opinion stating whether in his or her view the proposed action will affect the species or its habitat. If it will, the secretary must suggest modifications to the project that will remove these effects. During the consultation process, neither the agency nor its permittee may make any irreversible commitment of resources that would foreclose such modifications. Further, if the biological opinion concludes that the action will adversely affect the species or its habitat, the project must be altered in accordance with the opinion, or an exemption must be secured. By explicitly stating that a project cannot proceed in defiance of an unfavorable biological opinion, the amendments remove one source of ambiguity in the 1973 act.

But the amendments also include some noteworthy changes that bring flexibility to the act and allow incorporation of other considerations under certain circumstances. The impetus for these changes was the snail darter case, discussed above as TVA v. Hill. Many congressmen felt that the court's absolute interpretation of section 7 was not what they had intended when they passed the ESA, so the act was amended to allow tradeoffs among competing objectives. Congress ensured, however, that such tradeoffs would not be made lightly.

To balance endangered species protection against other considerations, the amendments established a process by which a project may be exempted from the requirements of the act. A seven-member Endangered Species Committee was set up to rule on exemptions. It consists of the secretary of agriculture, the secretary of the army, the chairman of the Council of Economic Advisers, the administrator of the Environmental Protection Agency, the secretary of interior, and the administrator of the National Oceanic and Atmospheric Administration. For each application for exemption, moreover, the president is to appoint

[60] 40 F.R. 870 (1970).

one individual from the state or states affected by the action under consideration.

The exemption process works in the following way. If the biological opinion rendered by FWS concludes that a federal action could "jeopardize the continued existence of any endangered or threatened species or destroy or adversely modify the critical habitat," any of the principals (the federal agency, the governor of the state in which the project is to take place, or the licensee) may apply to the secretary of interior for an exemption. Thereupon, a three-member review board is appointed to consider the application. After determining that an irresolvable conflict does in fact exist, and that the exemption applicant has carried out the consultation responsibilities in good faith, the review board prepares a report on the application for the Endangered Species Committee. Although it is not required, the review board may (and probably will) conduct one or more adjudicatory hearings. Upon receiving the review board's report, the committee may grant the exemption (possibly conditioned on the performance of certain enhancement measures) if five of its members so vote. Any outcome of the exemption process may be reviewed in the court of appeals.

Nonetheless, the exemption process could be less important than it seems. In the first place, Congress apparently envisioned that few exemptions would be considered, and fewer granted. The Endangered Species Committee is composed of seven high-ranking officials—presumably busy people with little time to be routinely involved with the Endangered Species Committee.

Moreover, the entire exemption process could cause significant delays, even though Congress did place time limits on each step. The time limits given in the amendments could take up to nine months from inception of a project to the rendering of the biological opinion. If an exemption is applied for, it will take an additional year. Thus, almost two years must pass before an irreversible commitment of resources can be made. This means that little work can be done on the project until the endangered species problem is resolved.

The actual delay could be even greater than these twenty-one months. First, of course, is the possibility of judicial review. Second, there is no sanction for missing a deadline. Many deadlines in other federal legislation are routinely missed by operating agencies. Third, the applicant is financially responsible for the mitigation or enhancement measures that the committee may require. As a result, the committee must have assurances that the funds are available and that such measures will be completed before the exemption can be granted. For federal agencies with development responsibility, this means that the funds for mitigation and enhancement measures must be authorized and appropriated by Congress.

The very limited experience since passage of the 1978 amendments tends to support these preceding assertions. Except for the Tellico and Grayrocks dams, where consideration by the Endangered Species Committee was mandatory, only one exemption has been sought: the Pittston refinery in Eastport, Maine. This refinery is subject to the Endangered Species Act because it must obtain an effluent discharge permit from the Environmental Protection Agency (EPA). In December 1978, FWS issued a biological opinion that completion of the project would jeopardize the continued existence of the bald eagle in Maine. EPA accordingly denied the permit. After Pittston applied for an exemption in January 1979, all parties agreed to a 90-day suspension of the exemption process so that another consultation, in search of a compromise, could take place. In May, however, FWS reaffirmed its earlier conclusion, and the review board resumed its processing of the exemption application. Several environmental groups immediately sued to halt the proceedings, claiming the EPA's internal appeals procedure had not been exhausted. Thus Pittston, which had first applied to EPA for a permit in early 1978, still must go through an EPA appeals procedure lasting several months before further action can be taken on its exemption application. This experience is not likely to make developers particularly eager to seek exemptions from the Endangered Species Committee.

The Fish and Wildlife Service also may have been anxious to avoid an irresolvable conflict that would require convening the Endangered Species Committee because such conflict might reopen the issue of endangered species protection in Congress. That this was no idle concern is evidenced by the Tellico Dam experience. As part of the Endangered Species Committee's investigation of the Tellico question, a benefit-cost analysis was undertaken by the Office of Policy Analysis in the Department of Interior.[61] This analysis showed that the net benefits of a "river development" alternative were almost equal to those of a "reservoir" alternative. Thereupon, the Endangered Species Committee denied Tellico an exemption to section 7 because a reasonable alternative existed. Senator Baker of Tennessee vigorously protested this decision, on the rather curious grounds that the Endangered Species Committee was not authorized to consider economic benefits in their decision making. Not long afterward, Congress exempted Tellico from the requirements of the act, and directed TVA to complete the project.[62] The

[61] "Tellico Dam and Reservoir," Report prepared for the Endangered Species Committee, January 1979.

[62] This provision was contained in the Energy and Water Development Appropriation Act of 1980, 93 Stat. 449.

Tellico case suggests that Congress will not be at all reluctant to overrule the committee, casting even further doubt on the viability of the exemption process. Indeed, if the mood of Congress is shifting away from support of environmental protection in favor of economic (and especially energy) development, it would probably not be a good time (from the point of view of FWS) for bringing attention to endangered species policy through rulings of the Endangered Species Committee.

Changes concerning the listing of species made in the 1978 amendments are also of great significance. First, where practicable, a critical habitat now must be designated at the same time a new species is listed. This designation obviously is not practicable for foreign species, but Congress clearly intended the great majority of domestic species to be included. The failure to designate critical habitat must be justified when the regulation is proposed. Second, in designating critical habitat, FWS must consider economic impact, and must apply a benefit–cost test to the designation of any area unless it is determined that its exclusion from critical habitat will result in the extinction of the species. Third, the amendments limit to two years the time between proposal and promulgation of a regulation to list a new species. If no regulation is promulgated within this period, the proposed listing must be withdrawn and cannot be reproposed unless new information becomes available. Fourth, the status of each listed species is to be reviewed every five years. Finally, the listing process itself was changed in important ways. The secretary of interior must give notice and hold hearings in or near potential critical habitats of proposed listings, and at the time of the proposal FWS must specify those activities that would adversely affect the habitat and therefore would face prohibition after the listing and habitat designation. New listing requirements will probably reduce significantly the rate at which new species are added to the list. Indeed, every change mentioned above works in this direction. It is impossible to say exactly how much the rate will decline, but an upper limit is the rate at which critical habitats are designated. If economic impact and local participation requirements play an important role, the actual rate may be considerably less than it has been.

The actual impact of the amendments on the listing of species and the designation of critical habitats has been surprisingly small. During 1979, about 70 species were added to the endangered and threatened lists, considerably more than had been added during the previous two years when the more stringent listing procedures did not apply. However, with one exception, the species added were ones for which the new listing procedures did not apply anyway. About half were foreign species, for which critical habitat designation is not applicable. The rest were mostly domestic plants. For these species, critical habitats were not designated on the grounds that restricting information on the location of the species would protect the plants from being taken.[63] During 1980, an additional 21 species were added to the list. In addition, critical habitats were designated for 12 newly listed species, a rate of critical habitat designation that was approximately the same as 1976–78.

The big falloff in activity to protect endangered species came, not with the change of legislation, but with the change in administration. Only four species were listed during 1981, all of which had been proposed during the Carter administration, and only one species has been listed in 1982. Compared to administrative intentions, in other words, statutory changes are still of secondary importance.

OPTIONS FOR PRESERVATION POLICY

In considering possible future changes in policies to preserve endangered species, it is important to keep in mind several points regarding the effects of current policy. In the first place, the alleged potential impacts of the Endangered Species Act on economic development have been largely unrealized. A quick survey of the experience with section 7 suggests that the aggregate economic costs of implementing the act have been small. To be sure, casual evidence of this sort can be misleading. On the one hand, it is unknown how many projects were altered, delayed, or abandoned in the planning stages as a result of uncertainties regarding the implementation of section 7. On the other hand, projects were affected by many regulations besides the Endangered Species Act. A proposed development challenged by section 7 is likely to be also affected by NEPA, the Wild and Scenic Rivers Act, designation of wilderness areas, or regulations to prevent significant deterioration of air quality, as well as many other regulations. In such cases, it is an overstatement to attribute all the costs of regulation to the Endangered Species Act.

It also should be noted that the costs that are imposed are very local. Measures designed to protect endangered species, especially those protecting habitat, are usually site-specific, and their implementation can fall heavily on particular individuals or firms. The passionate opposition the act has aroused is due to this uneven distribution of impacts, rather

[63] That this is no idle concern is evidenced by the experience with the Virginia roundleaf birch, thought to be extinct since 1914, but recently rediscovered. Shortly after its rediscovery, several trees were stolen and others damaged. (*Endangered Species Technical Bulletin* vol. 3, no. 5, p. 7).

than the aggregate effects. At the same time, many of the projects most affected by the act have been federally funded, a fact that should make the distribution argument much less compelling. Indeed, even on the basis of a fairly narrow definition of economic efficiency, one that does not count environmental costs, some of these projects should never have been authorized in the first place.

A second point to be made is that it is extremely difficult to assess the effectiveness of many actions taken to preserve a species. Often it is not known whether there is any protective action that will prevent extinction. Some biologists, for example, believe that the Colorado squawfish or the humpbacked chub may be doomed to extinction, at least in the wild, regardless of any action taken on their behalf.[64] Likewise, a species may survive even in the absence of any action. For instance, the population of whooping cranes in the wild has increased by more than fourfold in the past forty years, during a period when habitat now regarded as "critical" to the cranes' migration shrank by 50 percent.[65] Some measure of a policy's effectiveness may be given by a count of the number of species afforded protection or the area of protected habitat, but we should acknowledge how very crude such measures are.

Third, effectiveness, however measured, is not simply a statutory matter; it also depends on how statutes are implemented. It has already been noted how, under the Reagan administration, the listing of species and the designation of critical habitat has slowed to a crawl with no change in the underlying statute. Moreover, the budget for the Office of Endangered Species has fallen from $25 million for fiscal 1981 to a proposed level of $16 million for fiscal 1983, a level requiring substantial curtailment in listing and enforcement activities.[66] Finally, the massive die-off in species feared by many specialists before the end of the century is probably beyond the reach of any unilateral U.S. policy, given the fact that most species and certainly most endangered species are found in the tropical rain forests of the world. We will return to this point in closing.

---

[64] R. J. Behnke, "The Impacts of Habitat Alterations on the Endangered and Threatened Fishes of the Upper Colorado River Basin," in W. O. Spofford, A. L. Parker, and A. V. Kneese, eds., *Energy Development in the Southwest* (Washington, D.C., Resources for the Future, 1980) vol. 2, p. 212.

[65] Winston Harrington, "Endangered Species Policy and Water Resources Development," informal report, Los Alamos Scientific Laboratory, Los Alamos, N.M., pp. 42–43.

[66] "Endangered Species Act in Jeopardy," *Science* vol. 215 (March 5, 1982) p. 1212.

Reauthorization of the Endangered Species Act

When authority to expend funds to enforce the act expired in early 1982, an opportunity arose for amendments to be considered. Although opponents of the act attempted to restrict its scope or otherwise weaken its provisions, the act was reauthorized by Congress for three years with only marginal changes. The exemption process was streamlined somewhat, reducing the time involved from a maximum of a year to a maximum of about six months. The act also will allow early consultation with the Interior Department on whether an endangered species will be jeopardized by a project.

The exemption process was shortened because developers and others opposed to the act did not think the process as established by the 1978 amendments was working very well. Since 1978 only two cases have been referred to the committee—the same two required by the congressional mandate. But as the Pittston case makes clear, it is not the duration of the exemption process that discouraged it, but the difficulty of bringing a case before the committee to start with. The presumed "streamlining" of the process did not address this question of access. Nor is it altogether certain that the question should have been addressed. After all, the committee was never intended to be convened frequently; indeed, the difficulty of bringing a matter before the committee is in itself a strong incentive to reach an accommodation. It is unlikely, then, that these latest amendments will prove altogether satisfactory to developers, in which case the reauthorization will have postponed rather than resolved conflict over the Endangered Species Act.

It was argued above that the principal cause of dissatisfaction with section 7 is the localized costs of preserving habitat. One future change to the act that might mitigate such conflicts is to allow the government to compensate firms or individuals for losses caused by section 7.[67] Environmentalists ought to be amenable to this proposal, especially if it reduces the act's exposure to more fundamental change. Nonetheless, there are practical problems with compensation. For one thing, perverse incentives would be created if the government had to compensate developers for projects halted or amended to prevent damage to endangered species. Developers would have an interest in claiming to build such projects even if they had no real interest in doing so. Also, in an era of hundred-billion-dollar budget deficits, compensation schemes have limited political appeal.

---

[67] This has already been proposed by the National Forest Products Association. Ibid., p. 1213.

Global Aspects

In our emphasis on domestic issues and policies we have thus far largely neglected what most experts on extinction feel is, indeed, the major problem: the fact that most of the populations and species at risk are located in tropical moist forests, where the cost of preserving habitat may be high, and where what happens is beyond the reach of U.S. policy in any event. While the Endangered Species Act does have an international component that seeks to halt traffic in endangered specimens, it cannot address the problem of habitat modification except in the United States. (And, in any event, the 430 overseas species now on the endangered list seem puny compared with estimates of future extinctions.) Indeed, its value is largely symbolic. Having an effective endangered species policy of our own provides a moral basis for urging similar concerns upon others.

Measures to conserve the world's biological resources can be divided into two classes. In what are called *in situ* approaches, species are left where found in nature, preserved in more or less natural settings. *Ex situ* approaches, on the other hand, include the removal of species from their natural habitat, for preservation in permanent collections, such as in zoos and botanical gardens and the preservation of seeds and other genetic material in a controlled environment. The Atlas lion, for example, is extinct in the wild but maintained in zoo collections. Perhaps the most important *ex situ* approaches involve the maintenance of plant and animal germplasm for agriculture (e.g., seed collections), in which are kept wild or primitive varieties of crops and domestic animals.

Until recently, germplasm collection and maintenance has been rather haphazard and informal throughout the world. In the United States many private collections exist, assembled from all over the world by individual scientists and seed companies to meet research or commercial needs. In addition, the Agricultural Research Service of the U.S. Department of Agriculture operates the National Seed Storage Laboratory (NSSL), intended to provide backup storage for the private collections. Although this informal network of private collections has been instrumental in improving agricultural productivity, it has remained oriented toward the specific research needs of the collectors rather than preservation in its own right. In any event, familiar "free rider" problems discussed in chapter 1 would probably prevent the extent of germplasm conservation from being economically efficient.[68]

---

[68] It is perhaps not immediately obvious why the free rider problem arises in this context. The reason is that it is difficult to assign property rights to naturally occurring genetic

The apparent deficiencies of private germplasm collection led to the establishment in 1973 of the National Plant Germplasm System (NPGS). In part, this system is supposed to serve as a clearinghouse for users of germplasm by providing a centralized source of information on private germplasm collections, and to strengthen the ties between the NSSL and private collectors. NPGS is also establishing a network of germplasm banks, the first of which recently opened on the campus of Oregon State University. However, a recent report by GAO alleged that "insufficient management" was jeopardizing the viability of genetic resources.[69] Among the deficiencies cited by GAO were inadequate storage and insufficient resources for collection. Perhaps in response, federal spending on collection and storage of genetic material has been increased by one third in the proposed 1983 budget, one of the few nondefense increases.[70] The United States also contributes—both directly and indirectly through the World Bank and United Nations—to the International Board of Plant Genetic Resources (IBPGR), the international coordinator of germplasm collection and storage. About forty germplasm banks around the world are now part of the IBPGR system, storing over one million varieties of crop plants.[71] The principal advantage of *ex situ* collections is cost. Plants that can be preserved from seeds are quite inexpensive to maintain. Clonal propagation of plants that cannot be preserved by seeds is more costly, but usually inexpensive compared with the opportunity costs of maintaining habitat.[72] *Ex situ* collections are also valuable because they allow the assembly of genetic material from many disparate locations at a place where research is going on. Thus much field work can be avoided.

Unfortunately, *ex situ* preservation is feasible for only a small fraction of species. Most obviously, *ex situ* techniques cannot be used for species as yet undiscovered. For many known species, furthermore, long-term preservation *ex situ* is not yet guaranteed because their reproductive mechanisms are insufficiently understood. Even where feasible, moreover, *ex situ* preservation suffers from serious shortcomings. A germ-

---

material. Although hybrid plants not found naturally can be patented (over 4,000 such patents have been issued), naturally occurring specimens are not patentable. It is difficult to see how such a patent could be enforceable.

[69] Government Accounting Office, "Better Collection and Maintenance Procedures Needed to Help Protect Agriculture's Germplasm Resources," CED–82–7, December 4, 1981.

[70] *Wall Street Journal*, July 21, 1982, p. 54.

[71] Tim Griggs, "FAO Acts to Strengthen Seed Conservation," *International Agricultural Development* (June 1982) p. 14.

[72] Some *ex situ* techniques are rather expensive, however, for example, cryobiological preservation. Ibid., pp. 79–91.

plasm repository will ordinarily contain only a small fraction of the genotypes of the species unless the number of individuals kept is very large. In addition, conservation of a species outside its natural environment will very likely interrupt the evolutionary process. Particularly important for agricultural purposes is the danger that a species preserved *ex situ* will not evolve along with its predators.[73] Finally, we should note that while *ex situ* techniques may be the least expensive way to preserve an individual species, it is rarely the least expensive way to preserve an entire ecosystem, and indeed may not work at all for this purpose.

The above considerations suggest that no matter how successful and economically important *ex situ* preservation becomes, it can only be regarded as a supplement to, not a substitute for, habitat preservation as a means of preserving species. In other words, saving a substantial portion of the world's biological resources may well require setting aside extensive areas as nature preserves. Other questions then arise: How extensive must such areas be? Where should they be located? And who will pay the cost of maintaining them?

Probably the most urgent priority is the preservation of germplasm for agriculture, because it is on this resource that the world's future food supply largely depends. At present, only about 150 species are used worldwide in agriculture, with three species (wheat, rice, and maize) providing over half of human caloric intake.[74] Each of these 150 species evolved in a relatively small geographic area, and a substantial amount of overlap in the areas of various species can be found. In fact, twelve regions, often called Vavilov Centers after the Russian biologist who first studied them, are said to be the origin of most of the genetic diversity of agriculturally important plants.[75] Obviously, habitat preservation efforts should be concentrated in these regions, although determination of the precise areas that are the best candidates for preservation requires further study.

In the humid tropics, one suggested approach to preservation is found in the concept of "refugia."[76] It has recently been argued that during

---

[73] Robert and Christian Prescott-Allen, "The Case for in situ Conservation of Crop Genetic Resources," *Nature and Resources* (May–June 1982) p. 15.

[74] H.G. Wilkes, "New and Potential Crops, or What to Anticipate for the Future." Paper presented at the annual meeting of the American Association for the Advancement of Science, Toronto, Canada (January 1981).

[75] National Academy of Sciences, "Ecological Aspects of Development in the Humid Tropics," p. 78.

[76] T. E. Lovejoy, "Refugia, Refuges and Minimum Critical Size: Problems in the Conservation of Neotropical Herpetofauna," in W. E. Duellman, ed., *South American Herpetofauna: Its Origin, Evolution and Dispersal* (Lawrence, Kans., Museum of Natural History, University of Kansas, 1979).

the Ice Ages of the Pleistocene period, the tropics were much dryer than they are now, and tropical moist forests apparently survived only in small patches. Because they were safe harbors during the cold periods, these refugia are thought to contain relatively more species and in particular, more endemic species than other currently similar areas.[77] If they can be identified, these refugia would appear to be ideal candidates for preservation.

Both kinds of areas mentioned here—the refugia and the Vavilov Centers—are primarily located in developing countries where the need for preservation must compete against other land uses, especially food and fuelwood production. The policies of third world countries have, until recently, tended to promote habitat destruction. Brazil, for example, has made the opening of the Amazon region a matter of national pride. Consequently, land in the interior was made available to landless peasants much in the manner of our own Homestead Act. Developers of Amazon lands also receive generous tax breaks and import duty rebates.[78]

Nonetheless, there are signs that developing countries are becoming increasingly concerned about preservation of natural habitats. The Brazilian government recently purchased a section of primary forest in the state of Bahia that is especially rich in endemic species. In addition, several new conservation areas have recently been created in Brazil, including one of 22,000 square kilometers.[79] Most other developing countries are much more conservation-minded than before. An example is Indonesia, which has recently announced a plan to set aside 5 percent of the nation's land area—over ten million hectares—in parks and nature reserves.[80]

One reason for the interest of developing countries in conservation is in the potential economic value of biological resources. Until recently, diosgenin, a drug essential to the manufacture of cortisone and some birth control pills, could be obtained only from a plant indigenous to Mexico. The Mexican government has in the past few years raised the price from $5 per pound to $69 per pound, the latter a price at which synthetic substitutes become economically attractive. Other countries,

---

[77] G. Barney, *Global 2000,* vol. 2 (Washington, D.C., Council on Environmental Quality, 1979) p. 329.

[78] Myers, *Conversion of Tropical Moist Forests,* p. 123.

[79] Ibid.

[80] Robert Goodland, "Indonesia's Environmental Progress in Economic Development," in V. H. Sutlive, N. Altschuler, and N. Zamora, *Where Have All the Flowers Gone? Deforestation in the Third World,* Studies in Third World Societies No. 13, Department of Anthropology, College of William and Mary, Williamsburg, Va. (1981).

including Kenya and Ethiopia, have given the indication that they will charge for germplasm whatever the market will bear.[81] However, the poverty endemic to these countries makes it difficult for them to promulgate policies whose benefits are both uncertain and deferred. As in the United States, moreover, the costs of preservation will largely be borne in the vicinity of the area to be preserved. The present effects of preservation, in other words, may include considerable suffering for many people who already live in extreme poverty. As Myers points out, Indonesia's very strong preservationist policy is "an expansive gesture in a country with a per-capita gross national product of only $360."[82]

While the bulk of the world's germplasm resources are located in the third world, the principal users of these resources, at least for now, are the developed countries. This gives the developed nations a strong interest in preservation, and justifies actions by the western nations to assist in the preservation of endangered species and their habitat. Such actions can either actively discourage the destruction of habitat or taking of species, or they make habitat destruction unnecessary by substituting for the products that would be produced thereby. An example of the former is the CITES treaty discussed in the preceding section. Also, inasmuch as cattle production is one of the principal causes of habitat destruction in the Amazon, it has been proposed that the importation of beef from Brazil (or at least from the Amazon region) be banned.[83]

The trouble with such punitive measures is that they may generate hostility, especially if the target country does not agree that the species is endangered. The recent contretemps between the United States and Australia over importation of kangaroo products provides an example. In addition, unilateral or even multilateral actions to discourage markets in endangered species will not be fully effective if other countries are willing to provide markets. Even the CITES treaty is not as effective as it could be because some Western European nations are not signatories and have refused to restrict trade in endangered species.

The other approach would require the United States and other developed countries to provide aid to developing countries in return for actions by those countries to prevent further conversion of natural areas. In fact, "trades" of this sort already have been implemented through the World Bank, where loans to third world countries have often required an environmental component to project development plans. Many

---

[81] Myers, "The Exhausted Earth."
[82] Ibid.
[83] Douglas Share, "Hoofprints in the Forest," Office of Environmental Affairs, U.S. Department of State (1980).

observers feel that the financial assistance currently being extended to such countries is too small to make much difference in their preservation policies.[84] Moreover, recent trends, in the United States at least, are toward reduced funding, especially for multilateral institutions such as the World Bank.

The economic and political difficulties of preventing massive extinctions in tropical rain forests will perhaps engender a sentiment in the United States that such extinctions, while unfortunate, are not our problem. But they are, quite apart from any ethical responsibility we may feel. After all, the economic potential of a species does not end at national frontiers. As our earlier examples indicate, it is U.S. agriculture, industry, and science that stand to benefit greatly from the preservation of genetic information in other areas of the world especially rich in this information, and it is U.S. agriculture, industry, and science that will lose greatly if this information is destroyed.

[84] Myers, "The Exhausted Earth."

5

Marine Fisheries

Lee G. Anderson

In 1976 Congress passed the Fisheries Conservation and Management Act (FCMA), now officially called the Magnuson Act. The central theme of the law, which has become fundamental to fisheries management in the United States, is that the United States claims the right to manage, with certain exceptions, the living marine resources within 200 nautical miles of its shore. With its subsequent amendments, this law has made two significant changes in the utilization and management of fisheries. First, there now exists the potential for strong and unified management where previously international agreements, which by their nature are often weak and fragmented, were the only source of control. Second, the right to manage carries with it the right to utilize the stocks. Prior to the FCMA, about 70 percent of the fish landed in what is now the fisheries conservation and management zone of the United States was harvested by foreign boats. Therefore, the law represented an enormous potential gain to the United States.

This chapter reviews the major fisheries management problems in the United States and analyzes the policies and institutions that have been implemented under the FCMA to correct them. In particular, the chapter attempts to see if the management potential of the FCMA has been realized. The first section contains a brief description of how fisheries operate and their contribution to the U.S. economy. The special problems inherent in the utilization of open-access living resources are discussed and it is pointed out that fisheries will generally be overutilized in an economic sense, and often in a biological one. The second section discusses the realities of a regulated fishery and argues that existing fisheries regulations are often economically wasteful and sometimes even biologically ineffective as well—at least in the long run.

The third section describes current U.S. fishery management laws and institutions. It is pointed out that there is really no single coherent fisheries management policy as such, but rather a loosely structured apparatus or system that develops regulatory policy on a fishery-by-fishery basis, using vague national standards. Some of the actual regulations resulting from this process are analyzed and an attempt is made to explain why and in what way they reflect the system that generated them. The fifth section reviews briefly the health of the U.S. marine fisheries and some of the environmental factors that affect them. A final section provides some conclusions and tentative recommendations.

FISHERIES IN THE U.S. ECONOMY

Commercial fisheries have served an important role in the development of the United States and they are still a key component in the economic base of many regions. In 1980, the harvesting, processing, and marketing of commercial fish stocks contributed $7 billion to the gross national product (GNP) of the United States, less than one-third of 1 percent.[1] This small percentage of total GNP can be somewhat deceiving, however. For example, in Alaska, fisheries account for about 13 percent of gross product, and are an important part of the economy in sections of California, Louisiana, Texas, Massachusetts, and other coastal states.

When discussing U.S. fisheries, it is important to realize that total catch by weight has increased only by about half over the past thirty-five years, although its value has grown nearly tenfold as a result of increases in price (see table 5–1). During World War II, total domestic catch averaged somewhat more than 4 million pounds. Since 1975 it has increased 33 percent, reaching 6.5 million pounds in 1980. This is mostly because the FCMA limits the entry of foreign vessels in the waters adjacent to the United States. Thus, while total catch in the area has

---

[1]For another perspective on the role of fisheries in the economy, see G. Pontecorvo et al., "Contribution of the Ocean Sector to the United States Economy," *Science* vol. 208 (May 30, 1980) pp. 1000–1006.

TABLE 5–1. U.S. Landings of Fish and
Shellfish, 1945–80

Year	Total		Average price per pound (cents)
	Million pounds	Million dollars (current)	
1945	4,598	270	5.87
1946	4,467	313	7.01
1947	4,349	312	7.16
1948	4,513	371	8.22
1949	4,804	343	7.13
1950	4,901	347	7.09
1951	4,433	365	8.23
1952	4,432	364	8.20
1953	4,487	356	7.94
1954	4,762	359	7.55
1955	4,809	339	7.05
1956	5,268	372	7.06
1957	4,789	354	7.39
1958	4,747	373	7.86
1959	5,122	346	6.76
1960	4,942	354	7.15
1961	5,187	362	6.98
1962	5,354	396	7.40
1963	4,847	377	7.78
1964	4,541	389	8.57
1965	4,777	446	9.34
1966	4,366	472	10.81
1967	4,055	440	10.85
1968	4,160	497	11.95
1969	4,337	527	12.15
1970	4,917	613	12.47
1971	5,018	651	12.97
1972	4,806	748	15.56
1973	4,858	937	19.28
1974	4,967	932	18.76
1975	4,877	977	20.02
1976	5,388	1,349	25.03
1977	5,200	1,500	28.85
1978	6,100	1,900	31.15
1979	6,300	2,200	34.92
1980	6,500	2,200	33.85

Source: Department of Commerce, National Marine Fisheries Service, *Fisheries Statistics of the United States*, various issues.

Note: Does not include data on the Hawaii landings prior to 1948.

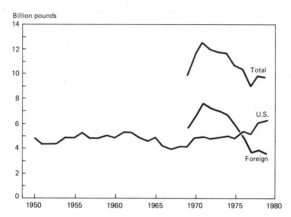

Figure 5–1. U.S. and foreign fish catch in U.S. waters, 1950–79. (Reproduced from Council on Environmental Quality, *Environmental Trends*, Washington, D.C., Government Printing Office, 1981, p. 8–13. Data from National Marine Fisheries Service, National Oceanic and Atmospheric Administration.)

not significantly increased, more of it is now being harvested by U.S. vessels and in 1977 U.S. landings exceeded foreign catch for the first time (see figure 5–1). This trend has continued. Nevertheless, foreign catch in the U.S. zone is still quite significant (about 45 percent of the total). It is technically possible for U.S. vessels to take up still more of the foreign catch and this is a tenet of U.S. policy. However, since there are no U.S. markets for the types of fish involved, and the existing U.S. fleet is not prepared to harvest for export, complete domestic utilization of the fishery is not imminent.

While replacement of foreign catch by domestic boats is an important aspect of fisheries management policy, and through it the United States has already achieved significant gains in landings, these gains did not come from increased total production. U.S. commercial fishermen have been able to maintain levels of production by substituting new species and exploiting the more traditional ones at faster rates. However, as figure 5–2 shows, several important commercial fisheries are showing signs of declining catch. Indeed, as many studies have shown,[2] most traditional fisheries in the world are at the point where no further increases in catch can be expected. In fact, if anything, stocks are overused

[2] See D.J. Garrod and J.G. Pope, "The Assessment of Complex Fisheries Resources," in *Economic Aspects of Fisheries Production* (Paris, Organization for Economic Cooperation and Development, 1972) p. 53.

in the sense that reductions in fishing effort may in the long run increase catch by allowing stock size to increase. This is certainly true for most U.S. fisheries, with the exception of Alaskan groundfish and a few others. Therefore, if there are further gains to be had from the FCMA, they will have to come from better management of existing stocks.

Although total catch has not varied much, both per capita and industrial consumption have increased. Thirty years ago, only 25 to 30 percent of the catch went into meal, oil, fish solubles, homogenized condensed fish, and animal food, while today it is approximately 50 percent. In the 1950s, average consumption of fish was 10.5 pounds per person, while today it is 13, compared with about 50 pounds of chicken and about 120 pounds of beef per person.

Generally, the total domestic use of fishery products has been at least

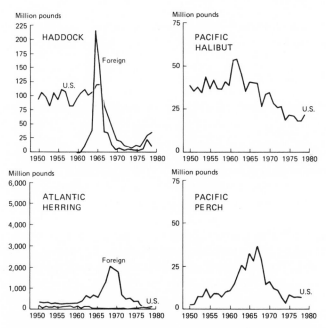

Figure 5–2. U.S. and foreign catch of selected fish species in U.S. waters, 1950–79. While substitution of new species and exploitation of the more traditional ones at faster rates have allowed U.S. commercial fishermen to maintain production, half the important commercial fisheries are showing signs of declining catches. (Charts reproduced from Council on Environmental Quality, *Environmental Trends,* Washington, D.C, Government Printing Office, 1981, p. 8–14. Data from National Marine Fisheries Service.)

double the amount of domestic landings; the difference is made up by imports. Although they are now less than U.S. landings, imports still exceed U.S. exports of fish. In the 1950s, they were, on the average, seven times greater than exports, but between 1976 and 1980 this ratio fell to 2.7.

As can be seen in table 5–2, total employment in fisheries-related industries has been rising steadily over the past two decades. Almost all of the additional employment has been in harvesting, with a significant increase following the passage of FCMA in 1976. At that time, many boats were added to the U.S. fleet in the hopes of increased catches once foreign fishing was eliminated. It is true that catch has increased, but whether the additional vessels were needed is still an unanswered question. As will be pointed out later, most fisheries tend to have fleets that are larger than necessary.

THE ECONOMICS AND OPERATION OF FISHERIES

Before turning to actual fisheries policy, it is useful to review the behavior of an uncontrolled fishery and the nature of the regulations that are often used to correct for abuses of open-access resources.[3]

The Operation of the Unregulated Fishery

In practice, a fishery can be very difficult to define because it often consists of many stocks of fish exploited by a variety of vessel types. In addition, these vessels can switch from stock to stock, depending upon prices, costs, biological availability, and other variables, even psychological ones. In this chapter, however, a fishery is considered to be a single biologically independent species harvested by similar vessels from a particular port. With some exceptions, the results obtained from analyzing such a fishery can be applied to most real world fisheries. One key to understanding the problems that arise in an uncontrolled fishery is the behavior of individual vessels and their effect on one another. This can be described in a fairly simple manner.

The amount of fish that can be harvested by a particular vessel depends upon where and when the vessel fishes, the type of gear it uses, and a

---

[3] An expanded treatment of these topics can be found in Lee G. Anderson, *Economics of Fisheries Management* (Baltimore, Md., Johns Hopkins University Press, 1977) chapters 2 and 4; Colin Clark, *Mathematical Bioeconomics* (New York, Wiley, 1976) chapters 1, 2, 3; and Rognvaldur Hannesson, *Economics of Fishing* (Bergen, Norway, Universitetsforlaget, 1978) chapter 2.

TABLE 5–2. Employment in Fisheries
Industries

Year	Fishermen	Processing, wholesaling
1960	130,431	93,625
1961	129,693	92,115
1962	126,333	90,993
1963	128,470	87,252
1964	127,875	83,976
1965	128,565	86,864
1966	135,636	88,748
1967	131,752	88,624
1968	127,924	88,742
1969	132,448	84,820
1970	140,538	86,813
1971	140,392	90,771
1972	139,119	91,268
1973	148,884	93,792
1974	161,361	92,118
1975	168,013	92,310
1976	173,610	91,863
1977	N.A.	96,041
1978	N.A.	N.A.
1979	184,000	93,054

Source: Fisheries Statistics of the United States, various issues.
N.A. = Not available.

number of other factors, including the skill of the captain and crew. In addition, of course, it depends upon the size of the fish stock. An important biological fact, however, is that, all else being equal, the equilibrium stock size and hence the long-term catch per vessel depends upon the total amount of fishing effort expended upon a stock. *In terms of our simple example, this means the more vessels that fish the stock, the lower the annual average catch per vessel.*

This is an interesting and important phenomenon because it means that to a very real degree, in the long term an individual boat cannot determine how much fish it will catch in any given year! A boat owner can control his fishing effort, but the amount of fish that will actually be harvested depends upon the size of the fish stock and the total number of vessels exploiting the stock. In this way the seemingly independent vessels of a fishery are actually interdependent through the stock size.

This interdependency helps to determine how many boats will actually constitute an unregulated fishery. Since fishermen, like other business-men, must cover all their costs in order to stay in business, when the number of boats in the fishery is in equilibrium, the annual revenue per boat will be equal to annual costs. In other words, any new boats would depress everyone else's catch to the point that *all* boats would lose money. Consider the hypothetical example in table 5–3. Suppose the annual cost of operating a vessel, including normal return on investment and wages that could be earned elsewhere, is $80,000. As the introduction to this book points out, economists refer to this as opportunity cost. Suppose also that with 45 vessels the average annual catch per vessel is 430 tons. If the price of fish is $200 per ton, this yields an annual revenue of $86,000. Since annual costs are assumed to be $80,000, all vessels in the fishery are, on the average, making $6,000 a year over and above all costs of fishing. This extra profit will tend to attract other vessels because potential owners will think they can earn more than enough to cover costs. However, as more vessels enter, the long-run catch per vessel will fall—not just for the new vessels, but for all vessels in the fishery. Notice from the table that if five extra boats enter the fishery, the catch per vessel falls to 400 tons per year, which will provide an annual revenue just equal to annual opportunity costs. All boats will be covering their costs but there will be no incentive for others to enter, and so, all else being equal, the fleet size will remain at 50.

There are two important features of this equilibrium. First, the stock can be driven to such a low level that problems with other important determinants of stock size can lead to serious depletion. For example, a temporary reduction in food supply may reduce the numbers of fish added to the stock (the recruitment rate) and thus reduce the stock to a danger level. This problem is all the more important when it is realized that as the price of fish goes up, or the cost of catching them goes down, it takes a smaller catch to allow each boat to cover its costs. Thus, it is economical for more boats to enter the fishery. In an unregulated fishery, this will decrease the stock size and could lead to collapse of the fishery.

There are many examples of such collapses, including the California sardine, the South African pilchard, the Atlanto-Scandian herring, and the temporary decline of the Atlantic haddock. Table 5–4 shows the dramatic case of the Peruvian anchoveta. The tendency demonstrated in this fishery for vessels to increase until total catch falls off is becoming

TABLE 5–3. Hypothetical Fishery

Boats	Average catch per vessel	Price	Revenue per boat	Cost per boat
45	430	$200	$86,000	$80,000
50	400	$200	$80,000	$80,000

TABLE 5–4. The Peruvian Anchoveta
Fishery, 1959–78

Year	Number of boats	Number of fishing days	Catch (million tons)
1959	414	294	1.91
1960	667	279	2.93
1961	756	298	4.58
1962	1,069	294	6.27
1963	1,655	269	6.42
1964	1,744	297	8.86
1965	1,623	265	7.23
1966	1,650	190	8.53
1967	1,569	170	9.82
1968	1,490	167	10.26
1969	1,455	162	8.96
1970	1,499	180	12.27
1971	1,473	89	10.28
1972	1,399	89	4.45
1973	1,256	27	1.78
1974	—[a]	—	4.00
1975	—	—	3.30
1976	—	—	4.30
1977	—	—	0.80
1978	—	—	0.50

Source: Colin W. Clark, "Bioeconomics of the Ocean,"
Bioscience vol. 31, no. 3 (March 1981) p. 233.
[a] Missing data not currently available.

very familiar in fisheries around the world. It should be noted that the exact cause of the 1973 collapse of the anchoveta fishery has not been determined, but it is likely that an incursion of warm tropical waters (called the El Niño) further decreased already overfished anchoveta stocks.

A second problem with the equilibrium in table 5–3 is that it does not represent a very efficient use of society's resources because the fishing vessels behave independently even though the productive effort makes them interdependent. To be specific, as new boats enter the fishery, they consider their own revenues and costs but do not consider how their entry will affect the catch of all the other boats. Because of this, too many vessels will enter.

This is illustrated in table 5–5. Note what happens if the fleet is reduced from 50 to 45. There is an economic gain of $400,000 to society because the resources used to produce that fishing effort (which has an opportunity cost of $400,000) can now be used to produce other goods and services in the economy. On the other hand, there is a loss to the

TABLE 5-5. Economic Efficiency Effect of
Reducing Fleet by 5 Boats

Annual gain
The resources used to operate five boats can be used elsewhere in economy
5 × $80,000 = + $400,000
Annual loss
Total catch falls by 650 tons
i.e.,
50 boats at 400 tons/year = 20,000
45 boats at 430 tons/year = 19,350
decrease of 650 × $200 = − $130,000
Net gain + $270,000

economy of $130,000 because total catch falls by 650 tons. However, when both of these effects are considered, the value of goods and services in the economy as a whole increases by $270,000. It is important to note that in some cases reducing the number of vessels can actually *increase* total catch if the increase in catch per vessel more than makes up for the reduction in fleet size. In those cases there are only positive effects because the value of fishery output goes up and, in addition, resources are freed to produce other goods and services.

Looking at the same thing in reverse, it can be seen that expanding the fleet from 45 to 50, as would normally occur in the absence of regulation, is not efficient. This is because although $130,000 worth of fish would be caught, there would be a loss in production elsewhere in the economy of $400,000.

It must be emphasized that the gain from controlling fishing effort does not come without losses. The reduction in effort will often mean that less fish will be available and, if the reduction in output is large enough, the catch that is taken may command a higher price. Under proper regulation, of course, these costs are more than offset by the increase in the value of goods and services produced elsewhere in the economy. However, since the benefits of sound regulation are spread across the country, with each individual reaping small gains, while the costs fall on a relatively small group of fishermen and processors, it can be politically most difficult to regulate effectively.

Although these are hypothetical numbers, studies have shown that similar economic gains are possible from proper regulation in existing fisheries. For example, Gulland and Carroz have shown that fishing effort could be reduced by 10 to 20 percent in the North Atlantic cod fishery without a reduction in catch; this would result in a savings of approximately $130 to $260 million per year in 1981 prices. Similarly,

Crutchfield and Pontecorvo have estimated that proper regulation in the Puget Sound salmon fishery could save between $13 and $18 million per year in 1981 prices.[4]

To ensure that a fishery is operating at peak economic efficiency, the fleet size must be reduced so long as the savings that result when boats are retired exceed the value of the fish that would have been caught. When no further economic gains can be made by reducing fleet size, the fishery is said to be producing the maximum economic yield (MEY).

Complexity of the Marine Environment

Another element that must be considered in fisheries management is the complexity of the marine environment. It is important at this point to stress the fact that, for the purposes of this discussion, the biology and some of the economics provided here are enormously simplified. The complexities that actually exist make the problem of fisheries management much more difficult than might be imagined from this discussion.

First of all, it is hard to do justice to the intricate population dynamics of fish stocks.[5] The stock size of a given species depends on a number of things besides the amount of fishing effort expended on it. These include predator and prey relationships, annual fecundity, direction and magnitude of ocean currents, food supply, habitat, disease, and other phenomena. Many of these factors are not clearly understood. This means that there really is no simple, deterministic relationship between average yield and effort. There is actually a great deal of uncertainty involved and although the inverse relationship between number of vessels and average catch may be generally representative of many fisheries, catch at any given level of effort will probably vary widely, depending upon other variables.

The biological and economic or technological interrelationships among different species further complicate the population dynamics of individual species. Various species compete with each other for food or habitat, or may prey upon one another. Furthermore, the harvest of one species often results in the simultaneous harvest, or at least mortality, of others

[4] See J.A. Gulland and J.E. Carroz, "Management of Fishery Resources," in *Advances in Marine Biology* (New York, Academic Press) vol. 6, pp. 1–71, and J.A. Crutchfield and Giulio Pontecorvo, *The Pacific Salmon Fisheries* (Baltimore, Md., Johns Hopkins University Press for Resources for the Future, 1969).

[5] See Lloyd M. Dickie, "Perspectives on Fisheries and Implications for Management," *Journal of the Fisheries Research Board of Canada* vol. 36, no. 7 (1979) pp. 836–844 and "Effects of Fishery Regulations on the Catch of Fish," in *Economic Effects of Fishery Regulation,* Fisheries Report no. 5 (Rome, Food and Agricultural Organization, 1962).

(one of the best-known cases is that of the dolphin that are caught in tuna nets). Therefore, it is necessary to understand the basic ecology of the marine environment rather than simply the growth of a particular species. This emphasizes the complexity of the management problem, but it also implies that managing fisheries on a species-by-species basis can be very difficult. A total ecological approach may be necessary for proper management.

Another important issue is the definition of fishing effort.[6] This is a function of the size of the boat; the type, size, and amount of gear; the time, location, and expertise of captain and crew; as well as a good number of other factors. In order to properly understand the effect of fishing on stock size, it is important to know how much effort is being expended. However, unless effort can be meaningfully measured, it may be impossible to know just how much is being exerted at any one time and, equally important, how effort changes over time.

In addition, there is also a general lack of data about fish stocks and their environment. For one thing, it is expensive to collect data on marine-based populations, much more so than for comparable work on land. It is possible to collect useful data from fishermen, and indeed most of what data there are come from them, but fishermen have a natural tendency to misrepresent catch or effort levels, especially if there are quotas or other such regulations in effect. In most cases, therefore, management must proceed with very little information about what is happening to the fish stock. Since additional information is costly, it is important to design policies that are manageable even when information is less than perfect.[7]

REGULATION AND ECONOMIC EFFICIENCY

The preceding discussion suggests that if economic efficiency were the only objective of fisheries management, the appropriate policy would be relatively straightforward. First, some control would be potentially beneficial because, left to its own devices, an open-access fishery would probably operate in an inefficient manner. There would be net gains, however, only if the costs of the entire regulation program were less than the benefits of controlling entry.

---

[6] See S. Cunningham and D. Whitemarsh, "Fishing Effort and Fisheries Policy," *Marine Policy* no. 4 (1980) pp. 309–317; and B. Rothschild, "An Exposition on the Measurement of Fishing Effort," *Fishery Bulletin* vol. 70, no. 3 (1972) pp. 671–679.

[7] See J. Donaldson and G. Pontecorvo, "Economic Rationalization of Fisheries," *Ocean Development and International Law* vol. 8, no. 2 (1980) pp. 149–170.

Second, in order to achieve all the potential net benefits, effort should be reduced from the open-access level to the point of maximum economic yield in such a way that the cost of catching the allowed yield is as low as possible. The importance of the last condition cannot be overemphasized. Fully efficient management of fisheries harvest entails two things: catch must be limited to the optimal level and that catch should be harvested in the most inexpensive manner possible. Regulating a fishery to accomplish this dual objective can be a difficult task, and as the discussion that follows indicates, many current regulatory approaches are incapable of doing so. Some even have trouble in permanently reducing effective fishing effort, as will be demonstrated later.[8]

The most common tools of fishery regulation are total quotas, closed seasons and areas, and gear restrictions. Each has problems which can be analyzed in terms of the previous discussion. Consider first total quotas. Assume that a management agency decides to limit catch to the economically efficient level. On the surface, this appears to be a plausible way to regulate. Note, however, that if effort is reduced, the new equilibrium average revenue will be higher than the average cost. That is, to the degree that catch restrictions are successful, the stock size will increase and hence catch and revenue per vessel will go up. Seeing the potential profits, other boats will be motivated to enter the fishery and those already fishing will try to catch more. With the total quota in effect, however, the boats will have to be prepared to take their catch as quickly as possible because all fishing ceases when the limit is reached. They will use bigger boats, more nets, and additional equipment, which can only mean an increase in the annual cost of maintaining and operating a representative vessel. A successful quota, therefore, sows the seeds of its own destruction as far as economic efficiency is concerned. The resulting profits encourage activities that will increase costs until they equal average revenue and hence all profits are once again removed. The desired catch will be achieved, but at a higher cost than is necessary.

Closed seasons and closed areas have the same problem. In addition, they cannot even guarantee that the proper amount of fish will be har-

---

[8] For a more detailed analysis of these points, see Lee G. Anderson, *Economics of Fisheries Management,* chapter 4; Peter H. Pearse, ed., Symposium on Managing Fishing Effort, *Journal of the Fisheries Research Board of Canada* vol. 6, no. 7 (1979) pp. 711–866; Bruce R. Rettig, ed., *Limited Entry as a Fishery Management Tool* (Seattle, University of Washington Press, 1980); Lee G. Anderson, "A Comparison of Limited Entry Fisheries Management Schemes," and Colin W. Clark, "Fishery Management and Fishing Rights," in *Report of the ACMRR Working Party on the Scientific Basis of Determining Management Measures,* Fisheries Report no. 23 (Rome, Food and Agricultural Organization, 1980) pp. 47–74 and pp. 101–113, respectively.

vested. If a management agency wanted to achieve the optimal yield by these methods, it would have to reduce the length of the season or the areas in which fishing can take place so that the amount of fishing that could be done in the allowed time or area would result in the desired catch. In the very short run this may be effective because fishermen will have no way to adjust their rate of fishing. However, as the stock increases as a result of the reduced effort, the resulting extra profits will encourage fishermen to increase the amount of effort. Because of limits on time and area, this can only be done by increasing the annual cost of this effort. The end result is a fleet with the capacity to harvest more than the optimal catch and which tends to harvest fish at a higher average cost than is necessary. Therefore, not only does economic inefficiency result, but the biological effectiveness of the regulation is eroded as well.

This type of regulation often results in a race between the fishermen, who are motivated to increase their catching power, and the regulator, who must then impose further restrictions. The Pacific halibut fishery provides a good example.[9] Before regulation, the normal season was several months. But as fishermen adapted to successively shorter seasons by improving their vessels and equipment, the season was finally restricted to several weeks.

Under gear restrictions, regulators try to limit catch by restricting the type or amount of equipment that the fishermen can use. To the extent that these restrictions affect the fishermen's ability to operate, they will increase the annual cost of maintaining and operating a vessel. With the increased costs, some vessels will be forced to leave the fishery. A new equilibrium will be achieved when the fleet has decreased sufficiently to increase catch per vessel to cover the higher costs. Under these regulations, therefore, the fleet will operate at a lower level of effort. However, the fish that are caught will not be harvested as cheaply as possible. In addition, these measures usually only have a short-term effect. As fishermen adjust to input restrictions, they learn how to increase their fishing power within the constraints of the controls. Here again, there will often be a race between regulators and fishermen, with the former trying to reduce the effectiveness of the latter, while the latter try to increase their fishing power subject to the constraints, and in doing so increase cost per boat.

Taxes, individual quotas, and licenses (sometimes considered together as "limited entry" approaches) can also be used to encourage the desirable amount of fishing. If a tax were levied on each ton of fish har-

---

[9] See James A. Crutchfield and Arnold Zellner, "Economic Aspects of the Pacific Halibut Fishery," *Fisheries Industrial Research* vol. 1, no. 1 (1962) pp. 1–174.

vested, annual revenue per boat after taxes would be decreased; in turn this would reduce the number of boats since revenues will no longer cover costs. The reduction in the fleet would continue until average revenue per boat again equaled average cost. Under the tax approach, the fishermen will have an incentive to keep costs as low as possible; thus the actual cost of catching the fish will be minimized. It is important to note, however, that the tax approach is very unpopular with fishermen. Moreover, it can also be difficult to implement because changes in prices and/or costs will necessitate a change in the tax rate in order to keep the fleet at the desired level.

Individual (as opposed to total) quotas could also be used as a regulatory device. After the desired total catch is determined, it could be divided into shares which would be assigned to individual fishermen. These shares would give each of them the right to harvest a certain amount of fish each year. Since each can catch only a specified amount, it would be to the individual fisherman's advantage to take the allowable catch as cheaply as possible. Under an ideal individual quota system, the allotted shares would be freely transferable between fishermen, so that those who are more efficient could purchase the right to harvest from others. This would further decrease the real cost of harvesting the allotted catch while at the same time benefitting both the buyer and the seller of the quotas.

License programs—the only type of limited entry regulation that has actually been implemented—forbid fishing to those not specifically licensed to do so. The object is to set the number of licenses so that those allowed to fish will harvest the optimal catch. The problems with this approach are not difficult to discern. For example, if boats are licensed, and if the restriction on the number of boats is successful in increasing the profitability of the fishery, then the participants will have an incentive to increase their fishing power by manipulating unlicensed inputs, such as size of boat, fish-finding equipment, and so on. Where such substitutions are possible, therefore, limited license programs are very similar in design and effect to limitations on gear. Measures to prevent fishermen from increasing their catch by attaching the licenses to specifically defined units of fishing effort (i.e., a boat of specific length with a certain amount of gear) might work, but would require an accurate definition of a unit of effort, especially in a fleet composed of different types and ages of vessels. In addition, they may also inhibit technological advance. (See the references in footnote 8 for detailed discussions of how license programs have introduced these problems.)

In summary, limited entry approaches differ from total quotas, closed seasons and areas, and gear restrictions. They have the potential to minimize the costs of harvesting the desired catch. This is especially true of taxes and individual quotas. There are other differences among them, however, including ease of implementation, political acceptability, and the distribution of costs and benefits among fishermen and general consumers. In actual fisheries management in the United States, it is usually the latter that determine which type of regulation is selected.

It is hard to explain exactly why the pattern of regulation has developed as it has. However, the explanation may be that the individuals responsible for the original programs were primarily biologists or industry representatives with no training in fisheries economics. They viewed the problem as one of reducing catch, with no consideration for economic efficiency. In addition, in the realm of international management, the only types of control that could be agreed upon were those which were viewed as helping the stocks without favoring any one nation. Total quotas, closed seasons and areas, and gear restrictions were fairly easy to implement and yet appeared to accomplish these objectives.

Once the pattern was set, it was hard to break, even after jurisdiction was extended. Fisheries administrators were not easily convinced that economic efficiency was important and therefore there was no real incentive to look at other types of regulation. Employment, nondiscriminatory access to the stocks, the way of life in fishing communities, as well as concern with biological aspects of conservation, were deemed more important.

Furthermore, many fishermen and fisheries administrators feel that fisheries are the last frontier and that fishing should be an inalienable right. They therefore opposed individual quotas and limited licenses. Hard to believe as it may seem, private property rights in fisheries were viewed as socialistic even though they are an integral part of the market system! In addition, individual quotas and licenses were opposed because no one relished the possibility that they personally would be precluded from free entry to the fishery. Similarly, taxes were not popular for obvious reasons.

Because of industry opposition and a lack of support for efficiency as a primary objective of management, limited entry programs have not been widely implemented. Licenses have been tried in several instances, but the programs usually amount to prevention of further entry into an already overcapitalized fleet, with little effective effort to reduce fleet size. The fact that license programs are closer to normal practice than taxes or individual quotas may explain why they have been adopted. Unfortunately, however, because license programs are similar to gear restriction programs when inputs can be easily substituted for one another, the former are generally less effective in obtaining efficiency than taxes or individual quotas.

FISHERIES MANAGEMENT IN THE UNITED STATES: LAWS AND INSTITUTIONS

The main pillar upon which U.S. fisheries management is built is the Fisheries Conservation and Management Act of 1976. With this act, the United States reversed its earlier position and claimed management and conservation rights over the living resources in the area between 3 and 200 miles from its shore.[10] The United States previously opposed similar laws passed in Central and South America, which extended national jurisdiction over fish ştocks beyond 12 miles, but came to accept this principle when U.S. coastal stocks were heavily fished by foreign boats.

Previous to the FCMA, fishing in the area beyond 12 miles was regulated by a number of international fisheries organizations, with individual countries applying restrictions to their own fishermen in the event of overfishing. While these organizations had the authority to inspect all boats fishing in their areas for suspected violations, they had little real power because they were without enforcement capability.

The FCMA has been praised in the United States both for its claim to the living wealth off our shores and for creating an authority with the potential to manage this valuable resource.[11] It should be remembered, however, that the key word is potential. Because of the difficulties of managing a marine fishery and the unresolved conflicts over the proper objectives of management, effective management was not achieved when states had sole control over inshore fisheries, and it is doubtful whether it has been fully achieved in the fisheries zones created by the FCMA.

According to the act, the first national standard for fishery conservation and management is:[12]

> Conservation and management measures shall prevent overfishing while achieving, on a continuing basis, the optimum yield. . . . The

[10] Highly migratory species such as tuna were exempted and for anadromous species such as salmon, the right to manage was claimed for as far as they range. The area from shore to 3 miles was already subject to U.S. rule although fisheries management authority was vested in the various states.

[11] See Ross D. Eckert, *The Enclosure of Ocean Resources* (Stanford, Calif., Hoover Institution Press, 1979).

[12] See Fisheries and Conservation Act of 1976, Public Law 94–265 (as amended by Public Law, 95–354 and 96–61) Title III, section 301 (a) and section 3(18).

term "optimum" with respect to the yield from any fishery means the amount of fish—(A) which will provide the greatest overall benefit to the nation with particular reference to food production and recreational opportunities and (B) which is prescribed as such on the basis of maximum sustainable yield from such fishery as modified by any relevant economic, social, or ecological factor.

Conservation and management measures shall, where practicable, promote efficiency in the utilization of fishery resources except that no such measure shall have economic allocation as its sole purpose.

Conservation and management measures shall, where practicable, minimize costs and avoid unnecessary duplications.

To the extent practical . . . interrelated stocks of fish shall be managed as a unit or in close coordination.

The first two of these national standards appears to establish economic efficiency as an important objective of fisheries management in the United States. However, the phrase "where practicable" certainly has the potential of weakening this objective, depending upon its interpretation. The third directive is in recognition of the difficulties of managing individual species.

As the law was first written, the difference between "optimal yield" and the expected domestic annual harvest of each species or group of species was to be made available by the State Department to foreign nations who had traditionally harvested that species and who met certain other requirements. However, these foreign boats were required to pay certain vessel fees and "poundage" taxes on their allowable catch. There have been subsequent changes in the law that require domestic processing capacity to be utilized before turning to foreign processors (regardless of the relative costs of the two) and provisions have also been made for eventually phasing out foreign fishing when there are specified increases in domestic capacity.

The most important operational elements of the FCMA are the regional fisheries management councils, whose task it is to prepare plans determining how much of each species will be harvested, and how this will be done. The eight councils and the species under their control are described in table 5–6. Each has the responsibility of managing the species within its geographical area, but where species are important in two or more areas, they are jointly managed by the respective councils, although one may be designated as the lead council. While they are important, the councils are only one part of a complex system through which fisheries management policy in the United States is determined. The schematic diagram in figure 5–3 is useful in describing the councils and the rest of the system.

TABLE 5–6. Regional Fisheries Councils

Council	States	Species
New England	Maine, New Hampshire, Massachusetts, Rhode Island, and Connecticut	Atlantic groundfish, Atlantic herring, sharks, sea scallops, swordfish, redfish, billfish, hake, pollock, red crabs, and American lobster.
Mid-Atlantic	New York, New Jersey, Pennsylvania, Delaware, Maryland, and Virginia	Surf clam and ocean quahog, Atlantic mackerel, butterfish, squid, sharks, bluefish, swordfish, scup, dogfish, billfish, other flounder, sea bass, tile fish, sea scallops.
South Atlantic	North Carolina, South Carolina, Georgia, and Florida	Billfish, coastal migratory pelagics, sharks, swordfish, corals, spiny lobster, tropical reef fish, calico scallops, sea scallops, shrimp, and coastal herring.
Caribbean	Virgin Islands, and Puerto Rico	Spiny lobster, shallow water reef fish, swordfish, migratory pelagics, mollusks, billfish, corals, deep water reef fish, bait fishes, sharks, and rays.
Gulf	Texas, Louisiana, Mississippi, Alabama, and Florida	Groundfish, calico scallops, shrimp, coastal migratory pelagics, reef fish, corals, squids, spiny lobster, sharks, stone crab, sponges, billfish, coastal herring, swordfish, and tropical reef fish.
Pacific	California, Oregon, Washington, and Idaho	Salmon, anchovy, groundfish, pink shrimp, billfish, herring.
North Pacific	Alaska, Washington, and Oregon	Tanner crab, Gulf of Alaska groundfish, king crab, high sea salmon, scallops, Bering Sea groundfish, Bering Sea clam, Bering Sea herring, Bering Sea shrimp, corals, dungeness crab, shrimp, and snails.
Western Pacific	Hawaii, American Samoa, and Guam	Billfish, bottomfish, precious corals, seamount resources, and spiny lobster.

According to the law, basic responsibility for preparing management plans is vested in the councils. Half of the council members are the secretaries for natural resources (or the equivalent) in the states in the particular region, along with the regional director of the National Marine Fisheries Service of the Department of Commerce. The other half are "interested and knowledgeable members of the public" who are nominated by the governors of each member state and selected by the secretary of commerce. In addition, individuals from the U.S. Coast Guard and the Department of State are nonvoting members of the councils.

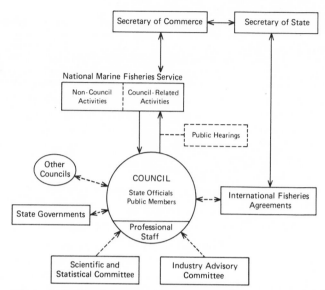

Figure 5–3. The fisheries management system in the United States centers around the individual management councils, but their activities are related to the other councils, state governments, National Marine Fisheries Service, and the departments of Commerce and State.

Since the number of states in each region is not equal, council membership varies between eight and sixteen people.

The makeup of the councils is obviously quite important in determining what kinds of plans are developed. It is, therefore, interesting that the public members have predominantly been representatives of harvestors, processors, distributors, or some other aspect of the fishing industry.[13] Individuals who might represent other or more general interests—consumer advocates, professional biologists, economists, or planners, for example—have been notable by their absence.

The main work of the councils is done by a full-time professional staff consisting of an executive director and others with training in biology, law, planning, and economics. The councils usually meet once a month for two or three days, under the direction of a chairperson elected from their midst, to review and approve the work done by the staff, to discuss future activities, and to vote on policy issues.

---

[13] For more on this, see G. Pontecorvo, "Fisheries Management and the General Welfare: Implications for the New Structure," *Washington Law Review* vol. 52, no. 3 (July 1977) pp. 641–656.

Although each council has the same organizational structure, they often differ widely in the way they operate. For example, some councils issue contracts to consulting firms or universities to write the plans. Others set up special task forces consisting of council members, scientific and statistical committee members, industry representatives, and NMFS and council staff people to write the plan. In some councils the staff has primary responsibility for writing plans. Finally, some councils actually write important sections of their plans during regular council meetings. The result is that the plans prepared by the councils have sometimes been quite different.

However it is developed, each fishery management plan must be discussed in open public hearings and must be published in the *Federal Register*. The council must respond in writing to any written comments that result, and often does so in an appendix to the final plan. It should come as no surprise that these comments come almost exclusively from representatives of the industry. Industry people have more to gain from the costs of preparing such formal comments, since a specific proposal could significantly affect their profits. By contrast, isolated individuals may gain very little from advocating economic efficiency even though the gains to the whole economy are quite large.

Although there is no room for a discussion of their respective roles, the involvement of other actors in the formulation of management plans is clear from figure 5–3. The most important of these are the commerce department's National Marine Fisheries Service (NMFS), which must ultimately approve, implement, and (with the Coast Guard) enforce all plans; state governments and international agencies, which have jurisdiction over species within three and beyond 200 miles from shore, respectively; and the scientific and industry advisory committees. It should be obvious that this system is very complex, and, as will be seen below, has implications for the type of policies that are actually produced.

HOW THE SYSTEM WORKS AND WHAT IT PRODUCES

Workings

Each council has the responsibility of preparing annual or biennial plans for the species under its control, although the possibility of establishing permanent plans based on biological and economic variables has been discussed. Even though the councils have been in operation about five years, none have completed plans for all the species under their jurisdictions. The workload of the councils is substantial and all are revising their existing plans and developing others.

On the surface, most councils use the following procedure for developing fishery management plans.[14] First, the objectives for management are determined. Within the constraints set, the councils can choose any objective they feel appropriate for the fishery involved and the particular problems it faces. The real problem is specifying objectives that have operational significance (a goal to "improve the fishery" is not of much use in choosing among specific management techniques). In the event that there are conflicting objectives, the council must place relative weights on them so that appropriate tradeoffs can be made.

The next step is to identify a set of alternative plans which will specify optimal yield and identify how harvest will be limited to that level. Finally, the plan which most nearly achieves the stated objectives is selected. If the objectives are reasonable, if the range of alternatives considered is broad and imaginative, and if the analysis used to compare the alternative plans and the objectives is correctly done, a suitable management plan will result.

In reality, of course, the system does not operate this straightforwardly. One sometimes gets the feeling that a particular plan is chosen in advance and that the desired yield, objectives, and other components are then selected to ensure that the favored alternative emerges victorious. This is especially true when the pursuit of one objective—say efficiency—might impose job losses or other distributional problems on certain parts of the fleet. With respect to the tradeoff between economic efficiency and distributional issues, the latter implicitly appear to be more important, as one would expect given the influence of industry representatives in the planning process. In fact, one council made the conscious decision that economic efficiency was to be of no concern in the development of plans.[15]

---

[14] NMFS has issued operational guidelines; in addition, several studies on how to develop proper plans in a manner that is consistent with the law have been done under the auspices of NMFS and the various councils. For example, see *Guidelines for Fishery Management Plans* (Washington, D.C., National Marine Fisheries Service, 1981); Lee G. Anderson, ed., *Economic Analysis for Fisheries Management Plans* (Ann Arbor, Mich., Ann Arbor Science Publishers, 1981); R.C. Hennemuth et al., Overview Document, Phase I: *Northeast Fishery Management Task Force* (Woods Hole, Mass., National Marine Fisheries Service, 1980); and M.K. Orbach, ed., *Report of National Workshop on the Concept of Optimum Yield in Fisheries Management* (Washington, D.C., U.S. Department of Commerce, 1977).

[15] On two separate occasions the Mid-Atlantic Council voted down resolutions from its scientific and statistical committee to the effect that, all else being equal, regulations should not make the cost of producing fish higher than necessary. See minutes of the Mid-Atlantic Council, July 1980, and September 1980, pp. 3–5.

Another reason why the above procedure is not followed as rigorously as need be is the bureaucratic motivation of the main agencies in the management system. For instance, one reason for rejecting an economic efficiency objective is that according to the FCMA and NMFS procedures, a main criterion for plan approval is how well the selected management policy achieves the stated objectives. Therefore why include an efficiency objective when it can be difficult to judge different options against it? The business of the council is to produce plans and thus they are loath to do something that will make their job more difficult.

Also, since it is industry that is most likely to protest, there is a tendency for the plans to be written so as to minimize potential complaints, lawsuits, and other procedures that can make the work of the councils more burdensome and increase the probability of a negative review from NMFS. Therefore, economic efficiency and other important management issues which are of little concern to those likely to complain may not receive appropriate consideration.

On the other hand, NMFS has taken the position that as long as the plans meet the stated objectives and unless they blatantly violate one of the national standards, the plan will be approved. It is unlikely that a plan will be disapproved on grounds of inadequate objectives. NMFS too is in the business of producing plans and they do not want to stand in the way of implementation, especially over issues concerning income distribution or other politically sensitive topics. This is an important point. Secretarial approval of plans does provide the opportunity for consistency and also can ensure that purely regional interests do not prevail in fisheries policy. If, in fact, the review system is lax in this regard, some of the potential benefits of the FCMA will be lost.

While NMFS has been reluctant to refuse approval because of inadequate consideration of efficiency, they frequently do disapprove plans because of procedural issues.[16] This has created animosity between the councils and NMFS, with the former sometimes accusing the latter of trying to regain some of the preeminence they lost with the passage of the FCMA. NMFS counters such arguments by emphasizing that rejections on procedural grounds are appropriate because they will prevent potential lawsuits. This ill will can certainly affect the smooth operation of the system. In addition, these rejections have caused the councils to be even more concerned with the necessity of preparing plans that will

[16] See A.D. Chandler, "Bureaucratic Red Tape Stifles FCMA's Effectiveness," *National Fisherman*, vol. 61, no. 11 (March 1981) p. 28; and B. Morehead, "South Atlantic Fishery Plans Stifled by Foot-Dragging Bureaucrats," *National Fisherman*, vol. 62, no. 4 (August 1981) p. 34.

be approved and hence they are less willing to look at economic efficiency matters.

To summarize, the organization of the U.S. fisheries management system (including the conflicts between the principal actors), as well as the ambitious goals it sets for itself, makes it unlikely that all goals will be realized.

Results

It is impossible to review and evaluate here each of the plans produced by the various councils. However, a brief discussion of two management plans may give a feeling for the types of regulations that are produced by the system which the FCMA created.

The Atlantic surf clam is found in the inshore shallow waters from Long Island to Cape Hatteras (N.C.). Prior to the FCMA, the usual pattern of exploitation was to locate a productive area and to harvest it until it was no longer profitable to do so or until a more productive area was found. The main fishing activity moved back and forth between New Jersey and Virginia. Although the states had some control over the harvesting of surf clams in their areas, there was effectively no real limit on harvest. The main objectives of the Surf Clam and Ocean Quahog management plan developed under FCMA were to rebuild the depleted surf clam stock with a minimum of economic disruption to the industry, and at the same time to allow for the orderly development of the fishery for quahogs, an offshore species that had not been heavily fished up to that time.[17]

Because the capacity of the fleet was at that time several times larger than the allowable harvest, a moratorium on new entry was instituted. Annual and quarterly quotas on total catch were specified to smooth harvest throughout the year. Also, the days per week and the hours per day that could be fished were controlled and fishing was restricted in areas where young clams were predominant.

There are several interesting things about the way the fishery operated in the following years. Initially the boats were allowed to operate four days per week but when it became obvious that the quarterly quota would be obtained very early in the period, the number of allowable

---

[17] See Mid-Atlantic Fisheries Management Council, "Final Environmental Impact Statement/Fisheries Management Plan for Surf Clams and Ocean Quahogs," (Dover, Delaware, October 1977); and Ivar E. Strand, Jr., James E. Kirkley, and Kenneth E. McConnell, "Economic Analysis of the Management of Atlantic Surf Clams," in Lee G. Anderson, ed., *Economic Analysis for Fisheries Management Plans* (Ann Arbor, Mich., Ann Arbor Science Publishers, 1981).

days fished was reduced until each boat could only fish one specified 24-hour period per week. This was clearly not the most inexpensive way to harvest the allowable catch since it required a large fleet to stand idle six days a week. The moratorium on new entry was a step in the right direction, but efficient management also required a reduction in fleet size. Instead, the council spread the allowable catch over the existing fleet because that was more palatable to the industry.

In the current plan, vessels that do not make an annual minimum catch will lose their license. This may result in a numerically smaller fleet, but because the boats removed are likely to be the smallest, the effective size of the fleet will probably not be significantly reduced.

The limitations on allowable fishing effort created some problems, however. If bad weather or mechanical problems prevented a boat from going out on its designated day, fishing for that week was not possible. As complaints grew louder, the plan was modified to allow for a "fallback" fishing day under certain circumstances. This demonstrates that the plan was flexible enough to accommodate change, although, to be taken seriously, the pressure for such change generally had to come from the regulated parties. For example, the inefficiency of the redundant vessels was not opposed by the industry for reasons discussed above, and there has been no move to correct for it.

Given the conceptual appeal of individual quotas, it is interesting to note that the Mid-Atlantic Council considered such a method for managing surf clams and quahogs. It became apparent, however, that a lack of data on catch in previous years would make it very difficult to apportion the prospective individual quotas on historical catches. If such a system were implemented, it was determined that catches for the next year would have to be used as the standard of comparison. Therefore all fishermen would be motivated to increase their catch for the next year. Vessels that previously only used one dredge would double their capacity by adding another. Thus, an already oversized fleet might become even larger. This is a good example of the perverse incentives which well-intentioned policy can sometimes create. Although the individual quotas were never instituted (mainly because a specific program which was acceptable to the industry could not be found), their mere consideration may have doubled the size of the fleet. Such effects must be taken into account in policy design, and more is said about this later.

Consider next the management plan for cod, haddock, and yellowtail flounder prepared by the New England Council. These three species are among the most important of the fifteen or so which comprise the New England groundfishery. It is believed that there are two fairly distinct stocks of yellowtail and cod, but only one stock of haddock.

The two stocks of yellowtail are thought to be located east and west of 69° west longitude, while the two stocks of cod are found in the Gulf of Maine and on Georges Bank respectively.

The fleet that harvests these three species comes mostly from New England and it also harvests other species during certain parts of the year. Because of the biological relationships between these species, as well as certain economic phenomena, this particular fishery is perhaps one of the most difficult and challenging to manage.

The plan for cod, haddock, and yellowtail was initiated in 1977 and established a total quota for each of the stocks of fish. Fishing licenses were required, but they were easily available and there was no moratorium on entry as there was in the surf clam and ocean quahog fishery. It was soon discovered that with the existing fleet and the many new entrants, the annual quota would be harvested very early in the year. This infuriated fishermen. In the following year the quota was caught early in the year but because absolute closure of the fishery would cause hardships for the industry, the council adopted a policy which effectively turned back the clock and started the fishing year and quota over again. While this may have protected employment in the short run, if continually repeated it would have serious consequences on the long-run productivity of the fishery.

Eventually the quarterly quotas were further subdivided by vessel size, and other stipulations were introduced which limited catch per boat trip. These limits were particularly wasteful of resources since boats had to return to port before they would normally have done so and hence wasted fuel and other resources. These allocation methods were not enough to subdue the loud voices heard at most council meetings concerning the perceived inequities of the plan. Larger, newer boats needed substantial catches in order to pay their mortgages; smaller boats felt unable to get a fair share of the total quota since they could not fish in stormy weather. The quarterly quota allocation by vessel size did not solve either of these problems since, if the smaller boats and fixed gear vessels did not harvest their allocation, it was given to the larger boat categories rather than reserved for the following quarter. Trip limits based on the number of crew members were then instituted, presumably to allow the larger boats to catch more. The effect of doing so was predictable. Many boats increased the size of their crews in order to increase their allowable catch.

The system deteriorated still further. Toward the end of a quarter, it was possible for small boats to be forbidden to fish for yellowtail flounder west of the 69° meridian because their share of that quarterly quota was used up, but permitted to harvest them east of that line. At the same time, medium boats might be forbidden to fish for flounder on either side of the line while big boats could fish anywhere for flounder. The rules for cod and haddock, which are caught in the same nets, could be different. Vessels were subject to different rules if they fished in state waters before or after fishing beyond the 3-mile line. Since it was impossible to tell where a fish was caught, enforcement was all but impossible. Finally, complaints led to changes in both total quotas and the rules to enforce them. Neither fisherman nor regulator knew what was going on.

It is small wonder that the council is now considering an interim plan with no controls at all aside from limits on the mesh in nets and the establishment of protected areas for small fish. Such a plan may have some weaknesses but it will no doubt be easier to operate. To be fair to the New England Council, it must be remembered that for reasons already mentioned, the Atlantic groundfishery is very difficult to understand and manage. Further, the council has never been pleased with the original management plan and it has endeavored to improve it.

Nevertheless, at least through its first few years, the fishery management system created by the FCMA has not produced adequate policy. At the very least, many of the specific regulations adopted by the regional councils have had an adverse effect on economic efficiency. Some lapses in policy may have even threatened fish stocks. However, one cannot judge all councils and all fisheries management plans on the basis of those discussed above. Some, such as the northern anchovy management plan prepared by the Pacific Council,[18] contain excellent economic analysis. In addition, the Pacific Council is currently considering individual quotas as an adjunct to an existing state-imposed moratorium on entry in the Pacific salmon fishery. Clearly, management plans can and do vary among councils and in some instances they come closer to achieving the full potential for proper management provided by the FCMA. There is, nevertheless, reason to be concerned about the system's ability to achieve its full potential.

CURRENT HEALTH OF FISHERIES AND ENVIRONMENTAL THREATS

The preceding sections have reviewed the principles behind efficient fisheries regulation and the extent to which actual policy, as expressed

[18] See D.D. Huppert, "Economic Analysis for Northern Anchovy Management," in Lee G. Anderson, ed., *Economic Analysis for Fisheries Management Plans* (Ann Arbor, Mich., Ann Arbor Science Publishers, 1981).

through FCMA, embodies these principles. Before concluding, it seems prudent to very briefly review the overall health of U.S. marine fisheries and identify factors other than fishing effort that might affect these important resources.

While increases in all fish stocks will always be welcomed, and while some stocks are lower than appropriate for maximum economic yield, very few species appear in danger of severe biological depletion. There are exceptions, however. The herring stocks off Georges Bank in the North Atlantic are so depleted that there has been virtually no commercial catch since 1977. Whether this is due to overfishing or prolonged recruitment failure[19] unrelated to fishing is not clear, although chances appear good that stocks will recover. Pacific salmon stocks have also declined over the past decade. This is probably due not only to overfishing but also to hydroelectric facilities, which impede spawning, as well as poor grazing, logging, and mining practices, which can also affect breeding habitat. There is still a very active commercial and recreational salmon fishery, however.

With respect to these currently reduced stocks, it is important to remember that at any point a number of stocks would be expected to be below their average size while others will be above it, and that these relative positions can and do change. For example, in 1975 there was considerable concern over the Atlantic haddock stocks and yet they are now apparently healthy again. Bearing these points in mind, from a broad perspective the biological health of U.S. fish stocks is good, although there is certainly room for improvement.

To this point in the discussion, overfishing has been treated as the only human threat to marine fisheries. While that is indeed the preeminent threat, it is true that other human activities, such as offshore energy exploration and extraction, ocean shipping, waste disposal, and hydroelectric power generation can all affect fish stocks. Perhaps the most notable of these potential threats is the oil drilling that is beginning to take place in the Georges Bank area off the southeast coasts of Rhode Island and Massachusetts. Environmentalists and fishermen object strenuously to the Department of Interior's decision to lease offshore tracts in this area, claiming not only that potential spills and toxic drilling brines may damage stocks, but also that drilling platforms may snag fishing nets and otherwise impede harvesting. These risks are too great, the critics argue, to justify the development of petroleum reserves in the midst of a highly productive commercial fishery.

---

[19] That is, there would be a drop in the total weight of fish entering the catchable population during a given period.

On the other hand, it is hard to deny the attractiveness of potentially new offshore domestic petroleum and natural gas reserves, reserves which the Interior Department estimates may be worth $1.5 trillion.[20] Moreover, the risks associated with petroleum exploration and other human activity are not well understood. Thus, valuable opportunities may be forgone to avoid risks that many believe are trivial; but just possibly, a very small addition to the nation's oil and gas reserves may be proven and developed at the cost of substantial fishery disruption. For present purposes, it is only possible to identify such conflicts and express confidence that they will continue to arise wherever human activity has the potential to significantly affect marine fisheries.

CONCLUSIONS AND RECOMMENDATIONS

Although marine fisheries do not make a major contribution to the gross national product, they are vital to an industry upon which many individuals and several geographical regions depend. If unregulated, this fishing industry might expand to a point which is at the very least uneconomic, and which might even threaten the long-term commercial viability of certain fish stocks.

The United States passed what is now called the Magnuson Fisheries Conservation and Management Act in 1976 so as to better manage an important natural resource. Previous to this law, offshore fisheries were regulated by international agencies. Under this management structure, regulation was motivated by purely biological goals and by the need to achieve international agreement. As a result, the particular controls used resulted in further diseconomies. Regulations have tended to encourage fleets which have more equipment than is necessary to economically harvest the species they are after. In a world where resources were plentiful and economic growth was steady and substantial, such inefficiencies could be overlooked. This hardly characterizes the United States today; hence the importance of considering the efficiency effects of regulation.

There are methods which appear capable of improving the efficiency with which marine fisheries are regulated. Referred to as limited entry approaches, they include license programs, taxes per unit of catch, and the allocation of individual catch quotas.

The fisheries management system which has been instituted as a result of the FCMA and its amendments is a relatively loose one, subject to

[20] *New York Times,* Nov. 25, 1981, p. A1.

pressure from many sides and within, but having only very general operational guidelines. The types of regulations that result depend, in part, upon the types of pressures exerted as management plans progress through the system. At present there is a tendency for industry views to dominate. There certainly has been a limited willingness to directly confront the issues of economic efficiency and implement effective regulations.[21] Controlling entry by taxation is obviously not very popular with the industry. The individual quota system and, to a certain extent limited licensing, would involve a new conception of the right to fish which many fishermen and fishery administrators find objectionable. In addition, fishermen are unsure whether they will be among those allocated a quota.

Thus, while the FCMA carries with it the potential for efficient management, even partial fulfillment of this potential has yet to be realized. This is partly the result of the system by which the management plans are produced. It does afford the possibility for different groups to make their views known and their influence felt, but as the system is set up, industry views predominate. Although they cannot run the system, they have the power to prevent implementation of regulations to which they object. To a large degree this is why limited entry type regimes have not been implemented.

The situation might improve if consumer interests were given as much weight as those of the fishing industry. As it now stands, employment and distributional effects may very likely be given too much weight in the formulation of plans. While these considerations must obviously be an important part of any management plan, they should be balanced against the other important objectives of public policy, including efficiency. As has been pointed out, efficiency can only be achieved if the optimal catch is obtained at a minimum cost, including the costs of regulation. FCMA is in its youth, however, and it should be possible to accommodate these and other changes as the act and its implementation mature.

---

[21] In fact, one member of the New England Fisheries Management Council went so far as to say, "No one who's involved in this fisheries regulation thinks that economic efficiency is what you're after. What you're after is a continuation of a way of life." See Michael Blumstein, "Fishing: A Bitter Harvest," *New York Times*, September 4, 1982, p. 27.

6

The Global Climate

John W. Firor and Paul R. Portney

Although it is not frequently discussed as a natural resource, climate shares many characteristics with agricultural lands, fresh water supplies, parks and wilderness areas, forests and fisheries, and other important natural resources.[1] Like agricultural land and fresh water, climate can be thought of as a factor of production—for example, each crop has a range of temperature and rainfall outside of which it does not prosper. Like parks and wilderness areas, climate can enhance the attractiveness of a region—some people trade away a range of job opportunities to live in places they consider to have pleasant climates. Like forests and fisheries, climate is a renewable resource, one which, if properly "managed," can provide benefits for the indefinite future.

Climate today also shares another characteristic with more conventional natural resources—it can be affected by human activity.[2] Just as

---

[1] Climate at a locality is usually defined as the long-term average (by convention, the thirty-year average) of physical properties that describe the weather—temperature, atmospheric pressure, rainfall, winds—and their variation from month to month and year to year. Note that with this definition, an unusually cold or dry year at a particular place is not a "climate change," but an example of "climate variability." In this chapter, however, "climate change" is used simply to mean any change in an average measure of these properties that takes place over a year or longer.

[2] See, for example, Geophysics Research Board, *Energy and Climate* (Washington, D.C., National Academy of Sciences, 1977).

agricultural land can be degraded by cropping customs which lead to erosion, climate can be affected by man. Stratospheric pollution modifies the ultraviolet absorptive capacity of the atmosphere and rainfall patterns are changed by irrigation and deforestation.

It may only be in its variability that climate seems different from other natural resources. The amount of metal in an unmined ore deposit does not change with time, and soil types or even forest areas change only very slowly, but climate changes in both time and space and affects human activities in a variety of ways. This variability, coupled with the global nature of climate and the long time spans over which climate changes and their effects occur, makes the policy issues which arise difficult to understand and describe and difficult to resolve.

CLIMATE AND HUMAN ACTIVITY

This chapter concentrates on two important ways in which human activity can affect climate. The first, and better known, of these is the effect of increasing concentrations of carbon dioxide (CO_2) and other gases on the average temperature of the world. The second is the effect of complex, manmade chemicals called chlorofluorocarbons (or CFCs) on the amount of damaging ultraviolet radiation that reaches the earth from the sun.

These two cases are selected as important examples, but a wide variety of other human activities can also affect local, regional, or global climate. Some of these impacts are quite direct, as in cities where the release of heat keeps the air warmer than in the surrounding countryside. Some are indirect as, for example, when particulate pollution supplies the nuclei for ice formation in clouds, thus influencing precipitation.

Normal agricultural activity can also affect climate in several ways. When forested areas are converted to fields, the reflectivity of the earth's surface is increased, thus exerting a cooling effect, but also decreasing humidity. The widespread application of fertilizers may change climate by introducing into the atmosphere oxides of nitrogen, which affect radiation balances.

Urban areas can also significantly influence local or perhaps even regional climates through a combination of heat release and pollution. Such a situation occurs in Indiana, where the growth of the Chicago–Gary metropolitan area and its industrial activity increased rainfall in

LaPorte.[3] Similar changes in rainfall have been observed in the Houston metropolitan area, although they are attributed as much to changes in wind flow as a result of the construction of tall buildings as to the release of gases, aerosols, or heat from the urbanized area.[4] However, such changes are limited and do not affect climate on a global scale.

Finally, in addition to all these inadvertent effects, throughout the ages people have attempted deliberately to influence climate to their advantage. There is little empirical evidence to support the efficacy of prayers, rain dances, or even cloud seeding to increase rainfall, but wind breaks, houses, furnaces, and air conditioners are effective in modifying the climate of at least a small portion of the atmosphere.

One point, touched on earlier, should be emphasized before turning to the effects of carbon dioxide and chlorofluorocarbons on global climate. It is essential to understand that all human activities affecting climate take place against a background of natural climate fluctuations which can occur from year to year, century to century, or over hundreds of thousands of years. For instance, during the so-called Altithermal or (Hypsithermal) Period, between 4,000 and 8,000 years ago, the average surface temperature of the earth was apparently about 2° C to 4° C warmer than it is now. More recently, the average temperature of the Northern Hemisphere increased about 0.6° C between 1890 and 1940, cooled about 0.3° C between 1940 and 1970, and increased again by 0.1° C between 1970 and 1980. The global mean temperature appears to have followed a similar pattern (see figure 6–1).[5]

This observation about the natural or background variation in climate is important for two reasons. First, by examining what is known about human and other living things in earlier, climatologically different periods, it may be possible to infer some of the changes that would accompany climatic regimes altered by human activity. Such an exercise may also suggest ways to adapt to the changes. Second, this natural variation may for a time—perhaps a considerable time—mask or hide any variation in climate caused by CO_2, CFCs, or other substances created by human activities. This inability to distinguish new perturbations from background fluctuations is extremely important—it makes policy issues more difficult to describe, much less easy to resolve, and

[3] Stanley A. Changnon, Jr., "More on the La Porte Anomaly: A Review" *Bulletin of the American Meteorological Society* (July 1980) pp. 702–722.

[4] Joseph L. Goldman, "Urbanization and Climate Change," in Terry A. Ferrar, ed., *The Urban Costs of Climate Modification* (New York, Wiley, 1976) p. 63.

[5] J.W. Hansen, D. Johnson, A. Lacis, S. Lebedeff, P. Lee, D. Rind, and G. Russell, "Climate Impact of Increasing Atmospheric Carbon Dioxide" *Science* vol. 213, no. 4511 (August 28, 1981) pp. 957–966.

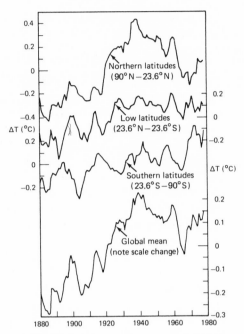

Figure 6–1. Observed surface air temperature trends for three latitude bands and the entire globe. (From J. W. Hansen, "Climate Impact of Increasing Atmospheric Carbon Dioxide," *Science* vol. 213, no. 4511 (August 28, 1981) p. 961. Copyright © 1981, American Association for the Advancement of Science.)

places a very high premium on credible scientific insight into future changes in the atmosphere.

Carbon Dioxide and the "Greenhouse" Effect

Eighty years have passed since the first predictions of global warming and other climate changes caused by increasing concentrations of CO_2. It is only within the past twenty years, however, that the scientific community has begun to take this potential problem seriously.[6] The policy implications of carbon dioxide-induced warming are an even newer subject of inquiry.[7] In 1981, in fact, the "CO_2 problem"—as it is coming

[6] See, for example, Geophysics Research Board, *Energy and Climate.*
[7] William W. Kellogg and Robert Schware, *Climate Change and Society: Consequences of Increasing Atmospheric Carbon Dioxide* (Boulder, Col., Westview, 1981).

to be known—was for the first time the subject of an extensive government report.[8] The possibility of global warming is now attracting increasing attention.

While the CO_2 problem is extremely complicated, it can be described in a reasonably simple way. Carbon dioxide is one of a number of gases which occur naturally in the earth's atmosphere (it constitutes 0.034 percent of the atmosphere). As its atmospheric concentration increases, which it appears to have done, it is believed that the temperature of the earth's surface will increase. This is because while carbon dioxide permits much of the incoming solar radiation (visible light) to reach the earth, it traps outgoing terrestrial (or infrared) radiation, slowing down the cooling of the earth's surface. The temperature increases that are expected to result will vary about the earth, some regions warming much more than the average, some perhaps cooling. The global distribution of the warming is quite uncertain except that it is likely that the polar regions will warm more than the equator—by as much as two or three times. This reduced temperature differential between equator and poles will in turn affect wind direction and velocity, and hence precipitation and cloud cover.

What has happened to atmospheric concentrations of CO_2 and other infrared-absorbing gases so far and what have these gases to do with human activity? Although there are no reliable observations, atmospheric concentrations of carbon dioxide about 100 years ago, at about the start of the industrial revolution, are estimated to have been on the order of 270 to 290 parts per million (ppm). By 1958, when fairly detailed records began to be kept at a number of locations, including the observatory at Mauna Loa, Hawaii, this concentration had risen about 12 percent, to approximately 314 ppm. By 1980, the readings at Mauna Loa averaged 338 ppm, about 8 percent higher than the 1958 readings and more than 20 percent above the hypothesized concentration in 1880 (see figure 6–2). Readings from other stations during the period 1958 to 1976 confirm the increase in atmospheric concentrations of CO_2 found at Mauna Loa (see figure 6–3).

This increase in the atmospheric concentrations of CO_2 may be due to a number of factors, but there is fairly broad consensus that its primary cause is the combustion of fossil fuels. When coal, oil, and natural gas are burned, they give off trapped carbon in the form of carbon dioxide, which is released to the atmosphere. In 1980, for example, some 20 billion (20^9) metric tons of carbon dioxide were placed in the atmosphere by this process worldwide.

[8] Council on Environmental Quality, *Global Energy Futures and the Carbon Dioxide Problem* (Washington, D.C., U.S. Government Printing Office, 1981).

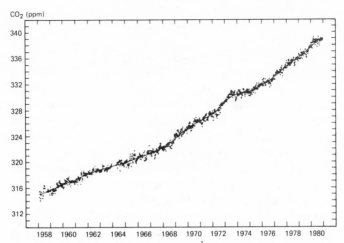

Figure 6–2. Monthly averages of atmospheric CO_2 concentrations at Mauna Loa, Hawaii, with average seasonal effect removed. (Reproduced from Council on Environmental Quality, *Global Energy Futures and the Carbon Dioxide Problem*, Washington, D.C., Government Printing Office, 1981. Original data from R. B. Bacastow, C. D. Keeling, and T. P. Whorf, "Seasonal Amplitude in Atmospheric CO_2 Concentrations at Mauna Loa, Hawaii, 1959–1980," paper presented at World Meteorological Organization conference on analysis and interpretation of atmospheric CO_2 data, Bern, Switzerland, 1981.)

Coal, which is nearly pure carbon, is almost completely converted to carbon dioxide when it is burned; oil and gas contain hydrogen in addition to carbon, hence both carbon dioxide and water are released when they are burned. For the same amount of heat produced, oil and gas produce less carbon dioxide than does coal, since some of the energy released from oil and gas comes from the reaction of hydrogen with air. The synthetic fuels, on the other hand, require extensive processing and as a result produce even more CO_2 for a fixed heat output than does coal. Natural gas is the lowest CO_2 producer (25 percent less than fuel oil), while synthetic gas from coal produces 80 percent more than fuel oil.

Not all the CO_2 placed in the atmosphere by human activity remains there. Over the past few decades, accurate values are available for both the amount (and type) of fossil fuel used and the amount of CO_2 in the atmosphere. The comparison indicates that about half of the CO_2 produced by the burning of fossil fuels is retained in the atmosphere, the rest being taken up by the oceans and perhaps by other processes. Table 6–1 summarizes the CO_2 released during energy generation in 1980, the

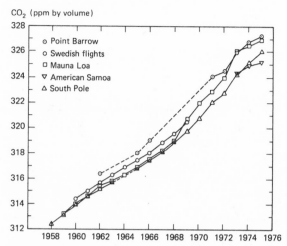

Figure 6–3. Long-term rise in atmospheric carbon dioxide content as indicated by various collection points. (From William W. Kellogg and Robert Schware, *Climate Change and Society: Consequences of Increasing Atmospheric Carbon Dioxide,* Boulder, Colo., Westview, 1981, p. 36.)

amount added to the air, and also indicates the potential future CO_2 release from recoverable fossil fuel deposits.

In order to estimate the amount of CO_2 that will be placed in the atmosphere in coming years, it would be necessary to know, among other things, how much, and what kind of, fossil fuel will be burned in the future. The rate of fuel use depends on many factors, but it is clear from the size of the reserves listed in table 6–1 that as far as CO_2 is concerned, major attention should be focused on future use of coal and, conceivably, synthetics.

The reason for much of the concern about the CO_2 problem is this: according to present knowledge, if growth of worldwide fossil fuel use continues at its present rate, the atmospheric concentration of CO_2 will be double that of the preindustrial (or 1880) period sometime around the year 2025. Even if the growth rate falls to 2 percent per year, the doubling would occur around 2050. If fossil fuel use remained constant at today's level (an unlikely occurrence, even given reduced rates of growth of energy use resulting from higher prices), a doubling would occur toward the end of the 2100s.

This doubling of atmospheric CO_2 is interesting because the temperature and other climate changes thought to be associated with such a level would be large enough to have significant impacts. Specifically, a

TABLE 6–1. Energy Supplied and CO_2 Released by Fuels, 1980

Fuel	Energy supplied[a] 10^{19} joules	Energy supplied[a] (%)	CO_2 release per unit energy (oil = 1)	Airborne CO_2 added[a] (%)	Airborne CO_2 added[a] (ppm)	CO_2 added (total ppm)	Potential airborne CO_2 in virgin reservoirs[b] (ppm)
Oil	12	40	1	50	0.7	11	70
Coal	7	24	5/4	35	0.5	26	1000
Gas	5	16	3/4	15	0.2	5	50
Oil shale, tar sands, heavy oil	0	0	7/4	0	0	0	100
Nuclear, solar, wood, hydroelectric	6	20	0	0	0	0	0
Total	30	100	—	100	1.4	42	1200

Source: J.W. Hansen, D. Johnson, A. Lacis, S. Lebedeff, P. Lee, D. Rind, and G. Russell, "Climate Impact of Increasing Atmospheric Carbon Dioxide," Science vol. 213, no. 4511 (August 28, 1981) p. 964. (Copyright © 1981, American Association for the Advancement of Science.)

[a] Based on late 1970s.

[b] Reservoir estimates assume that half the coal above 3,000 feet can be recovered and that oil recovery rates will increase from 25 to 30 percent to 40 percent. Estimate for unconventional fossil fuels may be low if techniques are developed for economic extraction of "synthetic oil" from deposits that are deep or of marginal energy content. It is assumed that the airborne fraction of released CO_2 is fixed.

doubling of atmospheric CO_2 is now generally believed sufficient to increase average global temperature by about 3° C ± 1.5° C. Also, as temperature increases, the snow and ice around the poles will retreat, uncovering dark land or ocean, which in turn will absorb more sunlight. Therefore, as noted above, at the North Pole and, to a lesser extent, the South Pole—the warming would be much more pronounced, as figure 6–4 indicates. In fact, at the poles the warming could be as much as 11° C.

As mentioned earlier, in addition to CO_2, other gases released as a result of human activity add to the climate effects of CO_2. They include methane (CH_4), nitrous oxide (N_2O), and two chlorofluorocarbons— CF_2Cl_2 and $CFCl_3$, all of which can warm the surface of the earth by enhancing the greenhouse effect. Carbon monoxide (CO), methane (CH_4), and nitric oxide (NO) can warm the climate indirectly by enhancing the production in the lower atmosphere of ozone (O_3), another infrared-absorbing gas. Chlorofluorocarbons (CFCs) and ozone will be discussed later in this chapter in connection with changes in the stratosphere, about 7 miles above the surface of the earth. Here they are regarded as just two infrared-absorbing gases which can magnify the "CO_2 problem." These gases at present appear in the atmosphere in concentrations far below that of CO_2, but their strong infrared-absorbing capability creates a combined effect which needs to be considered.

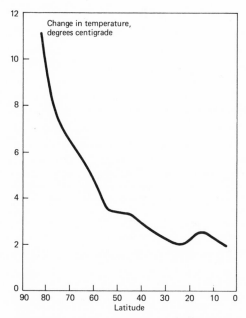

Figure 6–4. Estimated effect of doubling of atmospheric carbon dioxide on surface temperatures, by latitude. (From S. Manabe and R. T. Wetherald, "The Effects of Doubling the CO_2 Concentration on the Climate of a General Circulation Model," *Journal of Atmospheric Science* vol. 32 (1975) pp. 3–15.

Estimating the amounts of these substances which will be released and which will remain in the air is more difficult than for CO_2, since less is known about the processes that remove these gases from the atmosphere. It is interesting to note that the source for several of these gases, CH_4, CO, NO, and part of the N_2O is the same as for CO_2— fossil fuels. Some N_2O comes from the use of fertilizers, and the CFCs are used as refrigerants, propellants, and in various industrial processes. The estimates of the climate impacts of given amounts of these substances contain uncertainties similar to those for CO_2, but the most recent estimate of the combined effect of these trace gases is that they will increase the warming produced by CO_2 by about 50 percent, so the 3° C warming associated with doubled CO_2 becomes 4.5° C with the additional influence of these trace gases.[9]

[9] V. Ramanathan, "Climatic Effects of Anthropogenic Trace Gases," in W. Bach, et al., eds. *Interactions of Energy and Climate* (Boston, Reidel, 1980) pp. 269–280.

Even though there is a growing consensus on the global warming associated with a CO_2 doubling, specific changes in climate (precipitation, wind velocity, cloud cover) are hard to predict, even more so if regional or local detail is desired. Using large computer models of the global climate, and inferring certain past conditions when the globe was warmer, some scientists have hazarded guesses about how climate might differ with a CO_2 doubling. Two such "scenarios" are illustrated in figures 6–5 and 6–6. Note that both figures suggest drier weather for most of the United States and large parts of the Soviet Union. Africa, the Middle East, Southeast Asia, Central America, and a large part of South America are predicted to become wetter in the event of a CO_2 doubling.

While it is always dangerous to draw conclusions based on such uncertain predictions, it appears that the most highly productive agricultural regions of the world would shift toward the North and South poles if a doubling of CO_2 were to occur. Table 6–2 illustrates what might happen in such an event to the countries which produce the world's supplies of wheat, rice, corn, and barley. For instance, in 1978, the USSR produced 27.3 percent of the world's wheat, while China produced 10 percent. According to these speculations about the effects of a CO_2 doubling on precipitation, all of the USSR's wheat lands would become drier than they are now, and 75 percent of China's wheat lands would be wetter. In other countries producing (27 percent of) wheat, about 80 percent would become wetter and 20 percent drier. Because different crops respond differently to changed climatic conditions, it is difficult to predict changes in the agricultural output of individual countries. Nevertheless, several major crops (wheat, corn, oats) are known to be sensitive to growing season precipitation, so that reductions in rainfall would be accompanied by decreases in crop yields.[10]

In spite of the many potentially serious effects of a CO_2 doubling, no effect has received more attention, or caused more alarm, than the potential melting of polar ice and its attendant increase in sea level. Critics of increasing fossil fuel use (or proponents of nuclear power) are quick to conjure up visions of coastal high-rise dwellers stepping off their balconies into salt water. Although it should be viewed warily, this possibility cannot be dismissed out of hand. There is enough water in all polar ice to increase the sea level by perhaps 300 feet, but this ice would take thousands of years to melt. However, eleven million people in the United States alone are located in areas no higher than 15 feet

[10] For a discussion of crop yields, see Asit K. Biswas, "Crop-Climate Models: A Review of the State of the Art," in Jesse Ausubel and Asit Biswas, eds., *Climatic Constraints and Human Activities* (Oxford, Pergamon, 1980) pp. 75–92.

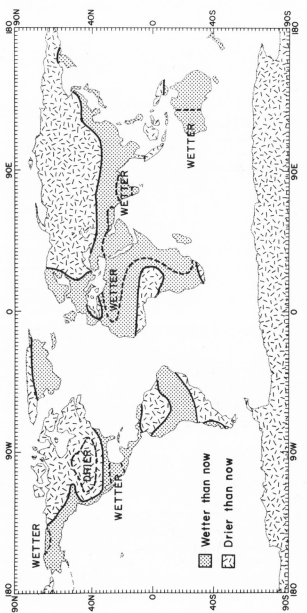

Figure 6–5. Scenario of possible soil moisture patterns on a warmer earth. Based on paleoclimatic reconstruction, comparisons of recent warm and cold years in the northern hemisphere, and a climate model experiment. (From William W. Kellogg and Robert Schware, *Climate Change and Society: Consequences of Increasing Atmospheric Carbon Dioxide*, Boulder, Colo., Westview, 1981, p. 49.)

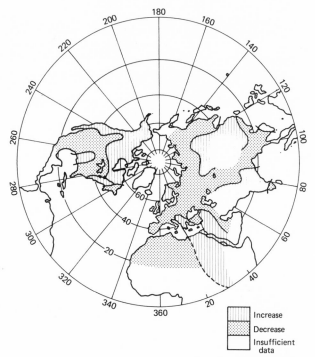

Figure 6–6. Mean annual precipitation changes from cold to warm years. Past temperature changes of as little as 0.6° C have caused geographical changes in precipitation. (From T. M. L. Wigley, et al., "Scenario for a Warm, High-CO$_2$ World," *Nature* vol. 283, no. 10 (1980). Copyright © 1980, Macmillan Journals, Ltd., reprinted with permission.)

above sea level, and there are portions of the Antarctic ice sheet that are potentially subject to more rapid breakup, so the possible consequences of a substantial warming are easy to imagine.[11]

How likely are such increases in sea level, and over what length of time would they take place? According to most estimates, a 2° C average increase in global temperature would warm the Antarctic by about 5° C. Since the summertime temperature there is about − 5° C, this increase would apparently be sufficient to begin the melting and disintegration of the West Antarctic ice sheet. Most models foresee a 2° C increase in global temperatures sometime in the next century, perhaps in its early

[11] S. Schneider and R. Chen, "Carbon Dioxide Warming and Coastline Flooding: Physical Factors and Climatic Impact," *Annual Review of Energy* vol. 5 (1980) pp. 107–140.

TABLE 6–2. Current World Production and
Projected Soil Moisture Changes for
Some Major Crops in a Warming
Trend

Cropland	Current % of world output, 1978	% of land to become: Wetter	% of land to become: Drier
Wheat			
USSR	27.3		100
U.S.	11.1		100
China	10.0	75	25
India	7.0	100	
France	4.8	100	
Canada	4.7		100
Australia	4.1	100	
Turkey	3.7	100	
Other	27.3	80	20
Corn (maize)			
U.S.	49.5	20	80
China	9.1	80	20
Brazil	3.7	60	40
Romania	2.8	100	
South Africa	2.7		100
Argentina	2.7		100
Mexico	2.6	100	
France	2.6		100
USSR	2.5	100	
Other	21.8	80	20
Rice			
China	35.0	100	
India	21.8	100	
Indonesia	6.8		100
Bangladesh	5.0	100	
Thailand	4.5	100	
Japan	4.2	100	
Burma	2.7	100	
Vietnam	2.6	100	
Other	18.2	40	60
Barley			
USSR	31.6		100
China	10.1	100	
France	5.8	100	
Canada	5.3		100
U.K.	5.0	100	
U.S.	5.0		100
West Germany	4.4	100	
Romania	4.0	100	
Denmark	3.2	100	
Other	25.6	80	20

Source: Adapted from William Kellogg and Robert Schware,
*Climate Change and Society: Consequences of Increasing Carbon
Dioxide* (Boulder, Col., Westview, 1981).

decades. The breakup of the West Antarctic ice sheet would increase sea level 5 to 6 meters, or 16 to 20 feet. Thus, there is a legitimate reason to be concerned about the possible eventual increase in sea level if CO_2 concentrations in the atmosphere continue to increase.

Nevertheless, the seriousness of such an event would depend in large part on the speed with which it might occur. If the rise in sea level were to take place gradually (over a period of several hundred years or more), the consequences would be much less severe than if the entire change took only a decade or so. First of all, existing human activity could gradually be shifted away from low-lying areas and at least certain new activities prohibited or discouraged. More important, perhaps, some preventive or defensive actions could be taken for activities which are important but difficult to shift. After all, large parts of the Netherlands which are below sea level are protected by dikes; similarly, New Orleans and other U.S. cities are at least partially below sea level, but are protected from flooding by levees and dikes. Given enough time, many areas too valuable to concede to the ocean might be at least partially protected from rising sea levels.

This is *not* to suggest that one should be indifferent to the potential sea level consequences of CO_2 buildup; nor does it imply that the cost of defensive measures would be small—it would most assuredly not be. It is intended to make a point we will return to later, however: the ideal response to the CO_2 problem, and other climate-related problems as well, will no doubt include some preventive measures as well as some based on adaptation to climate change.

We will return to the carbon dioxide problem in a later section devoted to possible policy responses. For the time being, however, let us turn to chlorofluorocarbons and the problems they may pose for climate and, hence, mankind.

Chlorofluorocarbons

Chlorofluorocarbons, or CFCs, are manmade chemical compounds containing chlorine, fluorine, carbon, and sometimes hydrogen. Because of their desirable chemical properties—they are much less flammable, corrosive, and directly injurious to human health than the substances they replaced—CFCs have come to be used in a wide variety of applications. They are used as a refrigerant in chillers, freezers, and home and automobile air conditioners; as a solvent to clean integrated circuits, metals, and clothes; as a blowing agent in the manufacture of both flexible and rigid foams for furniture, carpets, and packing insulation; and as an important component in other products ranging from air horns on

TABLE 6–3. Estimated CFC Production and Nonaerosol End Use, 1976
(millions of pounds)

Use	CFC–11	CFC–12	CFC–22	CFC–113	Total	Total minus CFC–22
Analyzed applications						
Flexible foam	34	—	—	—	34	34
Solvents	—	—	—	69	69	69
Rigid foams						
Urethane	35	2	—	—	37	37
Nonurethane	2	21	—	—	23	23
Mobile air conditioning	—	90	—	—	90	90
Other refrigeration						
Chillers	8	5	3	—	16	13
Home refrigerators and freezers	—	6	—	—	6	6
Retail food	—	11	1	—	12	11
Miscellaneous						
Liquid fast freezing	—	6	—	—	6	6
Sterilants	—	13	—	—	13	13
Others	1	3	—	—	4	4
Total	80	157	4	69	310	306
Other applications						
Home air conditioning	—	—	46	—	46	—
Supermarket air conditioning	—	—	29	—	29	—
Other	19	32	38	—	89	51
Total	19	32	113	0	164	51
Total domestic production	256	393	170	72	891	721
Sales for nonaerosol use[a]	99	189	117	69	474	357

Source: Adele Palmer, William Mooz, Timothy Quinn, and Kathleen Wolf, "Economic Implications of Regulating Chlorofluorocarbon Emissions from Nonaerosol Applications," Research Report R–2524–EPA prepared for the Environmental Protection Agency, June 1980, p. 35.

Notes: Estimates of total domestic production and sales for nonaerosol use are based on data supplied by the CFC producers. Usage levels in the analyzed applications are based on data developed by Rand and International Research and Technology Corp. (IR&T). Usage levels for other applications were obtained from the Dupont Co. Total domestic production includes production for aerosol use.

[a] Sales for nonaerosol use equal production minus internal use by the CFC producers, exports, and emissions during packaging and transport to users. Imports should be included, but data were not available for most of the CFCs. Uses reported for individual applications exclude: 1 million pounds of CFC–114 used mostly in chillers; 5 million pounds each of CFC–22 and CFC–115 used to form CFC–502 used in retail food refrigeration; and less than 1 million pounds of CFC–12 used to form CFC–500 used in chillers.

trucks to propellants in spray deodorants.[12] Table 6–3 indicates the use distribution of the estimated 891 million pounds of CFCs produced in the United States in 1976.

CFCs are produced and used worldwide. The United States accounts for about one-third of world usage of CFCs, so we concentrate on

[12] For a more complete discussion of the properties of CFCs, see National Academy of Sciences, *Stratospheric Ozone Depletion by Halocarbons: Chemistry and Transport* (Washington, D.C., NAS, 1979).

domestic policy here. A later section mentions several difficulties arising out of the international nature of the CFC problem.

There are two different, albeit related, problems thought to be associated with the production and use of CFCs. The first has been described here as part of the CO_2 problem—that is, CFCs are among the trace gases which contribute to atmospheric warming. The second, and better known, of these problems has to do with the eventual fate of the CFCs that escape into the atmosphere. Because they are chemically very stable, CFCs do not break down easily—in fact, some of them may live more than 100 years in the lowest layer of the atmosphere (the troposphere).[13] Some fraction of these CFCs work their way higher into the second layer of the atmosphere—the stratosphere—where, under the influence of sunlight, they break down, releasing atoms of chlorine. Chlorine, in turn, is particularly effective in dissociating or breaking up ozone molecules, which shield the earth from damaging ultraviolet solar radiation. Thus, this CFC effect is one of ozone depletion and its impacts on plant and animal life.[14]

The problem of CFC/ozone depletion is much more complex than those of either the CFC or CO_2 greenhouse effects. The former involves more than 100 chemical reactions, at least some of which actually help *create* rather than destroy ozone. The possibility of stratospheric ozone depletion by CFCs was first raised in 1974.[15] Gradually, the empirical information to test the validity of the ozone depletion theory is becoming available, along with better information about past and future worldwide production of certain CFCs. Table 6–4 shows the 1950–80 global production trend for F–11 and F–12, the two most important types of CFCs.

The decline in production that began about 1975 reflects the phasing out of aerosol uses of CFCs. This decline would be even greater were it not for the rapid growth rate for nonaerosol uses of CFCs in the United States and elsewhere. On account of this latter trend, it was recently estimated that between 1980 and 1990, purchases in the United States of four major types of CFCs would increase 68 percent in the

[13] The exact lifetimes are still controversial. See ibid., p. 56. For arguments in favor of a shorter lifetime, see E.I. DuPont de Nemours and Company, *Fluorocarbon/Ozone Update: The Chlorofluororcarbon/Ozone Depletion Theory—A Status Report* (Wilmington, Del., October 1980).

[14] The reader should be careful not to confuse the "good" stratospheric ozone which shields the earth from harmful radiation with the "bad" ozone which, along with other photochemical oxidants often found at ground level in the troposphere, may be responsible for adverse human health effects, property and crop damage, and other environmental disamenities. It will no doubt occur to the reader, as it has to us, that what is needed is a way to pump the unwanted, low-level concentration of ozone up to the stratosphere where it could do some good!

[15] M.J. Molina and F.S. Rowland, "Stratospheric Sink for Chlorofluoromethanes—Chlorine Atom Catalyzed Destruction of Ozone," *Nature* vol. 249 (1974) pp. 810–812.

absence of further regulation. Since the decline in aerosol uses will no doubt slow (because some aerosol uses are not easily replaced), continued growth in nonaerosol uses implies growth in total CFC output.

Although not all CFCs produced or used in a particular year escape into the atmosphere, eventually they will. This may take some time in the case of the CFCs used in rigid polyurethane foam or coolants, for example, but even these will eventually work their way into the atmosphere. During the time between production and escape, CFCs can be thought of as being stored in a "bank." Unfortunately, this bank is now and apparently will continue to be well stocked. Table 6–5 shows recent estimates of the size of the CFC bank in the United States by product area for the years 1976 and 1990. If the estimates are correct, by 1990 there will be nearly 2 billion pounds of CFCs in the United States alone that will be released in later years. This is about five years' worth of CFCs at current production levels. It makes it clear that CFC emissions would not cease for some time even if all new production and use were suspended everywhere.

Until recently, no studies had detected any apparent ozone depletion in the atmosphere. However, very preliminary measurements by the National Aeronautics and Space Administration have recently detected some ozone depletion at about 30 kilometers (18.6 miles) above the earth's surface.[16] Moreover, these measurements appear to be consistent with the ozone depletion hypothesized as a result of CFC use to date.

It remains to be seen if these estimates withstand scrutiny. Such measurements are difficult to make because of the large natural variability of ozone concentrations. Even if the measurements are correct, of course, and represent a trend toward ozone depletion, it does not necessarily imply that CFCs are the culprit.

It is even more difficult to calculate the eventual depletion in ozone expected to result from a given level of CFC production and use. Following a four-year period in which estimates fluctuated up and down, the National Academy of Sciences (NAS) attempted in 1979 to synthesize the current state of knowledge.[17] The NAS concluded,

> If the worldwide release of various types of CFMs were to continue at 1977 levels, the most probable value of eventual ozone depletion would be 16% (reduction of worldwide ozone to 84% of what it otherwise would have been). . . . The depletion would reach one quarter of its eventual value in about 15 years, and half of it in about 35 years.

[16] Colin Norman, Satellite Data Indicate Ozone Depletion," news report in *Science* vol. 213 (September 4, 1981) pp. 1088–1089.
[17] National Academy of Sciences, *Stratospheric Ozone Depletion*, p. 10.

TABLE 6–4. Fluorocarbon Production and Release Summary—
World Total

(million kilograms)

	CFC–11				
	Annual		Cumulative		
Year	Production	Released	Production	Released	Unreleased
1950	6.6	5.4	18.6	14.4	4.1
1951	9.1	7.5	27.6	21.9	5.7
1952	13.6	10.8	41.2	32.7	8.5
1953	17.3	14.7	58.5	47.4	11.1
1954	20.9	18.3	79.4	65.7	13.7
1955	26.3	22.6	105.6	88.3	17.4
1956	32.5	28.2	138.1	116.5	21.6
1957	33.9	31.6	172.0	148.1	23.9
1958	29.5	29.7	201.6	177.8	23.8
1959	35.6	30.3	237.1	208.1	29.0
1960	49.7	39.7	286.9	247.9	39.0
1961	60.5	51.2	347.3	299.0	48.3
1962	78.1	64.1	425.4	363.1	62.3
1963	93.3	78.5	518.7	441.7	77.0
1964	111.1	93.2	629.8	534.9	94.9
1965	122.8	106.3	752.6	641.2	111.4
1966	141.0	119.0	893.7	760.2	133.4
1967	159.8	135.1	1053.4	895.3	158.1
1968	184.8	154.6	1238.2	1049.9	188.3
1969	219.8	180.2	1458.0	1230.1	228.0
1970	241.1	205.1	1699.1	1435.2	263.9
1971	266.6	225.4	1965.7	1660.6	305.1
1972	310.5	253.8	2276.2	1914.5	361.7
1973	354.3	290.6	2630.5	2205.0	425.5
1974	377.6	320.9	3008.1	2526.0	482.1
1975	323.5	312.9	3331.6	2838.8	492.7
1976	349.9	304.1	3681.5	3142.9	538.6
1977	332.2	306.4	4013.7	3449.3	564.4
1978	321.2	291.0	4334.9	3740.3	594.6
1979	302.0	272.0	4636.9	4012.3	624.7
1980	302.2	257.4	4939.1	4269.7	669.4

Moreover, according to the 1979 NAS report, if the worldwide release of CFCs were to increase at 7 percent per year between 1980 and 2000, the chance of a 30 percent depletion of stratospheric ozone would be three in four (a 75 percent likelihood).

However, still more recent research[18] summarized in a NASA report (primarily involving the numerical constants governing chemical reac-

[18] National Aeronautics and Space Administration, "Present State of Knowledge of the Upper Atmosphere: An Assessment Report" (Washington, D.C., January 1982).

| CFC–12 | | | | |
| Annual | | Cumulative | | |
Production	Released	Production	Released	Unreleased
34.6	27.1	198.3	129.5	68.8
36.2	30.2	234.5	159.6	74.9
37.2	31.5	271.7	191.1	80.6
46.5	35.5	318.2	226.6	91.6
49.1	40.3	367.4	266.9	100.4
57.6	45.2	425.0	312.1	112.9
68.7	52.6	493.6	364.7	129.0
74.2	59.8	567.8	424.5	143.3
73.4	62.6	641.2	487.1	154.2
87.6	69.6	728.8	556.7	172.1
99.4	83.2	828.3	639.9	188.3
108.5	93.2	936.8	733.2	203.6
128.1	107.1	1064.9	840.3	224.6
146.4	125.8	1211.3	966.1	245.1
170.1	146.6	1381.4	1112.7	268.7
190.1	165.6	1571.4	1278.4	293.1
216.2	184.3	1787.6	1462.7	324.9
242.8	208.3	2030.4	1670.9	359.4
278.8	238.0	2309.2	1909.0	400.2
311.4	270.0	2620.6	2179.0	441.6
336.9	296.2	2957.5	2475.2	482.3
360.5	319.1	3318.1	2794.3	523.7
401.7	348.3	3719.7	3142.6	577.1
447.5	386.2	4167.2	3528.8	638.4
473.6	420.3	4640.8	3949.1	691.7
418.6	412.0	5059.4	4361.1	698.3
449.8	395.7	5509.3	4756.8	752.4
424.4	376.5	5933.6	5133.4	800.3
414.1	347.6	6347.7	5481.0	866.8
400.3	338.0	6748.0	5818.9	929.1
393.4	333.7	7141.4	6152.6	988.8

Source: Chemical Manufacturers Association, Washington, D.C.

tions) suggests that the eventual ozone depletion associated with CFCs may be less than that estimated in the 1979 NAS report. According to these more recent calculations, if the worldwide use of all CFCs continues at present levels, stratospheric ozone depletion will eventually reach about 5 to 9 percent (compared with 16 percent in the NAS study). The NASA report comments that other chlorine compounds released to the atmosphere (carbon tetrachloride, methyl chloroform, and so on) could increase the size of the depletion by one third. Thus, although the "consensus" depletion estimates have been revised downward, they

TABLE 6–5. Estimated Size of the CFC Bank in
1976 and 1990 (Excluding CFC–22)

Product area	CFC bank (millions of lbs)	
	1976	1990
Rigid foams		
Urethane	230	1,156
Nonurethane	20	135
Mobile air conditioning	222	384
Other refrigeration		
Chillers	59	89
Home refrigerators and freezers	86	104
Retail food store devices	56	81
Total	673	1,949

Source: Adele Palmer, William Mooz, Timothy Quinn, and Kathleen Wolf, "Economic Implications of Regulating Chlorofluorocarbon Emissions from Nonaerosol Applications," Research Report R–2524–EPA prepared for the Environmental Protection Agency, June 1980, p. 8.

still imply an appreciable reduction in ozone if CFC use stays constant, and a large reduction if CFC use grows.

The eventual extent of ozone depletion is important because it determines how much additional damaging ultraviolet radiation (DUV) reaches the earth. This in turn is of concern for a number of reasons. First, and perhaps most important, DUV is of the wavelength believed to be the prime cause of both fatal and nonfatal skin cancers.[19] It is difficult to determine the likely increase in skin cancers for a given increase in DUV because other factors besides radiation affect incidence. These include susceptibility (which is strongly linked to skin color) and other characteristics of population and location.

However, new evidence from both animal studies and epidemiological investigations of human populations has given scientists an improved understanding of radiation-induced carcinogenesis.[20] Current best estimates are that each 1 percent reduction in stratospheric ozone through its effect on DUV will result in a 2 to 5 percent increase in basal cell skin cancers and a 4 to 10 percent increase in squamous cell skin cancers

[19] DUV radiation has wavelength ranges of 290–320 nanometers (a nanometer is a billionth, or 10^{-9}, of a meter).

[20] This new evidence is discussed in some detail in Causes and Effects of Stratospheric Ozone Reduction: An Update, a report prepared by the Committee on Chemistry and Physics of Ozone Depletion and the Committee on the Biological Effects of Increased Solar Ultraviolet Radiation, National Research Council, National Academy of Sciences (Washington, D.C., NAS, 1982).

(both types are serious although treatable and usually are not fatal). Thus, a 5 to 9 percent reduction in stratospheric ozone might be expected to result in a 10 to 45 percent increase in basal cell skin cancers, and a 20 to 90 percent increase in squamous cell cancers. Even greater increases in these nonmelanoma skin cancers would result if CFC emissions continued to grow at their present rate of about 7 percent annually. Regardless of where in these ranges the "true" numbers lie, one implication of ozone depletion is an increase of many thousands in the number of nonmelanoma skin cancers. While some of these would no doubt involve fairly minor surgery, other cases would produce more serious consequences.

The relationship between DUV and the much more serious melanoma skin cancers is less well established. Yet if they increased in response to expected ozone depletion in the same proportion as nonmelanomas, eventually several thousand additional cancer deaths could be expected each year in the United States.

In addition to these adverse health effects, increased DUV also appears to hamper human immunological response. It is also associated with a number of serious effects on the nonhuman environment, which cannot be detailed here. Suffice it to say that DUV can damage the genetic coding in the cells of plants; cause cancers in some animals, including cattle; impair the reproductive ability of certain aquatic species such as shrimp and crabs; and kill other species directly.

CHARACTERISTICS OF CLIMATE PROBLEMS

Before discussing policies to deal with CO_2 and CFC-related problems, it may be useful to identify several common characteristics that make these problems so intractable. This will go some way toward explaining the relative absence of policies that deal with climate changes.

Uncertainty

The first and by far the most vexing characteristic of the two climate problems discussed here is uncertainty. It arises at almost every step in the chain of events that must occur if human activity is to pose a serious threat to the global climate. In fact, in many ways uncertainty grows, or "cascades," from one link in the chain to the next.[21]

[21] William W. Kellogg, "Modeling the Prospects for Climate Change: Current State of the Art and Implications," paper presented at RFF/National Climate Workshop on Economic Methodologies for Climate Change, April 1980.

Consider the CO_2 problem. The links in this chain might be described as follows: (1) individuals and organizations decide to burn a certain amount of fossil fuel each year, which (2) releases a quantity of CO_2 into the atmosphere, of which (3) a fraction is taken up by the oceans, plants, and so on, leaving (4) an increased total atmospheric CO_2 content, which (5) increases the temperature at various places on the globe and the global mean temperature, so that (6) wind, cloud, and precipitation patterns are modified, thus (7) changing plant and animal growth, and many other features of the environment experienced by people, leading to (8) adaptation to adverse effects or making use of beneficial effects. A similar chain, differing only in (1) and (4), can be described for each of the other infrared-absorbing gases that may be found in the atmosphere.

It is fair to say that less is known about the later steps in this chain than the earlier ones. *But note that even step (1) is subject to considerable uncertainty.* The slowdown over the past five years in the growth rate of energy use in general, and fossil fuels in particular, has caught many experts by surprise. Whereas U.S. annual energy use in the year 2000 was predicted to be 160 quads ten years ago, it is now predicted to be on the order of 95 quads.[22] If prices rise sharply again, demand may be further reduced. (On the other hand, of course, if real prices stay constant or continue to fall, there may be a resurgence in energy consumption.) The point is simply that there is uncertainty even at the starting point of the analysis, and that uncertainty grows.

The amount of warming associated with a given CO_2 increase is still debated among atmospheric scientists, and while maps showing lower soil moisture in midlatitudes associated with warmer climates are used to estimate crop decreases, some argue that elevated CO_2 levels will lead to enhanced agricultural outputs.[23] There is disagreement about the extent to which cropping patterns can be changed, new hybrids developed which are better adapted to possible new climatic conditions, oceanic encroachment prevented or moderated, and so on. These and other uncertainties—such as the background of natural climate changes against which these effects take place—greatly complicate attempts to determine what *could* happen and what is *likely* to happen.

Similar uncertainties bedevil decision-making regarding CFCs. Here the chain can be described as follows: (1) CFCs are released into the

[22] For a discussion of trends in forecasts of U.S. energy demand in the year 2000, see A.B. Lovins, "Economically Efficient Energy Futures," in Wilfrid Bach, et al., eds., *Interactions of Energy and Climate* (Boston, Reidel, 1980).

[23] Sylvan H. Wittwer, "Environmental and Social Consequences of a Possible CO_2-Induced Climate Change on Agriculture," paper presented at the Annual Meeting of the American Association for the Advancement of Science, San Francisco, January 5, 1980.

atmosphere at some rate; (2) some of these are removed in sinks; (3) certain amounts stay in the troposphere and eventually work their way into the stratosphere; (4) these CFCs react with sunlight to produce chlorine; (5) chlorine enters into a complex, many-component reaction in which ozone is created and destroyed, but the addition of chlorine pushes the reactions toward less ozone; (6) more DUV reaches the surface of the earth; (7) the DUV affects plants, animals, people in various ways; and (8) certain adaptations take place. Again, uncertainty appears to increase at later stages in this chain, but it is hardly the case that the initial steps are well understood. For example, some have claimed that a relatively quick depletion of the fluoride ores that provide the raw material for CFCs will limit their manufacture, while others take issue with this projection.

The complexity of stratospheric chemistry, and the uncertainties it creates, is illustrated by the changes that have taken place in the debate over supersonic flight and stratospheric ozone. Beginning in 1970, Congress became concerned that the development and operation of a fleet of supersonic transport airplanes (SSTs) would deplete ozone in the stratosphere because planes emit oxides of nitrogen. As a result, Congress authorized funds for research on the subject, and the Climate Impact Assessment Program (CIAP) was launched. Four years later, in December 1974, the final report was submitted. It concluded that while climatic effects resulting from SSTs would be hard to detect, the proposed U.S. fleet of 500 SSTs would damage the ozone layer. This potential damage was cited by critics of the SST proposal and, along with economic arguments, was successful in helping kill it.

No more than five years later, however, the National Academy of Sciences was able to conclude with little controversy that, "the effect of nitrogen oxides—emitted in the exhausts of high-flying aircraft and by the natural degradation of nitrogen fertilizers—is probably now quite small and not of immediate concern." The shift of scientific opinion resulted from a steadily increasing understanding about the number and variety of interactions considered to be important in the stratosphere and an improved knowledge of the relevant reaction rates. This example illustrates how quickly apparently serious climate problems can be relegated to the status of nonproblems through the accumulation of scientific evidence. Such possibilities have to be kept in mind in designing appropriate responses to the problems that CO_2 and CFCs appear to pose.

One final observation about uncertainty is in order here. Researchers may differ on the undesirability of a doubling of atmospheric CO_2, but they are in rather close agreement that this doubling will eventually be reached, perhaps early in the next century, unless measures are taken to reduce fossil fuel use. Similarly, while significant CFC-induced ozone depletion may be somewhat more uncertain than CO_2 doubling, the possibility of its occurring is not all that small—in 1979 the NAS estimated that there was a 95 percent probability that eventual depletion will be between 5 and 28 percent. Thus, we are discussing events which have a more than small possibility of occurring.

On the other hand, it is extremely important to keep in mind that some of the possible effects discussed are just that—possible, not necessarily likely. When all the attention is devoted to the worst-case outcome, as it often is, people tend to lose sight of the fact that it is but one of many possible outcomes, some much more likely than the "catastrophic" one. A simple example may illustrate this point. Suppose the realization of a bad outcome requires an unfortunate turn at each of four independent links in a chain of events like that discussed above. If the probability of each unfortunate turn is one in ten, then the probability of the bad outcome is 0.0001, or one in ten thousand. This might be a risk worth heeding, of course, especially if the consequences would be quite bad, but it would be far from a likely occurrence. It is important to keep this perspective in mind when considering appropriate policy measures.

Most studies of the CO_2 and CFC problems, however, have not intentionally discussed worst-case scenarios. Usually a scientist will attempt to give a most likely value for a particular effect and include error estimates around this value to show the range of uncertainty. To the extent that scientists are successful in this attempt, the upper limit value is just as likely as the lower limit. For example, if a temperature change of $4°$ C $±$ $2°$ C is given, a $6°$ C change has a likelihood similar to that of $2°$ C. Whether those people who study possible disadvantageous environmental changes arising from human activity tend to lean toward the worst case might make an interesting psychological study, but until it is shown that they do, we perhaps can do no better than assume when a particular issue is studied that both "better case" and "worst case" outcomes are possible and plan policy accordingly. In the two problems described in this chapter, this approach would mean that the breakup of the West Antarctic ice sheet, or a very large increase in malignant melanoma cancers, should be kept in mind as possible occurrences, to be avoided if at all possible.

Even in these extreme cases, however, preventive or ameliorative measures are conceivable. In the case of increased DUV, such measures may amount to no more than the increased use of protective clothing by sensitive individuals. With respect to rising sea levels, certain measures were discussed that may be quite feasible, given enough time to respond. The point is *not* that these problems should be ignored or treated lightly. Indeed, the opposite is argued below. Rather, we are suggesting that these climate problems are amenable to analysis and control measures, and should be approached in the same way that less "exotic" environmental and natural resource problems can be approached.

Distant Horizons and Valuation Problems

Some of the serious effects of the problems just discussed are not expected to become manifest for tens or perhaps hundreds of years, if at all. This makes dealing with them difficult for both political and economic reasons. Political myopia—the tendency to focus on the most immediate problems, regardless of their long-run implications—is well known. It is hard to get possible temperature changes in the year 2025, or increases in DUV-related damage ten years after that onto a legislative agenda filled with controversies over next year's defense authorizations, or a regulatory agenda driven by a multitude of congressionally mandated deadlines. In fact, this orientation toward the present accounts for the attempts by some to raise the climate problems discussed here, and others, to "catastrophe status." In this way, it is hoped, policymakers will direct some attention to the problems.

The distant horizon of at least some of the potential climate effects creates an economic problem, as well. In trying to evaluate programs for which benefits and costs are spread over many years, it is customary for future effects to be *discounted,* or reduced, when they are compared with present effects. This is not because the present generation values itself more highly than its eventual successors, but rather because, at some positive rate of interest, the present generation can invest some amount less than a dollar in order to have a dollar available in some future year. Thus, it might sometimes be better to invest the money that might otherwise be used to prevent a problem in order to have a large sum available in the future to deal with the problem, and perhaps to address others as well.

The implications of discounting are clear for the climate problems under consideration in this chapter. Benefits or costs that will not appear for twenty or thirty years, much less several hundred years, look very small in comparison with more immediate costs and benefits. Thus, a regulatory program to prevent CO_2 or CFC releases which requires society to bear costs immediately may not look efficient (or socially worthwhile) if the benefits will not arise for many years. This may be true even if the benefits are very great but quite distant.

But just as scientists may disagree on the size or timing of an atmospheric change, so too do economists often disagree about the rate at which future costs and benefits should be discounted—some believe the rate should be zero. In addition, this whole discussion assumes that the effects that may be felt many years from now can be expressed in dollar terms—this is logically prior to discounting. Yet some of the changes that might result from climate alteration could be so large as to render traditional benefit-cost analysis inapplicable. Thus, shifts in cropping patterns, industrial production, and other human activities affected by climate changes might be so significant as to defy conventional valuation. Moreover, even where standard valuation techniques can be used, it is very difficult to place values on certain occurrences. For instance, how would one value the increased likelihood of contracting a fatal skin cancer? Or the chance of damage to an aquatic ecosystem? Or the added recreational opportunities that might result from warming? If valuation is impossible, the problems of discounting are moot.

The Distribution of Climate Effects

Still another factor adding to the difficulty of addressing climate problems is the uneven distribution of possible consequences, as can be seen from figures 6–5 and 6–6. Some areas will become wetter, while others are likely to be drier. By the same token, some areas will probably cool in spite of the overall warming that might take place. Depending on both existing and altered conditions, then, as well as the pattern of agricultural and industrial activities among regions and countries, some areas will be better off after a warming while other areas will be worse off; even within an area some individuals could benefit from the change while some would suffer.

To see the obstacles this raises for any effort to arrange preventive action, consider that such action would be difficult to secure and maintain even if *all* countries were harmed by warming. In that case, it would be tempting for any one country to cheat on an agreement, say, to restrict fossil fuel use since it could save money by doing so while at the same time enjoying the protection against adverse climate change that would result if all other countries stuck to the agreement. The problems are magnified considerably when some areas will benefit from warming—in this case, preventive actions by certain regions might make other regions worse off; in cases like these, it is extraordinarily difficult to secure cooperation.

This is especially true with respect to the CO_2 problem. Developing countries will no doubt be loath to restrict use of the fossil fuel resources they may now be in a position to exploit simply because the developed countries have used too much. It would be as if the United States were asking them to remain poor because of the problems it caused while getting rich. Nevertheless, the developing countries' share of annual global carbon emissions increased from about 7 percent in 1950 to 19 percent by 1976 (see table 6–6). If fossil fuel use in developing countries continues to increase in the future, it will be difficult to secure an agreement to limit carbon release if such a step is deemed necessary.

Conflicting Goals

A final impediment to the formulation of a "climate policy" is the sometimes conflicting set of goals which the United States and other countries pursue. For instance, oil supply disruptions in 1973 and 1979 and the price increases that resulted have led the United States to conclude that it must make better use of its vast reserves of coal. Yet as we have seen (table 6–1), coal combustion releases more CO_2 per unit of heat obtained than fuel oil or natural gas. Synthetic fuels (which have been given a tentative blessing by the current and past administrations) release even more CO_2. Thus, an attempt to slow down the buildup of atmospheric CO_2 may conflict with the goal of greater energy independence.

In addition, solutions to the problems of CO_2 and CFCs will cost money and will require constraints on industrial and household activities. They will come at a time when the existing corpus of environmental regulation is under attack for exacerbating an already disappointingly sluggish economy.[24] Thus, the prospect of additional controls may not be greeted warmly, especially in view of the scientific uncertainties surrounding the problems. These controls could be quite expensive. For example, one estimate has pegged at \$540 billion (1975\$) the present value of the cost of preventing a 50 percent increase in atmospheric concentrations of CO_2.[25] The analogous figure for a program designed

[24] See Henry M. Peskin, Paul R. Portney, and Allen V. Kneese, eds., *Environmental Regulation and the U.S. Economy* (Baltimore, Md., Johns Hopkins University Press for Resources for the Future, 1981).
[25] William Nordhaus, *The Efficient Use of Energy Resources* (New Haven, Conn., Yale University Press, 1979) p. 154.

TABLE 6–6. Fraction of Carbon Emissions (%) by
Developed and Developing Countries,
1950–76

Year	Global emissions (10⁹ tons carbon)	Developed[a]	Developing[b]
1950	1.57	93	7
1951	1.71	92	8
1952	1.74	91	9
1953	1.79	91	9
1954	1.83	90	10
1955	2.01	90	10
1956	2.12	90	10
1957	2.19	89	11
1958	2.30	86	14
1959	2.42	82	18
1960	2.59	81	19
1961	2.53	85	15
1962	2.66	86	14
1963	2.82	86	14
1964	2.96	85	15
1965	3.09	85	15
1966	3.26	84	16
1967	3.28	86	14
1968	3.51	85	15
1969	3.74	85	15
1970	3.93	84	16
1971	4.06	84	16
1972	4.24	83	17
1973	4.46	83	17
1974	4.47	82	18
1975	4.51	81	19
1976	4.76	81	19

Source: William W. Kellogg and Robert Schware, *Climate Change and Society: Consequences of Increasing Atmospheric Carbon Dioxide* (Boulder, Col, Westview, 1981) p. 148.

Note: Values were derived from United Nations fuel use tables.

[a] Includes centrally planned economies in Europe.

[b] Includes centrally planned economies in Asia.

to prevent a doubling (or a 100 percent increase) is $87 billion. Other estimates vary, of course, but it is clear that the control of CO_2 releases will be expensive, an expense that will increase sharply with the degree of control required.

Although controlling CFC emissions is less formidable than limiting CO_2, it too will require scarce resources. A study recently estimated how much it would cost the United States to limit CFC emissions between 1980 and 1990 to their 1980 level (instead of allowing emissions to grow as they would without such a "cap").[26] The present discounted value of these costs for the ten-year period using the most inexpensive means possible was $304 million. In addition, a limit on CFC production and use would create wealth transfers between individuals of as much as $2 billion over the same period. While these are not costs to society as a whole, they are losses to particular individuals who will be sure to resist them. Any attempt to limit CFC production on a worldwide basis would obviously be more expensive and more difficult to arrange.

In addition to the direct costs of CFC controls—for example, higher prices for products which must use more expensive substitutes for CFCs— indirect costs must also be taken into account. These *may* include less effective refrigeration, cleaning, insulation, and packaging. While it is difficult to place dollar values on these possible consequences of CFC limitations, they too are legitimate costs of such controls.

In short, then, CFC and CO_2 control measures will be costly. These costs are hard to quantify because they depend on the degree of control, the rate at which it is introduced, the ease with which substitutions and adjustments can be made. It does appear certain, however, that such controls would conflict with other important goals. If so, some accommodation of interests will have to be struck.

CLIMATE CHANGE AND PUBLIC POLICY

Current Actions

In contrast to the natural resources discussed in previous chapters, there are few laws or policies having to do with climate. A small beginning came in 1978 with the signing of the National Climate Program Act, setting up a National Climate Program Office and providing a focus for CO_2 studies. Later, the Energy Security Act of 1980 authorized $3 million for a study of carbon dioxide buildup in the atmosphere and its potential consequences. As a result of the budget reductions sought by the Reagan administration in 1981, no new money was appropriated for the study. Toward the end of 1981, however, the Climate Research Board of the National Academy of Sciences began work on a two-year, $0.5 million study for the Department of Energy, the National Science Foundation, and the White House Office of Science and Technology Policy.

[26] Adele Palmer and Timothy Quinn, "Allocating Chlorofluorocarbon Permits: Who Gains, Who Loses, and What Is the Cost?" Rand Report R-2806-EPA, prepared for the Environmental Protection Agency, June 1981.

Although there is little policy directed explicitly at carbon dioxide buildup, it is important to recognize that other energy policies may have important implications for this problem. For instance, the deregulation of the prices of crude oil and gasoline in the Carter and Reagan administrations, respectively, contributed to higher prices and reduced consumption of gasoline and other crude oil products. This, in turn, has reduced CO_2 emissions from the levels that would have been reached at the previous prices. Similarly, the eventual decontrol of natural gas prices may further dampen demand for energy and reduce CO_2 emissions in the process. Also, environmental controls—like those protecting air quality—that slow down the consumption of fuels by electric utilities, other industrial facilities, or households also reduce CO_2 emissions at the same time. So, too, would policies that make it more expensive to mine coal (such as reclamation requirements) or to drill for oil (as in environmentally sensitive marine or terrestrial ecosystems). In short, a number of environmental and other policies indirectly limit CO_2 emissions.

On the other hand, government policies could conceivably increase the rate at which CO_2 is released into the atmosphere in the United States. For instance, the large-scale substitution of coal for natural gas or fuel oil in utility and other industrial boilers would imply greater CO_2 emissions per unit of energy used. By the same token, efforts by the federal government to speed the development of shale oil or "heavy" oil reserves would have even greater effects on CO_2 emissions. Each unit of energy from these sources contributes more than twice as much CO_2 to the atmosphere as a unit of energy supplied by natural gas, and 75 percent more CO_2 than a unit of fuel oil (see table 6–1).

Also, government policies toward energy conservation can have an important effect on CO_2 emissions. Obviously, if a unit of energy can be conserved as easily and inexpensively as a new unit of energy can be produced, it is better from the standpoint of CO_2 emissions to make use of the conservation alternative. The lack of CO_2 or other pollutant emissions, then, is one of the attractive features of energy conservation. One of the first steps taken by the Reagan adminitration was to drastically reduce federal funding of the conservation programs at the Department of Energy. To the extent that these programs were effective in promoting conservation (and this is certainly a fair question for debate), these cuts may mean more energy use and more CO_2 emissions. It is impossible, however, to venture quantitative estimates of the size of these effects.

Finally, no carbon dioxide is released through nuclear fission or fusion. Thus, policies which directly or indirectly encourage the substitution of nuclear power for fossil fuel combustion help combat global warming.

Against this quite attractive feature, of course, must be weighed the problems attending nuclear power. These include reactor safety as well as the risks of transporting and safely disposing of reactor wastes.

In contrast to CO_2, the United States has taken some regulatory action regarding chlorofluorocarbons. In 1978, the Environmental Protection Agency announced a ban on almost all uses of CFCs as propellants in aerosol sprays. This ban has reduced the U.S. share of worldwide CFC production from about one-half to about one-third. However, only a few other countries have taken similar control actions—Canada, Sweden, West Germany, and the Netherlands have adopted partial bans on aerosol uses, limited CFC production capacity, or have agreed to participate in meetings aimed at reducing CFC emissions. It is most unfortunate that more international cooperation has not been forthcoming. Even if the United States reduced its CFC emissions by 70 percent (a very substantial cutback), eventual worldwide ozone depletion would only be reduced from 32 to 26 percent as long as the rest of the world took no control measures. Thus, there is little incentive for the United States to take control measures if the rest of the world does not—if it did, it would bear a very large share of the costs, but receive few benefits because ozone depletion would continue to be fueled by worldwide CFC emissions.

Nevertheless, in an October 7, 1980, Advance Notice of Proposed Rulemaking (a warning that new regulation might be issued), EPA announced that it was considering additional controls on CFCs, controls that would be directed at nonaerosol uses. At that time, EPA also announced that if additional regulations were proposed, the agency would favor the use of limitations on total CFC production which allowed individual producers and/or users to sell the right to produce or use CFCs among themselves. The favor with which EPA treated such a marketable permit system is traceable to the considerable cost savings it would allow when compared with mandatory bans on certain uses of CFCs.

As this book went to press, however, EPA had proposed no new regulations governing nonaerosol uses. In fact, momentum appears to have swung somewhat in the opposite direction. Legislation has been introduced in both the Senate and House of Representatives that, if passed into law, would prohibit further regulation of CFCs until ozone depletion is actually detected or until CFC-producing countries around the world reached agreement on the need for reducing emissions. At the same time, a lobbying organization—the Alliance for Responsible CFC Policy—formed to agitate against additional CFC controls and has emphasized the many uncertainties in present knowledge concerning the

CFC/ozone depletion hypothesis. It appears unlikely that any further CFC regulation will soon be forthcoming.

Recommendations

Our first recommendation is a very direct one. *It is that the climate problems discussed here must be given more attention than they have been receiving.* This is so for a number of reasons.

First, it should be clear from this discussion that a genuine, serious problem may well exist. The global climate may warm, in the next eighty years, at a rate five or six times faster than any change of similar length experienced in the past 6,000 years.

There is a second reason why climate problems should be given more attention. Although their adverse effects may take some time to appear, both the CO_2 and the CFC problems will be difficult to reverse or "shut down" if and when it is decided to do something about them. This is true for CFCs because of the existence of banked emissions—CFCs would continue to be released for a number of years even if all new production were to cease. Hence, we cannot wait for irrefutable evidence before we act and expect that shutting down production of CFCs will prevent any future releases to the atmosphere.

A similar mechanism is at work in the CO_2 problem. Once in the atmosphere, excess CO_2 will remain there for hundreds of years. Furthermore, the oceans store some of the heat produced by the CO_2 greenhouse effect, delaying the realization that the earth is entering a warmer era. This "flywheel effect," as it has been called, must be taken into account in deciding how much time there is to observe temperature changes before it is necessary to act to slow the release of CO_2 into the atmosphere.

In light of the uncertainties about the form and distribution of the CO_2-induced climate change, it seems wise in developing long-term plans to allow for the possibility of such a change. For instance, by starting now gradually to reduce new construction in low-lying coastal areas, it is possible to limit the capital infrastructure that would be at risk in the event of rising sea level. In fact, such actions may be desirable quite apart from the protection they would afford against warming. Development of barrier islands has often been cited as environmentally destructive, and federal flood insurance is already under attack for encouraging the rebuilding of flood-damaged homes that will inevitably be destroyed again. By restricting new building in coastal areas, the country might not only buy some social insurance against CO_2-induced warming, but may also satisfy less speculative and shorter term objectives as well.

Our second recommendation follows directly from the first. It should be clear that the greatest barriers to effective planning—either to temper the extent of induced climate change or to prepare to live with the change—are the uncertainties involved in foreseeing the amount, kind, and timing of the change in a convincing way. *Reducing these uncertainties should, therefore, be a steady policy for some years to come.* The best way to learn more about climate problems is to study them, and this requires the commitment of resources to research. The importance of research is well illustrated by several cases alluded to above. As scientists came to improve their understanding of the interaction between oxides of nitrogen and those of chlorine, they downgraded the SST/ozone depletion problem. Similarly, new knowledge about chemical reactions has from time to time both raised and lowered the estimate of the eventual ozone depletion that would result from continued CFC releases at present levels.

In spite of reductions in federal government spending, CFC-related research appears to be holding its own. In fiscal year 1981, about $20 million was spent on scientific research related to CFCs, with NASA contributing about $12 million of that, and EPA, the National Oceanic and Atmospheric Administration (NOAA), and the Department of Transportation accounting for most of the rest. This total was scheduled to increase by about 30 percent in 1982, largely as a result of an increase in NASA's CFC research budget to nearly $20 million. Most of this money was devoted to the ozone depletion aspect of the CFC problem.

The research picture is less favorable with respect to CO_2 and other "greenhouse" gases. In fiscal year 1982, the federal government spent about $21.5 million on research related to CO_2, about $12 million of which came from the Department of Energy (DOE). The tentative funding for FY 1983 was on the order of $17 million, with DOE's share declining slightly to $8 million. Other research in 1983 will be funded by the National Oceanic and Atmospheric Administration (about $2.2 million), the National Science Foundation (about $5 million), and the U.S. Geological Survey ($0.5 million). However, the DOE activities are slated to be decreased and dispersed to other agencies; almost all studies of socioeconomic consequences of the climate shifts that may occur as a result of CO_2 accumulation in the atmosphere have been eliminated; the National Climate Program Office has not received much funding or attention. In other areas the picture is similar—studies of techniques to shift from fossil fuels to conservation or other energy sources have been drastically reduced. In light of the magnitude of the potential problem and its national and international scope, there should be strong, steady federal research funding.

Our third recommendation has to do with steps that might be taken to forestall the kinds of climate changes discussed above. The country ought to be engaged now in a search for what might be called low-cost insurance policies against adverse climate change. That is, a process should be underway to rank the various means available to reduce emissions of CFCs or CO_2. For instance, certain nonaerosol applications of CFCs appear to lend themselves to the substitution of other chemicals for CFCs (flexible foams, cleaning agents, and sterilization are the best examples) in the same way aerosol uses were easily eliminated. If the cost of making these substitutions is small, it might be wise to begin doing so as a hedge against the possibility that CFCs are more harmful than is now thought to be the case. At the same time, the United States should continue to press in international forums for the worldwide elimination of all aerosol uses, since reasonably available substitutes for CFCs do exist.

An analogous search should be underway for means of reducing emissions of CO_2 into the atmosphere. One of the most promising means may be energy conservation. Although estimates differ considerably, some studies conclude that U.S. energy needs can be reduced appreciably at little or no additional cost.[27] In other words, these studies find that not only can investments in insulation, cogeneration, and other conservation measures reduce energy use, but they can also reduce energy bills by as much or more than they cost. Still another way of putting this is the following: not only might certain energy conservation measures be socially efficient (by taking CO_2 risks into account), they might also be *privately* efficient (and save money for energy users). Even if energy conservation is not attractive from the standpoint of private profitability, or even socially profitable when one takes into account the commonly recognized external costs associated with energy extraction and use, the fact that conservation *also* implies reduced CO_2 emissions might tip the balance in its favor. This seems an inappropriate time to pull back so precipitously from research on conservation.

The measures just discussed are aimed at avoiding at least some of the climate changes that would otherwise take place. A "balanced portfolio" of protective measures should also include some aimed at adapting to climate changes that may be inevitable or too expensive to prevent. In fact, most studies of the socioeconomic impacts of potential climate

[27] Many references to studies on influencing energy demand can be found in Bach, *Interactions of Energy and Climate.*

TABLE 6–7. Some Major U.S. Crops and the Extent to Which They Are Dominated by a Few Varieties

	Hectares (millions) 1976	Value ($ millions) 1976	Total varieties	Major varieties	Hectarage, % of major varieties
Corn	33,664	14,742	197	6	71
Wheat	28,662	6,201	269	10	55
Soybean	20,009	8,487	62	6	56
Cotton	4,411	3,350	50	3	53
Rice	1,012	770	14	4	65
Potato	556	1,182	82	4	72
Peanut	611	749	15	9	95
Peas	51	22	50	2	96

Source: Norman Myers, The Sinking Ark (Oxford, Pergamon, 1979) p. 36.

change emphasize adaptation rather than prevention. This makes some sense since, for many activities likely to be affected by climate change, adaptation may be effective and relatively inexpensive.

The most obvious area where such adaptation might occur is agriculture. In fact, it has been suggested that it might be possible to gain some insight about future agricultural adaptation to climate changes by examining past responses to alterations in growing conditions. Such an examination might suggest ways to facilitate the desired adaptation and lessen unproductive efforts if climate changes significantly.

One adjustment mechanism that has been used for centuries is plant breeding—selecting those varieties that provide resistance to specific pests and that thrive in specific soil and climate conditions. This sort of selection operates best when there are a number of native varieties to choose from. The demands of modern agriculture, however, operate against diversity. In the United States, 40 percent of red winter wheat acreage is planted with just two varieties and their derivatives.[28] At least half and as much as 96 percent of all U.S. crop production is derived from a few major varieties (see table 6–7).[29] When one considers the huge acreages of genetically uniform crops that are planted in this country, a climate change that alters growing conditions or introduces new disease strains might have profound and serious consequences.

One of the best forms of insurance against such a catastrophe is a gene pool. Native varieties become extinct once they are replaced by a "bred" seed and thus can only be saved by storage in a germplasm bank. The U.S. Department of Agriculture has been collecting and cataloging

[28] National Academy of Sciences, Genetic Vulnerability of Major Crops (Washington, D.C., 1972).
[29] Norman Myers, The Sinking Ark (Oxford, Pergamon, 1979).

new seed varieties since 1888, resulting in an enormous potential pool. In recent years, however, the program has received relatively little attention, and seed varieties as well as viability have been lost. A recent review of the system has emphasized the importance of improving the organization and management of the germplasm bank and upgrading its collection, maintenance, and storage procedures.[30]

There are several characteristics of a society that enhance its ability to adapt to change, including its level of economic well-being, the education of its labor force, the flexibility of its capital stock, and its technological sophistication.[31] Unfortunately, these characteristics are not easily or quickly altered. Perhaps the best that can be hoped for is that increasing awareness of potential climate changes will impress on individuals the need for flexibility in their personal and business plans. Surely no good farmer would lock himself into a cropping pattern if he were aware of potential climate changes that might adversely affect this pattern. Thus, basic scientific information that is well disseminated is sure to influence individual decision-making even when it does no more than raise the possibility of climatic disturbance.

CONCLUSIONS

The climate problems discussed above are among the most vexing natural resource problems mankind faces. This is so primarily because of their uncertainty. Indeed, reasonable people disagree not only on the magnitude of key links in the CO_2 or CFC chains, but sometimes even about the direction of effects. In addition, the global scope of the problems and the distant date at which certain effects will be felt add to the scientific and political complications of policymaking.

In spite of the uncertainties, global warming and ozone depletion deserve more serious attention than they are getting. This is partly because of the problem society may have in reversing both effects when and if a decision to do so is made. In fact, the emerging consensus about the likelihood of a significant, CO_2-induced global warming suggests that some measures should perhaps be taken now. These might include additional efforts at energy conservation as well as attempts to increase the adaptability of plants and animals, including man, to climate change.

[30] General Accounting Office, *Better Collection and Maintenance Procedures Needed to Help Protect Agriculture's Germplasm Resources.* Report to the Secretary of Agriculture (Washington, D.C., U.S. General Accounting Office, 1981). See chapter 4 for a more detailed discussion of germplasm and its potential.

[31] Lester Lave, "A More Feasible Social Response," *Technology Review* vol. 84, no. 2 (November/December 1981) pp. 23–31.

With respect to CFCs, two steps seem wise. First, the United States should be working diligently in international forums to effect a coordinated worldwide response to the threats CFCs pose. Second, serious consideration should be given to the least costly additional restrictions on domestic CFC use. While it may still be somewhat premature to take new regulatory action, a contingency plan should exist in case new studies reaffirm the seriousness of the problem.

7

Water Supplies

Kenneth D. Frederick

The adequacy of our water resources has emerged as one of the nation's principal resource concerns in the 1980s. These concerns have been articulated and spread through extensive newspaper, magazine, and television coverage of current and future water problems. For example, the February 23, 1981 cover of *Newsweek* depicted the United States covered with parched earth and asked "Are we running out of water?" The accompanying article, "The Browning of America," noted that "Drought, waste and pollution threaten a water shortage whose impact may rival the energy crisis." The title of a feature article in the June 29, 1981 *U.S. News and World Report* asked a similar question while a subheading responded that "nearly every part of the United States faces serious water troubles—either lack of supply or doubtful purity. Experts warn that time for remedies is rapidly running out." These are just two of many such articles appearing in the last year or so.

Water problems tend to be regional or even local in nature since water is a bulky resource in relation to its value and since transporting it long distances out of natural channels is costly and uneconomic for most uses. Nevertheless, there are a number of legitimate national water concerns. In particular, questions have been raised about water supplies to meet future food and energy needs, the burgeoning growth of cities and towns in semiarid regions, and the recreational demands of a population that has more leisure and more interest in outdoor sports.

216

This chapter analyzes the problems associated with the availability of water in the United States. It begins by detailing the various sources and uses of water in this country and then addresses water availability on the one hand and agricultural output and energy development on the other. This is followed by a section pointing out the link between water availability and water quality. A discussion of the laws, policies, and institutions which affect water availability in the United States precedes the conclusions and recommendations.

NATURE AND IMPORTANCE OF THE RESOURCE

Supplies

Water is the nation's most abundant resource. Precipitation within the forty-eight conterminous states averages 30 inches per year or 4,200 billion gallons per day (bgd).[1] Even larger quantities of fresh water are stored in the nation's surface and underground reservoirs. Surface reservoirs contain about 150 trillion gallons of fresh water and the water stored in the nation's aquifers (i.e., subterranean bodies of unconsolidated material such as rock, sand, and soil) is more than 200 times surface storage. Estimates of the water stored within 2,500 feet of the land surface of the conterminous United States range from 33,000 trillion to 59,000 trillion gallons. The lower estimate exceeds the nation's cumulative precipitation over two decades and is roughly equivalent to the cumulative discharge of the Mississippi River over the past 200 years.[2]

It is the hydrological cycle that makes water a renewable resource that can literally be used over and over again. Solar radiation draws water from surface water bodies (especially the oceans) and plants, leaving behind salts and other impurities that may have diminished the quality of the water. The cleansed water is moved in vapor form into the atmosphere by the winds until it condenses into water droplets and is precipitated as rain, snow, or hail. The process continues indefinitely with no significant change in the amount of water within the global system. However, the location of the water, both in the atmosphere and where it precipitates to the ground, is highly variable (see chapter 6 for a discussion of activities which can alter local climates).

Figure 7–1 shows the disposition of precipitation within the conterminous United States, assuming 1975 demand and average rainfall. Nearly

[1] All references to water supply and demand in the United States are for the forty-eight conterminous states.

[2] U.S. Water Resources Council, *The Nation's Water Resources, 1975–2000* (Washington, D.C.) vol. 1, summary, pp. 12–20.

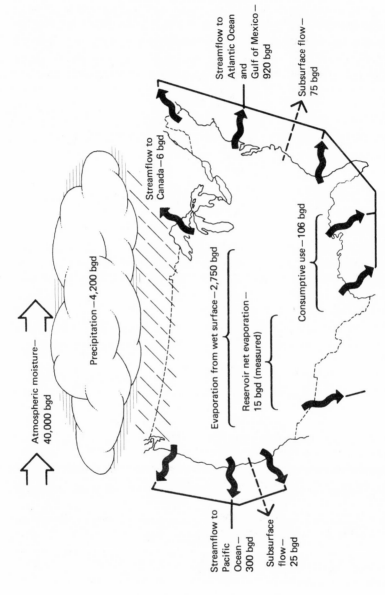

Figure 7-1. Water supply and use in the United States (billions of gallons per day). (Redrawn from the U.S. Water Resources Council, *Second National Water Assessment, 1975–2000* Washington, D.C.).

two-thirds of precipitation is almost immediately returned to the atmosphere through evaporation from wet surfaces or transpiration by vegetation. Although this water is considered to be lost for use, transpiration by trees and crops is vital to the well-being of all forms of life. Moreover, some transpiration is influenced by the crops and trees man chooses to plant and the nonuseful vegetation he chooses to eliminate. Nevertheless, only the remaining 35 percent of the precipitation is considered potential supply. Of this, 91 percent flows in surface or subsurface streams to saltwater bodies, 1 percent is evaporated from reservoirs, and less than 1 percent flows to Canada and Mexico. Only 106 billion gallons per day or 7 percent of this potential is purposefully consumed within the country.

Use

Water is one of the earth's most important and versatile resources. Neither plants nor animals can survive very long without it, and water is used in virtually everything man does. It is used more than any other material by industry, it is used both directly and indirectly to produce energy, it provides the basis of much of our outdoor recreation, is an important part of our transportation, and serves as a vehicle for disposing of society's wastes.

Water uses are differentiated as to whether or not they involve withdrawing water from a natural channel. Offstream water use by function for the forty-eight conterminous states is summarized in table 7–1. The portion of water withdrawn for offstream uses that is actually consumed (consumption is defined as water withdrawn but not returned to a surface or groundwater source) varies widely, depending on the use. Less than one-third of total freshwater withdrawals are consumed, but the range varies from less than 2 percent for steam electric generation to 100 percent for livestock use.

Irrigation, which accounts for nearly half of annual water withdrawals and more than four-fifths of consumption, is the dominant offstream water use. A more than doubling of irrigated acreage since 1950 has made irrigation water an important factor in the production of the nation's food and fiber. Irrigated land, which was about 60 million acres, accounted for about one-seventh of the nation's cropland and one-fourth of the value of the nation's crops in 1977.[3]

Domestic and manufacturing uses each account for about 6 percent of total consumption while no other use accounts for much more than

[3] Acreage data are based on Soil Conservation Service, "1977 Natural Resources Inventory," revised February 1980.

TABLE 7–1. Offstream Water Use: Total Freshwater Withdrawals and Consumption, by Functional Use for the Conterminous Forty-eight States as of 1975

	Withdrawals		Consumption	
Use	Billion gallons per day	% of total	Billion gallons per day	% of total
Domestic	22.7	6.8	6.2	5.9
Commercial	5.5	1.6	1.1	1.0
Manufacturing	50.8	15.1	6.0	5.7
Agriculture				
Irrigation	156.8	46.8	85.6	81.1
Livestock	1.9	0.6	1.9	1.8
Steam electric generation	88.9	26.5	1.4	1.3
Minerals industry	7.0	2.1	2.2	2.1
Public lands and others	1.9	0.6	1.2	1.1
Total	335.4	100.0	105.6	100.0

Source: U.S. Water Resources Council, The Nation's Water Resources, 1975–2000 (Washington, D.C.) vol. 3, appendix II, p. 40.

2 percent. Per capita domestic water withdrawals in 1975 exceeded 100 gallons per day, nearly three-fourths of which was for drinking, cooking, washing, and sanitary needs.[4] Not only are the quantities of water used for manufacturing and mining small relative to those consumed for irrigation, the quality of this water does not always have to be high. Nevertheless, water is an important input to these sectors, as has been demonstrated by concerns that failure to secure water rights may prevent western energy resources from being developed on a timely basis.

If the only uses for water were those summarized in table 7–1, there would be little cause for concern regarding supplies, at least from a national perspective. For instance, consumption accounts for only 2.5 percent of total precipitation and 7.3 percent of that portion of rainfall potentially available for use. However, there are important nonconsumptive or instream uses of water. Navigation requires minimum streamflows; freshwater flows into estuaries are essential to the ecology and often to the economic vitality of those areas; free-flowing rivers and streams are essential to fish, wildlife, recreation, and other amenity services; and rivers and streams have long served as sources of power and vehicles for disposing of society's wastes. These uses represent additional but generally unquantified demands on the nation's water resources.

[4] U.S. Water Resources Council, The Nation's Water Resources, 1975–2000, vol. 1, p. 32.

The Second National Water Assessment represents the first government effort to examine instream flow needs nationwide.[5] Many of these uses are complementary in their demands on water, and to simplify the task of quantifying instream needs, the Second Assessment focused on streamflow levels needed to maintain fish and wildlife populations and for navigation. In all subregions, the fish and wildlife use was dominant in that the quantities of water required to satisfy these needs also were sufficient to meet minimum navigation requirements. Thus, the Assessment's instream flow needs were estimated as the monthly flows required to support wildlife and outdoor recreation; these needs are estimated at nearly 10 times offstream consumption for the forty-eight states. The nation's total water use, defined as the sum of instream use and offstream consumption, is about 87 percent of assessed streamflow (i.e., the flow that would be available in a year with average precipitation if consumption and groundwater mining were eliminated but 1975 water transfers and reservoirs were maintained) (see table 7–2).

Complications in Satisfying Water Needs

The preceding sketch of the nation's average, aggregate water supplies and uses ignores several factors important for identifying and assessing the adequacy of water supplies. Most water needs are time and location specific and they do not necessarily coincide with natural supply availability. In fact, per capita water consumption in the seventeen western states is more than twelve times that in the much more amply watered eastern states,[6] and the periods of heaviest precipitation may not correspond to the periods of greatest need. Nor are all instream water uses mutually compatible. Of particular concern are the conflicts between use of water bodies to dispose of wastes and their use for other purposes, especially recreation, fish and wildlife, and other amenities.

Table 7–2 presents data on the use and supply of water for eighteen water resource regions covering the forty-eight conterminous states.[7]

---

[5] An earlier Resources for the Future study by Nathaniel Wollman and Gilbert W. Bonem, *The Outlook for Water: Quality, Quantity and National Growth* (Baltimore, Md., Johns Hopkins University Press for Resources for the Future, 1971) estimates the water flows needed to maintain certain water quality standards.

[6] C. Richard Murray and E. Bodette Reeves, *Estimated Use of Water in the United States in 1975*, U.S. Geological Survey Circular 765, 1977, p. 8.

[7] Water use and supply data are available for regions divided along hydrological boundaries. The Second National Water Assessment divides the nation into 106 water resources subregions, which are grouped into 21 major water resources regions. Eighteen of these regions and 99 of these subregions comprise the conterminous United States; the other regions are Alaska, Hawaii, and the Caribbean area.

TABLE 7–2. Annual Average Water Use and Streamflow Data by Water
Resource Regions, 1975

Water resource region	Instream use (bgd)	Offstream use (bgd)	Instream as a percent of total use	Assessed streamflow at outflow point (bgd)	Total use as percent of assessed streamflow
1 New England	69.0	0.5	99	78.7	89
2 Mid Atlantic	68.8	1.8	97	81.0	87
3 South Atlantic–Gulf	188.7	4.9	97	232.5	83
4 Great Lakes	64.0	2.6	96	75.3	88
5 Ohio	160.5	2.1	99	180.1	90
6 Tennessee	38.5	0.3	99	41.1	95
7 Upper Mississippi	110.8	16.6	87	135.1	94
8 Lower Mississippi	359.0	30.8	92	455.4	86
9 Souris–Red–Rainy	3.7	0.1	97	6.1	62
10 Missouri	34.0	15.5	69	57.0	87
11 Arkansas–White–Red	46.2	8.1	85	65.2	83
12 Texas Gulf	22.9	11.3	67	34.0	101
13 Rio Grande	2.3	4.2	35	4.8	136
14 Upper Colorado	7.9	2.4	77	12.4	84
15 Lower Colorado	6.9	7.0	50	6.2	225
16 Great Basin	3.4	3.8	47	5.8	125
17 Pacific Northwest	214.0	11.9	95	266.6	84
18 California	32.6	26.6	55	71.8	82
Regions 1–18[a]	1,035.2	105.6	91	1,318.1	87

Source: U.S. Water Resources Council, The Nation's Water Resources, 1975–2000 (Washington, D.C.) vol. 3, appendix II, pp. 106–107.

[a] Instream uses and assessed streamflows are not additive for all regions since one region's flow may be input to another (e.g., the Upper Colorado flows into the Lower Colorado).

These data reveal several significant regional differences as well as a number of potential problem areas. The first three columns of table 7–2 indicate a marked regional difference in the relative importance of instream and offstream uses. Instream uses are particularly dominant in the relatively well-watered East and Northwest. They account for at least 95 percent of the total use in eight water resource regions. In contrast, offstream uses are much higher relative to streamflows in the arid and semiarid West.

A comparison of total water use with assessed streamflow provides one indication of potential regional water supply problems. Total water use exceeds streamflow in four western water resource regions, implying that some of the uses identified in the Second Assessment are not being met or that water stocks are being depleted. In the Lower Colorado basin, offstream use alone exceeds streamflow and total use is more than twice streamflow. A more detailed regional look indicates that water use exceeds streamflow in twenty-four western subregions. These subregions, which comprise the shaded area in figure 7–2, extend from

Central California and Nevada through most of Arizona, New Mexico, Texas, Oklahoma, Kansas, Nebraska, and eastern Colorado.

Focusing on average annual precipitation and streamflow presents an overly optimistic picture of U.S. water supplies. Underlying the average are periods of droughts and floods which are only partially offset by available water storage facilities. Thus, average annual streamflow figures suggest a theoretical upper limit for long-term surface supplies which will never be reached. Only 675 bgd, less than half of the potential supply identified in figure 7–1, actually is available for intensive beneficial uses in 95 out of 100 years with existing surface storage facilities.[8]

Although additional storage capacity is being constructed, sizable increases in usable supplies through new dams and reservoirs will be less common in the future and offset in part by sedimentation, which is reducing the effective capacity of existing reservoirs. (See chapter 8 for a discussion of erosion.) Both the direct and indirect costs of new water storage projects are rising. In general, the best sites for dams and reservoirs have been used, making additional construction more expensive per unit of storage. More important, the indirect costs of additional dams are rising as society places a higher value on the instream uses of this water and on the environmental amenities attached to natural watercourses as opposed to reservoirs and canals. Furthermore, surface storage, especially in arid areas, increases evaporation losses, which in turn reduces effective water availability.

The variability of annual streamflows within the eighteen water resource regions is illustrated in table 7–3, which shows wet, dry, and very dry year flows as a percentage of the average annual flow. For the forty-eight states, wet year streamflows are 59 percent above the average while dry year flows are 28 percent less and very dry year flows are 45 percent less than the average. Large variations in annual streamflows are particularly common in the West. Excluding the Pacific Northwest, western streamflows as a percent of the average range from 188 percent in a wet year to 61 percent in a dry year and 36 percent in a very dry year.[9] These percentage variations from the average are 66 percent greater in wet years and 52 percent greater in very dry years in these western water resource regions than they are in the rest of the nation. Moreover, seasonal fluctuations, which add to the uncertainty of supply, often are more pronounced in the arid and semiarid West.

Although the focus of this chapter is on water supply issues, supply cannot be divorced completely from water quality considerations. One of the earliest uses of water was as a medium for waste disposal. The

---

[8] U.S. Water Resources Council, *The Nation's Water Resources, 1975–2000*, vol. 1, pp. 12–13.

[9] These data refer to water resource regions 10 to 16 and 18.

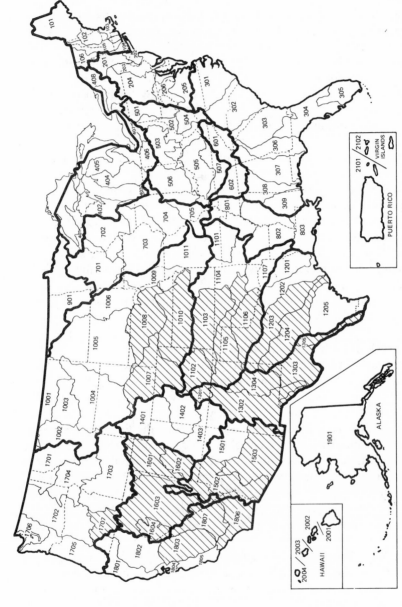

Figure 7-2. Water resource subregions where total water use exceeds streamflows in an average year. (Data from U.S. Water Resources Council, *Second National Water Assessment, 1975–2000*, Washington, D.C.)

TABLE 7–3. Variability of Surface Water Supplies: Wet, Dry, and Very Dry Year Streamflows as a Percentage of Average Year Streamflows

Region	Wet year[a]	Dry year[b]	Very dry year[c]
1 New England	138	80	62
2 Mid Atlantic	145	77	61
3 South Atlantic–Gulf	156	72	53
4 Great Lakes	143	79	62
5 Ohio	143	79	59
6 Tennessee	142	88	77
7 Upper Mississippi	156	76	54
8 Lower Mississippi	175	65	47
9 Souris–Red–Rainy	190	57	30
10 Missouri	168	68	40
11 Arkansas–White–Red	193	60	35
12 Texas Gulf	220	43	22
13 Rio Grande	367	25	17
14 Upper Colorado	156	70	39
15 Lower Colorado	106	88	75
16 Great Basin	181	62	46
17 Pacific Northwest	135	84	70
18 California	184	63	41
Regions 1–18	159	72	55

Source: U.S. Water Resources Council, *The Nation's Water Resources, 1975–2000* (Washington, D.C.) vol. 1, pp. 14–15.

[a] A wet year is one in which the flow will be exceeded in only 5 of every 100 years.

[b] A dry year is one in which the flow will be exceeded in 80 of every 100 years.

[c] A very dry year is one in which the flow will be exceeded in 95 of every 100 years.

capacity of lakes, rivers, and streams to assimilate waste is large. As long as the wastes do not exceed this capacity, disposal is not competitive with several other nonconsumptive uses of the water and society benefits from an inexpensive means of waste disposal. Once this capacity is exceeded, however, the indirect costs of this use rise rapidly. In many parts of the nation, the assimilative capacity of lakes, rivers, and streams has been grossly violated by growth in the quantity, toxicity, and persistence of the pollutants introduced, either intentionally or inadvertently. Major water bodies became less desirable or even unusable for drinking water, recreation, and many other uses where the value of water is sensitive to the quality. Thus, degradation adds to the pressures on the availability of supply.

Groundwater provides an additional source of supply as well as a means of compensating for fluctuations in precipitation. Indeed, these vast subterranean supplies provided 24 percent of the nation's freshwater withdrawals in 1975.[10] About 39 percent of the country's irrigation water is pumped from the ground, and many small towns rely on groundwater for all their water needs.[11] Even though it will be feasible to extract only a small fraction of the water stored within 2,500 feet of the surface, this still leaves enormous quantities that can be withdrawn economically. Nevertheless, there are factors restricting the role of groundwater in meeting the country's water needs. Ground and surface water supplies generally are interrelated. In an average year groundwater that emerges as natural springs or other seepage supplies about 30 percent of the country's streamflow.[12] Consequently, in some areas a primary effect of pumping groundwater is to deplete neighboring surface flows. In such cases, groundwater adds little or nothing to usable supplies.

Conversely, aquifers are recharged from the downward percolation of surface waters. Although most aquifers receive some recharge from the infiltration of surface waters, groundwater withdrawals may exceed recharge. If this occurs over the long term, the aquifer is being mined or overdrawn, and water costs rise as pumping depths increase and well yields decline. Furthermore, there may be indirect costs such as subsidence or saltwater intrusion associated with mining. Subsidence is particularly serious when urban areas are affected. In the Houston–Pasadena area of Texas and in Las Vegas, city streets and buildings have been threatened. Saltwater intrusion occurs when the fresh water of coastal aquifers is mined and replaced by seawater. As a wedge of saltwater intrudes into the aquifer, the value of the remaining fresh water as well as the storage value of the aquifer may be destroyed. Saltwater intrusion is a problem along parts of both the California and Texas coasts.

MAJOR ISSUES

Water and Food

An adequate and timely supply of water is essential to high-yield agriculture. In most years precipitation alone permits good yields throughout most of the East but in the West will support only the most water-

---

[10] U.S. Water Resources Council, *The Nation's Water Resources, 1975–2000*, vol. 1, p. 25.

[11] Murray and Reeves, *Estimated Use of Water in the United States in 1975*, p. 25.

[12] U.S. Water Resources Council, *The Nation's Water Resources, 1975–2000*, vol. 1, p. 18.

conserving plants. With water, vast areas in the arid and semiarid West could be converted into highly productive agricultural areas. Indeed, about 50 million acres in the West are irrigated. Although this is only one-fifth of that region's total cropland and pasture use, more than one-half of the value of the West's agricultural production comes from these lands.[13]

Past expansion of western irrigation was spurred by access to inexpensive water. The earliest farmers were granted rights in perpetuity to neighboring surface waters. Federal water projects provided enormous subsidies for transporting water to more distant fields and, until the early 1970s, low energy prices kept the cost of pumping groundwater low. This expansion, however, has been the principal factor in the region's transition from a situation in which water could be obtained readily at low cost to one in which supplies are becoming both more expensive and more difficult to secure.

Future changes in agricultural production will be dictated by very different conditions. Total water use now exceeds streamflows throughout the areas with the longest growing seasons; the opportunities for developing new irrigation water supplies through federal projects are much more limited and costly; 22 million acre-feet of water are being mined annually from western aquifers; the combination of higher pumping distances and energy prices have made groundwater much more expensive; and nonagricultural demands for scarce water supplies are increasing rapidly. As the consumer of 90 percent of the West's water, and as a relatively low-value user, irrigation is the sector most acutely affected by changes in the water situation.

While water undoubtedly will constrain the future growth of western irrigation, doubts have also arisen about the adequacy of western water to sustain *current* levels of irrigation. According to a recent magazine report, "Excessive pumping of underground water pools in arid Western states is forcing a return to marginal dry-land farming after decades of spectacular crop yields made possible by flooding fields with cheap water. Many farmers may be forced out of business because they cannot afford to bid for water supplies against cash-rich energy companies."[14]

The transition from abundance to scarcity has not been an abrupt one. It has been under way for at least several decades at varying rates and intensities in different parts of the West. Surface waters were the first to be developed but there has been virtually no increase in total western surface water withdrawals for irrigation since the mid-1950s. In

[13] U.S. Department of Agriculture, Soil Conservation Service, "Basic Statistics: 1977 National Resources Inventory (NRI)," revised February 1980, table 3.

[14] *U.S. News and World Report*, June 29, 1981, p. 34.

view of other in- and offstream pressures on these resources, no significant future increases are likely. On the other hand, major decreases in
surface irrigation have not occurred and are unlikely to for at least a
few more decades. Farmers have the most senior rights to most of the
water, and the dominance of irrigation in western water use suggests
that large percentage increases in nonagricultural uses can be met with
small percentage reductions in irrigation use.

Groundwater has been the source for the expansion of western irrigation for nearly two decades, and virtually all of the increases and most
of the decreases in irrigation over the next two decades are likely to
involve groundwater. While groundwater costs are sensitive to rising
energy prices and pumping depths, significant increases in agricultural
prices could offset these negative impacts and thereby encourage development of new irrigated lands and slow the decline in irrigated farming in areas with significant groundwater mining.

Despite the higher water costs and the limits on developing new supplies, some net expansion of western irrigated acreage is likely for at
least another decade or two, even in the absence of higher crop prices.
Water is still available at acceptable costs for irrigation in Nebraska and
some other, more northern regions. The expansion of irrigated acreage
in these regions should continue to more than offset declines in areas
where irrigation is declining because of diversion to nonagricultural uses
or groundwater mining. With no change in real crop prices, western
irrigated acreage might increase about 3 million acres or 6 percent over
the next two to three decades. A 25 percent increase in real crop prices
could add another 4.5 million acres to the total. Such changes are small
compared with the doubling of acreage from 1950 to 1977 and the 21
percent rise from 1967 to 1977. But acreage data alone reflect only a
part of irrigation's potential contribution to the nation's agricultural
growth.

The principal changes in western irrigation in the coming decades are
likely to be qualitative rather than quantitative in nature. Higher water
costs and more limited access to new supplies will make water-saving
investments and management practices more profitable. Although there
are no substitutes for water in the biological processes, there are numerous opportunities where inputs such as capital, labor, and improved
irrigation and agronomic management can save water. A 1979 government task force report concluded that in addition to "on-going programs,
public and private investments of up to five billion dollars should be
made over the next three decades to implement needed water conservation measures." According to the report, these investments could
"result in decreasing gross annual diversions by 15 to 20 million acre-

feet and making two to five million acre-feet of water available for new uses."[15] Nonstructural measures may prove to be even more important than structural alternatives for improving the returns to water in irrigation. Improved scheduling of irrigation, higher value or less water-using crops, tillage practices designed to conserve soil moisture, and seed varieties offering higher returns to water are just some of the measures that will become increasingly attractive to farmers confronted with high water costs.

While the overall potential for increasing irrigated production without increases in total water use is great, the extent to which this potential is realized will depend in large part on the institutions and policies affecting water use. The policies needed to ensure the realization of this potential, as well as a timely supply of water for other uses, are considered in a subsequent section.

Irrigation's contribution to U.S. agriculture is not limited to what happens in the West. Even in humid areas, irrigation improves yields by protecting against dry periods, encouraging use of fertilizers, pesticides, and other yield-increasing inputs, and in some cases making it possible to double-crop the land.

Unlike the situation in the West, conditions have become more favorable for irrigation in the East.[16] Water supplies are seldom a serious constraint since the amounts applied are less and the available supplies are greater. Moreover, energy is not as important to water costs since the quantities of water applied are much less than in arid areas. Technological improvements have made irrigation less expensive and more versatile, and the increasing cost and productivity of complementary inputs such as fertilizer, pesticides, machinery, and land increase the incentive to reduce the risk of water shortages.

Since rainfall in the East is adequate for good yields in most years, irrigation is profitable only in certain situations, such as rice fields, on high-value crops for which the difference in value between irrigated and dryland yields is sufficient to justify the added costs of irrigation, where it permits double-cropping, or on sandy soils which do not retain water

[15] U.S. Department of Interior, U.S. Department of Agriculture, Environmental Protection Agency, *Irrigation Water Use and Management: An InterAgency Task Force Report* (June 1979), p. ix.

[16] Two studies examining various aspects of eastern irrigation are James C. Hanson and James Pagano, "Growth and Prospects for Irrigation in the Eastern United States" and Robert M. Shulstad, Ralph May, Billy Herrington, and Jon M. Erstine, "The Economic Potential for the Expansion of Irrigation in the Mississippi Delta Region." Both studies are included in Pierre Crosson, project director, "Summary of Trends in U.S. Irrigation: Three Regional Studies," a Resources for the Future report to the Environmental Protection Agency's Environmental Research Laboratory, Athens, Georgia, George Bailey, project officer, June 1981.

well. Such situations were largely responsible for the expansion of eastern irrigation from about 1.5 million acres or 6 percent of the national total in 1950, to over 10 million acres or 17 percent of total irrigated acreage in 1977. Recent research suggests that conditions continue to favor the spread of eastern irrigation, especially within the Mississippi Delta and the areas in the Southeast and the Lake States with sandy soils.[17]

In conclusion, while water scarcity will markedly slow the expansion of irrigated acreage in the West, the value of production from these lands will continue to grow as farmers respond to opportunities for increasing the returns to water. Furthermore, both the acreage and the value of the products grown under irrigation in the East will continue to expand rapidly. Water is becoming an increasingly valuable resource and changes in the availability and demand for water will impose higher costs on some farmers. But water scarcity does not appear to pose any special threat to the nation's agricultural production. As we point out later, the real threat to irrigation's long-term contribution to U.S. agriculture will come if the country attempts to maintain a system of water institutions and laws which were developed during conditions of abundance. If this occurs, the opportunities and incentives for the wise use of scarce water supplies will be limited, along with irrigation's contribution to the nation's and the world's food and fiber needs.

Water and Energy

The 1970s brought turbulence, uncertainty, and rising costs to global energy markets. As the United States sought to establish secure supplies and contain the rise in prices, attention focused on developing the nation's vast coal and shale oil resources, most of which are located in the West.

The mining, conversion to liquid or gaseous fuels, and transport of these energy resources all require water. Water consumption with anticipated standard-sized plants and current technology is about 21 gallons for extracting a ton of coal, 107 gallons for extracting a barrel of petroleum through liquefaction, and 240 gallons for transporting a ton of coal through a slurry pipeline.[18] Applying these ratios to some of the ambitious schemes proposed for developing domestic energy resources implies major new demands on water supplies, much of which would come in areas where water demands already are pressing upon available supplies. Indeed, some analysts have concluded that water may constrain

[17] Ibid.
[18] Derived from data in the Aerospace Corporation, *Water-Related Constraints on Energy Production*. Aerospace Report no. ATR-89 (9409)-1, pp. 4-1 and 4-2 (June 1978).

the development of these energy resources.[19] Others fear that diverting water to energy development poses serious problems for meeting agricultural demands.[20]

Energy projects have always withdrawn large quantities of water, although consumption has been relatively small. In 1975, for example, energy uses accounted for more than one-fourth of the nation's water withdrawals, but only 3 percent of the consumption. This discrepancy is attributable to steam electric generation, which uses large volumes of water for cooling. Under prevailing technologies, this use consumes only 1 to 2 percent of the water withdrawn. Thus, while steam electric generation accounts for nearly 95 percent of energy-related withdrawals, it consumes only 44 percent of the total water consumed in energy production (see table 7–4). The mining of fuel minerals and the manufacture of petroleum account for more than half of the water consumed for energy purposes, but this amounts to less than 2 percent of total offstream consumption.

The eastern part of the nation withdraws ten times as much water for energy as does the West but, because of the dominance of steam electric uses in the East, total water consumption for energy is actually higher in the West. However, energy uses of water are relatively more important in the East, where they account for 54 percent of withdrawals and 9 percent of consumption. In comparison, energy uses account for only 4 percent of withdrawals and 2 percent of consumption in the West.

Projections in the Second National Water Assessment suggest that the consumption of water for energy purposes will increase more than threefold by the turn of the century, while withdrawals will decline by about 10 percent as a result of expected advances in cooling technology. Despite the rapid projected growth of consumption for energy, the Assessment's projections are not particularly alarming in terms of their total demands on water. They imply water for energy will rise to 10 percent of total offstream consumption for the forty-eight states, but only 5 percent in the water-scarce West.

There was concern that the Assessment had not taken adequate account of all likely energy developments and associated water require-

[19] For example, John Harte and Mohamed El-Gasseir in "Energy and Water" (*Science*, vol. 199, February 10, 1978, p. 623) conclude "that water consumption requirements place serious constraints on the future level of development of many of this country's energy options." John F. O'Leary while serving as deputy secretary of the Department of Energy noted that the constraint on the production of oil shale will not be derived from demand or resource constraints, but will be associated with water. See John F. O'Leary, "Water for Energy," p. 41 in Deborah M. Sluyter and Dabney Hart, eds., *Symposium on National Water Policy: Proceedings and Workshop Papers*, sponsored by the Mitre Corporation, June 1978, M78–54.

[20] *U.S. News and World Report*, June 29, 1981, p. 35.

TABLE 7–4. Water Use For Energy 1975, 1985, 2000
(billions of gallons per day)

	Withdrawals			Consumption		
	1975	1985	2000	1975	1985	2000
East (water resource regions 1–8)						
Second Assessment estimates of water for energy						
Steam electric	83.5	86.2	70.4	1.0	2.8	7.5
Mining fuels	1.0	1.3	1.6	0.3	0.4	0.5
Petroleum manufacturing	1.9	0.7	0.5	0.2	0.3	0.4
Subtotal	86.4	88.2	72.5	1.5	3.5	8.4
Aerospace Report estimates of additional water for energy[a]	—	—	—	—	1.4	6.9
Total water for energy uses	86.4	—	—	1.5	4.9	15.3
West (water resource regions 9–18)						
Second Assessment estimates of water for energy						
Steam electric	5.4	8.6	9.1	0.4	1.2	3.0
Mining fuels	1.6	1.8	1.9	1.0	1.2	1.3
Petroleum manufacturing	0.6	0.8	0.7	0.3	0.4	0.6
Subtotal	7.6	11.2	11.7	1.7	2.8	4.9
Aerospace Report estimates of additional water for energy[a]	—	—	—	—	0.7	4.4
Total water for energy uses	7.6	—	—	1.7	3.5	9.3
48 states (water resource regions 1–18)						
Second Assessment estimates of water for energy						
Steam electric	38.9	94.8	79.5	1.4	4.1	10.5
Mining fuels	2.5	3.1	3.5	1.3	1.6	1.8
Petroleum manufacturing	2.5	1.5	1.2	0.5	0.7	1.0
Subtotal	93.9	99.4	84.2	3.2	6.4	13.3
Aerospace Report estimates of additional water for energy[a]	—	—	—	—	2.1	11.4
Total water for energy uses	93.9	—	—	3.2	8.5	24.7

Sources: Second Assessment data are from U.S. Water Resources Council, *The Nation's Water Resources, 1975–2000*, vol. 3, appendix II, table II–4. Aerospace Report estimates are from Aerospace Corporation, *Water-Related Constraints on Energy Production*, Aerospace Report No. ATR-78(9409)-1, June 1978, table 6–2.

Note: Totals may not add due to rounding.

[a] The Aerospace Report does not provide water withdrawal projections.

ments. This led to a supplementary study by the Aerospace Corporation, which accepted all the Assessment's water supply data and all the demand projections except those relating to energy.[21] Using four federally generated energy development scenarios, the Aerospace report (AR) determined the maximum feasible limits for energy development and

[21] Aerospace Corporation, *Water-Related Constraints on Energy Production*.

the associated water requirements, assuming standard-sized plants and no special provisions to adopt water-conserving technologies.

The AR assumptions add 2.2 bgd or 35 percent by 1985 and 11.4 bgd or 86 percent by 2000 to the Assessment's projected levels of water consumption for energy purposes (see table 7–4). If realized, energy uses would account for 17 percent of the nation's and 38 percent of the East's total offstream water consumption. Within the West, water for energy rises from the 1975 level of about 2 percent of total offstream water consumption to nearly 4 percent by 1985 and 9 percent by 2000 under the AR assumptions. Furthermore, the energy demands would be localized, and within the affected regions major new demands on water supplies are implied. Where demand already exceeds renewable supplies, any increase requires either compensating reductions among other users or additional groundwater mining.

Projections such as those in the AR study underlie some of the concerns that water will either be insufficient to develop domestic energy resources or will be diverted in such large quantities from farming that the nation's ability to meet future agricultural demands will be seriously impaired. Several points are relevant for assessing these concerns.

- Development of energy resources in many areas of the West will require diverting water from other uses. Generally the water will come from agricultural or, where available, instream uses.

- If market forces are allowed to operate, water will be transferred from agricultural to energy users since the latter group can afford much higher water prices. Such transfers already have taken place in some areas, with positive benefits to both groups. Such sales have enabled farmers to earn more for their water rights than they ever could expect to earn in agricultural pursuits.

- Transfers of water rights from agricultural to energy uses will drastically alter the character of some communities. Within these communities, groups dependent on agriculture but lacking water rights to sell will be adversely affected by the transfers. The economic impacts need not be a matter of public concern since there will be numerous opportunities for these people to benefit from the changes. The potential environmental impacts, however, may be an item of legitimate public concern and action.

- The quantities of water likely to be shifted from current uses to energy are exaggerated by projections such as those in the AR study. First, the AR projections are for *maximum feasible* (as opposed to likely) energy development scenarios. More important, the quantities likely to be used for extracting, processing, and transporting a given energy output are overstated. Historically there have been few incentives to conserve water, and projections of water use which assume no change in the input of water per unit of energy output are reasonable only if water remains a virtually free resource. But if energy users bid water away from agriculture, this will create incentives to conserve. As with irrigation, there are numerous opportunities for conserving on water use for energy production and these opportunities become increasingly profitable as water costs rise.[22] Furthermore, new demands on water traditionally used in agriculture may be curtailed by having energy users exploit groundwater sources that are too deep or brackish for agriculture.

• While agricultural production will be adversely affected by transferring water to other uses, the impacts on national farm output will be negligible. The amounts of water that might be diverted from irrigation will be large in terms of the quantities available within affected locations but they will represent only a minor part of total irrigation water. And if rising energy demands lead farmers to view water as a more valuable resource, the negative impacts of transfers on agricultural output will be mitigated by water conservation practices among irrigators.

In summary, water supplies appear adequate to meet all probable needs for developing domestic energy resources. Whether or not supplies are made available to energy developers on a timely basis depends largely on institutional factors. Thus, our conclusion as to the impacts of water on energy development parallels that for western irrigation—the real threat that water availability poses to timely development of domestic energy resources (or to the future role of western irrigation) will come if the nation attempts to maintain a system of water institutions and laws which are appropriate only for conditions of abundance.

WATER QUALITY AND ADEQUACY OF SUPPLIES

Pollution

Water is seldom perfectly pure. Fortunately, it need not be so for most of its uses. However, very often quality affects the suitability of water

[22] For an examination of some of the water-conserving technologies available to energy producers, see David Abbey, "Energy Production and Water Resources in the Colorado River Basin," *Natural Resources Journal* vol. 19 (April 1979), University of New Mexico School of Law (Resources for the Future Reprint 170).

for certain uses. In some instances natural factors can affect water quality, but the major problems arise as a result of human activity. As the
introduction to this volume points out, we cannot go into great detail
here on traditional environmental policy, of which water pollution control is a major part.[23] Nevertheless, it may be useful to touch briefly on
the major impacts of pollution on water quality and availability.

Pollution of surface waters (lakes, streams, and rivers) comes from
three major sources: industrial manufacturing concerns that discharge
directly; municipal sewage treatment plants that serve households and
some commercial and industrial polluters; and an amalgam of what are
called nonpoint sources, consisting of farms, feedlots, streets and park-
ing lots, and other open areas from which pollution runs off into receiving waters. These sources all discharge both "conventional" pollutants, such as suspended sediments, bacteria, and oxygen-demanding
substances, as well as more longer lived and more dangerous toxic substances—heavy metals, pesticides, and inorganic chemical compounds
are the best-known examples. Both forms of pollutants can make water
unsafe for instream recreation and for commercial fishing and shellfish
harvesting. They necessitate expensive treatment if water is to be used
for drinking or as an input in some commercial or industrial process,
and degrade its value as an amenity resource.

Generally speaking, pollution does not reduce the amount of surface
water available. Rather, it makes many uses more expensive because
of the additional treatment required. However, when a particular body
of water is seriously contaminated by toxic substances (as in the case of
polychlorinated biphenyls in the Hudson River, or the pesticide Kepone
in Virginia's James River), there is a "loss" of water for at least some
important instream uses such as commercial and sport fishing.

The Clean Water Act, discussed briefly below, has been in place since
1972 and is the major federal statute regulating both the point and
nonpoint sources of conventional and toxic water pollutants. The data
necessary to evaluate the success of this act in cleaning up surface waters
are distressingly poor. Nevertheless, the data that do exist seem to
indicate that while certain bodies of water have improved significantly
during the time the act has been in place, the general trend in overall
water quality has been more or less constant.[24]

A more serious concern at this time may be the possible contamination
of groundwater supplies. To date, such contamination has been iden-

---

[23] For such a discussion, see A. M. Freeman, "Air and Water Pollution Policy," in Paul
R. Portney, ed., *Current Issues in U.S. Environmental Policy* (Baltimore, Md., Johns
Hopkins University Press for Resources for the Future, 1978) pp. 12–67.
[24] See *Environmental Quality: 1980*, the eleventh Annual Report of the Council on
Environmental Quality, p. 100.

tified in only a small percentage of the nation's aquifers. However, since water quality is not monitored in most aquifers, the problem may already be more extensive than is realized. Moreover, chemical and other wastes that have yet to be disposed of properly will continue to pose a potentially serious threat to the nation's groundwater. These wastes can originate from private or public sources, from onsite disposal at industrial facilities, from septic tanks, and from oil and mineral extraction and conversion.

Although no data are available on national trends in groundwater quality, there is considerable evidence to suggest that it is a serious problem in some communities, perhaps even some states. This is particularly worrisome since half of the nation's population relies on groundwater as the principal source of drinking water, and since once an aquifer is contaminated, it is effectively lost as a source of drinking water. Centuries may be required for natural restoration of groundwater quality, during which time water may have to be imported from other areas or subjected to very sophisticated and expensive treatment techniques.

The best-known example of local contamination of groundwater occurred at Love Canal, New York. There, of course, contamination also involved soil and both home and school sites. More recently, Atlantic City, New Jersey, has begun searching for a muncipal water supply to avoid the toxic chemical contamination which has already cost the neighboring town of Farmington its entire supply.[25] Recent surveys of underground well water in Michigan, New York, Massachusetts, and California have turned up varying degrees of chemical contamination—in some cases the levels of certain chemicals have been found to be several orders of magnitude greater than the presumably "safe" maximum levels established by the states.[26] To repeat, there is little evidence available to suggest that a serious *national* groundwater quality problem exists. But the existence of extremely serious local problems, coupled with a lack of comprehensive nationwide monitoring, suggests that close attention should be paid to groundwater quality.

Salinity

Another water quality problem, salinity stemming from irrigation, has been cited as an important cause of the collapse of several major civilizations.[27] While there is no reason to believe a similar fate will befall the United States, salinity is a threat to some of the West's major

[25] *New York Times*, November 4, 1981, p. B1

[26] For a longer discussion, see "Contamination of Groundwater by Toxic Organic Chemicals," Council on Environmental Quality, January 1981.

[27] Erik P. Eckholm, *Losing Ground: Environmental Stress and World Food Prospects* (Washington, D.C., Worldwatch Institute, 1976) pp. 114–119.

irrigated areas. Salts inhibit plant growth and in extreme cases render the land unsuitable for farming.

All irrigation water contains salts and these salt concentrations increase as water evaporates, is consumed by plants, or passes over saline soils. Salts can be flushed from the root zones if drainage is adequate and additional water is applied, but this seldom eliminates the problem since the salts washed off one farmer's land frequently add to the salts of downstream users. And in areas with poor drainage, the water tables rise over time with repeated irrigation. Once the water table reaches the root zone, capillary action carries water close to the surface, where it evaporates and leaves a salt residue. In time, this process may destroy the productivity of the land.

All western river basins except the Columbia are confronted with high and generally rising salt levels. In some areas salt concentrations in either the water or the soils are approaching levels that threaten the viability of traditional forms of irrigated agriculture. Overall, about one-fourth to one-third of all irrigated land in the West is so threatened.[28] The Lower Colorado River Basin and the west side of the San Joaquin Valley in California exemplify two types of salinity problems. In the Colorado Basin, the salt content of the river progressively increases downstream due to the salt-concentrating effects of irrigation and the addition of salts picked up as the water passes over saline formations. Annual damages from salinity in the Colorado River have been estimated to be between $75 and $104 million in 1980 and could rise to between $122 and $165 million in 2000 if no control measures are taken. While most of the damage would be incurred by municipal and industrial users, farmers would face decreased crop yields, increased leaching requirements, and higher management costs.[29] In the San Joaquin Valley, on the other hand, poor drainage prevents salt-laden waters from being carried away from the fields. High water tables already threaten the productivity of about 400,000 acres and ultimately more than 1 million acres in the valley may be similarly affected.[30]

Improved farm management practices can help reduce the levels of and problems resulting from salts. For example, efficient water and agronomic management can reduce (but not eliminate) salt concentrations by limiting evaporation and evapotranspiration. Curtailing the water

[28] Personal conversation with Jan van Schilfgaarde, Director, U.S. Salinity Laboratory, Riverside, California, February 1980.

[29] U.S. Department of Interior and U.S. Department of Agriculture, *Final Environmental Statement: Colorado River Water Quality Improvement Program*, vol. I (May 1977) section 1 (Washington, D.C.).

[30] U.S. Department of Interior, California Department of Water Resources, and California State Water Resources Control Board, *San Joaquin Valley InterAgency Drainage Program, Final Report*, June 1979.

applied for leaching reduces the dissolution of salts from the soil, to the benefit of downstream irrigators. While reduced leaching leaves salts in the farmer's soils, research results suggest that the damage from these salts can be kept within acceptable levels through careful water management.[31]

Since farm-level water and agronomic management practices alone will not eliminate salinity problems, additional steps may be required to preserve the long-term productivity of irrigated agriculture in some areas. Engineering solutions such as desalting plants or basin-wide drainage systems have been proposed, but their costs are high. Four initial salt control projects costing a total of $125 million have been proposed for the Colorado, while a $1.3 billion drainage system has been proposed for carrying salt-laden waters out of the San Joaquin Valley.[32]

Improved basin-wide water management offers at least a partial alternative for mitigating salinity problems. Where poor drainage prevents salt-laden waters from being carried away from a field, artificial drainage is required to prevent eventual loss of productivity. But the extent of the drainage needs can be greatly reduced through good management. For example, drainage needs in the San Joaquin Valley could be reduced to one-third or less of current levels and a long-term equilibrium reached through an integrated irrigation system whereby the best water is used first on salt-sensitive crops, with the increasingly salt-laden runoff applied to increasingly salt-tolerant crops. The remaining highly saline waters would be reduced to quantities that could be disposed of through a greatly scaled-down drainage system or perhaps in evaporation ponds.[33]

Barley has long been grown successfully with salt levels that would kill most plants and scientists have developed varieties of other crops with high tolerance to salt, such as wheat and tomatoes. Genetic research to combine salt tolerance, high yield, and desirable market characteristics in a single variety is likely to further expand the opportunities for successful irrigation with saline water and soil and to become increasingly important to the future of irrigated agriculture.[34] Nevertheless, a major

---

[31] Jan van Schilfgaarde, "Minimizing Salt in Return Flow by Improving Irrigation Efficiency," pp. 81–98, in James P. Law, Jr. and Gaylord V. Skogerboe, eds., *Irrigation Return Flow Quality Management: Proceedings of a National Conference*, May 16–19, 1977 (Fort Collins, Colorado State University, 1977).

[32] U.S. Department of Interior and U.S. Department of Agriculture, *Final Environmental Statement: Colorado River Water Quality Improvement Program*, vol. I, section 1; and U.S. Department of Interior and others, *San Joaquin Valley Inter-Agency Drainage Program*, pp. 1–3.

[33] Personal communication with Jan van Schilfgaarde in February 1980 and October 1980.

[34] Emanuel Epstein, Jack C. Norlyn, Dale W. Rush, Ralph W. Kingsley, David B. Kelley, Glen A. Cunningham, Anne F. Wrona, "Saline Culture of Crops: A Genetic Approach," *Science* vol. 210, October 24, 1980, pp. 399–404.

and perhaps insurmountable difficulty in implementing a basin-wide management scheme would be to get some farmers to accept lower quality water.

WATER POLICIES AND INSTITUTIONS

Introduction

The very nature of water resources and the problems inherent in valuing the benefits and costs of many possible uses create special problems for the management of these resources. While the hydrological cycle makes water renewable, it also makes it fugitive in time and space. As water flows from one property to another, supplies are accessible to many but belong to no one until they are withdrawn for use. Thus, water supplies are common property resources and suffer from some of the problems alluded to in the introduction to this volume.

Water management problems are accented because a user seldom bears the full costs of use (see the discussion of externalities in chapter 1). For instance, virtually all the costs of using a stream for waste disposal are borne by those downstream rather than by the polluter. Even when a farmer spends sizable sums to pump groundwater, these costs do not include the impacts on neighboring or potential future users associated with use of a common aquifer. When the capacity of streams to assimilate wastes, or the rates of natural recharge to groundwater stocks are exceeded, the costs not borne by the users can be substantial. Consequently, when left to private decisions, water use tends to exceed socially desirable levels. On the other hand, it is extremely difficult to determine what the socially desirable uses of water should be. This requires some determination of the benefits and costs of alternative uses, as well as a knowledge of the distribution of these good and bad effects.

In part because of the limitations of the market mechanism for allocating common property resources, water seldom is allocated through markets in the manner of most resources. Instead, government laws, institutions, and regulations control the distribution and use of water. There has been no effort to impose a single regulatory system over the nation's waters; the federal role is limited largely to ensuring sufficient water for federal and Indian lands, federal water projects, environmental requirements, and the negotiation and enforcement of international and interstate water agreements. The states establish the principal controls over water use. A variety of state institutions, laws, and regulations have emerged, reflecting variations among states in the supply and demand for water and in their views of property rights and the role of government.

The State Role

SURFACE WATER.   Although each state has adopted a somewhat unique approach, one of two basic doctrines—riparian rights or prior appropriation—underlies state surface water law. The doctrine of riparian rights holds that the owner of land adjacent to a water body has the right to make use of that water. Under this doctrine, the right is inseparable from the land and the owners can make any "reasonable" use of the water on the riparian land that does not unduly inconvenience other riparian owners. There is no priority in right among riparian users, and all such users share in reducing consumption in time of shortage. The riparian doctrine is used in the relatively water-abundant eastern states, and it provided the legal basis for the earliest water diversions in the western states.

Since western streams are not as numerous or reliably watered, and since development has been more dependent on large water diversions in the West than in the East, western development soon required diverting water beyond the riparian lands and increasing the assurance of supply. These needs led to development and adoption of the doctrine of prior appropriation, which establishes the basic principle of "first in time, first in right." In contrast to the riparian doctrine, appropriative water rights are not tied to use on land bordering a stream or pond nor are shortages shared equally. Appropriation rights are acquired by diverting water from its natural channel and putting it to some "beneficial" use. The diverter can then apply for a permit authorizing similar annual diversions for as long as the use remains beneficial. The right has priority over (is senior to) all rights acquired afterward and is junior to all previously acquired rights. Thus, in time of shortage, the full burden of the shortfall is borne by the holders of the junior water rights. All seventeen western states have adopted the appropriation doctrine as the basis of their water law, although several of these states also have retained elements of the riparian doctrine.

While state water laws and institutions have evolved in response to changing needs, further adjustments are needed if the nation's waters are to be efficiently utilized and not become a major obstacle to further regional development. Current and anticipated conditions in many states now differ from those prevailing when most existing water laws were written, the water rights acquired, and the water distribution organizations established. Increasing demands on eastern water supplies have started to focus on deficiencies of the riparian doctrine for allocating water when demand starts pressing upon supply. Even though the West started adjusting to similar pressures a century ago, the most pressing needs for reform of water law and institutions still are found in the West where continued development is becoming increasingly dependent on improving the efficiency with which its waters are utilized.

Several features of western water law limit the incentives to conserve water or transfer it to more highly valued uses. The beneficial use provisions, although intended to prevent wasteful water use, actually have the opposite effect in some states. For example, farmers may be discouraged from temporarily transferring water rights to other parties for fear that the transfer will be construed as evidence the water no longer can be put to beneficial use in farming and thereby serve as the basis for loss of the water rights. Similarly, farmers may not initiate measures to conserve water for fear that the water savings might be declared in surplus of the amount that is beneficially used.

Irrigation water rights are appurtenant (or tied) to the land specified in the permit and cannot be changed without approval of the agency granting the permit. The original intent of these provisions was to help prevent fraudulent land and water sales common to early settlement schemes. However, to the extent that appurtenancy provisions impair water transfers to alternative lands and uses, they may deter efficient water uses. A few states continue to use a relatively strict application of their appurtenancy provisions, but most permit water transfers so long as the rights of third parties (i.e., those who are not a direct part of the transfer) are not impaired.

Protecting the rights of third parties is perhaps the most important obstacle to water transfers. In general, transfers of appropriative rights are prohibited if the rights of third parties are expected to be impaired. But in view of the common property nature of the resource, transfers which have no impact on the quantity or quality of either the surface or groundwater flows of some nonparticipating party are rare. Efforts to resolve potential conflicts can be time consuming and expensive, especially if litigation is involved, and these costs often exceed the benefits of the transfer.[35]

GROUNDWATER.   Initially, groundwater pumping did not lead to obvious conflicts requiring government intervention. Consequently, the earliest legal doctrine governing groundwater use was that of absolute ownership in which economic factors imposed the only constraint on a landowner's use of the underlying waters. Uncontrolled pumping, how-

---

[35] Some illustrations of the kinds of inefficiencies that result from existing interpretation of water law in many states are presented in The John Muir Institute, *Institutional Constraints on Alternative Water for Energy: A Guidebook for Regional Assessments*, prepared for the U.S. Department of Energy, DOE/EV/10180–01 (November 1980) pp. 53–63.

ever, contributed to a variety of problems. Where groundwater withdrawal exceeds recharge, higher pumping lifts coupled with lower well yields push up water costs; sea water may intrude into and contaminate an aquifer; or overlying and neighboring lands may subside. Since many aquifers are interconnected with surface flows, groundwater pumping may jeopardize the rights of surface water users. The emergence of such problems, along with improved knowledge of groundwater hydrology, has brought greater appreciation of the need for better groundwater management.

With the exception of Texas, the western states have abandoned the doctrine of absolute ownership of groundwater. Most western states now employ the doctrine of prior appropriation to ground as well as to surface waters. The basic principle is to grant groundwater permits only where use does not adversely affect prior groundwater appropriations and where the water will be beneficially used. In practice, however, there are wide variations among the states in the application of the doctrine. It is seldom applied to prevent groundwater depletion and the negative impacts groundwater mining may impose on all users of an aquifer. However, Arizona's new Groundwater Management Act, which establishes active management areas and imposes strict limitations on groundwater use in these areas, may be the start of a move toward more comprehensive management of the groundwaters that are being depleted.

The costs of installing and operating a well and pump have been the principal regulators of groundwater use. In recent years, high energy costs have encouraged irrigators to adopt a variety of water-saving techniques. These costs, together with the greater control groundwater users have over the timing and quantity of withdrawals, explain why groundwater generally is used more efficiently than surface water in western irrigation. Nevertheless, in view of the common property nature of most aquifers, private pumping costs generally are less than social costs. The difference between private and social groundwater costs depends significantly on the characteristics of the aquifer. If lateral water movement is very slow or negligible, as with the Ogallala aquifer underlying the High Plains, the impacts on others are small. But where lateral flow is significant, the effects of an individual's pumping are spread over a wide area and the distortions between private and social costs may be important. In these cases, the "use it or lose it" view toward water resources prevails and current use exceeds socially efficient levels. Efforts to curb such misuses of groundwater have been limited to restrictions on pumping and drilling imposed by some states. While such restrictions tend to protect existing users from the additional damage that might be imposed by new users, they do not provide for an efficient long-term use of scarce groundwater resources.

Further inefficiencies in groundwater use result from restrictions some states have imposed on transfers of pumping permits from irrigation to nonagricultural uses. In particular, such restrictions have added to the problem some energy companies have had in securing needed water rights.[36]

Federal Water Projects

Two federal agencies—The Corps of Engineers and the Bureau of Reclamation—have provided much of the planning, financing, and construction of the nation's major water development projects. Since political considerations often preempt economic criteria in the selection of projects undertaken by these agencies, enormous sums of public funds have been spent on projects of questionable merit. Furthermore, some of these projects, especially irrigation projects, contribute to the inefficient use of the nation's water resources. Support for these statements is readily found by examining the activities of the Bureau of Reclamation.

The Bureau was established in 1902 to encourage settlement of the arid West through irrigation. By 1980, federal projects supplied either full or supplementary irrigation water to over 11 million acres, a considerable testament to the success of the 1902 legislation. This achievement has not come cheaply, however. Although the initial legislation stipulated that farmers be charged enough to recover all construction costs except interest, the intent bears little relation to what has transpired.[37]

The costs and problems of establishing irrigation on previously unfarmed arid lands were much greater than anticipated, and many farmers were unable to meet repayment requirements. Relief came with the 1914 Reclamation Extension Act, which increased the repayment period from ten to twenty years and provided a five-year grace period. New irrigators paid 5 percent of the costs up front and the balance in fifteen annual installments beginning in the sixth year. But even these more lenient repayment schedules were not met by many farmers, and the 1914 legislation proved to be just the first of a series of legislative and administrative adjustments providing enormous subsidies for federal

---

[36] Ibid.

[37] Exempting interest is a tremendous subsidy in itself. Imagine, for example, how small a homeowner's monthly mortgage payments would be if it were only necessary to repay the principal of a loan over its lifetime. Typically, total interest payments will be two or three times the amount of the principal.

irrigation projects. In 1926 about $17.3 million or 13 percent of the costs on twenty-one projects were written off and the repayment period was extended to forty years on all projects. The policy of not charging interest remained intact.

Further relief came when the Reclamation Project Act of 1939 specified that irrigators were responsible only for that portion of the debt they were able to repay. While implementation of the ability-to-pay criterion has been very beneficial to the farmers, an even more important concession has been fixing the rates charged farmers so that there is no adjustment for inflation throughout the repayment period, which extends as long as fifty years, with a ten-year grace period. Thus, almost regardless of the initial rates charged farmers, enormous subsidies are assured.

Estimates of the level of subsidy provided to those using federal irrigation water vary depending in part on the projects considered and the interest rate used to discount future payments by irrigators. In all cases, however, dispassionate analysis indicates the subsidies have been extraordinarily generous. Analysis of eighteen irrigation districts by the U.S. Department of Interior shows an average subsidy of $792 per acre in 1978 dollars. The range in the subsidy varies widely among projects. varying from $58 per acre for Moon Lake, a small project receiving only supplemental water, to $1,787 per acre for the Wellton–Mohawk district. The subsidy ranges from 57 percent of the total project costs for Moon Lake to 97 percent for the East Columbia basin.[38] An alternative estimate of irrigation subsidies suggests that at current collection rates and costs, farmers will repay only 3.3 percent of the $3.62 billion the Bureau has spent for irrigation construction.[39] In some cases the effects of inflation on long-term fixed charges have reduced the rates paid by irrigators below the point where they even cover the project's operating and maintenance costs.

A 1981 General Accounting Office (GAO) report to the Congress suggests that high subsidy levels will continue with new water projects.[40] The GAO report summarizes their assessment of six Bureau of Reclamation projects under construction. The total cost of these projects exceeds $2.1 billion, nearly half of which is attributed to irrigation facilities. Using a 7.5 percent discount rate, the fees established by the

[38] U.S. Department of Interior. Water and Power Resources Service. *Acreage Limitation*, Interim Report. March 1980, pp. 37–42.
[39] E? Phillip LeVeen, "Reclamation Policy at a Crossroads," in *Public Affairs Report*, Bulletin of the Institute of Governmental Studies, University of California, Berkeley (October 1978) vol. 19, no. 5, pp. 2–3.
[40] U.S. General Accounting Office. *Federal Charges for Irrigation Projects Reviewed Do Not Cover Costs*, PAD–81–97, March 3, 1981.

Bureau imply irrigation subsidies ranging from 92.2 to 97.8 percent of the construction costs. The estimated costs of water delivered from these federal projects range from $54 an acre-foot for the Fryingpan–Arkansas project, which distributes supplementary water through existing facilities, to $130 an acre-foot for the Pollock–Herreid project. Yet the charges to recover the construction costs of this water range from 27 cents (only 7 cents according to GAO calculations) to $9.82 cents per acre-foot.

As noted earlier, the damage of these projects extends beyond the waste of federal funds at a time when the budget is very tight indeed. The farmers fortunate enough to be serviced with this highly subsidized water must use the water on their farms or lose it. Thus, there are no incentives to conserve this water and no opportunities to put it to non-agricultural uses. Consequently, federal irrigation projects have created, at enormous public cost, isolated areas within the water-scarce West where water is viewed and treated as virtually a free resource. Of course, this extravagance adds to the overall problems of water scarcity in the West.

One of the more controversial aspects of the federal water projects has been the Bureau of Reclamation's failure to enforce provisions of the 1902 Reclamation Act limiting an individual to 160 acres and a farm couple to 320 acres of land receiving federal water. Congress's initial intent to provide water solely for small family farms has been violated in practice through lax enforcement of the law and loose administrative practices which permit unlimited leasing and multiple ownership arrangements. While the great majority of farm operations comply with a 160- or 320-acre limitation, much of the irrigable land is operated in larger units. Of the 126,000 owners of 8.8 million irrigated acres supposedly subject to acreage limitations, nearly 91 percent own 160 acres or less and 98 percent own 320 acres or less. The remaining 2 percent, however, own 27 percent of the land. The 340 largest owners (comprising less than one-third of 1 percent of the farmers receiving water from federal projects) own 11 percent of the land receiving subsidized water.[41]

The Bureau of Reclamation's procedures allowing such large holdings to receive subsidized water were challenged in 1977 when National Land for People (a small public interest organization centered in Fresno, California and consisting largely of small farmers and their sympathizers) brought suit against the federal government over violations of the acreage limitation provisions of the 1902 legislation. The court ruled in favor of the plaintiffs and issued an injunction against sales of excess lands until the Congress changed the law or the Department of Interior altered its

[41] U.S. Department of Agriculture, *Farmline*, vol. 1, no. 6 (September 1980) p. 4.

rules and regulations. Interior proposed new rules in 1978, but actual changes in the rules have been stalled until at least mid-1982 pending final comments on a court-mandated environmental impact statement. In the meantime, Congress has considered several proposed changes in the 1902 law that would increase the acreage limitations.

Resolution of the acreage limitation issue is likely to eventually reduce the subsidized water provided the very large landowners. (Secretary of Interior Watt has supported charging farmers the full cost for acreages in excess of those stipulated by Congress.) Nevertheless, the changes are not likely to have any significant impact on the farm output grown with this water or the efficiency of its use. Proponents of eliminating or relaxing the acreage provisions have claimed there are significant economies of scale to be gained by allowing large farmers to use the water. A recent U.S. Department of Agriculture study, however, suggests that 98 percent of the cost advantages achieved by larger operations are captured by farms of 320 to 640 acres.[42] All the legislation under consideration by the Congress as well as the Department of Interior's proposed changes in the rules and regulations would permit the use of federally subsidized water on operations of this size.

Although the acreage limitation issue is essentially a question of who receives the subsidized water, the debate over this issue has focused national attention on the appropriateness of federal financing of irrigation projects and the manner in which they are administered. As noted earlier, an important part of the subsidy results from setting water rates for long periods, with no provision for interim adjustment. In response to the pressures of public scrutiny, new contracts negotiated by the Bureau of Reclamation call for adjusting water prices every five years to allow for rising operation and maintenance costs. These changes are not retroactive, and thus only affect new contracts or old contracts as they expire. In California, over 80 percent of the water delivered under current contracts will not be renegotiated until the 1992–96 period. Even then, federally supplied water will remain grossly underpriced unless much more sweeping policy changes are made.

Water for Federal and Indian Lands

Water rights for federal lands were not specified when, in the nineteenth century, the states were granted jurisdiction over all nonnavigable waters

---

[42] U.S. Department of Agriculture, *The U.S. Department of the Interior's Proposed Rules for Enforcement of the Reclamation Act of 1902: An Economic Impact Analysis*, ESCS–04 (Washington, D.C.) 1980.

in the public domain. Nor were the water rights of Indian lands specified when the reservations were established. These oversights became the origin of much anxiety since the states proceeded to grant water rights without any special regard to the rights of federal and Indian lands. The 1908 U.S. Supreme Court ruling in *Winters vs. United States* provides a legal basis for Indian water rights. The Winters doctrine, which has been supported in subsequent judicial rulings, holds that when the federal government withdrew lands for any purpose, it at the same time implicitly withdrew unappropriated waters from the public domain to accomplish this purpose. Accordingly, Indian water rights have a senior claim to western waters dating from the time a reservation was created. Furthermore, several Supreme Court decisions since 1955 suggested that all federal lands have reserved water rights.[43] Since these rights would be senior to those of most other users, Indian and federal claims to western waters threatened the existing allocation systems established by the western states. Although the legitimacy of Indian and federal claims has been established in principle, these rights have not been quantified. Even though current use for these purposes is small, the Indian claims at least are potentially large.[44]

In recognition that uncertainties created by unresolved Indian and federal water claims are detrimental to western development, the Carter administration announced in 1977 its intent to resolve quickly the quantity of water claimed for these lands. The Reagan administration has taken the position that there are no federal "nonreserved" water rights and that "federal agencies must acquire water as would any other private claimant within the various states."[45] Nonetheless, the uncertainties at least concerning Indian claims are likely to remain for many years to come. Currently federal policy is to allow concerned parties to negotiate a settlement on a case-by-case basis and let the courts resolve any differences. In the meantime, a cloud of uncertainty envelops western water use and adds to the risks borne by investors dependent on its use.

[43] Heidi Topp Brooks, "Reserved Water Rights and Our National Lands," *Natural Resources Journal* vol. 19 (April 1979) pp. 433–435.

[44] See Allen V. Kneese and F. Lee Brown, *The Southwest Under Stress: National Resource Issues in a Regional Setting* (Baltimore, Md., Johns Hopkins University Press for Resources for the Future, 1981) pp. 70–94.

[45] Secretary of the Interior James Watt told the western governors on September 11, 1981 that "federal land managers must follow State water laws and procedures except where Congress has specifically established a water right or where Congress has explicitly set aside a federal land area with a reserved water right . . ." See *Federal Lands*, September 21, 1981 (published by McGraw-Hill) p. 9. In June 1982 the U.S. Attorney General, William French Smith, confirmed that the Department of Justice supported the view that there are no federal nonreserved water rights.

CONCLUSIONS AND RECOMMENDATIONS

The United States is not running out of water. Supplies appear adequate to meet both existing needs as well as possible additional ones arising from energy development, the expansion of irrigated agriculture, growing household and industrial demands, and even an increasing national appetite for outdoor recreation and amenity resources.

This optimistic forecast depends upon a number of important qualifications. The first is this: the growing and increasingly more competitive demands for water cannot be met successfully until and unless it is recognized that water is a scarce resource which will not be used efficiently under existing institutional arrangements. Water simply must be priced more rationally and exchanged more freely among alternative users. Unless users pay a price for water that is more nearly in accord with its opportunity cost, they will have little or no incentive to take the many available conservation measures that would free up existing water supplies for the new uses mentioned above. And unless water is exchanged more freely among users in marketlike settings, it will not be put to its most socially valuable uses.

Although marketlike exchange has many desirable features, the common property nature of both surface and groundwaters limits the utility of an unfettered market system for allocating scarce water resources. Nevertheless, the federal and especially state governments can create and oversee the operation of pseudo-markets where normal markets would not arise naturally or where, for reasons discussed in chapter 1, they would not result in wise resource use. One example of a marketlike mechanism is "water banking," a scheme to facilitate water transfers in areas where it is scarce.[46] The bank would be a state-sanctioned agency established in a particular water district to serve as a broker in arranging transfers between users and to determine the effects of such transfers on third parties. However, water banking would have to be classified as a beneficial use to avoid forfeiture under the appropriation doctrine. Under such a scheme, water prices would be determined by supply and demand, with the buyer's and seller's prices differing by an assessment to cover legitimate third-party effects as well as transfer costs. As in most markets, participation would be voluntary, but the opportunity to sell water without fear of losing the rights to it would provide a great incentive to conservation that is now absent.

[46] A water banking scheme is proposed and described in Sotirios Angelides and Eugene Bardach, *Water Banking: How to Stop Wasting Agricultural Water*, Institute for Contemporary Studies, San Francisco, California, 1978.

As indicated above, groundwater generally is used more efficiently than surface water. Nevertheless, social costs often exceed private costs because of the external effects on others. In theory, a tax on pumping could adjust for such differences. In practice, however, such a tax would encounter strong resistance, and it would be very difficult to determine the correct tax rate. Well or pumping quotas are a more acceptable means of limiting overpumping since they have the political advantage of protecting the early users. Many states permit the formation of special local districts to regulate groundwater; such districts are common in areas with critical groundwater problems—California, Texas, Nebraska, Kansas, and Colorado, for instance. Although the controls established by these districts are unlikely to result in a socially optimal groundwater use over time, there is evidence that the regulated outcome better approximates the social optimum than does a policy of unrestricted pumping.[47]

In some situations, major improvements in water management are possible through conjunctive management of ground and surface water resources. This generally involves utilizing surface water supplies whenever they are available, either for direct delivery to users or to recharge groundwater stocks. Groundwater serves as a reserve and becomes the main source of supply when the less expensive but fugitive surface waters are insufficient to meet demand. Conjunctive management has been employed successfully by some local water agencies in California for some years, but it is the exception rather than the rule.

Our dictum about rational water pricing applies not only to natural surface and groundwater supplies, but also to the water which the federal government makes available through reclamation projects. Massive subsidies to water use (95 percent, or more in some cases, as pointed out above) are hard to justify even in a rapidly growing economy which is generating considerable tax revenues. They are nearly scandalous at a time when badly needed social programs are being cut in an all-out effort to reduce the size of government spending. Once again, users should pay the full social costs of the water they receive. This includes both principal *and* interest, where the latter should reflect the true cost of money to the government rather than some artificially low rate. The sooner the Corps of Engineers and the Bureau of Reclamation begin more sensible water pricing, the sooner will water conservation measures begin to be adopted.

[47] Jay E. Noel, B. Delworth Gardner, and Charles V. Moore, "Optimal Regional Conjunctive Water Management," *American Journal of Agricultural Economics* vol. 62, no. 3 (August 1980) pp. 489–498.

There are other possibilities for augmenting or stretching supplies in water-scarce areas. Dams and reservoirs can increase water availability for specific purposes such as irrigation, and interbasin transfers can relocate water to more closely approximate demand. Structural measures, however, no longer offer a source of inexpensive water for the West. The best dam sites already have been exploited, ecological and aesthetic costs at certain sites are significant, and the costs of increasing usable supplies through impoundment are high. For example, the dams and reservoirs under consideration in California will cost $200 to $300 per acre-foot of water added to effective supply. Such costs are about an order of magnitude above the prices currently paid by California farmers receiving water through state projects and nearly two orders of magnitude above the highly subsidized rates charged those fortunate enough to receive water from federal projects. Interbasin transfers tend to be even more costly. For instance, it would cost $360 to $880 per acre-foot to bring water into the High Plains, where current use is depleting groundwater stocks.[48] Furthermore, these costs assume water has no value in its current use and location. The increasing value of instream uses makes such an assumption increasingly difficult to justify, however.

Nontraditional methods of increasing water supplies include weather modification, icebergs, and desalinization. Weather modification is the only method with potential for providing relatively inexpensive water in selected areas. Studies suggest winter cloud seeding within the mountain ranges of the Upper Colorado Basin might add 1.4 to 2.3 million acre-feet of water a year at a cost of about $5 to $10 per acre-foot.[49] However, major institutional obstacles may prevent adoption of any sizable cloud seeding program even if scientists and economists can agree it makes sense. Compensating the losers (whether real or imagined), dealing with the concerns of people downwind from the seeding, and allocating the additional water pose major challenges to use of weather modification for enhancing water supplies.

The enormous quantities of fresh water trapped as polar ice have attracted the interest of some arid areas. Precise cost estimates for the transportation and use of icebergs await resolution of some outstanding technical problems. Even if "iceberg harvesting" appears promising after examination of technical, economic, and environmental factors, inter-

---

[48] Based on the Corps of Engineers estimates for the Six-State High Plains-Ogallala Aquifer Regional Resources Study, Congressional Briefing, February 25, 1981, p. 25.

[49] Personal communication with Bernie Silverman, Chief Atmospheric Water Resources Management, Water and Power Resources Service, Denver, February 1980.

national political and legal issues concerning resource rights could prevent their use.

Costs impose the principal constraint to desalinization as a means of increasing freshwater supplies. There are several processes for desalting but the least expensive methods cost $250 to $300 per acre-foot even when the process starts with waters with salt levels well below those of sea water and ends with less than pure water.[50] These are plant-site costs, and delivery costs would be additional. Although such costs can be justified in isolated instances, they far exceed the marginal value of water even in the arid West.

Another important qualification to our optimistic conclusion concerns water quality. If discharges of conventional or toxic pollutants increase—either because of relaxations in current standards or an unwillingness or inability to enforce them—at least certain kinds of water availability problems could reoccur. The most likely problems would involve forgone instream uses, probably recreational and commercial fishing losses. However, a failure to control certain toxic substances could have even wider public health effects if sources of municipal drinking water are affected.

The Clean Water Act—which directs EPA to establish discharge standards for tens of thousands of individual water polluters—is the most important water quality statute. Unfortunately, a number of analyses have suggested serious shortcomings with the act—shortcomings related to the controls imposed on both industrial and municipal polluters.[51] Moreover, these analyses have suggested that much more effort should be going into the control of nonpoint sources. Almost everyone who has reviewed the act agrees that much more water quality can be "produced" by the existing funds. The Clean Water Act is up for reauthorization in 1982 and this may provide the occasion to review these and other issues which affect water quality.

As suggested above, the quality of groundwater supplies also has an important bearing on overall water availability. Moreover, there is evidence of serious local groundwater contamination problems. Since monitoring has been very limited, there is cause for concern that these

---

[50] U.S. Bureau of Reclamation, California Department of Water Resources and California State Water Resources Control Board, *Agricultural Drainage and Salt Management in the San Joaquin Valley*, June 1979, pp. 8–4 and 8–5.

[51] For instance, see A. M. Freeman, "Air and Water Pollution Policy," in Paul Portney, ed., *Current Issues in U.S. Environmental Policy* (Baltimore, Md., Johns Hopkins University Press for Resources for the Future, 1978); Charles Schultze and Allen Kneese, *Pollution, Prices and Public Policy* (Washington, D.C., Brookings Institution, 1975); and David Harrison and Robert Leone, "Federal Water Pollution Control Policy," draft manuscript prepared for the American Enterprise Institute, Washington, D.C., 1981.

problems may be much more extensive and serious than currently realized.

One difficulty with management of groundwater quality is that authority for it exists under at least three, and perhaps four, statutes administered by EPA. Under the Resource Conservation and Recovery Act (RCRA) of 1976, EPA is to promulgate either design or performance standards that must be met by hazardous and other waste disposal sites. In part these regulations are intended to prevent the future contamination of underground aquifers by pollutants leaching from such sites. Under the so-called "Superfund" act passed by Congress in 1980, EPA is to begin identifying and cleaning up abandoned waste disposal sites which may be contributing to current groundwater contamination and other problems. Finally, under the "underground injection control" provisions of the Safe Drinking Water Act of 1974, EPA is to regulate the practice by which the muds and brines which are by-products of energy exploration are disposed of in deep shafts drilled in the earth. These latter regulations are clearly related to drinking water protection, but have the obvious effect of preserving aquifers used for other purposes as well.

Because of these conflicting and overlapping authorities, the Carter administration tried to develop an overall groundwater strategy. Apparently wishing to begin afresh, the Reagan administration is making its own examination of such a coordinated approach. This is being made difficult, however, by the pressure EPA is facing from both Congress and the courts to issue regulations under RCRA, a law which is now more than five years old but which has yet to be translated into meaningful controls on waste disposal sites. Several of the key issues to be determined in any groundwater protection strategy are, first, whether zero degradation of groundwater will be the goal (as opposed, say, to establishing a limit on the amount of degradation permitted); and, second, whether aquifers that are not used as drinking water sources might be used as underground waste disposal sites. Clearly, the final decision will have considerable bearing on both the quality and quantity of groundwater available, not only for current use, but for future generations as well.

8

Agricultural Land

Pierre R. Crosson with Ruth B. Haas

Recently, increasing concern has been expressed about the adequacy of agricultural land in the United States. Specifically, will there be enough land to meet mounting demands on it over the long term? The question is not new, but three events in the 1970s gave it fresh urgency: (1) the very rapid growth of agricultural exports and the possibility of additional demand for corn to produce ethanol; (2) an apparent slowdown in the rate of yield increases per acre of cropland; and (3) the publication of a Department of Agriculture report showing that between 1967 and 1975 some 3 million acres of rural land were converted annually to urban, transportation, and similar uses, which in most cases removed this land permanently from agriculture.[1]

The growth in export demand, coupled with reduced growth of yields, combined to increase the amount of land in crops by about 60 million acres between 1972 and 1981; expectations are that demand for such land will continue to grow. However, the withdrawal of land from farming suggests that the increased demand will encounter a steadily diminishing supply. For many, the implication is a looming cropland crisis requiring a mobilization of effort at all levels of government. The remedy

---

[1] R. Dideriksen, A.R. Hidlebaugh, and K.O. Schmude, *Potential Cropland Study*, Statistical Bulletin 578 (Washington, D.C., U.S. Department of Agriculture, 1977).

most frequently proposed, as in the National Agricultural Lands Study, is to slow the conversion of agricultural land to nonagricultural uses.[2]

Are the fears about U.S. agricultural land justified? If a problem does exist, what are the most effective policies for dealing with it? This chapter is addressed to these questions. The discussion is in three parts: (1) an identification of the issues surrounding the adequacy of agricultural land; (2) a review of the evidence bearing on the problem; and (3) an appraisal of policies for dealing with it.

NATURE OF THE PROBLEM

Some of the current discussion about agricultural land suggests that the problem lies in its gradual disappearance. In this view, the nation's stock of agricultural land is fixed at so many acres. Consequently, conversions to nonagricultural uses reduce the amount available for agriculture. If, at the same time, the demand for such land is increasing, eventually there will not be "enough" to meet all the demands upon it.

Unfortunately, this is not a useful way of defining the problem. It ignores the fact that society's interest lies, not in the physical quantity of land available, but rather in the goods and services which the land provides. The quantity of these goods and services can be expanded almost indefinitely if society is willing to bear the cost of doing so. The question, therefore, can properly be framed in either of two ways: Will the supply of agricultural land be adequate to meet all the demands on it at socially acceptable costs? Or, what will be the social and economic costs of meeting varying levels of demand for the goods and services provided by the land?

This view of the problem treats agricultural land as a factor of production. It implies that the adequacy of such land cannot be evaluated independently of the other inputs which are joined with the land to produce goods and services. If the price of land rises but is offset by a decline in the prices of complementary inputs, such as fertilizer or pesticides, then it is likely that the supply of land will be considered "adequate," despite its higher price. If the combination of higher land prices and other costs results in more expensive goods and services, then society is likely to see a problem, and one component of the problem will be the higher price of agricultural land.

The main products of agricultural land are food and fiber, but it also yields intangible values, for example, the pleasures derived from open

[2] Available from the U.S. Government Printing Office, Washington, D.C.

space and from the opportunity to live in a rural setting. Conversion of agricultural land to nonagricultural uses may imperil these values, and judgments of its adequacy must take account of this.

There are, therefore, two aspects to the adequacy question. One is the role of the land in the nation's capacity to produce food and fiber. This is referred to as the capacity issue. The second is the land's role in producing intangible values and is described as the amenity issue.

REVIEW OF THE EVIDENCE

The Capacity Issue

Three factors are particularly relevant to the capacity issue: the growth in demand for food and fiber; the trend in per acre productivity of cropland (yields); and the present and potential supply of cropland.

DEMAND FOR FOOD AND FIBER.   As for any factor of production, the demand for agricultural land is what economists call a derived demand. It depends on the demand for food, fiber, and other services provided by the land. In the United States, foreign demand for food and feedgrains has come to play an important role in the demand for agricultural land. In 1949, some 45 million acres, 13 percent of all cropland harvested that year, were used to grow crops that were eventually exported. While cropland devoted to export production increased by about 1.3 million acres per year from 1949 to 1970, the annual increase from 1970 to 1980 was 6.6 million acres. In 1980, 138 million acres of cropland were in production for export, 39 percent of the cropland harvested that year.[3] Rising foreign demand for wheat, corn, and soybeans was the main reason for this increase (see table 8–1).

The accelerated growth of U.S. grain exports in the 1970s reflected both fast-rising world trade in these crops and increasing U.S. penetration of world markets. Growing world trade also spurred exports of soybeans and soybean products, even though increasing competition from Brazil and Argentina, particularly Brazil, reduced the U.S. share from about 90 to 70 percent. Trade in both these items was stimulated by increasing income and population in the developing countries, particularly in the so-called middle-income countries such as Mexico and Korea, and in the OPEC countries. The rise in per capita income pro-

[3] U.S. Department of Agriculture, *Economic Indicators of the Farm Sector: Production and Efficiency Statistics*, Statistical Bulletin 679 (Washington, D.C., U.S. Department of Agriculture, 1982).

TABLE 8–1. Production, Exports, and Yields of Wheat, Corn, and
            Soybeans, Selected Years

	1948/1950[a]	1970/1972[a]	1978/1980[a]
Wheat			
Production (million metric tons)	31.6	41.0	57.0
Exports (million metric tons)	10.6	22.6	37.1
Export (percent of production)	33.5	55.1	65.2
Yields (kilos/acre)	45.0	88.6	90.0
Corn			
Production (million metric tons)	79.2	129.9	185.0
Exports (million metric tons)	2.9	21.8	60.2
Export (percent of production)	3.7	16.8	32.5
Yields (kilos/acre)	101.1	218.4	256.1
Soybeans			
Production (million metric tons)	6.7	32.5	54.0
Exports[b] (million metric tons)	27.7	17.1	29.8
Export (percent of production)	10.4	52.6	55.2
Yields (kilos/acre)	59.7	74.7	80.2

Sources: U.S. Department of Agriculture, *Agricultural Statistics*, 1952, 1973 and for 1978–
79 figures, 1980; 1980 figures are from *Agricultural Outlook*, December 1981. Original data
are in bushels. One metric ton of wheat and soybeans equals 36.75 bushels. One metric ton
of corn equals 39.38 bushels.

[a] Three-year averages are used to smooth annual fluctuations.

[b] Includes oil and meal expressed as bean equivalents.

duced increased demands for meat, especially poultry, and fledgling
meat products industries were established. The result was a growth in
demand for corn and soybean meal for animal feed. Japanese imports
of corn and soybeans increased for the same reason. Finally, both the
Soviet Union and China emerged as important net importers of grain
in the 1970s, reflecting government decisions to improve diets and the
inability of domestic production to meet all of the increase in demand.

U.S. shares of world trade in grains rose in the 1970s, and at the end
of the decade were almost 45 percent for wheat and about 70 percent
for feedgrains. The reasons for the increased shares are not entirely
clear, but there is no doubt that a major factor was the decline in the
international value of the dollar after 1971, which greatly improved the
competitiveness of U.S. exports.

Projections of export demand vary, but all agree that exports will
continue to be a dynamic element in the growth of crop production.
The export figures in table 8–2 are based on World Bank projections
of world population and income growth and on assumptions about trade
policies in the European Community, Japan, the Soviet Union, and
China. No specific crop prices are assumed. However, comparison of
the projections in table 8–2 with a set made using the USDA's National
Interregional Agricultural Projections (NIRAP) model, which incor-

TABLE 8–2. Production, Exports, and
Domestic Use of Wheat,
Feedgrains, Soybeans, and
Cotton

(million metric tons)

	1978/80[a]	2010
Wheat		
Production	57.0	98
Exports	37.0	70
Domestic use	20.0	28
Feedgrains		
Production	219.3	354
Exports	67.0	167
Domestic use	152.3	187
Soybeans		
Production	53.8	120
Exports	29.4	76
Domestic use	24.4	44
Cotton		
Production	2.7	3.5–3.9
Exports	1.5	Not projected
Domestic use	1.2	Not projected

Sources: 1978/80 figures derived from U.S. Department of Agriculture, *Agricultural Outlook*, December 1981. 2010 from Pierre R. Crosson and Sterling Brubaker, *Resource and Environmental Effects of U.S. Agriculture* (Washington, D.C., Resources for the Future, 1982).

Notes: Feedgrains are corn, grain sorghum, oats, and barley, with corn by far the most important. Soybean exports include the bean equivalent of oil and meal. For all commodities, domestic use includes the change in stocks.

[a] Three-year averages were used to smooth annual fluctuations.

porates prices, suggests that the projections here are consistent with increases in real crop prices of 25–30 percent.[4]

CROP YIELDS.   How much land would be needed to satisfy the projected levels of production? The answer depends in large part on the trend in crop yields. From before World War I until the late 1940s, crop

---

[4] The projections for domestic demand make no special allowance for demand for corn to produce ethanol. While there was much enthusiasm for gasohol in 1981, the resource and federal budget costs of reaching a legislated goal of 10 billion gallons of ethanol by 1990 have been found to be high (Fred Sanderson, "Benefits and Costs of the U.S. Gasohol Program," *Resources* No. 67, available from Resources for the Future, Washington, D.C.).

TABLE 8–3. Crop Yields and Total Agricultural
Productivity in the United States

Years	Yields	Productivity (1967 = 100)	Average annual percent increase from previous period	
			Yields	Productivity
1910/14	56.4	49.8	—	—
1946/50	69.8	71.0	0.6	1.0
1968/72	108.0	105.4	2.0	1.8
1977/80	120.3	116.0	1.3	1.1

Source: U.S. Department of Agriculture, *Economic Indicators of the Farm Sector: Production and Efficiency Statistics, 1980*. ERS, Statistical Bulletin 679 (Washington, D.C.).

yields and total productivity (the ratio of total output to total input) increased at average annual rates of 0.6 and 1.0 percent respectively. From the late 1940s to the early 1970s, both yields and productivity increased dramatically faster, as table 8–3 shows. The development of new seed varieties, fertilizers, pesticides, improved irrigation methods, and low prices for these inputs underlay this improved performance as farmers found it profitable to substitute these inputs for land.

In recent years, however, the gains obtained through technological advances seem to have tapered off (table 8–3). There are a number of reasons for this. An important one was that in the 1970s fertilizer prices rose relative to prices of crops and to the value of land in agricultural production. Consequently, the substitution of fertilizer for land was no longer as profitable as it had been. However, price is but one factor affecting the amount of fertilizer used per acre. Its productivity at the margin of use also is important. Early in the postwar period, the amount of fertilizer used per acre was low and fertilizer-responsive varieties of corn and other crops promised high returns to increased use. By the early 1970s, the amount of fertilizer applied per acre had increased substantially, and the gains from additional amounts were much less than before. The combination of higher fertilizer prices and lower marginal productivity caused much slower growth in per acre applications of fertilizer in the 1970s compared with the two previous decades. This undoubtedly contributed to slower yield growth in that decade.

However, the incorporation of less productive land into crop production also was a factor. Yields on land held out of production in the 1960s were 10 to 20 percent lower than those on land in production.[5]

[5] P. Weisberger, *Productivity of Converted Cropland*, Economic Research Service, Statistical Bulletin 398 (Washington, D.C., U.S. Department of Agriculture, 1969).

All of the inferior land was brought back into production in the 1970s, and this contributed to the slower growth of yields in the decade.[6]

But what about future trends in yields? If wheat and feedgrain yields were to grow at the rates of the late '40s to the early '70s, the production levels projected for those crops in table 8–2 could be achieved with less land than in 1980. Soybean production would require more land, but overall there would be little, if any, increase in the demand for cropland and little concern about the adequacy of agricultural land, even if nonagricultural conversions continued at recent rates.

However, present evidence suggests that a return to the pre-1970s growth in yield for wheat and feedgrains is unlikely over the next several decades. Two of the conditions that prompted reductions in fertilizer use in the 1970s—rising prices and lower marginal productivity—appear likely to persist into the foreseeable future. Rising prices for natural gas will tend to increase nitrogen fertilizer prices, as will rising costs of constructing fertilizer plants.[7] Almost 100 percent of the land in corn now is fertilized at close to optimum rates and while there is a greater potential for expanded fertilization of wheat and soybeans, it is much less than in the pre-1970 period.[8] Without more fertilizer-responsive varieties of these crops, and of corn, than now appear on the horizon, per acre fertilization is not likely to increase faster than the relatively slow rates of the 1970s, with concomitant effects on yields.

In western states, rising energy prices, combined with declining water tables and increasing competition for water for nonagricultural uses, are likely to increase the costs of irrigation, slowing its expansion.[9] There is potential for irrigated wheat and soybeans in the Mississippi Delta and corn in the Southeast; nonetheless, it is likely that, nationally, irrigation will contribute less to yield growth over the next several decades than in the previous three.

The prospective conditions affecting fertilizer use, yield potential of new seed varieties, and irrigation suggest that in the foreseeable future farmers will respond to rising crop demand with a relatively low rate of substitution of nonland inputs as in the 1970s. This would make yield growth similar to that in the 1970s, and less than the growth of crop demand. Additional land thus would be required, which also would

[6] Pierre R. Crosson and Sterling Brubaker, *Resource and Environmental Effects of U.S. Agriculture* (Washington, D.C., Resources for the Future, 1982).

[7] Ibid.

[8] Earl O. Heady, "The Adequacy of Agricultural Land: A Demand-Supply Perspective," in Pierre R. Crosson, ed., *The Cropland Crisis: Myth or Reality?* (Baltimore, Md., Johns Hopkins University Press for Resources for the Future, 1982).

[9] Kenneth Frederick, "Irrigation and the Adequacy of Agricultural Land," in Crosson, ed., *The Cropland Crisis*. See also chapter 7 in this volume.

depress yield growth since this land will be less productive. There no doubt are exceptions, but as a general rule farmers use their most productive land first.

On balance, it appears that yields of grains and soybeans are likely to grow between 1 and 2 percent from the late 1970s to 2010, with the most probable rate in the lower part of the range. In work done at RFF, yields were projected to grow from 1976/80 to 2010 as follows (annual rates): wheat 0.7 percent; feedgrains 1.2 percent; and soybeans 1.0 percent.[10]

These projections, when combined with projected levels of output (table 8–2), imply that 320 million acres of wheat, feedgrains, and soybeans will be harvested in 2010, an increase of 80 million acres from 1980. Some of the increase may be met by shifting to these crops some cropland now in less intensive uses, for example, hay and fallow. Allowing for this, and also for land on which crops are lost and which is idle for a variety of reasons, total demand for cropland in 2010 is projected at 477 million acres, 64 million more than in 1977.

SUPPLY OF CROPLAND.   Where would the additional land come from? The general answer is, from those lands now in pasture, forest, and range which would give the highest net return when converted to crops. More specifically, the National Resource Inventory (NRI), done by the U.S. Soil Conservation Service (SCS) in 1977, identifies 127 million acres of pasture, range, forest, and "other" land judged to have medium to high potential for conversion to cropland under yield and price conditions that existed in 1976. The fact that the definition of this land specifically incorporates economic criteria makes the 127 million acres, although only a rough estimate, the best available measure of the supply of additional cropland.[11]

What then can be said about the economic supply of cropland? No definite answer is possible, but it appears likely that the supply can be expanded enough to accommodate the projected demand. The production projections (table 8–2) probably imply rising real prices of grains and soybeans, which would favor conversion of land now in forest, pasture, and range. The supply of land in such uses of would be reduced, but this is unlikely to have much effect on the price of that land (its

---

[10] Crosson and Brubaker, *Resource and Environmental Effects*.

[11] The NRI also found 115 million acres of prime farmland not in crops in 1977. Only 48 million acres of this had high to medium potential for conversion to crops under the economic criteria defining potential. The rest had the physical characteristics necessary for crop production, but would not pass the economic test. Since farmers' decisions to convert land to crops are based on economic considerations, the NRI's estimate of potential cropland is a better estimate of additional supply than its estimate of prime land not already in crops.

opportunity cost in crop production). First, the proportion of forest, range, and pasture land with potential for crop production is small relative to the total supply (less than 5 percent for nonfederal and federal forest land and less than 17 percent for nonfederal and federal range and pasture land). Second, studies show that prospective increases in demand for forest products and services and beef could be accommodated by modest increases in the productivity of forest, range, and meadowland, even if all of that land with the potential for crops were converted.[12]

The supply of cropland and potential cropland is influenced by the growing demand for land for urban and other nonagricultural uses. The discussion that followed release of *The Potential Cropland Study*, cited earlier, often failed to note that only 675,000 of the 3 million acres of rural land converted were cropland. Accurate data on the amount which was potential cropland are not available, but within the USDA, 200,000 acres is taken as a reasonable approximation.[13] Thus, well under a million acres of cropland and potential cropland were converted annually to nonagricultural uses between 1967 and 1975.[14] The cumulative total for the eight years—approximately 7 million acres—was a little over 1 percent of the nation's supply of cropland and potential cropland in the 1970s.

It frequently is argued that these numbers understate the true loss of cropland because the spread of nonagricultural land use is uneven, creating small pockets of cropland which cannot be farmed as efficiently as before. The result is the so-called impermanence syndrome. Owners of these lands are hampered, for example, by ordinances restricting the movement of farm machinery on local roads or against early morning noise. Crops are damaged by vandals and farm animals attacked by dogs. In these circumstances the productivity of farming declines, and while the land may remain classified as cropland or potential cropland, it no longer contributes, or has the potential to contribute, to crop production as much as it once did.

[12] For forestland, see William F. Hyde, *Timber Supply, Land Allocation, and Economic Efficiency* (Baltimore, Md., Johns Hopkins University Press for Resources for the Future, 1980). For range and pastureland, see U.S. Forest Service, "An Assessment of the Forest and Range Land Situation in the United States," review draft, no date (Washington, D.C.) pp. 259–266.

[13] Robert Boxley, "Competition for Agricultural Land to the Year 2000," in Committee on Agriculture, Nutrition and Forestry, U.S. Senate, *Agricultural Land Availability*, Papers on the Supply and Demand for Agricultural Lands in the United States (Washington, D.C., U.S. Government Printing Office, 1981).

[14] Fischel makes a persuasive argument that even this figure greatly overstates the loss of cropland and potential cropland [W.A. Fischel, "The Urbanization of Agricultural Land: a Review of the National Agricultural Lands Study," *Land Economics* vol. 58, no. 2 (May 1982) pp. 236–259.]

The impermanence syndrome seems real, but there are no good estimates of how much land is affected by it. Even if it equals the amount of cropland and potential cropland converted, however, the total amount of land involved from 1967 to 1975 would be only a little more than 2 percent of the nation's cropland and potential cropland in the 1970s. This is a small amount.

The key question is the future magnitude of this change and its effects on agricultural land prices. Judgments about this depend to a large extent upon expectations about future rates of conversion to nonagricultural uses. The main variables are the rate at which nonagricultural economic activity spreads into rural areas, the rate of household formation, preferences of households between rural and urban areas as places to live, and the expansion of land-absorbing infrastructure.

In a careful study prepared for the National Agricultural Lands Study, Brown and Beale concluded that the net outcome of these forces would be a slower rate of conversion of land to nonagricultural uses in the 1980s and 1990s than in the late 1960s and early 1970s.[15] They give several reasons. One is that the federal highway system now is substantially complete. They also note that the loss of agricultural land to the construction of reservoirs is likely to be less in the future than in the 1960s and 1970s. They expect that after 1984 the rate of household formation will decline sharply relative to the 1960s and 1970s, indicating a decline in residential demand for agricultural land if householders' preferences between rural and urban areas remain the same as in the 1970s.

If Brown and Beale are right, the future rate of conversion of cropland and potential cropland to nonagricultural uses will be less than the 875,000 acres per year experienced from 1967 to 1975. For purposes of discussion, I assume 750,000 acres per year. In this case, some 25 million acres of present and potential cropland will be converted to nonagricultural uses between 1977 and 2010. Adding this to the projected additional 64 million acres demanded for crop production indicates that roughly 90 million acres of potential cropland now in pasture, forest, and range will be converted, well within the 127 million acres of such land found by the NRI in 1977.

FUTURE COSTS. In the projected scenario, there appears to be no problem of the physical availability of land. But what will it cost to meet

---

[15] David L. Brown and Calvin L. Beale, "Sociodemographic Influences on Land Use in Nonmetropolitan America," in Committee on Agriculture, Nutrition and Forestry, U.S. Senate, *Agricultural Land Availability*.

the demand for land, and what effect will this have on the cost of producing food and fiber?

While the demands for land for nonagricultural uses will grow more slowly in the future, they will help drive up the price of land remaining in crops around urban areas. That land will shift into higher valued crops, for example, vegetables and horticultural crops, in order to accommodate the higher price of land. The crops that were economic at lower land prices, such as grains, will be moved to more distant, less valuable land. This process has been going on for a long time, but until the early 1970s the demand for land for grain production was declining, so the displacement of this production by urban expansion did not press heavily on the supply of cropland. The rise in the cost of agricultural land around urban areas therefore probably had relatively small impact on the cost of land in grain and soybean production.

In the projected scenario, however, the displacement of grain and soybean production by urban expansion occurs at a time when the demand for land to produce these crops is rising sharply. The rising costs of agricultural land around urban areas, therefore, will tend more strongly than in the past to increase the cost of land in grains and soybeans, and farmers growing these crops will be unable to avoid these costs by moving further out.

The rising demand for cropland also will tend to increase production costs because the quality of the potential cropland is inferior to that of land currently in production. The USDA measures land by capability classes I–VIII, with quality for crop production diminishing in ascending order:[16]

Class	Definition
I	Soils have few limitations that restrict their use.
II	Soils have moderate limitations that reduce the choice of plants.
III	Soils have severe limitations that reduce the choice of plants.
IV	Soils have very severe limitations that reduce the choice of plants.
V	Soils are not likely to erode but have other limitations, impractical to remove, that limit their use.
VI	Soils have severe limitations that make them generally unsuitable for cultivation.

[16] U.S. Department of Agriculture, RCA 1980 appraisal (Washington, D.C., 1981) part I, p. 53.

Class	Definition
VII	Soils have very severe limitations that make them unsuitable for cultivation.
VIII	Soils and landforms have limitations that nearly preclude their use for commercial crop production.

The principal limitations referred to are erosiveness, poor drainage, stoniness, and climate. All of these limitations can be reduced, even climate (e.g., with irrigation), but always at a cost. In general, these costs rise as the quality of the land declines. Since the quality of potential cropland generally is lower than that of present cropland (table 8–4), costs of production on the potential cropland would be higher than on that now farmed. Rising real prices of key nonland inputs, particularly energy, fertilizer, and irrigation water, suggest that these also will tend to increase crop production costs.

It is likely that the expansion of cropland also would entail higher external costs of crop production (i.e., those not borne by the farmer or consumers). The most important of these costs will come from erosion since erosion hazard is greater on the potential cropland than on present cropland (tables 8–4 and 8–5).[17]

The effects of erosion on crop yields have long been of concern, but studies of these effects are relatively few and limited to small areas, usually under experimental conditions. There are no reliable estimates at the national level. A major problem in estimating the impact of erosion on yields is that whatever they may have been in the past, these effects have been swamped by the yield-increasing effects of advancing technology. Still, despite the lack of convincing evidence, it is hard to avoid concluding that an increase in erosion like that projected in table 8–5 would take a toll on the productivity of the land.

There is not enough information to allow accurate estimates of how much damage cropland erosion causes through siltation of lakes, reservoirs, and harbors, increased flooding, and impaired water quality. Whatever these damages now are, table 8–5 suggests that under the projected scenario they will be substantially higher by 2010 (see pages 280–281).

Present levels of fertilizer use do not appear to impose major external costs, and the slow growth in use projected for the future is not expected to change this.[18] Farm consumption of insecticides is expected to decline, primarily because of the spread of integrated pest management practices

---

[17] Crosson and Brubaker, *Resource and Environmental Effects*.
[18] Ibid.

TABLE 8–4. Cropland and Potential Cropland by Land
Capability Class in 1977

Land capability class	Cropland		Potential cropland[a]	
	Acres (millions)	Percent of total	Acres (millions)	Percent of total
I	31.5	7.6	3.2	2.6
II	187.8	45.5	39.6	32.6
III	131.7	31.9	47.5	39.1
Total, I–III	351.0	85.0	110.3	74.3
IV–VIII	62.2	15.0	31.2	25.7
Total, all classes	413.2	100.0	121.5	100.0

Inherent Potential Erosion[b]
(tons/acre)

24.8 cropland   36.6 potential cropland

Source: National Resources Inventory.

[a] Potential cropland is land in forest, pasture, and range that could be economically converted to crops under conditions prevailing in 1976.

[b] The amount of erosion that would occur if the land were in bare fallow. Calculated by the Universal Soil Loss Equation.

TABLE 8–5. Erosion from Cropland and Sediment
Delivered in the United States

	1977	2010
Erosion		
Total (million tons)	1,907.0	3,537.0
Per acre (tons)	4.6	8.3
Sediment delivered (million tons)	748.3	1,449.8

Sources: Erosion in 1977 from the National Resources Inventory; erosion in 2010 and sediment delivered in 1977 and 2010 from Pierre R. Crosson and Sterling Brubaker, Resource and Environmental Effects of U.S. Agriculture (Washington, D.C., Resources for the Future, 1982).

Notes: Data are for the forty-eight contiguous states. Erosion is by water. Wind erosion in the Plains region was 891 million tons in 1977.

in cotton production. Herbicide use is likely to rise significantly because more land will be in crops and because conservation tillage, which uses relatively large amounts of herbicides to control weeds, is likely to spread. On present evidence, herbicides do not appear to pose a serious threat to the environment, although more research is needed in this area.

The prospect, then, is for rising real costs of crop production, including those paid by the farmer as well as external costs of erosion paid by the general public. Increasing land costs will contribute to this but they are by no means its sole cause. No attempt is made here to estimate how much agricultural production costs might rise. Conceivably, they could increase enough to reduce the growth of demand below that projected in table 8–2. Export demand in particular would grow more slowly if production costs, and hence prices, were to rise steeply. For purposes of discussion here, I assume that in the projected scenario production costs rise no more than 25 to 30 percent from 1980 to 2010. (This refers to costs paid by farmers, not erosion costs.)

Does the prospect of rising costs indicate a problem of agricultural land in meeting future crop demands? There is no certain answer, but two things can be said. First, if there is a problem of agricultural land, it is only part of a larger one—namely, the prospect of rising costs of production. Second, the main cause of the problem, if there is one, is the increasing demand for land for crop production, not the conversion of land to nonagricultural uses. Both of these points have implications for the discussion of policy issues in the last section.

The Amenity Issue

Although the capacity issue dominates the discussion of the adequacy of agricultural land, it is clear that the possible loss of amenity values is of concern to many people. Amenity values are not easily defined, let alone measured. What, specifically, are the values of a "rural life-style" and how should these values be weighted relative to others that are both tangible and intangible? Another problem is that amenity is to a large extent in the eye of the beholder, and there are many beholders. One man's amenity is another man's eyesore. There is substantial agreement, if not a consensus, that people should have access to open space at reasonable cost in time and effort. Moreover, polls show that more people prefer to live in a rural setting than actually live there and the "rural turnaround" of the 1970s indicates that an increasing number of them are acting upon this preference.[19] Ironically, the "turnaround" is one of the reasons for the conversion of agricultural land to nonagricultural (residential) uses.

Aside from the values attached to open space and rural living, it is difficult to discern a common pattern in the amenity values people wish to obtain from agricultural land. Accordingly, it is difficult to form a judgment about either their present status or future prospects. A number of points can be made, however.

[19] See Brown and Beale, "Sociodemographic Influences."

1. The number of people living on farms declined from 15.3 percent of the total population in 1950 to 3.4 percent in 1979, reflecting massive migration from agricultural to nonagricultural activities. To the extent that farm dwellers reap amenity value from contact with the land, that value must have declined. However, the movement from the farm was primarily a voluntary response to the greater economic opportunities available outside agriculture. The loss of amenity value was an inevitable consequence of a freely taken decision. In a society based on the principle that people should be free to choose how to manage their lives, the loss cannot be regarded as a social problem requiring a public response.

2. Although migrating farm dwellers lost some of the amenity values of open space, these values have probably increased for the nonfarm population. In the early 1980s, more nonfarm people had more access to open space than twenty to twenty-five years ago. Not that there is more "open space," whatever that means. But the combination of the interstate highway system, greater per capita income, and more leisure time means that people now can more often and more speedily enjoy the pleasures of a day in the country than previously.

3. The rural turnaround indicates that during the 1970s the number of nonfarm people benefiting from rural life-styles increased.

4. Urban expansion undoubtedly has created adjustment problems in areas that are shifting from predominantly agricultural to predominantly nonagricultural bases. The "impermanence syndrome" is real. The adjustment problems it represents are caused in part, however, by precisely those people seeking the values of a rural, but nonagricultural, lifestyle.

5. Continued urban and surburban growth will diminish the total amount of open space available in the future, since the nation's land base is fixed. Even if the conversion of rural land to nonagricultural uses continues at 3 million acres per year, which for reasons already given is doubtful, the total amount converted from 1977 to 2010, 66 million acres, would be only 3.6 percent of the present stock of rural nonfederal land plus federal land in range and forest in the forty-eight contiguous states. Moreover, a significant fraction of the conversions will be made by people seeking the values of a rural lifestyle. And rising per capita income and leisure time will continue to facilitate access to open space by urban dwellers.

These points indicate that, from a national perspective, the loss of amenity values from conversion of agricultural land is of secondary importance. The loss may be keenly felt by some people in urban areas, but it is essentially a local issue.

POLICY ISSUES

Introduction

The projected increases in land devoted to crop production and non-agricultural uses, and the attendant increases in costs, reflect primarily the future play of market forces. Is there an argument for public intervention to change the projected market outcome?

The American economy relies to a great extent on the market system to allocate scarce resources. It has long been recognized, however, that in specific instances markets may fail in this respect. In the case of agriculture, the amount of land allocated to agricultural production may be too much or too little relative to some hard-to-observe "ideal." Similarly, the market may overshoot or undershoot in the allocation of resources devoted to the development of substitutes for land in agricultural production.

The introduction to this volume discusses the general conditions under which the market system may fail to allocate resources efficiently. Such conditions may arise wherever economic activity generates external costs and benefits. Off-farm damage by erosion is a prime example of external costs resulting from agricultural production. As property rights of farmers and others are presently defined, those who bear the off-farm costs of erosion generally cannot obtain compensation from the farmer imposing them. Thus, the farmer has no incentive to prevent these costs from occurring or to absorb them. Farm output, therefore, is higher and farm prices lower than if the market correctly registered off-farm erosion damage.

Amenity values provided by the view of a well-tended farm are an example of external benefits. These values are real, but farmers cannot charge for them so they are not reflected in the value of agricultural land. Consequently, the amount of land converted to nonagricultural uses may be greater than it would be if the land market captured amenity values.

Apart from externalities, the market may misjudge future demand for agricultural land. For example, the true social value of land will be understated if the market underestimates the future demand for food and fiber or overestimates the emergence of technological substitutes for land in production. In this case, the conversion of agricultural land to nonagricultural uses will be excessive and farmers will underinvest in practices to maintain long-term productivity. A caution is necessary here. It may well be that the market misjudges the future. However, it does not follow that those in a government agency necessarily would do a better job of forecasting, no matter how able and dedicated they are. The future is inherently uncertain. There is little reason to believe that public officials can foresee it any more clearly than farmers and others who comprise the land market, people whose very livelihood depends upon acquiring the best information about future conditions and acting wisely on it.

The problem would not arise at all if land, once developed, could easily be shifted back into agriculture. Many feel, however, that certain land uses are irreversible as far as future reconversions to agriculture are concerned. In many cases where land was converted to shopping centers or residential development, for instance, this is no doubt true. Yet it is also true that if future food prices rose enough, some land now considered unusable for agriculture would no doubt be brought (back) into cultivation. In economically declining areas, strong agricultural demand might even induce agricultural conversion of land now in commercial, industrial, and residential uses. The argument for "irreversible" losses can be overdone.

Markets may also fail to allocate enough resources to research and development of new agricultural technologies. If agricultural land becomes more scarce, as the projected scenario indicates, private firms will have an incentive to develop technologies which substitute for land. However, some of the more promising technologies, for example, those that would rely on more efficient use of the sun's energy in photosynthesis, require advances in basic research. It often is difficult for private firms to capture enough of the payoff from such research to justify their investment in it. From a social standpoint, however, the payoff may return the investment manyfold. This is a clear case of market failure justifying public action.

The discussion indicates that in thinking about agricultural land policy issues, we should ask to what extent the projected scenario of rising land and production costs reflects various kinds of market failure.

Capacity

Is there a capacity problem requiring a public response? For agriculture as for any other economic sector, we know capacity is being approached when production costs begin to rise. But how much must costs rise before it becomes apparent that there is a problem? The answer is a matter of judgment, but a common criterion surely is the importance of the sector in which costs are rising. Agriculture, in particular food production, clearly is of key importance to the American economy, both domestically and internationally. The strong growth of the economy and relatively stable price level enjoyed from the end of World War II until the early 1970s owed much to the success of agriculture in meeting steadily rising demand, especially for exports, at declining real costs. The prospect of a steady continuation of the cost increases that began in the early 1970s is disquieting. It provides grounds for concern about efforts to control inflation and to maintain a strong balance of payments, and for the welfare of consumers, particularly the poor, both at home and abroad.

The projected scenario indicates an emerging problem of capacity. The conclusion reflects my judgment that the prospective increases in costs of agricultural production threaten the public welfare. Since the scenario assumes that most of the resources used in agriculturally related activities will continue to be allocated by private markets, market failure is implicit. Some specific forms of possible failure are considered below.

If one accepts that there is an emerging problem reflecting market failure, then there is a prima facie case for public intervention to correct the situation. A second condition of such intervention, however, is that it is possible to find cost-effective government policies to deal with the situation. The discussion in this section is addressed to this latter condition. Policies to limit the growth of demand and for dealing with possible inadequacies in the agricultural land market and in the markets for inputs which substitute for land are considered, as are erosion control policies. The overarching question is: Are there cost-effective policies which improve on market performance in easing pressures on the land and other agricultural resources?

POLICIES TO LIMIT DEMAND.   One way to alleviate these pressures is to limit the growth of crop demand. Because erosion and other external costs (e.g., those derived from fertilizer and pesticide pollution) are not reflected in crop prices, a case could be made for a tax on crops.[20] Such a tax, of course, would increase crop prices, dampen demand, and ease pressure on the resource base. Export demand is more price elastic than domestic demand, so exports, the main source of the prospective increase in demand, would be reduced proportionately more than domestic demand.

Although it is unassailable in principle, a tax on crops would face serious practical difficulties. Erosion and other environmental costs are

[20] Seitz argues for a tax on crop exports as a source of revenue to finance erosion control practices. However, in principle such a tax on total crop production, not just exports, can be justified as a way of reflecting the social costs of erosion and other environmental damages of crop production. [Wesley D. Seitz, "Viewpoint: A Conservation Tariff," *Journal of Soil and Water Conservation* vol. 36, no. 3 (May-June 1981) pp. 120–121.]

hard to measure. This would lead to great uncertainty about the proper level of the tax. There also would be political problems. Some crops cause more environmental damage than others; for example, corn is much more erosive than wheat and could justifiably be taxed more than wheat. Corn farmers would complain of discrimination, but the tax differential would be defensible. Among corn farmers, however, the tax would be inequitable because some of them cause far more erosion than others. The lesser offenders would have a strong case against the tax. Probably no tax is completely fair, but one that is blatantly inequitable is particularly hard to defend.

Export quotas would limit the growth of demand, but are an unattractive way of achieving this. Aside from their high domestic political costs—farmers would oppose them fiercely—export quotas infringe upon the deeply held American commitment to free trade. No commitment is beyond modification as conditions change, but this one has served the country well. Departing from it by imposing quotas on agricultural exports would raise questions abroad about the overall thrust of American trade policy and weaken our efforts to promote a more generally open world trading system.

It appears that the unfavorable economics of ethanol production from grain would reduce this source of crop demand to insignificance by 2010.[21] At this writing, however, the 1980 legislation setting a goal of 10 billion gallons of ethanol by 1990 was still on the books, as was the waiver of the federal gasoline tax on gasohol. Other federal incentives to gasohol production also remain in effect. Given the mounting pressure on agricultural resources, it makes no sense to subsidize an additional major increase in crop demand. Given the importance of energy and uncertainty about its long-term cost, maintenance of energy options has social value. The market may falter in providing these, and some low-level public support for ethanol production technology perhaps could be justified on these grounds. But Sanderson's analysis indicates that the present program should be scaled back considerably, if not eliminated.

On balance, the country will be best served by letting the market determine the growth of crop demand. This means no policies to limit the expansion of exports or to stimulate ethanol production from grains. This is the posture assumed in the projections of crop production shown in table 8–2. Accepting it as in the nation's best interest, we must look to other policy options for easing the mounting pressure on land and other agricultural resources.

[21] See Sanderson, "Benefits and Costs of the U.S. Gasohol Program."

AGRICULTURAL LAND POLICIES.   Given the growth of demand, pressure on the cropland base can be reduced either by stimulating faster growth in grain and soybean yields or by slowing the conversion of cropland and potential cropland to nonagricultural uses. The latter approach is the one that has generated the most interest—it is recognized in the 1981 farm bill and most states and local jurisdictions have adopted measures along this line.

These measures include agricultural zoning, sometimes combined with a development permit system; agricultural districting; purchase of development rights; purchase and resale of development rights with restrictions on use; transfer of development rights; differential tax treatment of agricultural land; and so-called "right to farm" legislation.

Among these measures, agricultural zoning by local governments is by far the most widely used.[22] To date most zoning ordinances have sought to protect agricultural land by specifying minimum lot sizes, but many of these regulations were weakened by including an open-ended list of permitted nonfarm uses of the land. The development permit system requires a permit from a designated public agency before agricultural land can be turned to some other use. The system is used in conjunction with zoning, but as of 1980 had been adopted only in Vermont and California.

Oregon is the only state so far to take the lead in requiring local jurisdictions to adopt zoning to keep agricultural land in agriculture. All class I–IV soils in farming are to remain in that use, and in eastern Oregon this applies also to classes V and VI. With minor exceptions, provision of additional public services is confined to present urban areas. It seems clear that if the program is followed rigorously, it will slow the conversion of agricultural land in Oregon.

While it is still too early to judge the effectiveness of agricultural zoning, a general problem is that when the value of the zoned land increases, zoning ordinances are changed to accommodate the higher valued use. There are exceptions of course, Central Park in New York City being the most conspicuous. Conceivably Oregon's approach may spread, but the record shows that in general zoning succumbs to market power.

Agricultural districting and right to farm legislation are state level measures designed to protect farming against some of the threats of urban encroachment, for example, by prohibiting ordinances against the noise or odors associated with farming, avoiding special assessments particularly burdensome to agriculture, and controlling public services

[22] *National Agricultural Lands Study*, p. 64. This account of measures to slow the conversion of agricultural land is based on the NALS.

likely to induce urban expansion. Six states have agricultural districts and 16 have right-to-farm legislation. Except for New York's districting law, the programs are too recent for accurate evaluation. The New York law has provided modest protection to farmers against special assessments and eminent domain proceedings but has been relatively ineffective in slowing the conversion of agricultural land.[23]

The basic idea of purchase of development rights is to buy out the farmer at a price reflecting the nonagricultural value of his land on condition that the land continue in farming. The main problem with the programs is that they are expensive. New Jersey abandoned a PDR program when it became clear that the $5 million provided would not purchase a significant amount of farmland. So far, four states and 17 local jurisdictions have adopted programs for purchase, or purchase and resale, with restrictions on use.

Only a few local jurisdictions have adopted programs for the transfer of development rights and they have not been very successful in slowing conversions.[24] In these programs certain areas are designated as agricultural districts and others as development districts. Farmers in agricultural districts are given development rights which they can sell for use in development districts. When the farmer sells, however, he must keep an equivalent portion of his land in agriculture, or in a use compatible with agriculture.

Since farmland earns much less than land in urban uses, changes in property tax assessments to reflect urban values will ultimately force farmers to sell. All states but Kansas and Georgia give some sort of preference to farmers when it comes to property taxes. Typically, such tax relief takes the form of assessments at agricultural value or deferments until the land is sold for conversion. Again, while the programs have had some effect in slowing conversions, the market still determines the farmer's choices and when the price is right, he will sell.

The question, of course, is: How cost-effective are these measures? The answer is: Not very. Conversions would have to be slowed by millions of acres over the next several decades to make even a dent in the capacity problem, and the economic costs would be enormous. For example, assume that around urban areas, land in residences or shopping centers sells for $20,000 per acre more than the same land in crops (which is a conservative estimate). At 10 percent interest, this difference in capital value is the equivalent of $2,000 per acre per year in income yielded by the land. If over the next thirty years, 20 million acres of cropland which would otherwise be converted to nonagricultural uses

---

[23] Ibid.
[24] Ibid, p. 74.

were somehow kept in crop production, the contribution toward meeting the increased demand for cropland—60 to 65 million acres—would be relatively small. However, the cost to society in forgone income would be high: billions of dollars per year in 1981 dollars, mounting to $40 billion dollars per year at the end of the period.

There also would be a substantial redistribution of income. If zoning were the principal instrument used to hold cropland in crop production, farmers would be deprived of the capital gains that conversion of the land would yield them; and owners of land already in nonagricultural uses would enjoy greater increases in capital value than if more conversion were permitted. The amount of their gain would depend on the amount of land suitable for development and not restricted to agriculture. The larger the amount of such land, the larger the total supply of land for nonagricultural uses, hence the smaller the effect of the restrictions on the capital value of such land. The question is an empirical one, of course. But if the supply of unrestricted land which could be economically developed were large, why would there be so much pressure to convert agricultural land? It seems likely that restricting conversion of agricultural land would increase pressure for more intensive use of already developed land, driving up its price, to the benefit of its owners.

If purchase of development rights were the control instrument, farmers would gain more than they would if there were no limits on conversion. Whatever the instrument, or set of instruments, if they were successful enough to help solve the capacity problem, the value of land in nonagricultural uses would rise more than it otherwise would. Renters of the services of such land, for example, for residential housing, would pay more than they otherwise would, and owners of the land would receive correspondingly higher income. These effects are already observable in Oregon, according to a study of that state's system for preserving farmland.[25]

The high cost and income distribution consequences of measures to significantly slow the conversion of agricultural land would be acceptable if it were shown convincingly that there is a major failure of present land markets to anticipate future relative demands on the land. But no such showing has been made. The conclusion is inescapable that measures to slow the conversion of agricultural land have little promise and less justification for dealing with the capacity problem.

[25] A.E. Gamache, M.J. McCoy, W.M. Hobson, A.L. Johnson, P.M. Thompson, and V. Lentz, "Land Use Regulation in Oregon: an Evaluation," Discussion draft, 1981. Managed by Applied Economics, Lake Oswego, Oregon.

Technology as a Policy Instrument

The prospective increases in economic and environmental costs in part reflect a failure of markets to allocate enough resources to development of technologies which make more sparing use of land, fertilizer, fossil fuels, and water while still maintaining rapid productivity growth. There is much evidence that cost-effective policies can be devised to correct for this market failure. Studies of the returns to public investment in agricultural research show that they have been and are high.[26]

Historically, most of the basic research leading to technological advances in U.S. agriculture has been publicly funded. There usually is high uncertainty regarding the amount and timing of the payoff to such research, which makes it unattractive to private enterprise. More important, the knowledge gained may not be patentable, so the investor in such research cannot be assured of exclusive rights to returns from it. The research that led to the development of high-yield, fertilizer-responsive hybrid corn is the outstanding example of the powerful role federally funded research can play in agricultural development, but it is not unique.

Federal support for research to develop new agricultural technologies thus is a policy instrument. How should it be wielded? Given the characteristics of the emerging capacity problem, four lines of research look especially promising.

1. Any increase in crop yields and total productivity requires an increase in the amount of energy combined with the land or in the efficiency of the energy used. The prospective increases in real prices of energy and fertilizer indicate that simply increasing the amounts of these resources per acre of land is not the route to take. There is potential for increasing the efficiency with which purchased energy and fertilizer are used, but this is already reflected in the projections of crop yields given above.

Improvements in the photosynthetic capacity of main crops to capture the sun's energy and convert it into valuable plant material would increase yields without requiring proportional increases in inputs of purchased energy and fertilizer. Improvements in photosynthesis also would increase the attractiveness of enlarging the nitrogen-fixing capacity of plants. The biologically fixed nitrogen would substitute for increasingly expensive nitrogen fertilizers. However, the nitrogen-fixing process demands more plant energy. If photosynthetic efficiency were not im-

[26] R. Evenson, P. Waggoner, and V. Ruttan, "Economic Benefits from Research: An Example from Agriculture," *Science* vol. 205 (September 15, 1979) pp. 1101–1107.

proved, meeting nitrogen-fixing demands would reduce the energy supply available for valuable plant growth. In this case, crop yields might be lower with enhanced nitrogen fixation than if purchased fertilizers provided this nutrient.

Investment in these two areas, however, does not promise quick returns. They were not given high priority in the past and as a result, it will take time to build the stock of scientific talent and basic knowledge needed to achieve a major breakthrough.

2. Plant breeding has been an important source of higher yields and total productivity and there are promising lines still to be pursued in this area. Soybeans are a major land-using crop for which demand is rapidly increasing. In fact, land in soybeans is projected to exceed that in either corn or wheat by 15 to 20 million acres by 2010, even though the rate of yield increases of the last thirty years will continue.[27] Development of a soybean variety with a significantly higher yield potential that retains other valuable characteristics would make an important contribution to restraining the demand for agricultural land and the attendant increases in economic and external costs.

3. On land with moderate to steep slopes, conservation tillage greatly reduces erosion compared with conventional tillage. Conservation tillage can consist of any of a large number of tillage techniques, but all have three features in common: they do not use the moldboard plow; they leave enough crop residue on the soil surface to significantly reduce erosion; and they rely more on herbicides and less on cultivation to control weeds than conventional tillage. The prospective expansion of cropland implies that much land with high erosion potential will be shifted out of pasture, forest, and range to crops. The use of conservation tillage on this land would restrain the increase in erosion.

Conservation tillage spread rapidly in the 1970s, reflecting cost advantages in labor, energy, and equipment relative to conventional tillage. However, conservation tillage presently is not competitive with conventional tillage on poorly drained land, on land where weeds cannot be adequately controlled with herbicides, and in areas where the growing season is short. Research to overcome these limitations would have high payoff in reduced erosion damage.

4. The spread of conservation tillage implies increased use of herbicides because the technology relies more on herbicides and less on cultivation to control weeds than does conventional tillage. Present evidence does not indicate that the herbicides in wide use present serious threats to the environment.[28] With few exceptions, they are not mark-

[27] Crosson and Brubaker, *Resource and Environmental Effects.*
[28] Ibid.

edly toxic to animals when applied in generally used amounts, nor do they persist in the environment for long periods. Studies of their effects on soil microorganisms indicate that populations may be reduced immediately after application of herbicides, but they recover and show no permanent impairment of important functions, for example, fixing nitrogen.

Not all possible ways in which herbicides may affect soil organisms have been adequately investigated, however, nor have their effects on low trophic levels in aquatic environments been evaluated. Moreover, the increase in herbicide use implied by the spread of conservation tillage is large enough to cause concern if there is a possibility of threshold effects on the environment. The current lack of evidence of strong adverse effects may be because these thresholds have not been crossed.

The advantages of conservation tillage in controlling erosion are so strong that research to extend the technology should be pushed. In order to avoid unpleasant surprises, however, research on the ways in which herbicides may adversely affect the environment should be an integral part of this effort.

Development of technologies along these lines would reduce pressure on the land and other increasingly expensive resources, thus contributing to solution of the capacity problem. Since much of the research needed to develop the technologies is not likely to be undertaken by the private sector, the federal government could properly take the lead through its own research facilities and by giving support to others through the land grant college system. This would involve no major break with traditional federal government practice, only an increase in the level of effort. Short of much more analysis, no precise estimate of the needed level of effort is possible. However, such an effort would be only a minute fraction of the cost of slowing conversion of agricultural land, and the likelihood of success would be far higher.

Erosion Control Policies

It will be some years before there is a payoff to investment in research to extend the limits of conservation tillage. Meanwhile, there is an erosion problem to be dealt with.

In thinking about erosion control policies, it is essential to distinguish clearly between off-farm costs and on-farm costs. The off-farm damages to water and air quality are unambiguous examples of external costs. They are imposed on those who must use the sediment-laden waters or dust-filled air in an institutional setting that does not provide for compensation from the farmers responsible. This is a clear case of market failure.

There is a much less clear case for public intervention to limit on-farm costs of erosion—productivity loss—because unlike off-farm damages, the farmer bears the cost of such erosion-induced losses. Why should the market fail to register these costs and induce farmers to respond properly to them?

One possibility is that the market underestimates future demands on the land or overestimates the rate of development of technological substitutes for it. This clearly can happen, but as was pointed out above, it is not clear that those who would substitute their judgment for the market's can read the future more accurately.

It also may be argued that the farmer does not plan as far into the future as society and thus does not worry about the long-term effects of erosion on productivity. The difference in time horizons is real, but it need not lead to this result. Since the price of land reflects its future productivity, erosion that affects productivity, even if it is in the distant future, will lower the current price of the land. If erosion control costs less than the reduction in price, the farmer will have an incentive to adopt control measures. This assumes that the land market is working; if it is not, the farmer may underinvest (or overinvest) in erosion control, but the difference between private and social time horizons is not the reason for the error.

It sometimes is argued that farmers are simply ignorant of the long-term effects of erosion on productivity, but it is doubtful that this is so. The farmers responsible for most crop production in the United States today are sophisticated businessmen with a substantial investment in the land. They have a strong incentive to protect that investment. If they permit erosion to reduce productivity, it almost surely is because the cost of control exceeds the productivity loss.

Most tenant farmers, and there are a substantial number, operate on short-term leases, so are not likely to be sensitive to long-term effects of erosion on productivity. However, there is every reason to believe that the owner, even if he is an absentee landlord, will take these effects seriously, if in fact they are serious, and make arrangements with the tenant to control them.

If capital markets are not working properly, farmers may not be able to get the credit they need to finance erosion control measures, or if they have high fixed costs and limited profit margins, they may feel pressured to maximize short-term gains even at the expense of longer term deterioration of the land.

Clearly, farmers may receive faulty price signals which cause them to underinvest in erosion control, or institutional constraints may prevent them from responding appropriately even when the signals are right.

But it is an open question as to how pervasive these conditions are in American agriculture. Accordingly, it is difficult to build a strong case for public intervention to induce or require farmers to control erosion to protect productivity.

Although the case for policies to control off-farm damage of erosion is much stronger than the case for policies to reduce productivity loss, the latter traditionally has provided the main rationale for intervention. Indeed, until the emergence of the environmental movement in the 1960s and the realization that sediment is a principal contributor to water pollution, avoidance of productivity loss was the only rationale for erosion control policies.

These policies always were based on the principle that farmers must be induced to voluntarily adopt erosion control practices. The U.S. Department of Agriculture (USDA), which administered the policies, relied on education, persuasion, and sharing the costs of such practices as terracing with the farmer. No farmer, however, no matter how much erosion he caused, was required to accept the USDA's advice or enter into cost-sharing contracts. The General Accounting Office (GAO) appraised the effectiveness of these policies in controlling erosion, and found them wanting.[29]

The U.S. Environmental Protection Agency (EPA) is responsible for policies to improve water quality. However, under section 208 of the Clean Water Act of 1972, control of nonpoint sources of water pollution (which include but are not limited to agriculture) is delegated to the states, subject to approval of state control plans by the EPA. Section 208 conveys authority to control erosion where it is shown to be a source of water pollution. It appears that this authority permits regulatory approaches of the sort the EPA has used to deal with industrial and municipal polluters. However, the states have not used these approaches in their 208 plans, and the EPA has accepted this. Instead, the plans rely on traditional programs to induce voluntary adoption of erosion control practices.

Informed members of Congress, the soil conservation community, and probably also the USDA all feel that traditional erosion control policies have fallen short. Congressional dissatisfaction was a major reason for passage of the Soil and Water Resources Conservation Act of 1977. The act requires the USDA to appraise the soil and water resources situation of the country every five years and to submit recommendations for improvement to the Congress. The first appraisal (henceforth called RCA) was completed in 1981; and in October of that

---

[29] General Accounting Office, *To Protect Tomorrow's Food Supply, Soil Conservation Needs Priority Attention* (CED–77–30) (Washington, D.C., 1977).

year Secretary of Agriculture Block submitted a conservation program for congressional consideration.[30]

Top priority was given to erosion controls to protect productivity. There was scarcely any mention of reducing off-farm erosion damage. In its main objective, therefore, the secretary's program was not new. However, its approaches would differ in significant respects from those traditionally followed. Conservation efforts would be more carefully targeted on the areas where the erosion problem is most serious, unlike traditional programs. In addition, the proposed program put greater emphasis on state and local initiatives in developing conservation programs, and would support these initiatives with matching funds from block grants. This deemphasis of the federal role reflected the Reagan administration's general thrust to shift authority to state and local jurisdictions.

The proposed program also would put relatively more resources into research on conservation technologies, especially conservation tillage, and on technical assistance, and less on cost-sharing than the traditional program. The reasons for this shift in emphasis were nowhere stated explicitly. However, federal spending on cost-sharing has been declining for over a decade, and the new program may simply project this trend. It also is consistent with the enhanced role of state and local governments since much of their increased contribution would go to support cost-sharing programs.

Finally, the proposed program flirted cautiously with the concept of cross-compliance, the notion that to receive benefits of various government programs, commodity price supports, for example, farmers must agree to adopt conservation practices. The USDA's program proposed a pilot project that would tie access to loans from the Farmers' Home Administration to adoption of conservation practices.

The proposed program contained some novel elements which promised to do a better job than traditional approaches in controlling erosion. Even if program goals are met, however, total erosion at the end of five years (with the 1981 level of funding) would be only about 16 percent less than in 1977, and only about 7 percent less than if traditional programs were continued. At the end of fifty years, total erosion would be 18 percent less than in 1977 and 25 percent less than with traditional programs.

[30] The program is described briefly in Secretary Block's statement before the Senate Committee on Agriculture, Nutrition and Forestry, October 28, 1981, and at greater length in U.S. Department of Agriculture, "RCA 1981 Program Report and Environmental Impact Statement," revised draft (Washington, D.C., 1981). In a speech before midwestern governors in July 1982, Secretary of Agriculture Block presented a somewhat revised program. However, the essential points described here were unchanged.

This would represent a significant achievement, but it is still likely to leave a serious erosion problem, given the scenario for the future developed earlier. In that scenario, erosion in 2010 is substantially higher than in 1977, even with continued spread of conservation tillage. The USDA's estimates of future erosion are based on crop export projections that now look too low. Had the projections made here been used, the estimates of erosion in Secretary Block's program document surely would have been higher relative to 1977 than they are now.

On balance, it appears that USDA's proposed program would yield marginal improvement over the traditional program. However, if the projected scenario develops, this is not likely to be enough. Erosion-induced productivity losses would be higher than at present, although for reasons given above, the case for public intervention to deal with productivity loss would still be clouded. Off-farm damages to water quality most likely would be significantly higher. There would be a strong case for more forceful intervention to reduce these damages than is contemplated in the USDA's program. Measures to regulate erosion akin to those now employed by the EPA in dealing with industrial and municipal polluters most likely would be required. A more palatable and in the long run probably more cost-effective approach, however, would be that suggested earlier: increased investment in research to develop land-saving, erosion-reducing technologies. This approach is only hinted at in the USDA's program document, and the regulatory approach is not even mentioned. Should the projected scenario develop, these neglected approaches will have to be considered sooner or later.

SUMMARY

Contrary to popular perceptions, the main pressures that American agriculture will face in the coming decades will not arise from land lost to urban or transportation uses. Rather, they will come from growing export demand and rising prices for fertilizer, energy, and water. The results of these trends will be increases in the economic as well as the environmental costs of production, particularly those costs arising from cropland erosion.

What can be done to offset these trends? In principle, restricting export crops would relieve some of the pressure, but it is a solution that would antagonize domestic farmers as well as our friends abroad. Clearly, however, there is little sense in subsidizing a grain-based gasohol program that makes additional claims on the land base.

One of the more promising and relatively unexplored means of relieving pressure is to increase research on land-saving technologies. These fall into two categories, those that reduce erosion per acre and those that reduce the demand for land by increasing yields. Among the technologies in the first category, conservation tillage holds much promise for reducing erosion but uses more herbicides than conventional tillage methods. While this does not seem to be a problem at present, further information on the effects of herbicides is needed.

Research on ways to improve the photosynthetic capacity of plants and the nitrogen-fixing capacity of soil bacteria holds promise for higher yields and lower costs.

The search for land-saving technologies will not yield quick returns. There are large gaps in basic knowledge and a scarcity of the necessary scientific talent, particularly for research on photosynthesis and biological nitrogen fixation. There is also insufficient funding. Private companies are understandably reluctant to pay for research when they cannot be assured of the results. This is one area where a good argument can be made for strong federal support. This sort of support developed high-yielding corn hybrids and it is not unreasonable to expect that it would lead to other innovative land-saving technologies. However, if this effort is to have any payoff, it must be started now.

The value of land lies, not in its physical quantity, but in the goods and services it provides—recreation and housing as well as food and fiber. This quantity can be expanded almost indefinitely if society is willing to pay the costs. The questions in the coming decades will be how much and what costs society is willing to pay.

9

Private Forests

Marion Clawson

As earlier chapters have indicated, there are important and often difficult problems associated with many of the country's natural resources. For this reason, it is nice to be able to conclude on a soundly optimistic note. The private forests of the United States, a sometimes overlooked but still important resource, appear to be in good shape. Some problems exist, of course, but they appear manageable. As a whole, forests are growing more wood than is being harvested, hence inventories of standing timber are accumulating rather than being drawn down.

This brief and final chapter indicates the importance of the private forests in the United States, both in terms of land use and as contributors to total timber growth and harvest. Several issues which have arisen in discussions of public policy regarding these forests are identified and some conclusions and recommendations offered.

THE IMPORTANCE OF PRIVATE FORESTS

Land Use

What the Forest Service defines as "commercial forests" occupy nearly one-fourth of the total land area of the forty-eight contiguous states,

283

TABLE 9–1. Area of Commercial Timberland, by
Ownership Class, in Sections of the United
States

(million acres)

Ownership class	1952	1962	1970	1977
United States				
National forest	94.7	96.9	94.6	88.7
Other public	49.0	44.8	47.0	45.0
Forest industry	59.5	61.6	67.0	68.8
Farmer	172.3	144.8	125.3	115.8
Other private	123.8	159.3	162.6	162.2
Total	499.3	509.4	496.4	480.5
South				
National forest	10.4	10.7	10.8	11.0
Other public	6.4	6.5	6.7	6.7
Forest industry	32.1	33.4	35.1	36.2
Farmer	91.3	73.0	62.8	55.9
Other private	51.9	76.3	77.1	78.2
Total	192.1	199.9	192.5	188.0
West				
National forest	74.0	75.9	73.4	67.9
Other public	21.5	20.2	20.1	19.6
Forest industry	13.5	14.1	14.5	14.6
Farmer	15.9	15.4	14.5	13.9
Other private	13.5	13.0	12.7	12.3
Total	138.4	138.6	135.3	128.3
North				
National forest	10.3	10.3	10.5	9.8
Other public	21.0	20.1	20.1	20.7
Forest industry	14.0	14.0	17.4	17.9
Farmer	65.1	56.5	47.9	46.0
Other private	58.4	70.0	72.7	71.7
Total	168.8	170.9	168.6	166.1

Source: Forest Service, *Review Draft, An Analysis of the Timber Situation
in the United States*, 1952–2030, U.S. Department of Agriculture, Forest Service, summer 1980. See appendix 3, table 4, pp. 22–25.

Note: West includes all forests west of the Great Plains; North includes all
forests east of the Great Plains and all states from Kansas–Missouri–Kentucky–
West Virginia–Maryland northward; South is the remaining states.

and small additional areas in Alaska and Hawaii (table 9–1). In addition,
less productive forests and forests reserved from cutting by law occupy
nearly half as much more land. Much of the noncommercial and some
of the commercial forests are used for livestock grazing, nearly all are
open for outdoor recreation and serve as a home for wildlife, all have
watershed values, and some have important mineral (including oil and
gas) developments also.

The definition of a "commercial" forest is a rather peculiar and unfortunate one—unfortunate because the term has economic connotations even though the definition is wholly biological. Because this definition underlies all the available data about forests, however, it is important to examine it briefly. Commercial forests are those that are capable of annually growing 20 or more cubic feet of potentially industrial wood per acre from a fully stocked natural stand at about the age of the maximum mean annual growth rate. This definition takes no account of fuelwood or other biomass, the costs of growing and harvesting timber (including road-building costs to reach the site), the quality and hence value of the wood, nor the environmental damages inherent in harvest. Publicly owned forested areas reserved from timber harvest by law (e.g., national parks) are also considered noncommercial regardless of their timber-growing potential. The reader should keep in mind that the forest land consistent with this definition is much greater than that which could be managed for wood production with any reasonable prospect of favorable economic return.

Of the 482 million acres of commercial forests in 1977, 134 million were publicly owned. About two-thirds of these were in the national forests and the other third was in other federal or state forests. About 69 million were owned by the forest industry firms and the remaining 278 million acres were nonindustrial private forests (including farm forests). This picture has remained relatively stable since 1952 when the first modern data on forest ownership were collected. Forest industry firms have increased their holdings about 12 percent since 1952, particularly in the South and Pacific Coast regions; to the extent the data are accurate, farmer-owned forests have declined by a full third in the same period, and the "other" ownerships have increased nearly as much as the farm ownership has declined. There have always been sharp regional differences in forest ownership patterns; publicly owned forests dominate the West, but they are small in the South and in the North where the nonindustrial private forests are dominant. Industrial forests are found in all productive areas.

From the standpoint of ownership and management, there are two distinctly different kinds of privately owned forests in the United States. Forest industry firms, most of which are vertically integrated, own about 14 percent of the commercial forests, from which they harvest logs for their own processing and subsequent sale. They may at times sell some of their logs, and most of these firms also buy logs from other private owners or from public agencies managing publicly owned forests. The larger of these firms, which dominate the industry, operate in most or all major forested regions of the country. Several have extensive forestry operations in other countries, and several also have extensive marketing organizations in wood-consuming countries. These firms are big business, in the American sense of the term. In 1980, International Paper was number 67 on *Fortune's* list of the 500 largest industrial firms, Georgia Pacific was number 68, Weyerhaeuser was number 83, and in all there were seventeen forest industry firms in the 500 list.

In contrast are the many privately owned forests, the owners of which have no processing or manufacturing facilities to turn their logs into lumber, plywood, paper, or any other industrial wood use. Except for the twin features of private ownership and a lack of processing facilities, these "other" forest owners have little in common. Many own only a few acres; the group is often referred to as "small private owners" but this is a misnomer, for some of the forests are large—up to half a million acres for one California firm. While most are individuals, some are corporations. Railroad companies, public utilities, and other land-owning companies may be included here. Some are clearly industrial but not wood-processing corporations. Some are farmers owning "woodlots." Many are residents of small towns and small cities in the generally forested regions, but some are residents of large cities, living hundreds of miles away from their forests. The average farm forest probably has between 100 and 150 acres, while the average nonfarm, nonindustrial private forest has somewhat less than 100 acres.

Timber Growth and Harvest

As table 9–2 indicates, the forest industry firms have achieved a much higher growth rate per acre of the larger sawlogs and of all usable timber than any other major class of forest owners. Because the area of forest land differs considerably by ownership, as shown in table 9–1, the total capacity to grow wood is not exactly the same as either the ownership or the output per acre would suggest. Although the area they own is smaller than that of the national forests, the forest industry firms in 1977 grew more wood than the national forests and grew nearly as much timber as the much greater area of all publicly owned forests.

The actual growth rate per acre and the capacity to grow timber per acre were each about average on the nonindustrial private forests as a whole. If it were possible to eliminate the probably extensive areas of relatively unproductive forests owned for nontimber reasons (e.g., personal recreation) from the data, the nonindustrial private forests that are held primarily for growing timber probably would compare favorably with the industrial forests and thus would be well ahead of the national forests in per-acre yields and productivity.

TABLE 9–2. Net Annual Growth per Acre of All Species,
Growing Stock and Sawtimber, by Major
Ownership Group

(cubic feet and board feet per acre)

Forest ownership	Actual net growth[a]				Potential capacity[b]
	1952	1962	1970	1977	
Growing stock, all species					
National forests	23	26	28	35	72
Other public	26	32	39	54	77
Forest industry	43	50	52	59	88
Other private	27	31	34	45	74
All	28	32	37	46	75
Sawtimber					
National forests	83	98	107	143	
Other public	87	109	130	184	
Forest industry	158	174	185	213	
Other private	81	89	108	140	
All	91	103	120	151	

Immediate source: Marion Clawson, *The Economics of U.S. Nonindustrial Private Forests*, Research Paper R–14 (Washington, D.C., Resources for the Future, 1979) pp. 86–93 and 153. Source of basic data, Forest Service reports on timber supply.

[a] Net growth is total or gross wood growth minus mortality from storms (blowdowns), fire, disease, and insects. Timber harvest is not deducted from gross growth to arrive at net growth.

[b] Potential capacity, or productivity, is the ability of the site to grow potentially usable industrial wood under defined management and at defined age of the stand. It is better understood as an index of capacity to grow wood than as an actual output; the latter may vary greatly, depending upon management of the forest.

Since 1952 the trend in annual wood growth per acre has been upward on forests of all ownerships. The actual rate of annual net wood growth per acre has been lowest on national forests, and the increase, both in absolute and relative terms, has been less for these forests than for any other ownership class. The industrial forests have produced the most wood per acre at every date for which data have been collected, but their growth rate for output per acre over the period 1952 to 1977 was not the highest because they started from a higher base. The nonindustrial private forests made an outstanding showing in 1977, both in terms of absolute volume of wood grown per acre and compared to their own earlier growth rate.

One popular picture is that the United States is depleting its forest resources by overcutting. As table 9–3 shows, exactly the reverse is true—inventories are building up because harvests have fallen short of net growth. For the United States as a whole, annual harvests have not

TABLE 9–3. Annual Removal of Timber as a Percentage of Net
Growth, Commercial Forests, by General
Ownership Class

	Softwood				Hardwood			
Forest ownership	1952	1962	1970	1977	1952	1962	1970	1977
Growing stock								
National forests	61	87	89	86	29	25	28	22
Other public	59	67	77	79	28	23	29	24
Forest industry	146	99	114	126	76	79	66	49
Other private	102	69	65	61	71	66	61	49
Total	100	80	83	82	66	61	56	45
Sawtimber								
National forests	93	133	129	108	43	34	44	33
Other public	79	91	105	109	38	24	36	32
Forest industry	199	138	152	171	94	85	73	65
Other private	126	79	74	69	89	76	76	64
Total	133	104	109	105	83	70	71	60

Immediate source: Marion Clawson, *The Economics of U.S. Nonindustrial Private Forests*, Research Paper R–14, (Washington, D.C., Resources for the Future, 1979) p. 184. Source of basic data, Forest Service reports on timber supply.

been as large as net annual growth in the years of record since 1952. Moreover, the margin between net growth and harvest has widened over this period. While there has been a tendency for all owners to harvest the larger softwood sawlogs faster than they were growing, hardwood sawlogs have not been harvested as fast as they were growing and thus inventories have built up. The smaller sized stock of both softwood and hardwood has been growing faster than the rate of harvest on forests of all ownerships and hence inventories have also increased for them.

To summarize, the privately owned forests of the United States are important, judged by any of several measures. They occupy a large area of land, they have a high capital value, and they produce a lot of wood for manufacture into various products. In addition, they are the basis for a great many jobs; the number of workers in "lumber and all wood products" (Standard Industrial Code 24) is somewhat less than one million for the country as a whole. However, this does not include other workers who are in supply support or marketing jobs related to forestry.

PROBLEMS OF THE PRIVATE FORESTS

As the introduction to this volume points out, one problem that often arises in the natural resource area is that of externalities—in particular, if a certain kind of land use confers benefits or costs on others that are not appropriable by owners. This is characteristically the case for private forests. Owners of these forests, both industrial and nonindustrial, are generally unable to capture for their own income the values of the nonwood annual outputs, such as water supply, protection of wildlife and its habitat, opportunities for outdoor recreation, and aesthetic enjoyment. All forest owners suffer from trespass for these uses particularly, but increasingly persons trespass to cut trees for fuel. Even when trespass does not exist in the legal sense, the forest landowner may be unable to capture much value from the nonwood outputs. Under the laws in all states, a forest owner is unable to capture the values in the water flowing out of the forest. Although charges may be made, under applicable laws, for permission to enter the forest, no charge can be made for harvesting the game itself, because that belongs to the state. While a forest owner is legally free to charge for outdoor recreation, in many cases the policing of property to prevent unauthorized use would be more expensive than the gains would warrant. Far more seriously, the attitude has grown up in many localities and regions that access to privately owned forests should be free to all interested parties.

In times past, some forest industry firms sought to close their lands to public access, including access by hunters; the public reaction was so hostile that today virtually every such firm makes its lands freely available to hunters and other groups. This is in spite of the fact that some visitors inflict damage, sometimes malicious damage, on the machinery or other property of the forest owner.

Trespass is a serious problem for the nonindustrial private forest owner as well—trespass into cabins, and over forest land, cutting of trees for fuel, and damaging other vegetation. For the nonindustrial private owner who seeks to use the forest for weekend or vacation recreation, trespass may be so serious as to destroy its value for this use.

The lack of financial repayment for the nonwood outputs of forests is a problem for publicly owned forests as well. The costs of managing public forests fall on taxpayers as a whole; the nonwood benefits are likely to accrue to self-selected groups within the general populace.

Without a monetary reward for providing nonwood outputs from the forest, private forest owners, both industrial and nonindustrial, have no incentive to invest in the production of such outputs or to manage the forest to produce more of them. For instance, in some forest situations, selective plantings of various species or selective harvests of commercial trees could increase the food supply or the protective cover, or both, for many species of animals and birds. But, aside from the possibilities of personal enjoyment, why should forest owners incur expenditures for these purposes when they can expect no financial return?

Forest owners may be restrained by law or by regulation from timber harvesting practices which might lower the quality of the water flowing from the forest. In this case, regulation replaces economic incentive, but compliance is likely to be minimal and perhaps grudging. Regulation may or may not prevent undesirable action; it cannot coax forth desired actions.

It is sometimes alleged that from the viewpoint of the nation, wood consumers, and the forest products industry, the supply of timber is inadequate, especially for the future. Ever since the turn of the century, there have been warnings of impending timber scarcity—timber "famine," in the words of Gifford Pinchot and President Theodore Roosevelt. Over the intervening decades, annual net timber growth has mounted greatly, increasing by three times since 1920, and the predicted timber shortages have not yet arisen. Nevertheless, the prospect of a smaller supply of timber than will be demanded at present prices is still an article of faith in the forestry profession.

In looking at future timber supply—including wood from which to make paper—the role of the nonindustrial private forests will be large, perhaps crucial. Virtually everyone agrees on that. Some observers think that owners will not respond soon enough or in sufficient degree to increased demand and higher prices. They argue that incentives for these owners to invest in growing more timber, or capital available to invest, will be lacking even though timber prices rise. Another aspect or variant of this view is that many of the nonindustrial forest owners will be unwilling to cut the trees which they grow, preferring instead to enjoy the standing trees for their aesthetic values. Others point to the outstanding production record of the nonindustrial private owners over the past twenty-five years, and argue that reaction to present wood prices will produce far more net annual growth in the future. They argue further that, sooner or later, all truly merchantable timber will be cut—by the next owner of the forest, if not by the present one. Only time will tell, of course, which view is right, but the past record suggests that an optimistic viewpoint is appropriate.

Another area of concern involves wood as an energy source. The energy "crisis" of recent years has focused the attention of many on the supply of fuelwood from forests, public and private. Much of the increased inventory of hardwoods consists of trees not valuable for industrial use but excellent for fuel. The typical householder buys a comparatively small amount of fuelwood, even when wood is the chief source of energy for residential heating. A large number of comparatively small consumers face a large number of comparatively small supply sources, in many situations. Specialized fuelwood harvesters and marketers serve to bridge the gap between forest owner and wood user, but it may be doubted that this process works very well, at least not yet. The wood user is concerned with good quality fuelwood at the best price; questions are seldom raised as to the source of the wood, and whether it was harvested legally with the consent of the forest owner. If the use of wood as a source of residential space heating is to increase over the next several years, better enforcement against illegal harvesting must become a reality. Nevertheless, this problem quite probably pales by comparison with, say, the adverse effects of wide-scale wood burning on ambient air quality.

Environmental controls designed to protect air and water quality affect both private forest owners and forest users. As in other areas, the objective of these controls is (or should be) to protect the environment from undesirable degradation at as little cost to society as possible. To the extent that the environmental limitations on new paper mills and other wood-processing plants *can* be reduced to the minimum necessary for environmental protection, the building of new processing plants will be encouraged and the markets for wood improved. As the demand for paper grows, including the export demand, the economic incentive for additional wood-processing plants will increase; if these plants can be built economically, this will do much to improve the outlook for increased wood production from the nonindustrial private forests.

Another issue that has received some attention concerns government subsidies to owners of private forests. Such subsidies have been greeted warmly by the companies that purchase timber for processing (since the government would be paying part of their costs), by many state foresters (who would allocate the subsidies, and thus gain "constituencies"), and by consulting foresters (who would benefit from expanded timber production). In addition, such an idea has attracted the approval of some pro-consumer groups who favor lower prices.

Nevertheless, these subsidies are ill-considered. First, such subsidies often go to owners who would have increased production on their own in response to market forces. Thus, the extra output induced by such subsidies may be small. Also, there are better ways to assist consumers who suffer when wood prices increase—direct financial aid being the most effective, since it can be funneled to the most needy. And in general, little is to be gained by shielding consumers or other purchasers of wood products from the true costs of production. Doing so blunts one of the most desirable features of a market system—the incentive it creates to economize on all resources, especially those which are becoming more scarce.

CONCLUSIONS

To summarize, then, the private forests of the United States appear to be in reasonably good shape. Among the problems that do exist, the most serious seems to be the lack of incentive on the part of private forest owners to upgrade or maintain the quality of the external benefits their forests provide. Alternatively, the problem could be viewed as a failure of individual users to pay forest owners for the enjoyment they derive from these lands. However, in view of the difficulty of excluding nonpayers from hunting, fishing, or recreating on these lands, and the hostility that would be created were it feasible to do so, it is difficult to envision any policy intervention that would considerably improve matters. The present arrangement may not be "optimal," but it is not working badly. In view of some of the other problems discussed in this volume, that is encouraging.

About the Contributors

Lee G. Anderson is an associate professor of economics and marine studies, University of Delaware.

Marion Clawson is a senior fellow emeritus in the Renewable Resources Division, Resources for the Future.

Pierre R. Crosson is a senior fellow in the Renewable Resources Division, RFF.

John W. Firor is the director of the Advanced Study Program, National Center for Atmospheric Research.

Anthony C. Fisher is a professor in the Energy and Resources Program, University of California at Berkeley.

Kenneth D. Frederick is a senior fellow and director of the Renewable Resources Division, RFF.

Ruth B. Haas is an editor in the Public Affairs Division, RFF.

Winston Harrington is a fellow in the Quality of the Environment Division, RFF.

Hans H. Landsberg is a senior fellow in the Center for Energy Policy Research, RFF.

Robert H. Nelson is an economic staff member, Office of Policy Analysis, U.S. Department of the Interior.

Paul R. Portney is a senior fellow in the Quality of the Environment Division, RFF.

John E. Tilton is a professor of mineral economics, Pennsylvania State University.

Index

The book was set on a Linotron 202 in Times Roman text and Palatino display type by FotoTypesetters Inc., Baltimore, Maryland. It was printed and bound by Optic Graphics, Glen Burnie, Maryland.